Audio Anecdotes II

Audio Anecdotes II
Tools, Tips, and Techniques for Digital Audio

Edited by

Ken Greenebaum

Ronen Barzel

CRC Press is an imprint of the
Taylor & Francis Group, an **informa** business

AN A K PETERS BOOK

First published 2004 by A K Peters, Ltd.

Published 2019 by CRC Press
Taylor & Francis Group
6000 Broken Sound Parkway NW, Suite 300
Boca Raton, FL 33487-2742

First issued in paperback 2019

No claim to original U.S. Government works

ISBN 13: 978-0-367-44654-3 (pbk)
ISBN 13: 978-1-56881-214-4 (hbk)

Visit the Taylor & Francis Web site at
http://www.taylorandfrancis.com

and the CRC Press Web site at
http://www.crcpress.com

Library of Congress Cataloging-in-Publication Data

Audio anecdotes : tools, tips, and techniques for digital audio / edited by Ken Greenebaum,
   Ronen Barzel.
      p. cm.
   Includes bibliographical references.
   ISBN 1-56881-214-0 (vol. 2)
      1. Sound–Recording and reproducing–Digital techniques. I. Greenebaum, Ken, 1966-
   II. Barzel, Ronen.

TK7881.4.A93 2003
621.389'3--dc22

                                                         2003057398

Cover Art: **Paul Klee, Alter Klang** (Ancient Sound).1925, 236 (x6) (accession nr. G 1960.25)
Oil on cardboard nailed onto frame, 38 x 38 cm
Permission by Kunstmuseum Basel, Bequest of Richard Doetsch-Benziger, Basel 1960
Photogarphy: Kunstmuseum Basel, Martin Bühler

(C) 2004 Artists Rights Society (ARS), New York / VG Bild-Kunst, Bonn

Cover Design by Darren Wotherspoon

Contents

Preface

The publication of *Audio Anecdotes II* follows closely behind that of *Audio Anecdotes I*, for which the editors have received positive feedback as well as some constructive criticism. We appreciate all comments and have tried to incorporate as many suggestions as possible into the second volume. Most significantly, we have incorporated an index and provide superior support for Apple's OS X based computers.

Audio Anecdotes I introduces fundamental digital audio concepts. This second volume continues to explore these topics at a deeper level and introduces new topics such as music theory.

My early explorations of digital media, the application of digital computer techniques to previously analog media, were enabled by the inexpensive and increasingly powerful microprocessor while at the same time frustrated by the lack of appropriate resources in the literature or in the form of accessible programs and implementations. The research literature was abstract, making it difficult to approach or apply; free implementations for experimentation were almost nonexistent. More surprisingly there was a lack of communication among the practitioners of the many diverse fields that relate to digital media: sound design, music composition, recording engineering, signal processing, cognitive psychology, software design, etc. As I entered the field as a professional, the dramatic gap between the state of digital media research and practice became even more apparent to me.

Audio Anecdotes is an attempt to address these concerns by providing a collection of articles written by experts, bridging many fields, and describing practical tools and techniques. Wherever possible, articles provide motivation, working examples (programs, source code, and media files), and a list of annotated references to allow the reader to dig deeper into the subject and ultimately to enhance their own applications and products.

Recalling my own experiences, I decided to share this material with those just starting out, students. I created and taught the class, "Introduction to Dynamic Sound Synthesis," at the DigiPen Institute of Technology (perhaps the first school to offer a computer science degree dedicated to game design and simulation), using *Audio Anecdotes* as the textbook. I was pleasantly surprised and encouraged by the large enrollment and the enthusiasm for the class.

It takes many people to produce a book such as this, and thanks are due to all whose participation has helped make it successful. It was wonderful for me to work with our contributors, all esteemed professionals in their respective fields, and with the ideas represented in this volume. I hope you, the reader, share my excitement.

Many people have helped create this second volume by allowing me to bounce ideas off them, by reading and re-reading drafts of articles, and by contributing code, editorial, and technical expertise. Unfortunately, there are too many to list them all here; however, some deserve special mention:

Technical help: Mike Gonzalez and Greg Silber. Special thanks to Howard Good for his tremendous help with all aspects of the CD-ROM.

Editorial help: Jeffrey Greenebaum, John Nordlinger, and David Thiel.

I also want to thank those not otherwise mentioned. Thanks to Alice, Klaus, and the rest of the wonderful A K Peters publishing family.

For my own articles in this book, I must thank all the people who have shared their ideas, inspired me with their enthusiasm, and sharpened my understanding with their questions. I am especially grateful to my colleagues at Microsoft and Silicon Graphics and my students at DigiPen.

Finally, thank you to all my dear friends and loved ones who have supported me during this project.

Ken Greenebaum
Redmond, Washington
May 2004

Introduction

Introduction

Welcome to the second volume of *Audio Anecdotes*! Those of you already familiar with the first volume will find a host of new content in a familiar format. Those of you new to *Audio Anecdotes* should be able to dive right in, but for the full experience please use *Audio Anecdotes II* in conjunction with *Audio Anecdotes I*. Articles in this volume expand on the introductory material found in *Audio Anecdotes I* and, whenever possible, reference related material from the first volume.

Similar to the original book, *Audio Anecdotes II* discusses creating, recording, processing, and analyzing many forms of sound and music. Opportunities presented by digital media are emphasized, as are the powerful techniques made possible by inexpensive and nearly ubiquitous digital computing.

Perhaps because hearing is a subtle sense, sound and hearing are often misunderstood or undervalued in our society. While the sound of a twig snapping causes us to quickly localize the sound and orient our head in the direction from which the snap came, we often find ourselves looking in a direction without consciously being aware of the events that caused us to do so. Similarly, we might not realize that it was a sound that awoke us suddenly from a deep sleep. Equally powerful but less easy to explain is the dramatic influence sound and music have on our emotions.

In this book we explore sound and our sense of hearing, the one sense which never sleeps and works omnidirectionally from a distance. *Audio Anecdotes* attempts to present opportunities to improve the audio experience where sound already exists, or to encourage the integration of sound into presently mute applications, leading to richer, more expressive, and more valuable applications.

Since most interactions in the real world involve sound, we feel that there are many opportunities!

Structure

Each volume of *Audio Anecdotes* is comprised of articles that cover a wide range of audio-related topics. The articles take a variety of forms: introductions, essays, in-depth technical explorations, presentation of tools and techniques, and postmortem analyses.

Many articles contain the authors' personal anecdotes and hard-earned experience from the trenches. We, therefore, encourage our readers to learn about the authors' backgrounds before diving into each article by consulting the biography section at the end of the book.

The subjects covered in our articles are deep and often could fill their own book. Consequently, the articles are designed to act as a jumping-off point for readers who wish to further explore the topic. Each article contains an annotated list of references that serves not so much to document the sources of the article, but to direct readers to significant texts and further sources of information on the topic area. Where possible, articles reference other articles in this or other *Audio Anecdotes* volumes.

Articles are grouped into chapters by topics organized to form an arc spanning:

- The fundamentals: the physics, measurement, and perception of sound

- Recording and playback of sound: whether of music, voice, or nature

- Synthesis: rendering sounds which never existed including the synthesis of musical instruments, voice, or noise (Foley Sound)

- Signal processing: the mathematical analysis and manipulation of sound

- Signal processing applications: from compression techniques to signal detection and recognition

- Computer techniques: efficiently implementing low latency high performance audio systems on digital computers

- Music theory: the mathematics of both western and non-western music

- Creative topics: composition and sound design

- Nature, mind, and body: how sound exists in nature and affects the mind and body

This arc is rooted in the belief that to understand any topic or to be able to make informed trade-offs in design, an understanding of the physics and human perception of the phenomena is required. Great engineering efforts such as the design of the telephone system, color television, and computer graphics all demonstrate a mastery of the interplay between physics and human perception. From the fundamentals, the arc extends to the abstract through the applied and the creative, to again revisit human perception from a different perspective.

While each *Audio Anecdotes* volume can't include articles covering every topic area, the articles are organized according to this arc. *Audio Anecdotes II* contains the chapters described in the following sections:

Chapter 1. Field Recording

This chapter expands on the recording fundamentals chapter in *Audio Anecdotes I*. This time we explore trading the controlled environment of the recording studio for recording in the great outdoors, complete with the resulting wind, ambient noise, and other challenges.

The first two articles provide colorful descriptions of the author's experiences with field recording. The last article describes use of binaural recording techniques in nature to capture and recreate the three-dimensional sonic experience of actually being there.

Chapter 2. Synthesis

In this volume we expand on the synthesis articles from the first volume by presenting three unconventional approaches to solving common synthesis challenges.

We begin with an article describing an inexpensive technique for creating rich, nonrepeating synthetic ambiences. The next two articles are complimentary and describe ways to translate analog synthesis techniques to digital computers while avoiding the pitfalls that more straightforward digital implementations encounter.

The first article of the pair describes a methodology for very efficiently generating band-limited oscillators. The other article presents an intriguing algorithm for performing subtractive synthesis without the use of the filters most of us naively think are required.

Chapter 3. Signal Processing

This chapter presents detailed descriptions and implementations for some of the most fundamental signal processing techniques: spectral filters and time/frequency transformations.

The first two articles demonstrate finite and infinite impulse response filters. The next article describes a method for converting analog filters to the digital domain. The final two articles begin by explaining the venerable Fourier transform and then describe implementations of the Fast Fourier Transform in both floating point and fixed point implementations.

Chapter 4. Spatialization

Spatialization refers to the ability to determine the location in space from which a sound emanates or to artificially make a sound appear to emanate from a specific location. This chapter describes two techniques for creating spatialized sound using loudspeakers.

The first article examines techniques commonly applied to spatialize sound in the common stereo loudspeaker configuration: balance, panning, and distance attenuation. The second article expands on the first by providing a mathematical framework for spatializing sound using arrays of loudspeakers of various geometries.

Chapter 5. Computer Techniques

While most of our articles explore algorithms and briefly describe the engineering techniques needed to implement them, this chapter focuses on the implementations themselves and the resulting implications. These articles continue where the computer techniques chapter from *Audio Anecdotes I* leaves off.

The first article describes how the role of the humble volume control has been changed by the digital convergence and how PC audio's migration away from the analog mixer has left us with applications that tend to shout. The second article suggests that uniformly measuring digital audio in units of frames can help eliminate a common source of frustration and bugs when developing digital audio applications. The final two articles explore the opportunities for applying advanced buffering and audio I/O techniques. One introduces the ring buffer FIFO and related algebra; the other wraps the buffer in a library interface to provide uniform access and advanced functionality like blocking or variable latency I/O.

Chapter 6. Computer Tools

This chapter introduces three sets of tools that we distribute on the CD-ROM accompanying this book.

The first article describes the SoX sound exchange library, which provides tools for converting and manipulating many audio file formats. This article compliments "Audio File Formats: A formal description based approach" from *Audio Anecdotes I*. Next an author from the first volume returns to describe the Synthesis Toolkit (STK), a diverse collection of synthesis and signal processing algorithms written in C++. The final article describes the QEDesign filter design package. This package helps design the IIR and FIR filters described in the spectral filtering articles found in Chapter 2.

Chapter 7. Music Theory

Music theory is a highly evolved, and somewhat baroque, system for useful for composing, classifying, and analyzing music. For nonmusicians, and even many musicians, all but the most basic music theory concepts can be a confusing mystery. Simple exercises like equating notes to frequencies or converting note duration to seconds require an understanding of deeper concepts like scales and time signatures.

This chapter provides an introduction to music theory in two comprehensive articles. The first article covers topics related to pitch and the second to rhythm and meter.

Chapter 8. Sound Design

Visualization is a well-understood concept. Charts and graphs are commonly used for compact and clear communication. Visual attributes such as color or size are often used to convey additional information. Photographs, paintings, or advertisements are generally carefully composed for specific effect. This chapter explores sonification and sound design, the audio analogues to visualization and visual design.

The first article compliments "Designing a Movie for Sound" from *Audio Anecdotes I* by exploring sound design and the role of sound in telling a story. The second introduces the field of audio display, using sound to communicate information. The final article describes an actual research study evaluating the effectiveness of various sonification techniques.

Chapter 9. Nature

In this last chapter we reach the end of our topic arc by exploring sound in nature.

The first article describes the intriguing phenomena of brainwave entrainment and presents potential applications. We conclude the book with an article introducing bioacoustics, the study of interactions between sound and living organisms. This article suggests that we still have much to learn by studying the diverse sonic adaptations in living creatures and reminds us that Leonardo da Vinci also looked to nature for inspiration.

Glossary, Contributor Biographies, and Index

Following the main chapters are an extensive glossary, defining many of the audio terms used throughout the book, contributor biographies, and an index.

CD-ROM

Audio Anecdotes II is accompanied by a CD-ROM containing supplemental materials to the articles including audio and video files and executable demos. The demos support the Windows, Mac, and Linux platforms. Wherever possible, articles reference these materials so that readers can immediately listen to examples or experiment with the concepts introduced in the articles. Please be sure to explore the CD-ROM's contents via the HTML based tour as well, since additional materials have been included. Programs are also distributed as source code that may be modified and incorporated into the reader's own projects.

This material is distributed on the CD-ROM as tar balls (tar'd compressed archives). A wizard-based installer is provided for automatic installation on our supported platforms. README files provide installation information if the installation wizard doesn't automatically start upon

CD-ROM insertion. Once installed on your computer, the demo material is organized by chapter and author.

Unless otherwise specified, the contents of the CD-ROM are protected by the BSD license, and the reader may use the source code provided on the CD-ROM for any purpose as long as the following statement is prominently displayed: This product includes code from *Audio Anecdotes II*, edited by Ken Greenebaum and Ronen Barzel, published by A K Peters, 2004. The code is to be used at your own risk: Ken Greenebaum, Ronen Barzel, and A K Peters make no claim regarding the suitability of this material for any use.

A Note on Patents and Trade Secrets

All of our authors have certified that their articles do not contain trade secrets. In some articles, authors have explicitly stated that the algorithms that they describe are patented. However, even algorithms that lack such statements may be under some form of patent protection. For many reasons, including the long gestation of patent applications (so-called submarine patents), we can not vouch for the suitability of using these algorithms for any use other than educational purposes.

Please Participate

Visit us at the *Audio Anecdotes* website (http://www.audioanecdotes.com) to find errata, download code updates, or find out what's new.

Audio Anecdotes was created as a forum to share tools and techniques with the greater audio community. The subjects covered in this volume only scratch the surface of topics that we would like to cover. If you have been inspired by *Audio Anecdotes*, we encourage you to share your own tools, techniques, or experiences. If you would like to contribute to a future volume, please send your name, email address, postal address, and brief concept to submission@audioanecdotes.com. If you find an error in the text or code, or have a code improvement, please send it to errata@audioanecdotes.com.

A Final Thought

We wanted to create a book that would be fun to leaf through or read cover-to-cover; a book that would be useful both as a reference and a source of creative inspiration. We hope that we have succeeded.

Field Recording

A Quick Field Recording Primer for the Adventurous Sound Effects Recordist

Mike Caviezel

1 Introduction

As an end user of sound effects, I know that having the right effect is very important to convey realism to a listener, or conversely, can aid in a listener's sense of imagination when viewing or hearing a scene. In short, sound effects are a very powerful creative tool; just ask any radio producer or film director. Unfortunately, as great as most sound effect CDs are, sometimes they just don't have the effect you're looking for. That's when it's time to get creative and make your own. As a recordist/editor of a few sound effects CDs myself, I've learned a few techniques, which we will be exploring in this article. These techniques can help you make field recordings that suit your production perfectly.

2 Field Gear

The first thing to determine is what kind of machine you want to record to, and what format you want to end up with. If you're going to be later editing these recordings using a computer-based Digital Audio Workstation (DAW), I strongly recommend using a digital recorder out in the field. Use of a DAT (Digital Audio Tape), Deva (portable hard disk recorder), or other digital device makes for good, clean recordings, and eases transfers later on. I recommend the HHB PortaDat; it's loaded with I/O features, isn't too heavy, has a timecode option, and has proven to be pretty bulletproof in my experience. Any recordist will appreciate the headroom that its two built-in mic preamps have, as well as the built-in limiter that you can switch in or out. The limiter has proven to be useful for those situations where you're not sure how loud something will be, but you know you're only going to get one take of it (such as the Kingdome in Seattle imploding). Most portable DAT recorders have some kind of mic preamp on them, but be sure to check whether or not they can supply phantom power for your condenser microphones.

Be sure that your DAT recorder can record at the sampling rate at which you'll be editing later! Sample rate conversion issues are not fun. If portability isn't an issue to you (i.e., you're not going to be physically running around recording stuff), a DA-88, ADAT or other digital multitrack can be kind of cool out in the field. These recorders give you the ability to capture up to eight different perspectives at once, which is something to think about for the not-too-distant 5.1 surround-sound future. Of course, supplying power to these AC powered devices then becomes an issue. In lieu of a reeeeaaallly long extension cord, a company called Galaxy Audio makes something called the Far Outlet, which is a relatively heavy rechargeable black battery and inverters that can supply 120V AC power to two devices at once. I personally have used a DA-88 along with a Mackie 1402 mixer plugged into a Far Outlet, and it worked great. For your portable DAT recorders, most ship with rechargeable batteries included, but a few companies make external portable batteries that can run for much longer than the stock recorder batteries.

Once you've decided on a recorder, it's time to pick your microphone(s). I generally choose to use stereo condensers for, in my experience, they capture more high-end detail than dynamic mics, and the stereo perspective can always be collapsed to mono later. For general, all-purpose stereo recording, I can recommend a few things. The Audio Technica 825 stereo microphone has two capsules configured in an X-Y cardioid pattern, and has been a good all-around workhorse for me. As a more expensive option, the Neumann RSM 191 stereo microphone has also given me outstanding results. This is a dual capsule MS (midside) mic, which gives you options like being able to vary the stereo width of the mic, and can also record a split MS signal with the ability to decode it later. For recording ambiences, I have yet to use anything that works as well as the RSM 191. Sennheiser also makes a cardioid stereo mic that I've gotten good results with, the MKE 44-P, which is also an X-Y setup. All of the above mics are condensers with high SPL ratings, and have some sort of attenuation switch (or pad). All of these microphones can be powered with AA or 9V batteries, and they can all be either mounted on a mic stand for studio use, or function as handheld mics, which we'll discuss next.

3 Don't Let that Mic Go Outside Naked

The best physical set-up for me when I've made field recordings is to wear my DAT recorder hanging at my side, slung over my shoulder, wearing my headphones normally, and carrying the microphone in my hand. To carry the mic noiselessly, you're going to need some kind of pistol grip mount with a shock-absorbing mic clip. This will then allow you to simply point the mic like a gun at your sound source, and also allows you to quickly move the mic around without any handling noise. You could simply hold the mic in your hand without a shock-mount, but I think you'll find that unless you keep your hand absolutely still, you're going to get low frequency bumps from moving the mic around, from the mic cable hitting the mic, and other unexpected handling noises. Having a pistol mount also opens up all kinds of options for wind protection, which is absolutely necessary for recording outside (especially here in the Pacific Northwest).

You can first start by fitting the mic capsule with the windscreen it came with, and putting it in the pistol grip. You can then cover the entire pistol-grip assembly with a zeppelin windshield. A zeppelin windshield looks just like it sounds—a big gray plastic tube shaped like a zeppelin, which has been specially made to allow wind protection without killing frequency response to the mic. For even more wind protection, you can then cover the zeppelin with a WindJammer. A WindJammer is basically a fur coat for your zeppelin, and that's exactly what it looks like, except it's been specially made to diffuse wind noise while still allowing good frequency response to your mic. You slide this thing over your zeppelin, zip it up, and you're ready to go. All of these wind protection measures applied at once may seem a bit extreme, but believe me, it's worth it. After having entire tapes ruined by wind noise, you'll know what I'm talking about. I never do outdoor recording anymore without my pistol grip, zeppelin, and WindJammer. The company that makes all of these products is Rycote, and they are your one-stop source for microphone wind protection. Their products have certainly saved my recordings more than a few times.

4   It's Noisy Outside—Use the Right Mic for Noise Rejection!

OK, so you've got your microphone assembly plugged into the preamps on your DAT player, you're hearing sound though your headphones (which should be completely closed-ear headphones to keep outside noises out of your ears), and everything's groovy. You load up a DAT, and you're ready to record. You walk outside of your suburban home, and let's say you want to record that woodpecker that's been banging away on your siding for the last three days. You walk up to him and start rolling tape. Once you turn the gain up to get a good recording level, you notice something. You're picking up not only the woodpecker, but you're also picking up cars driving by on the street, planes flying far overhead, other birds screeching and making noise, insects chirping. . . in short, it's not exactly an isolation booth with just you and the woodpecker. Welcome to the plague of every field recordist—extraneous noises from the outside environment.

Unless you're specifically trying to capture the overall ambience of where you're standing, unwanted noises from the environment around you will give you fits when you're trying to edit your effects later. Unfortunately, easy solutions are few and far between.

Using a mic with the right polar pattern for the job is crucial. With cardioid (front-facing pick-up pattern) mics, you can angle them so that your sound source is on-axis, with sounds to the rear (and sides, to a lesser degree) of the mic being rejected. With omni mics, nothing gets rejected. If you're using an omnidirectional mic to try and record isolated effects, be prepared for lots of extraneous noise in your recordings, which also means be prepared to do a lot of editing later. If, however, you are recording overall ambiences, then an omni mic might be exactly what you want. A good rule of thumb is: cardioid (or other highly directional) patterns for individual effects, omni patterns for ambiences.

The first thing to try is to get as close to the sound source as you can. Then, if you're using a cardiod mic, try angling your mic differently. You can easily lower your noise floor by pointing your mic so it still faces your sound source, but also so that it doesn't face the street, or the airport, or the elementary school down the street, or whatever happens to also be making noise.

Rejection can be pretty good with most stereo cardioid microphones. But if you really care about rejection, a shotgun microphone can offer a highly directional pick-up pattern, with amazing rejection of sounds to either side and to the rear of the microphone. Basically, these mics are designed to pick up whatever's directly in front of it, and that's it. There is a potential downside, though. Some people feel that certain shotgun mics don't have quite the fidelity that a standard hand-held mics have, so be sure and try before you buy. Also, a lot of shotgun mics are mono only, but if you care more about isolation and rejection than you do about mono versus stereo, then a shotgun mic may be your best bet.

If you can't get very close to your sound source, you also may want to consider a parabolic mic. A parabolic microphone is one of those mics that you see guys on TV carrying around the sidelines of football games, with what looks like a small satellite dish attached to it. They are highly directional mics, and the attached reflector dish allows them to pinpoint sound sources up to 200 feet away. Again, these are mono mics, but for isolating faraway sound sources, they're hard to beat.

John Klepko's article, "Understanding Microphones," (see *Audio Anecdotes I*), provides much more technical information about microphones that should help you understand and select an appropriate mic.

5 If It is Still Noisy, Find a Quieter Place ...

If you're recording a very loud sound source, your job just got a lot easier, as you can get away with setting your mic gain very low, while still getting a good recording level. If your source isn't very loud, then that is a much bigger can of worms. The more you increase the gain to get a good signal on tape, the more background elements you'll find buried in your sound. If your sound source is VERY quiet, you'll even hear the self-noise of the equipment you're using. You'll probably hear your own self-noise, too, such as your own breathing and your clothing. Always remember to wear clothes that don't make a lot of noise. Nothing is worse than having the perfect effect ruined by your coat rustling at the wrong moment, or your keys jingling in your pocket. Leave the loose change back in the car.

Clothing issues aside, for fighting background noise, many times the easiest solution is to find a quiet environment (where there's no wind, bugs, birds, planes, cars, etc.), and record your effects there. Places like that still exist, you know. It may mean sometimes driving out to the middle of nowhere, but many times it's the only way to record clean sound effects. Not having to edit background noises out of your effects can save you weeks, even months of editing time. You can also try recording at night, when traffic and other activity has died down. Obviously, you can also try recording your effects indoors whenever possible, but some things you just have to do in cooperation with Mother Nature.

6 Social Engineering

Cooperation with Mother Nature is one thing, but cooperation with other people is something else. An important thing to remember while walking around loaded up with your DAT rig is that most people who see you working won't know a cardioid microphone from a carotid artery, and will want to know what you're doing. The actual intent of this question is entirely dependent on the manner in which it is asked.

For instance, it could be, "Hey, what are you doing?" as in, "Wow, I'm curious about all that cool stuff you've got there," or it could be, "Hey, what are you doing!" as in, "Get off of my property!" or "You can't do that here!" At this moment, you'll need to break out your diplomatic people-handling skills (if you have any), or be prepared to leave your location immediately. Or possibly both.

You should definitely have some kind of statement ready, such as, "Oh, we're just recording some sound effects for a documentary" (or movie studio, or video game, or whatever you think will impress people, if your actual project doesn't seem glamorous enough). Then you can ask, "Is that OK? We'll stay totally out of the way." You can even offer them a copy of the finished product to help grease the wheels. Most of the time, once people hear the words "TV" or "movie" or "documentary," they'll be receptive. They may even go out of their way to accommodate you. People can be very friendly when they think they're going to be part of something famous. If you're making it up though, just be ready for the follow-up question, "Really? What movie?" or, "Wow! What TV show?"—just try and be believable.

However, if people don't want you recording there, there isn't much you can do. Even if you're on public property, some people will put up a stink about you being there. If you don't want them to get the police involved, the best solution is to quickly apologize and then leave the immediate area. Just go someplace where Mr. Party Pooper won't be offended. It could be around the block, or it could be a few miles away. As with most cases, just use your best judgement and a little common sense, and you should be fine.

But the best way to handle a confrontation is not to have one at all by getting permission from the relevant parties BEFOREHAND to do some recording there. Obviously, if you're out on a 20-mile stretch of country road, out in the middle of nowhere with nobody else around, you could probably get away with just showing up and recording; providing, of course, that you're not going to be recording explosions, car chases, starting forest fires, or anything else that could get you arrested. However, if you want to go wandering around a construction site recording the construction crew, you should probably warn the foreman beforehand so you don't get hurt by falling beams, etc.; again, the common sense rule should prevail.

If you're going to a paid event to try and record, it is definitely wise to get permission beforehand. If you don't get permission, you can always go sneaking around, but be ready for all sorts of possible unpleasant consequences, from being merely kicked out of the event to having your equipment confiscated! Besides, getting permission often will allow you access to areas and sounds that you could never get to just by sneaking around. If you're trying to stage complicated, dangerous effects where you know you'll need government permission (such as blowing things up, throwing cars off of cliffs, etc), you'll need to obtain a permit from the local county or city office. Many cities have media relations offices that deal specifically with issuing permits for filming and recording. They'll tell you everything you need to do in order to get your effects recorded legally. Plus, police officers are downright friendly when they know you've got a legal permit to be there.

7   Use Indexing and Timecode So You Can Find Your Sounds

OK, back to the technical stuff. So now you're out in the field, you've got all-access clearance, you're ready to go. Just before you press "Record," you should check your DAT player to see if it's set on Auto ID, or Manual ID. For those of you not familiar with these terms, having Auto ID engaged will mean the DAT player will drop an index point on the DAT whenever audio passes above a preset threshold, which your DAT manufacturer sets at the factory, and you usually can't adjust. Auto ID is fine for studio recordings, but horribly annoying for field recording. With Manual ID, the DAT will be indexed every time you start the DAT machine recording. For example: When you first start recording, it drops a ID. When you're done recording, you can then pause the tape or stop recording. When you take the machine out of pause, or resume recording, the machine will drop another ID. I wholeheartedly recommend using Manual ID, as your tape can be very frustrating to sort through later if your machine has dropped an ID number after every loud noise while using Auto ID. With Manual ID, it's much easier to skip around logically on your tape. In any case, Start IDs can be revised and edited after your content is recorded.

You should also make sure to start your tape recording from the very beginning to establish an Absolute Time Code (or ABS) on your tape. Once you stop recording, you should ALWAYS resume recording right where you stopped, if not a little bit before, in order to preserve your tape's ABS. Trust me, this is pretty important. It's much easier to find an effect later if you know what ABS time it happened versus just knowing your effect is somewhere in the 25 minutes of tape between index points 4 and 5 on your DAT. Once you start editing your effects, you'll be glad you had ABS all the way through your tape.

8 Be Creative, Climb a Tree

Now that you're up and recording, with all the technical elements in place, you can get creative with recording techniques. Don't be afraid to climb trees, fences, fire escapes, etc. if you think it'll give you a unique sound. Also, don't be afraid to put the mic in places that you physically can't get to, such as hanging a mic by its cable down a small hole, or strapping a mic to the exhaust pipe of a car, and then recording from inside the car (see article, "Holding on for Dear Life: Recording the Automobile," (page 13), for all the gory details). Be prepared to improvise. A little duct tape and some cable ties will go a long way towards helping you put your mic in places where you can't hold it yourself.

Sometimes it can be advantageous to bring a friend along to help you out. It's very tricky to try to stage effects by yourself, especially if you're holding the DAT rig and trying to be as quiet as possible. Just do whatever it takes to get the effect you want. It's easier to record it right the first time than to have to fix it later.

9 Before Going Home

Once you're finished recording and it's time to go home, take the tape out of the DAT player, set the write-protect tab on it, and label it right there. Don't lose it! Also, please make sure you leave with everything you came with.

When you're back home and unpacking the gear, take the time to clean everything up and start all the batteries recharging. That way, you know everything will be ready to go and working when you have to dash out the door to go record that marching band that's coming down the street (true story).

10 Have Fun!

To sum up my feelings about field recording, I think it's a lot of fun. When done properly, it can yield fantastic results, and can get you into cool places you never thought you'd be. Hopefully, my little tidbits of information can start you out on the right foot, and send you on your way to making great sound effects. Good luck!

Holding on for Dear Life: Recording the Automobile

Mike Caviezel

What's the craziest thing you can think of doing with a car? 360s, jumps, crashes, ridiculous high speeds?

Well, I've done just about everything you can do with an automobile, all while holding my breath and clutching my bulletproof Mackie mixer and Tascam D-98 multitrack. Challenging? Yes. Fun? Mostly yes. Motion-sickness-inducing? DEFINITELY. Ugh. I get green just thinking about it. But the end result was one of the most comprehensive set of car sounds on the planet (Wheels II, from Sound Ideas), and we (our small company team) accumulated some great car stories with which we can out-macho our gearhead friends.

1 Multitrack Multiperspective

When we first started planning our car projects, we knew we wanted to approach the recording from a unique perspective, literally. Most sound effect sets at the time contained a good deal of exterior car sounds, such as drive-bys, skids, etc., but what we wanted to capture (along with the exterior perspective) was what doing these stunts sounded like from a bunch of different perspectives all over the car. We also wanted to record and edit these tracks simultaneously, so that users of these effects could either use our mixes, or make their own mixes of each perspective. This meant finding a suitable multitrack unit that we wouldn't be afraid to strap in a car going 150+ mph. We thought the DA98 from Tascam looked pretty bulletproof, so we got one. We also bought a small Mackie mixer, and some microphones that we thought could take the abuse. Little did we know.

From there, we played around with our own cars a bit, holding microphones out of windows and such, and decided on four positions which sounded best:

- Driver's perspective. Stereo cardioid condenser mic mounted between the driver and passenger seats.

- Tire perspective. Stereo, with two small lavalier condenser mics strapped to the wheel well, on either side of the car, facing the road.

- Engine perspective. Mono, omnidirectional dynamic mic basically strapped to the engine block!

- Exhaust perspective. Mono, omnidirectional dynamic mic hanging under the rear bumper facing the exhaust pipe.

We also took into account the external perspectives to be recorded by people walking around with portable DAT rigs and stereo microphones.

2   Wind Noise

In our test recordings, we found that wind noise was definitely an issue to be reckoned with, especially with our tire mics. The only workable place to put them was in the wheel well facing towards the rear of the car, so any wind from driving would be deflected by the wheel well. This works great as long as there are no side winds, which of course there always are. At one point, we thought about abandoning our tire perspective altogether, but it made for such a cool stereo effect that we just had to have it.

This may seem severe as far as wind protection goes, but here's what it took to make it work: First, we ended up putting a small windscreen on each lavalier tire mic. Then, we punched a mic cable-sized hole in the bottom of a couple of empty Kodak film canisters. We put each mic in its own canister, facing the open end, with the cable trailing through our punched holes in the bottom. We then stuffed small pieces of acoustic foam into the canister, filling in around the mic. With the top of the mic flush with the open end of the film can, we shoved the whole assembly into a WindJammer (sort of a fuzzy acoustic windsock) and mounted it in the wheel well. When we first did this, we thought for sure that our fidelity, especially our high treble end, was going to be so reduced that it would be make for muffly, lifeless audio tracks. But surprisingly, we didn't compromise that much in the way of fidelity. Some of the high end definitely went away because of the canister and the foam, but it wasn't nearly as bad as we thought it was going to be. We were even able to add a little high end in the editing process, which helped out further.

3   Our Set-Up

Our technical set-up was as follows: All mics went into six channels of our Mackie 1402. Phantom power was provided by the mixer. To get our mic signals to tape, we went out of the channel inserts on the 1402 into the tape ins of our DA-98. This signal was pre-fader and pre-eq, so our level to tape was controlled by the mic gain knob at the top of the Mackie channel strip. Any eq we did was limited to high-pass (low cut) filtering via the bass rolloff switch on the mixer channel strip or on the mic itself. We would then take the tape outs from the DA-98 and plug them into channels 7-14 of the 1402, so the recordist could monitor either the input signal from the mics, or the signal coming back from tape. Both the 1402 and DA-98 were powered by a Galaxy Audio "Far Outlet," a large portable battery with integrated inverter that could supply AC to our two devices simultaneously for up to four hours.

We determined that the recordist should be in the back seat whenever possible, giving instructions to our driver, and holding onto the gear to make sure it wasn't rattling around. The recordist would sit down, put the Mackie on his lap, belt himself in, arm the DA-98, and watch levels as he went around the track, making adjustments when necessary. We tried never to change levels in the middle of an effect, as we knew it would give us headaches when we tried to edit them later. If something was distorted or was too low in level, we'd just do the effect again right then and there.

We found that absolutely everything in the interior of the car had to be shut off to make the interior as quiet as possible. This meant shutting up any humans inside the car as well, which definitely proved to be harder than it sounds (try not breathing hard or gasping/panicking when you're going into a hairpin turn at 90 mph). Anyway, once we got our recording method down, we were ready to try it for real.

4   Stunt Driving

While it would have been fun to try some stunt driving ourselves, we decided it would be in the company's best interest if we all actually LIVED through the experience, so we hired a stunt driver. He happened to be the son of the owner of the company where we were renting the cars. I don't think he ever told his dad just what we were going to be doing with those horribly expensive sportscars. I know I wouldn't have. Once we had our driver and cars lined up, we rented a local racetrack for a week or so, and got everything ready to roll.

5   The Plan

At 7:00 am on the first day of recording, we all showed up at the racetrack to start wiring our first car, a BMW four-door sedan. Once we attached all the mics to the car and safety-belted the multitrack in, it was time to decide who was going to get to ride inside, and who was going to put on a DAT rig and be outside. Well, we all kind of wanted to be the first guy to go riding, but the first guy to actually say so was Bob, a freelance recordist we had hired for the project. So we strapped Bob in, had the driver rev it hard a few times to make sure the levels were cool, and sent Bob down to the track with our driver in his dad's shiny green BMW. Sean (another company recordist) and I elected to camp out on the track with DAT rigs to get some drive-bys and any other external effects. The sequence of events was going to be: two laps around the tracks at a slow speed (10–20 mph); two laps at a medium speed (35–45 mph); and two laps as fast as our driver could safely go. Needless to say, we were all curious as to just how fast that would be. Then, we'd do some skids, peel-outs, S-curve effects, parking simulations, and anything else we could think of.

6   First Impressions

So the first two laps go by, no problem. At the end of the second lap, the car pulled over and shuts off. Bob rolls his window down and hands us his headphones so we can listen to the tapes. Everything sounds great, but upon sticking our heads into the car, we immediately notice that it's pretty hot and foggy in there. I guess driving around on a muggy early summer morning with all the windows rolled up and no fan going will do that. But other than looking a little sticky, Bob seemed OK. After we adjusted a few settings, we sent our boys out again for the medium and high speed laps. As the car came around the track and went roaring between Sean and me in the straightaway, we're both thinking, "Man, how cool is that?" This sentiment immediately changed when we saw Bob's face after the car pulled over, tires smoking from the fast laps. Bob didn't bother with the window, he just opened the door and leaned out, definitely a little green around the gills. We asked him how he felt, and he said that the straightaways are OK, but that the S-curves feel like a horrible G-force-laden ride at the fair that you can't stop. At that point, we reminded Bob that we still had the forward and reverse 180s to record. He said he'd be all right, he just needed a minute to get his composure. We did a few slow speed parking maneuvers, and when Bob was ready, he and the driver buckled up and went down the track 75 yards or so to do some 180s, with the car spinning out in front of Sean and me.

The effects were impressive. Our driver was pretty aggressive, so a few of the 180s ended up being almost 360s, which put the car about four feet away from where both Sean and I were standing, which was a little nerve-racking. Controlling the urge to run for your life while a car is seemingly spinning out of control towards you takes considerable willpower. Anyway, after a few vicious spins and burnouts, we were done. Bob opened the door, and he is Kermit-the Frog-style green this time. He staggers out of the car, a sweaty, nauseous mess. We ask him how he's doing, and he just waves his hand and shakes his head, not able to speak. After five minutes of laying down on the pavement outside the car, he finally rights himself and tells us all, "Never again." The driver thinks this is hilarious, and is laughing his head off, wanting to know who his next victim will be. As bad as Bob looks, my curiosity gets the better of me, and I volunteer to be the backseater for the next car. Bob asks me if I'm sure that's what I want to do. "Yep. I just gotta know," I foolishly reply.

7   My Turn

So we drive back to our staging area and wire up the next car, a two-door BMW with a higher horsepower engine than Bob's four-door BMW sedan. Cooool. We check levels, everything's OK, and I get strapped down into the backseat. I tell everyone not to worry, and we go out to the track to do our slow laps. Sure enough, the interior fogs up immediately, and both the driver and I start to break a sweat from the heat inside the car. But I'm OK so far. After the slow laps, we pull over to air the car out a bit, and the driver asks me if I'm alright. I say yes. He says, "That'll change." So we go out for the medium laps, and I begin to see what Bob is talking about. Going around a tight curve at 15 mph is one thing; going around it at 45 mph is something else entirely. You start to get pressed up against the side of the car, and all the recording gear starts to rattle a bit, so you have to hold the equipment in place with one half of your body while holding yourself in place with the other half, and you have to do it all noiselessly, as to not ruin your recording. Not to mention the increasing effect of G-forces on your stomach as you wind around turn after turn ... After the medium laps, we pull over to air the car out again, and my head is definitely swimming a bit. Sean and Bob walk over to see how I am, and I tell them I think I can make it. Bob merely laughs, as does the driver. Sean says, "You sure about this, man? You look kind of bad ..." "Just gimme a minute," I reply. Five minutes go by, and I'm feeling a little less queasy, so I give our driver the thumbs up, and off we go for our hot laps.

We peel out, and head down the straightaway. We accelerate up to about 110 mph quicker than I thought possible. During the straightaway, I'm thinking "Hey, this is fun! I've never been this fast in a car before!" Then all inklings of potentially having a good time disappeared as the driver launched us into Turn 1, a nearly 180-degree turn with a very short radius. The thing about riding with a stunt driver/race car driver is that they brake and accelerate in almost the opposite places that you, a normal human being, would choose. As we head into Turn 1, we're not slowing down. The wall is getting closer, and we're still not slowing down. The wall is right in our FACE, and we're not slowing down. The only thing I can think of is, "Well, at least I'm going to die in a nice car ..."

The one nice thing about intense fear is that it masks any underlying nausea you may have at the time. You're simply too frightened to get sick. Coming out of Turn 1, I tried to steady myself for the upcoming set of S-curves. Something you may not know about S-Curves: At 15 mph, they feel like a normal road; at 45 mph they feel like a bad carnival ride (Bob was right!); but at 75 mph, they feel like you've been jammed into a washing machine set on "maximum agitate." The bad thing about knowing you're not going to die is that your body then can release any pent-up queasiness. And we'd decided not to have a break between the two fast laps, lucky me. So as I was praying the driver would notice me turning colors and cut me a break on Lap 2, I think he must have smelled my fear, because we instead tore into the straightaway at 165 mph (I know, because I looked) to start our second lap. To be honest, I don't remember much about Lap 2. I was just trying not to throw up most of the time. I remember being vaguely scared going into Turn 1 again, which was kind of nice, but then the S-curves brought it all back again.

I somehow managed to make it through Lap 2 without losing my lunch in the car, and we finally ground to a halt next to Sean and Bob. I undid my seatbelt and basically fell out of the car onto the pavement. Sean came up to me and asked if I was OK. I've never wanted to vomit so much in my entire life, but I ended up holding back. After ten minutes of lying down, I was ready to talk, but there was no way I was going to make it through the upcoming spins and skids that we needed to do. I switched places with Sean, who, despite having seen both Bob and me go through the wringer, was still itching to go. Sean climbed in, we did the skids, no problem. He's ready to go again in the next car, a Dodge Viper. Turns out, Sean was the only one of us who was smart enough to take some Dramamine before coming out to the track today. Duh. He had a great time in the Viper, and even wanted the driver to take him on an extra hot lap, and he happily obliged. Hey, it wasn't his car ...

8   The Smoking Mic

As a side note, that turned out to be an expensive extra lap. As Sean pulled up from it with the tires smoking, he rolled down the window and asked if somebody could check our exhaust mic. He said it was making a funny noise, then it quit working altogether. We looked in the back of the car, and the apparent reason the exhaust mic wasn't working was that it had been burnt to a crisp, or at least the zeppelin windscreen that held the mic was. Once we took the zeppelin off, we saw that our $750 condenser mic had been reduced to a molten pile of metal by the heat from the exhaust pipe. Whoops! Guess we won't put our exhaust mic so close next time. As it turned out, we ran that particular car so hard that we had to get a new set of tires for it as well. From showroom tires to junkyard in under an hour. Expensive. But I think it was worth it to see that thing spin around in a 360, and then peel out as if its tail was on fire (which of course, it was).

9   Mostly Uneventful

After learning our lessons early, we were able to successfully record most of our cars that week fairly uneventfully. Some highlights: Getting up to 185 mph in a souped-up Porsche, which turned out to be our overall top speed of any car we recorded; recording two police cars simulating a high speed chase with a forced spinout finish, where one car bumped the other one from behind to stop it; dropping a VW Rabbit from 150 feet up onto concrete pavement; dropping the same car off of a cliff, and then into 15 feet of water suspended from a crane; nearly getting hit from outside the car while recording a stretch limo doing spins and 180s; and nearly flipping over an Isuzu Rodeo when our driver got a little too aggressive. But our scariest moment came while recording a 1963 Pontiac GTO muscle car.

Terry (another company member) had elected to ride in the GTO backseat, while Sean and I stood outside with the DAT rigs. All of our lap routines went smoothly, as did our spins and skids. Then we decided we wanted some high-speed, smoking-tire burnouts, along with some hard, tire-squealing braking stops.

The sequence of events was supposed to go like this: The GTO would start out in front of Sean and me, and peel out. It would then go down the track about 150 yards or so, and skid to a stop. Then it would turn around, peel out again, and then skid to a stop directly in front of Sean and me.

So Terry climbed in the back of our two-door GTO, braced himself appropriately, as there are no seatbelts in the back of most 1960 muscle cars, and gave the driver the OK. Sean and I started rolling tape, and the car peeled out, no problem. It went down the track about 150 yards, skided to a stop, and turned around. Sean and I got ready for our upcoming skid-stop, and gave Terry and our driver the "OK" wave. The car peels out, and IMMEDIATELY skided to a stop, a good 100 yards short of Sean and me. We kind of looked at each other a little confused, and began walking towards the GTO to see what went wrong. Before we could get there, the car came racing back to meet us. The driver hurriedly got out and said, "We need to check your buddy Terry out—I just put his head through the windshield." Yeah, sure. Ha-ha. Then we look at the windshield. The passenger side looks like somebody hit it with a large rock, with glass all over and a large hole in the center. Then Terry steped out of the car, looking a little dazed, and muttered "I gotta take a little breather, fellas..." His head wasn't bleeding, but the top of it was definitely bruised, and he was acting goofy enough to make us think he had a concussion. He claimed he was all right, but we watched him very closely. Once it was established that Terry was OK, we asked him and the driver what in the world had happened.

As it turned out, Terry didn't explain the sequence of events very clearly to the driver, who was not our usual stunt-driver, and didn't really know what to expect from us. Before we started our sequence, Terry told the driver to peel out, go down the track, skid to a stop, and turn around. The driver did exactly what Terry told him to, and Terry braced himself appropriately. Once they were turned around ready to come back to Sean and me, Terry told the driver to peel out, which he did. He then was going to tell the driver, "Now I want you to skid to a stop in front of Sean and Mike," but his sentence came out only as far as "Now I want you to skid to a stop...," and then the driver jammed on his brakes. Not ready for the sudden stop, Terry came flying over the passenger seat, which simply folded over, and smashed his head into the windshield. Thank God he was wearing headphones. The padded band of the Sony headphones he was wearing probably saved him from severe injury.

10   On the Tape . . .

He was rolling tape from inside the car the whole time, though. When we took the car back to the garage, we were all pretty curious as to what the whole thing sounded like. Sean put on the headphones and had the first listen. He made this awful face, took off his headphones, and said, "I don't really need to listen to that again." Then I took a turn. You could hear the whole thing. The actual impact sounded like someone throwing a hard melon against a glass window. Pretty rough. The next thing you hear is the driver saying, "Oh my God, man, are you OK? I'm so sorry! You told me to skid to a stop, so I did..." And then Terry mutters, "I meant DOWN THERE...Ahhh, my head..." And then more apologizing by the driver as he speeds back to Sean and me. Later, whenever we'd watch somebody listening to the tape, you could always tell that the impact had just happened, because the person listening to it always says something like "Oh my God!!!" and then made the same kind of awful face that Sean and I did when we first heard it. We didn't include the effect in the final product because it seemed a little too graphic, but the thought of thousands of listeners making that face still amuses me.

11   The Results

When we got the tapes back to our studio, we loaded them into our computer workstations (using Digidesign's Pro Tools as our audio editor), and started sifting through the material. To our slight surprise, and more than a few "whews," everything turned out pretty much as we expected.

The combination of the stereo "cockpit" mic with the engine, exhaust, and tire mics really made it sound like you were sitting in the driver's seat of that particular car, barreling around the track. We did have to doctor a few of the tracks that had problems, such as removing clicks and pops that would occur when rocks would hit the tire mics, and a few other anomalies, but nothing too problematic. We also had to try and remove bird chirps, airplanes, train whistles, clothing rustle, and other "extraneous" noises from our external perspective tracks, the ones that were recorded by the guys walking around with portable DAT rigs. However, we had shot so many different effects, that we could usually just find a decent take where there wasn't too much noise going on around us, and use that one with a minimum of editing.

After all the editing, listening, documenting, and mastering were completed, I listened to each CD (20 CDs in all, one car per disc) as a final quality check, and though I could still hear little things I might change about it, I was (and still am) pretty proud of that sound effects set. It's a shame about that exhaust mic, though. Should have kept it as a souvenir...

12   What We Learned

If there is one catchphrase to describe what we learned from our car experiences, it would have to be "Expect the unexpected." Obviously, we could've avoided a few problems if we'd have thought some things through a little more thoroughly, but the fundamental problem was that none of us really knew what to expect when we were recording. Nobody had ever really tried this before, not to this extent. Sure, we were somewhat prepared, but we had to fly by the seat of our pants on at least a few things every day. And some things you always have to learn the hard way. I guess that's true in most areas of audio, though. So for all you guerilla recordists out there, just remember: Always wear your seatbelt, and don't forget the Dramamine.

Audio examples are available on the accompanying CD-ROM.

A Brief Introduction to Binaural Recording

Gordon Hempton and Ken Greenebaum

This article provides a brief discussion of the equipment I use for binaural recording, my technique-of-choice for recording ambiences both wild and civil around the world for the past two decades.

1 What is Binaural Recording?

Binaural recording seeks only one objective—to replicate human hearing. In this sense, the field journals of naturalist John Muir—which include detailed descriptions of natural sounds as he heard them—might very well be considered one of the earliest binaural "recordings" of nature. His work is collected in the *Eight Wilderness Discovery Books* [1]. Had Muir been alive today he most certainly would be interested in binaural recording as a means to not only record the world in vivid detail, but also explore the sonic world.

A binaural microphone looks like a human head. It is made out of a well-engineered blob of flesh density rubber to separate two ears (each with a molded outer ear), and short auditory canals that lead to sensitive, low-noise transducers.

Sound must pass around the head, then reflect off the outer ears and finally enter the auditory canal before it is recorded. Each side of the head, left and right channels, records different arrival times and spectral content, thereby preserving all of the information that the brain uses to form a three-dimensional image or soundscape.

There's no doubt about it, binaural recordings offer convincing realities and first-time listeners to recordings of passing locomotives, wolf attacks, and make-out sessions are often unprepared.

Binaural is always my first choice when I want to record what it *feels* like to be in the real world, places like the Hoh Valley Rain Forest at Olympic National Park or Koln Cathedral in Germany. Binaural microphones produce great sound, capture incredible depth, and preserve the *maximum amount of information* that you can obtain on location over a two-channel system. In the studio, this information can be processed to create excellent mono or even 5.1 surround sound (reportedly better than any other two-channel source with transaural processors). It can also be made speaker-compatible. The information also provides you with the perfect reference for the recorded area's acoustics and can be used to create additional sound files that conform to those acoustics. Yet despite this versatility and excellent quality, binaural recording remains largely undiscovered.

Binaural technology was first developed in the 1960s, but was relegated to a curiosity. At that time, only stereo headphone users would receive the impression accurately, and speaker playback was less than satisfactory because phase cancellations removed much of the detail, making the recording sound *far-away*. These restrictions have largely been overcome by further refinements in design. (Please refer to Haferkorn's article "Head-Related Transfer Functions and the Physics of Spatial Hearing," (see *Audio Anecdotes III*), and Gehring's articles "Why 3D Sound through Headphones," (see *Audio Anecdotes III*), and "Interactive Entertainment with 3D Sound," (see *Audio Anecdotes III*), describing the mathematics, reproduction, and application of binaural hearing.)

2 Recommended Equipment

The Dimensional Stereo Microphone (DSM) systems manufactured by Sonic Studios offer binaural type recording with outstanding results using your head instead of a separate dummy head. It is about the price of a popular SLR 35mm camera, and the sound images are so hallucinogenic the picture pops right out in the listener's imagination. This "covert" system (they fit on glasses and dangle in front of your ears) is popular for recording in social environments where the recordist would like to get the natural activity of people rather than record a lot of questions about what he or she is doing. I use DSMs myself for almost all social settings to avoid drawing attention to myself. The drawback is size, which impacts the noise floor of the system significantly (quiet places will sound hissy.)

For quieter acoustic environments with delicate sounds such as individual leaf rustles or the flight of an insect, the noise floor of the system is crucial. To this end, there is Neumann's KU81i system (which is no longer manufactured, unfortunately).

But even this might not be enough when the dBs drop very low, and for that there is a make-shift design by Lang Elliot that uses Crown's SASS system retrofitted with a pair of Sennheiser MKH-20s. But I hesitate to mention it, since true binaural has excellent front-center detail (meaning that if an event is moving across the sound stage, say from left to right, through the stereo image it sounds natural and does not change frequency content based on movement, while if a system is flawed, it will have a dip in the center) and the SASS system does not. However, if the subject, such as a songbird, is at a distance of 200 feet or more (not too unreasonable with this system), the atmospheric attenuation will take out the highest frequencies, which most influence our perception of "front-center"—in other words, the SASS system has a weak center stage, but at a distance of 200 feet or more, that won't really matter.

The DSM system is under $1,000, the SASS-Sennheiser hybrid is around $3,500 (and requires tooling and assembly), and the Neumann KU81 system is around $4,000 used (if you are lucky enough to find one). There are other binaural systems, some good and some bad, but these three are the only ones that I have tried and liked. If you go out shopping for a "binaural" system, ask to test it first (expect to leave a healthy deposit) and then use it under real conditions. If you plan to use it outdoors, you absolutely need to judge the unit's sensitivity to temperature, humidity changes, and wind.

For a simple and less expensive start-up system, you can always go with *poor man's binaural*, which is a pair of cardioid microphones in an ORTF configuration (named for the Organisation de Radio et Television Francaise who pioneered this technique). Play with the spacing and the angles for what sounds best to you. Start with a spacing of 7.5 inches and an angle of 65 degrees and then, while wearing headphones, focus the image. You will notice that your preference may change as your brain learns how to process this new information.

3 In Conclusion

Binaural recording is a sensational means for recording the real world. It reproduces the full soundscape and teaches the sound recordist about acoustic environments.

My article, "Listening to Nature: Hearing is More than Meets the Eye" (see *Audio Anecdotes I*), describes my own recording work and philosophy.

Please be sure to listen to the environmental binaural recordings included on the CD-ROM accompanying this book.

Annotated Bibliography

[1] John Muir. *The Eight Wilderness Discovery Books* Seattle, WA: The Mountaineers Books, 1992.

John Muir (1838–1914) was a naturalist and a promoter for what has become our national parks system. This collection contains his beautifully detailed observations of nature.

[2] http://www.sonicstudios.com/. Sonic Studios web site.

Sonic Studios is a great source for portable binaural recording gear.

Synthesis

Ambient Synthesis with Random Sound Fields

Hesham Fouad

1 Introduction

Often the most challenging aspect of designing effective virtual acoustic environments is filling the silence that ensues when no other audio events are occurring. The state of complete silence that occurs in such an environment can be disturbing, as the real world is never completely silent. Ambience synthesis is the process of generating interesting (i.e., nonrepeating) detail that tends to be unsynchronized with events in the simulation. The technique presented in this article, Random Sound Fields (RSF), is such a process. It is suitable for modeling discrete sound events occurring at random positions over a well-defined volume with an incidence rate that can vary from periodic to pseudorandom.

One can imagine the problem of modeling the collective effect of a large number of field crickets in an open space, for example. A possible solution is to make use of an actual recording of field crickets and simply play back the recording in a looped fashion. The effect, however, will not be convincing. The looping of the sound will become apparent after a short time and worse yet, the spatial characteristics of sound will not be preserved. Another approach is to model each cricket as a discrete sound source with perhaps a script or some other control mechanism triggering each sound at a prescribed time. The sounds can then be spatially distributed within the virtual acoustic space. The problem here is that a large number of sound sources are required, and placing and controlling those sounds would be tedious and inflexible and the resultant model would be very computationally intensive. RSF offers a better alternative to those approaches in that it provides a way to model such an environment directly in a parametric fashion.

The idea of RSF is conceptually simple. A number of sound sources are placed within a user-defined virtual acoustic space delineated by a volume. At some point, each sound source is activated by placing it at a random location within the volume and starting it. The parameters to the model determine the shape and size of the volume and temporal characteristics of the activation of sound sources within the volume.

In order to implement an RSF, we need two functions: a shape function that determines the placement of sounds within the volume and an activation function that controls the temporal characteristics of the RSF.

2   The Shape Function

In its simplest form, a shape function can simply define an axis-aligned rectangular volume centered at some location C_x, C_y, C_z with spans along each of the principal axes S_x, S_y, S_z. The location of a sound source can then be determined using a random number generator R with values in the range of 0-1 as follows:

$$x = 2S_x R + (C_x - S_x)$$
$$y = 2S_y R + (C_y - S_y)$$
$$z = 2S_z R + (C_z - S_z)$$

Similar functions can be developed for any shape that can be described analytically or even shapes bounded by polygons. The latter case, however, is more complicated since it requires generating random points within a polyhedron. One way to do this is to generate random points within the polyhedron's bounding box followed by a point in a polyhedron test to insure that the point actually lies within the polyhedron. An efficient algorithm for a point in polyhedron test is described in [4]. The spatial distribution of sounds within the volume defined by the shape function is determined by the probability distribution generated by function R. If R produces a uniform probability distribution, then sounds will be equally likely to occur anywhere within the volume. A normal distribution, on the other hand, will tend to place sounds around the center of the volume.

3   The Activation Function

The temporal behavior of sounds within an RSF is determined by a periodic function that generates a pulse train with a user-specified period. A unique period can be specified for each sound source along with a starting offset such that synchronization requirements between sounds can be expressed. Birdcall behavior, for example, can be mimicked by assigning two birdcall sounds the same period and offsetting one of them to give the impression of a call being answered. Finally, the regularity imposed by the use of a periodic function can produce undesirable results, especially when modeling natural phenomenon. We counteract this by jittering the activation times specified by the pulse function. A jitter value is simply a random perturbation of a sound's activation time with a value whose magnitude ranges within a user specified maximum. As the jitter value is increased, the occurrence of a particular sound varies from a periodic pattern to a seemingly random one. Figure 1 depicts the activation times for a sound source with a period of 10 seconds, an offset of 0, and jitter values of 0, 1, 5, and 10 seconds. Each sound's behavior is, therefore, specified as a tuple consisting of the offset, period, and maximum jitter value (o, p, j). The activation times for each sound can then be expressed as the series,

$$S(n) = (n - 1)p + o - j + 2jR,$$

where n is the set of positive integers, and R is a random number generator.

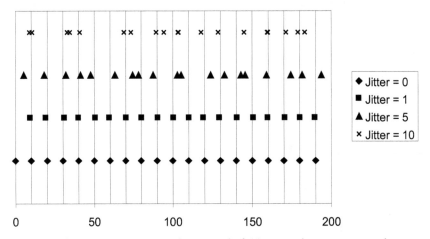

Figure 1. Activation times with a period of 10 sec and various jitter values.

4   Implementing RSF

The implementation of an RSF makes use of a timer mechanism that activates an update function on a regular basis. On each activation of the update function, the current time is compared to the next scheduled activation times of all the sound sources within the volume. If the current time is at or beyond the activation time of any sound, a new position is calculated; the next activation time is computed and stored; and finally the sound is moved to its new location and started. Since the timer takes discrete steps, it might overshoot the activate times. To avoid this, the timer steps should be small relative to the periods of the sounds in the RSF. Obviously, sounds should not be started in a looped (continuous play) fashion. Also, to avoid overlapping the sounds, and the period specified for a sound should be greater than its playback time.

The **Update** subroutine in Figure 2 implements a rectangular RSF volume with a uniform distribution function. We make use of a linked list of structures that maintain information about each sound's activation parameters, position, and state. We assume the caller has assembled the necessary records into a linked list. Upon the return of the **Update** subroutine, the caller makes use of the information contained in those structures to position and start sounds that have the *activate* flag set. The caller must reset the *activate* flag to 0 once a sound is activated. The **drand48** function is a random number generator that generates values ranging from 0 to 1. (See Ken Greenebaum's article "Sample Accurate Synchronization Using Pipelines: Put a Sample In and We Know When It Will Come Out" (see *Audio Anecdotes III*) for a discussion of sample-accurate scheduling of sound playback.)

```
#include <math.h>
#include <stdlib.h>
#define XEXT 10
#define YEXT 10
#define ZEXT 10

typedef struct SoundRec
{
    int soundId;
    float pos[3];
    int activate;
    long nextactive;
    long j, p, o;
```

```
    struct SoundRec *next;
} SOUNDREC;

void Update(SOUNDREC *sound, long time)
{
    static long n=0;
    SOUNDREC *sp = sound;

    while (sp != NULL)
    {
        if (sp->nextactive <= time)
        {
            // Calculate a random position within the volume
            sp->pos[0] = 2*XEXT*drand48()- XEXT;
            sp->pos[1] = 2*YEXT*drand48()- YEXT;
            sp->pos[2] = 2*ZEXT*drand48()- ZEXT;
            // Set the activate flag to indicate that the
            // sound should be activated
            sp->activate = 1;
            // Calculate the next activation time for this
            // sound
            sp->nextactive = (n - 1) * sp->p + sp->o
                           - sp->j + 2 * sp->j * drand48();
            // Must avoid negative activation times
            if (sp->nextactive < 0)
                sp->nextactive = 0;
        }
        sp = sp->next;
    }
    n++;
}
```

Figure 2. Random sound field implementation.

5   Conclusion

The RSF technique is both simple and effective for modeling a class of
ambient sounds. Producing convincing results with RSF usually requires
some experimentation with the timing parameters as well as the spatial
distribution and volume. In the end, however, convincing results can be

achieved with relatively little effort. As always, effective sound design is crucially important to the quality of the results produced. The type and combination of sounds used will determine the effectiveness of the sonic environment produced. RSF promotes experimentation as changing the sounds used and parameters to the model can be done easily.

Annotated Bibliography

[1] M. Back. "Micro-Narratives in Sound Design: Context, Character, and Caricature in Waveform Manipulation" In *Proceedings of the International Conference on Auditory Display, ICAD '96*, 1996.

An interesting paper on narrative structure in nonspeech audio.

[2] J. A. Ballas. "Delivery of Information through Sound." In *Auditory Display: Sonification, Audification, and Auditory Interfaces*, pp. 79–94, edited by Greg Kramer, Reading, MA: Addison-Wesley, 1992.

An important paper on the perception of everyday sounds.

[3] K. Greenebaum. "DirectAnimation—A New Approach to Multimedia." In *Proceedings of the International Conference on Auditory Display, ICAD '97*, November 1997.

This paper discusses a method of creating ambient sound through dynamic layering.

[4] J. Linhart, "A Quick Point in Polyhedron Test." *Computer Graphics* 14(1990), 445–447.

[5] N. E. Miner and T. P. Caudell. "Using Wavelets to Synthesize Stochastic-Based Sounds for Immersive Virtual Environments." In *Proceedings of the International Conference on Auditory Display, ICAD '97*, November 1997.

This paper presents an approach to synthesizing stochastic sounds like water flow, rainfall and wind using wavelets.

[6] R. M. Schafer. *Our Sonic Environment and The Soundscape, the Tuning of the World*. Rochester, VT: Destiny Books, 1994.

A seminal book about our sonic environment.

[7] E. Somers. "Abstract Sound Objects to Expand the Vocabulary of Sound Design for Visual and Theatrical Media." In *Proceedings of*

the International Conference on Auditory Display, ICAD 2000, April 2000.

This paper discusses sound design using abstract sonic objects. See also http://www.sandbook.com/dmusic.html for more information on Eric Somers' work in acoustic design.

[8] T. Takala, J. Hahn, L. Gritz, J. Geigel, J. W. Lee. "Using Physically-Based Models and Genetic Algorithms for Functional Composition of Sound Signals, Synchronized to Animated Motion." *International Computer Music Conference (ICMC)*, September, 1993.

This paper describes Timbre Trees, a functional approach to synthesizing classes of incidental sounds for use in Computer Animation and Virtual Environments.

Band Limited Oscillators Using Wave Table Synthesis

Phil Burk

1 Introduction

Generating an audio rate sawtooth waveform using an overly simple formula, the obvious approach, can result in frequencies above the Nyquist limit. These high frequencies fold back into the audible range creating unpleasant artifacts. This article describes an efficient algorithm using precalculated wave tables to generate band-limited sawtooths, which in turn may be used to generate other band-limited waveforms.

2 Cheap and Dirty Waveform Generation

Analog synthesizers use tone generators, called *oscillators*, to generate a few basic waveforms. These oscillators can in turn be used with other synthesis modules to produce complex sounds. Waveform oscillators are a fundamental building block of audio synthesis and most digital software synthesizers provide them.

It is very easy to digitally synthesize a waveform that looks like a sawtooth. Simply increment a value until it goes over the top, and then snap it back to the bottom. This value ranges between −1.0 and +1.0.

```
phase += 2.0 * frequency / sampleRate;
if( phase >= 1.0 )
    phase -= 2.0;
else if(( phase < -1.0 )
    phase += 2.0;
```

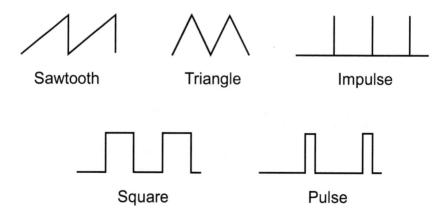

Sawtooth   Triangle   Impulse

Square   Pulse

Figure 1. How common waveforms would ideally appear on an oscilloscope.

I refer to the value as "phase" in the above code because this signal is often used as the angular phase position for various oscillators. For the purposes of this article, I will refer to the repeating sawtooth-like signal generated by this function as a *Phaser*. (This is not to be confused with *phasor* [4], which is a rotating vector described by the function e^{jwt}.)

Starting with a Phaser, you can easily generate the other waveforms. For example, to generate a square wave or a sine wave from a Phaser:

```
/* Use a comparator to generate a square wave. */
squareWave = (phase >= 0.0) ? 1.0 : -1.0;

/* Scale phase to 2 PI range and calculate sine wave. */
sineWave = sin(phase * PI);
```

3   Trouble in Paradise

This seems almost too good to be true. We can generate all the basic waveforms using very simple arithmetic. But there is a problem with this simplistic approach. The result may look like the desired waveform, but unfortunately it sounds terrible. If you listen to an analog synthesizer, and sweep a sawtooth oscillator from low to very high frequencies, it sounds continuous, nice and smooth. But a simple digital oscillator like the one above will sometimes produce multiple tones, and as you sweep it up, you can hear tones that sound like they are sweeping down. It basically sounds very "grungy" and "digital." This is the dirty part of "cheap and dirty." On the accompanying CD-ROM, you can find audio recordings of a simple Phaser sweeping up in pitch. Compare that to the recording of a band-limited sawtooth generated using the technique we are about to propose.

Example 1. Sounds

```
saw_bl_sweep.wav      = frequency sweep using new band
                        limited technique.
saw_phaser_sweep.wav = frequency sweep using simple Phaser.
saw_bl_735.wav        = fixed frequency using new band
                        limited technique.
saw_phaser_735.wav   = fixed frequency using simple Phaser.
```

You can also interact with an online software synthesizer that demonstrates a variety of band-limited and non-band-limited oscillators at: http://www.softsynth.com/jsyn/examples/.

Why does this grungy sound occur? And how can we solve this problem?

3.1 Fourier Analysis of a Sawtooth

We have learned from Fourier that any repeating waveform can be constructed from an infinite series of sines and cosines [2]. The formula for generating a sawtooth wave with an amplitude of 1.0 using a Fourier series is

$$f(x) = (2/\pi) * (\sin(x) - \sin(2x)/2 + \sin(3x)/3 - \sin(4x)/4 + ...).$$

Thus an idealized sawtooth waveform consists of an infinite series of sine waves. This means that an idealized sawtooth waveform contains frequencies stretching to infinity, but in increasingly smaller amounts. This is the source of the problem.

Please refer to Chamberlin's articles, "Floating Point Fast Fourier Transform" (page 101) and "Fast Fourier Transform Using Integer Math" (page 127), for more background on Fourier analysis.

3.2 Nyquist Limit

Einstein told us that objects cannot travel faster than the speed of light. Back in 1928, Henry Nyquist placed a similar limit on the audio world. He proved that you cannot represent frequencies higher than half the rate at which they are sampled. So if we have a sample rate of 44100 Hz,

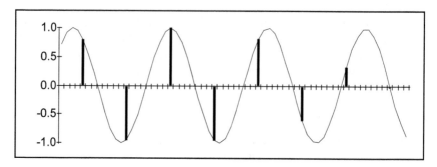

Figure 2. Sine wave near Nyquist Rate.

typical for audio CDs, then we cannot represent frequencies higher than 22050 Hz. This rate, SampleRate/2, is called the *Nyquist Rate*.

Be careful here. It is commonly thought that we can represent any frequencies up to the Nyquist Rate perfectly well. But that is not true in a practical sense. Consider a sine wave that is extremely close to the Nyquist Rate. If we sample that signal at the peaks and troughs, then we will have a good idea of that signal's amplitude. But if we sample it at a slightly different phase, then we may catch it closer to where the signal is crossing zero, so our data will indicate that the signal is lower than it actually is.

In Figure 2, we see that the sampled value is rising and falling as we catch the sine wave at various phases. According to Nyquist, it is theoretically possible to take those sampled values and reconstruct the original signal. But this requires a **perfect** low-pass filter that can analyze the signal over an infinite time. Such a filter does not exist. And if it did, the sharp cut-off would cause an undesirable ringing related to the Gibbs Phenomenon described later in this chapter. Also, most musical signals are short-lived, so even a perfect reconstruction filter would not have enough information to reproduce them perfectly.

To summarize, our ability to represent frequencies tapers off as we approach the Nyquist Rate. So when we synthesize a musical waveform, we have to start tapering off any high frequency partials before they reach the Nyquist Rate, and never try to include partials that exceed the Nyquist rate.

3.3   The Effect on Sound Quality

When we calculate a sawtooth using the simple Phaser technique from above, we are essentially sampling a mathematically ideal sawtooth wave.

Partial	Amplitude	Freq (ideal)	Freq (heard)
1	1.000	4300	4300
2	0.500	8600	8600
3	0.333	12900	12900
4	0.250	17200	17200
5	0.200	21500	21500
6	0.167	25800	18300
7	0.143	30100	14000
8	0.125	34400	9700
9	0.111	38700	5400
10	0.100	43000	1100

Table 1. The first 10 partials and their amplitudes of a 4300 Hz sawtooth wave sampled at 44110 Hz.

This ideal sawtooth contains infinite partials, which we cannot properly represent. The energy from these high frequencies has to go somewhere so it reappears as frequencies below the Nyquist Rate. This is called aliasing. A frequency that is supposed to be N Hz above the Nyquist Rate will actually be heard as a frequency N Hz below the Nyquist. For a 4300 Hz sawtooth wave sampled at 44100 Hz, the first 10 partials and their amplitudes are given in Table 1.

Notice that the tenth partial is ten percent of the amplitude of the fundamental, which is quite loud. And it will be heard at a lower frequency than the fundamental! This is unacceptable.

In the sound example, "saw_phaser_735.wav," you can hear the high order partials folded back into the audio range. Because the frequency chosen is close to an integer submultiple of the Nyquist Rate, the folded partials are closer in frequency to the original low-order partials. In fact, you can hear them beating together and causing a very fast tremolo.

4   Using Wave Table Synthesis to Solve the Problem

So how can we generate the audio waveforms we want without also generating these ugly artifacts? Clearly, we need to limit the production of the higher frequency partials. Using a low-pass filter won't work because, as we saw above, the undesirable partials wrap around and are interspersed among the desirable ones. So we need to avoid creating these partials in the first place. There are several ways to do this. After experimenting

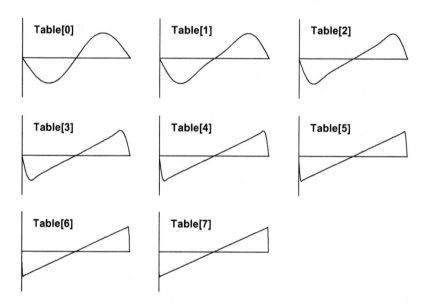

Figure 3. Waveforms for eight tables.

with several techniques when developing JSyn [1], I decided to solve the problem using wave table synthesis.

Wave table synthesis involves placing a precomputed waveform into a large array. Then a Phaser is generated as above. The Phaser is then used to calculate an index into the table. One can interpolate between adjacent values in the table to create a smooth output. This is a common technique used to generate sine-wave oscillators for use in FM synthesis.

The advantage of this technique is that very complex signals can be precomputed. In our case, we will calculate sawtooth waveforms containing all of the partials up to the Nyquist limit. We can use multiple tables and choose the best one depending on the oscillator frequency. The top wave table can contain a pure sine wave. It will be used when the frequency is between NyquistRate/2 and the NyquistRate. The next table will be for frequencies an octave lower and will contain a mixture of two sine waves corresponding to the first two terms of the Fourier expression. Each successive table will have twice as many partials.

In Figure 3 we can see the waveforms for eight tables. Notice how they progress from a pure sine wave to something very close to an ideal sawtooth wave as we add more partials.

5 Generating Tables

In JSyn, I use eight tables. For a 44100 Hz sample rate, this covers an eight-octave range from 86.1 Hz to 11025 Hz. Each table contains 1024 single precision floating point values. The tables occupy 8*1024*4=32768 bytes.

I could have precomputed the wave tables and compiled them with my program. But this would have added 32 kilobytes to JSyn. Since JSyn is downloaded as a browser plugin, I want to keep the size as small as possible. So I compute the wave tables when I launch JSyn.

To avoid a delay while initializing, this calculation needs to be very fast. My approach is to first calculate the top-level table, which is just a pure sine wave. For the other tables, I use that first sine table as a look-up table instead of making more calls to the sin() function. Since I am adding harmonics, I can index into that sine table using integers and do not have to interpolate between sine values.

Here is code to fill the top-level sine table. Notice that the phase is shifted by PI. This is so that the phase of the band-limited sawtooth will match that of the Phaser, allowing us to interpolate between them for low frequencies.

```
// Fill initial sine table with values for -PI to PI.
cycleSize = 1024;
for(j=0; j<tableSize; j++)
   table[j] =
      sin( ((((double)j)/(double)cycleSize )*PI*2) - PI );
```

Here is some code to fill the succeeding tables with partials scaled by 1/N:

```
// Build wave tables. Scale partials by 1/N.
for( i=1; i<numTables; i++ ){
   int numPartials;
   table = allTables[i];

   // Each table has twice as many partials as the previous.
   numPartials = 1 << i;

   // Add together partials for this table.
   for( k=0; k<numPartials; k++ ){
      double ampl;
      int sineIndex = 0;
```

```
        int partial = k+1;

        // Calculate amplitude for Nth partial
        ampl = 1.0 / partial;

        for( j=0; j<tableSize; j++ ){
            table[j] += ampl * sineTable[sineIndex];

            // Advance through sine table to generate harmonic
            // partial.
            sineIndex += partial;

            // Wrap index at end of cycle.
            if( sineIndex >= cycleSize )
                sineIndex -= cycleSize;
        }
    }
}
```

5.1   Normalization

We want the values in these wave tables to be between −1.0 and +1.0. In
order to guarantee that we need to normalize each table. This involves
scanning the table once to determine the maximum absolute value. Then
scanning the table a second time and dividing each of the values by that
maximum value.

5.2   Gibbs Phenomenon

When I first built these tables, I noticed that the waveforms looked a
little odd. The sawtooth was very wiggly near the corners and had a
bump right at the edge. This is known as the *Gibbs Phenomenon* [3]. It
is caused by the abrupt change in amplitude of the partials when we chop
off higher terms from the Fourier series. Figure 4 shows the fourth table
containing 16 partials showing the Gibbs effect.

   Besides looking odd, the Gibbs Phenomenon does have unpleasant
audible effects. When the frequency is smoothly changing, partials can
suddenly appear or disappear as they cross the Nyquist limit. This can
cause abrupt changes in timbre. Also, partials near the Nyquist limit are
not reproduced very well by real-world digital audio hardware and can
generate audible artifacts including beating. To eliminate these problems,

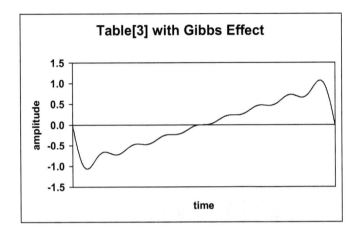

Figure 4. The fourth table containing 16 partials showing the Gibbs effect

we can gradually taper off the higher order partials by multiplying them by a *raised cosine window*. The raised cosine can be calculated as follows:

```
// This can be calculated once for each table
double kGibbs = PI / (2 * numPartials);

// This is calculated once for each partial in each table
double temp        = cos((partial-1) * kGibbs);
double raisedCosine = temp * temp; // Square it

// Calculate windowed amplitude for Nth partial
ampl = raisedCosine / partial;
```

Figure 5 is a chart of the first 16 partial's amplitudes that are used in the fourth table and the window that we multiply them by.

Figure 6 is the resulting table with the wiggles due to the Gibbs Phenomenon eliminated.

6   Scanning and Bilinear Interpolation

Now that we have the wave tables, we are ready to generate a band-limited sawtooth waveform. The basic steps are:

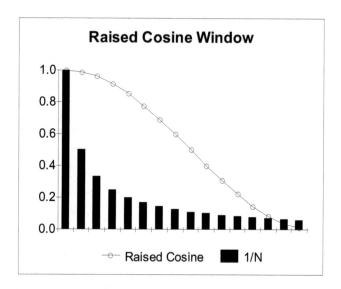

Figure 5. The first 16 partial amplitudes that are used in the fourth table the window we multiply them by.

(1) Generate sawtooth-like Phaser as above.

(2) Calculate base two logarithm of scaled oscillator frequency to determine which pair of octave tables to use.

(3) For each table, look up a waveform value based on phase. By interpolating between entries in a table, we can reduce quantization noise, which would add harmonic distortion to a signal.

(4) Interpolate between results of Step 3 based on log of frequency. By interpolating between the results of two adjacent tables, we can glide smoothly up or down in frequency without hearing abrupt discontinuities in amplitude or in spectral content, which would cause clicks.

These steps are explained in the following sections.

If you are not familiar with the term *interpolation*, it is a technique for smoothly transitioning between one value and another. Suppose we have two values, x_0 and x_1, and a fraction between 0.0 and 1.0. When the fraction is 0.0, we want the result, y, to be equal to x_0. When the fraction is 1.0, we want y to be equal to x_1. As the fraction moves from

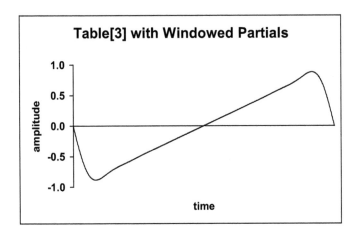

Figure 6. The resulting table of Figure 5 with the wiggles due to the Gibbs Phenomenon eliminated.

0.0 and 1.0, we want the value of y to move smoothly from x_0 and x_1. Here is an equation that will give us the desired behavior:

$$y = x_0 + fraction * (x_1 - x_0).$$

6.1 Logarithmic Scale

To determine which octave table we should use, we need a value, called *flevel*, that tells us which table to use, and how to interpolate between them. We want the value to be 0.0 when the frequency is NyquistRate/2 so that we will use table #0, the sine wave. It should then increase by one for each octave lower in frequency. We can calculate flevel as follows:

```
flevel = 0.0 - log2(4 * frequency / sampleRate)
```

In the code example on the CD you can find an optimized method for estimating this value that is based on dissecting the bits of the IEEE floating point number to get the base two exponent and a fraction.

6.2 Interpolating a Value from the Tables

There are then three possibilities for flevel. If flevel is less than zero, then we are in the range between Nyquist/2 and the Nyquist Rate. In this range, we interpolate between a pure sine wave for Nyquist/2 and a zero value. That way, we will have zero amplitude at the Nyquist Rate.

When we are at a frequency that falls between two tables, then we will look-up the value in both tables and interpolate between them.

The bottom table is very nearly a pure sawtooth wave. At the far end of the range (low frequencies), we run out of tables so we interpolate between the value of the top table (lowest frequency) and the Phaser that we are using as the basis for the oscillator. Since we want to interpolate over the range 0.0 Hz to the lowest frequency, we generate a fraction from the frequency directly instead of flevel.

These three cases based on flevel are handled in this code. This looks up the wave values and interpolates between adjacent table entries, then interpolates between the two tables.

```
// IMPORTANT: flevel increases with decreasing frequency
float highval; // sample corresponding to higher flevel
float lowval;  // sample corresponding to lower flevel

// Phase ranges from -1.0 to 1.0, table size is 1024.
fSampleIndex = 512 + (phase*512);
iSampleIndex = (int) fSampleIndex;

// Calculate fraction for interpolation between indexed
// samples.
sampleInterp = fSampleIndex - iSampleIndex;
iTableIndex = (int) flevel;
tableInterp = flevel - iTableIndex;

if (flevel < 0.0) // Frequency range is Nyquist to Nyquist/2
{
    lowval = 0;
    left = table[0][sampleIndex];
    right = table[0][sampleIndex+1];
    highval = left + (sampleInterp * (right-left));
}
else if (flevel < NumTables) // Range is Nyquist/2 to
                             // top-table
{
    left = table[iTableIndex][sampleIndex];
    right = table[iTableIndex][sampleIndex + 1];
    lowval = left + (sampleInterp * (right-left));
    left = table[iTableIndex + 1][sampleIndex];
    right = table[iTableIndex + 1][sampleIndex + 1];
```

```
   highval = left + (sampleInterp * (right-left));
}
else // Frequency range is top table frequency to zero.
{
   left = table[iTableIndex][sampleIndex];
   right = table[iTableIndex][sampleIndex + 1];
   lowval = left + (sampleInterp * (right-left));
   highval = phase;

   // Interpolation goes all the way to zero frequency so
   // can't use log.
   tableInterp = 1.0 - (frequency / topTableFrequency);
}

// Interpolate between values for adjacent frequencies.
value = lowval +(tableInterp * (highval-lowval));
```

An optimized version of this code appears on the CD-ROM.

7   Generating Other Waveforms

We can easily generate other band-limited waveforms using our band-limited sawtooth. Here are two examples:

Impulse waveform. To generate a band-limited impulse train, we simply differentiate the sawtooth waveform. When the sawtooth drops, we get our spike.

```
impulse = 0.5 * (sawtooth - sawtoothPrevious);
sawtoothPrevious = sawtooth;
```

Pulse and square waveform. A pulse waveform can be constructed by subtracting one sawtooth from another. The width is dependent on the phase difference. If the phase difference is 180 degrees, then you get a square wave. In this code fragment, the width, phase, and phaseInc are all fractions between −1.0 and +1.0. So we shift the phase 180 degrees by adding one.

```
// Calculate first sawtooth
val1 = SawtoothBL( phase );
```

```
// Generate second sawtooth offset by pulse width
phase2 = phase + 1.0 - width;

if( phase2 > 1.0 )
    phase2 -= 2.0;
val2 = SawtoothBL( phase2 );

// Need to adjust amplitude based on phaseInc
scale = 1.0 - fabs(phaseInc);
pulseWave = scale * (val - val2 - width);
```

7.1   Keep Those Old Oscillators

You might be tempted to get rid of the old non-band-limited oscillators now that we have band-limited versions. But hang onto them; they
are still useful. The non-band-limited impulse train is handy for getting
impulse responses from filters and other processing modules. The non-
band-limited pulse and square wave can be used to trigger logic modules.
And the non-band-limited sawtooth is very useful for driving waveshapers
thus making a wave-table oscillator.

8   Performance Measurements

Band limited waveforms sound better, but what do they cost in terms
of CPU time? I made some measurements using CSyn running on a
900 MHz Athlon Thunderbird. The test involved mixing more and more
oscillators together until the CPU utilization exceeded 80%. For each
oscillator, there is an accompanying adder used to mix the output with
the others. Table 2 shows the maximum number of oscillators that could
be generated using the simple "cheap and dirty" method, and the new
band-limited method.

The band-limited waveform generator consumes roughly three to five
times more CPU than the non-band-limited equivalent.

Max # Oscillators	Sawtooth	Square
Simple	323	285
Band-Limited	102	68

Table 2. Maximum numbers of oscillators that can be generated using the simple
and band-limited methods.

9 Code Example

A C code example has been provided on the CD-ROM, that calculates a band-limited sawtooth. A non-band-limited sawtooth is also generated. These two signals are swept across the frequency range so you can compare their sound quality. They are isolated in the left and right channels so you can use the balance knob on your mixer to fade back and forth between them. The difference will be quite obvious.

9.1 Using a Guard Point

You may notice in the code example that the period of the fundamental sine wave is 1024, but the table size is $1024+1 = 1025$. The extra point is called a guard point and is used to optimize interpolation. When interpolating between values within a table, we use the formula:

```
y = t[i] + fraction * (t[i+1] - t[i])
```

The index i can range from 0 to 1023. But at the end of the table, i+1 would be 1024. That would be past the end of the table if we only have 1024 values. We could check for this special case, and use t[0] instead of t[i+1] because the waveform is repetitive. But the conditional code would be inefficient. Instead we add an extra point and set it equal to t[0]. Then we always have a sample point one past our current index that we can use to interpolate quickly.

10 Other Solutions

John Lazzaro describes a different technique involving a closed form solution to series summation. See his article "Subtractive Synthesis without Filters" (page 55).

10.1 Band Limited Impulse Trains by Tim Stilson

Tim Stilson proposed [5] an alternative technique that involves calculating a Band Limited Impulse Train (BLIT). A sawtooth waveform can be generated by integrating the BLIT waveform. A pulse waveform can be generated by adding two BLITs offset in phase and then integrating the result. When integrating, you should multiply the sum by something like 0.999 each time to prevent an offset from building up. This is called a *leaky integrator*.

Calculating the BLIT is not very complex, but it involves two sine calculations, some multiplies, and a divide. You will probably want to interpolate between two BLITs with different numbers of harmonics to avoid pops when harmonics come in or go out. Obviously, the speed of the sine calculation has a big impact on the performance of this technique. I found that on my AMD Athlon-based PC, the wave table solution was somewhat faster than the BLIT technique. But the BLIT technique could probably be further optimized and may be faster than the wave table technique on some platforms.

11 Conclusion

This technique provides a very clean sounding set of basic waveform oscillators. They do require more CPU power than the "cheap and dirty" versions, but for professional music applications, they are worth the cost. Different techniques may be more or less efficient on different platforms. But the sonic quality is comparable so just use whichever one is fastest on your machine.

Annotated Bibliography

[1] Phil Burk. "JSyn – Audio Synthesis API for Java and C." *Proceedings of the 1998 International Computer Music Conference.* Available from World Wide Web http://www.softsynth.com/jsyn/, 1998.

A music software toolkit in Java written by the author of this article. The band-limited oscillator can heard in real-time using one of the example Applets.

[2] M.A. Khamsi. "Fourier Series: Basic Results." S.O.S. MAThematics. Available from World Wide Web http://www.sosmath.com/fourier/fourier1/fourier1.html.

The basic equations of Fourier analysis and synthesis with animated GIFs showing the synthesis of sawtooth and square waves.

[3] M.A. Khamsi. "Gibbs Phenomenon." S.O.S. MAThematics. Available from World Wide Web http://www.sosmath.com/fourier/fourier3/gibbs.html.

An explanation of why Fourier synthesis can cause odd bumps at the edges of waveforms.

[4] Ken Steiglitz. *A Digital Signal Processing Primer with Applications to Digital Audio and Computer Music.* Reading, MA: Addison-Wesley Publishing Co., 1996.

A very readable book on the math behind DSP, with a focus on music.

[5] Tim Stilson. "Alias-Free Digital Synthesis of Classic Analog Waveforms." *Proceedings of the 1996 International Computer Music Conference.* Available from World Wide Web http://ccrma-www.stanford.edu/~stilti/papers/Welcome.html, 1996.

A theoretical paper on waveform synthesis techniques focussing on the BLIT technique.

Subtractive Synthesis without Filters

John Lazzaro and John Wawrzynek

1 Introduction

The earliest commercially successful electronic music synthesizer keyboards used analog circuits to implement subtractive sound synthesis. These monophonic instruments, produced by manufacturers such as Moog, Arp, Emu, and Roland in the 1970s, produce signature sounds that remain musically useful to this day.

One approach to modeling the voices of these analog instruments on a digital computers is to emulate the signal processing performed by each oscillator, filter, and amplifier of the original instrument. Readers interested in taking this approach may consult [2].

In this article, we take a different approach. In Section 2, we analyze the basics of analog subtractive synthesis, using the simple patch of a square-wave oscillator processed by a low-pass filter with a dynamically variable cut-off frequency. In Section 3, we show how a single mathematical function can model both the oscillator and filter together, and describe an efficient formation for this function [4], [7]. Section 4 shows additional applications of this technique.

2 Subtractive Synthesis

The block diagram in Figure 1 shows the spectral processing that underlies subtractive synthesis. In this diagram, an oscillator with a fixed square waveform shape is coupled with a low-pass filter. Two properties of the system are open to dynamic control: the pitch of the oscillator and the

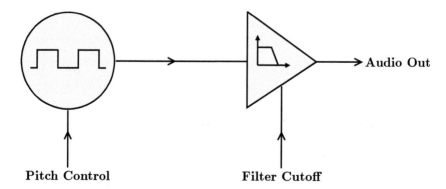

Figure 1. Block diagram for simple subtractive synthesis: a square wave oscillator processed by a low-pass filter whose cut-off frequency is under dynamic control.

cut-off frequency of the filter. Not shown are post-processing blocks to shape the amplitude envelope of the filter output.

Most of the 70s-era analog synthesizers are monophonic keyboard instruments. The keyboard input section of these instruments generates an analog voltage that codes the position of the currently depressed key. In a typical set-up, this signal provides the baseline oscillator pitch and filter cut-off control signals, so that the spectral signature of the sound scales across the keyboard.

To animate this static sound, oscillator pitch and filter frequency are dynamically varied around this baseline. Dynamic variation may be applied via specialized circuits (low-frequency oscillators, envelope generators triggered by a note depression) and by manual controllers (wheels, paddles, or joysticks that generate a continuous signal).

A square-wave oscillator generates a signal that can be described by this function, expressed as an infinite series:

$$\text{square}(p) = \sin(2\pi p) + \frac{1}{3}\sin(3 \cdot 2\pi p) + \frac{1}{5}\sin(5 \cdot 2\pi p) + \dots \quad (1)$$

We can write this function more compactly using summation notation:

$$\text{square}(p) = \sum_{k=0}^{\infty} \frac{1}{2k+1}\sin(2\pi(2k+1)p). \quad (2)$$

The function takes the phase pointer p as an argument. To produce one complete cycle of the square wave, p is swept from 0.0 to 1.0. To

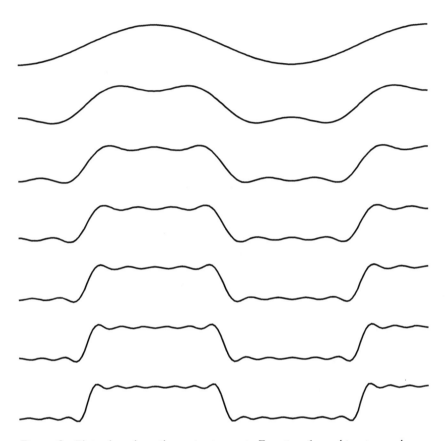

Figure 2. Plots show how the series terms in Equation 1 combine to produce a square wave. The top plot shows the first term of Equation 1, the second plot from the top shows the sum of the first two terms of Equation 1, the third plot from the top shows the sum of the first three terms of Equation 1, etc.

provide intuition that this series really does produce a square wave, we show in Figure 2 a set of waveforms, showing the result of summing the first two terms, first three terms, first four terms, etc. As we would expect from a sound with a clear pitch, a square wave produces a *harmonic series*—i.e., all sinusoidal frequencies are integral multiples of the lowest frequency component.

This series formulation lets us plot the spectrum of the square wave directly, by plotting the coefficients in front of each sine component. Figure 3(a) shows this spectral plot in decibel (dB) units, which correspond

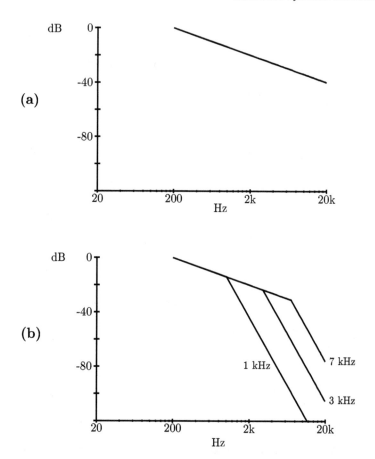

Figure 3. (a) Spectral shape of a 200 Hz square wave. (b) Spectral shape of a 200 Hz square wave, filtered by 24 dB/octave low-pass filters with cut-off frequencies of 1 kHz, 3 kHz, and 7 kHz as marked.

to how humans perceive relative amplitudes (a 10 dB amplitude increase approximately doubles the perceived loudness at a given frequency).

In Figure 3(b), we plot the spectrum for the complete system shown in Figure 1—a square-wave oscillator processed by low-pass filter—for several different values of the filter cut-off frequency. Dynamic variation of cut-off frequency acts to interpolate the spectrum between the shown patterns. For simplicity, Figure 3(b) draws filter responses using straight lines—real-world, low-pass filter responses have curved sections, and may even be nonmonotonic.

As we stated in the introduction, one approach to implementing sub-tractive synthesis on digital computers is to emulate the signal processing performed by each component of the instrument. For the simple system in Figure 1, independent modules for alias-free square-wave generation [6] and dynamic filters would be designed and interconnected.

In this article, however, we consider the problem at a higher level of abstraction. Three properties make the system shown in Figure 1 a good framework for analog musical instruments:

(1) The type of spectral variation shown in Figure 3(b) is musically interesting.

(2) This spectral variation occurs by varying a single parameter in a monotonic way.

(3) The method efficiently maps into analog circuits.

In the Section 3, we present a digital synthesis method that maintains properties [1] and [2] above, while mapping efficiently onto the digital abstraction.

3 Subtractive Synthesis without Filters

Our goal in this section is to find a single simple algorithm to compute both the oscillator and filter blocks in Figure 1. One way to approach this problem is to modify the square-wave generation function shown in Equation 2, so that it incorporates low-pass filtering. The function shown below is an example of this method; this function is a simplified form of a library function contained in the MPEG-4 Structured Audio signal processing language [5], [1]:

$$B(p, a) = \frac{1 - |a|}{1 - |a^{H+1}|} \sum_{k=0}^{H} a^k \cos(2\pi(k+1)p). \qquad (3)$$

Like Equation 2, this series is a harmonic series, and it uses a phase pointer p to plot out one complete cycle of the waveform over the range $0.0 \le p \le 1.0$. For compactness, this equation uses the cosine function $(\cos(x) = \sin(x + \pi/2))$ instead of the sine function. However, the key difference between this function and Equation 2 is the new parameter a, which has a role similar to the filter cut-off frequency in the system shown in Figure 1.

Examining Equation 3, we see that a is used to implement parametric scaling: Each sine component $2\pi(k+1)p$ is scaled by the value a^k. Figure 4(a) shows the low-pass spectral shapes that this equation generates, for values of a in the range $0.0 < a < 1.0$.

Equation 3 is a finite series summation, whose scaling formula has been carefully chosen to have a special property. Namely, by using the series summation techniques described in [3], [4], and [7], it is possible to derive an exact closed form solution for Equation 3:

$$B(p,a) = \frac{(1 - a\cos(\theta))(S_1 \cos(\theta) - S_2 \cos(N\theta))}{1 - 2a\cos(\theta) + a^2}$$
$$+ \frac{-a\sin(\theta)(S_2 \sin(N\theta) - S_1 \sin(\theta))}{1 - 2a\cos(\theta) + a^2}, \quad (4)$$

where

$$\theta = 2\pi p$$

$$N = H + 2$$

$$S_1 = \frac{1 - |a|}{1 - |a^{H+1}|}$$

$$S_2 = \frac{1 - |a|}{(1/a^{H+1}) - (|a^{H+1}|/a^{H+1})}.$$

By using Equation 4, we can generate a waveform value using an amount of computation that is independent of the number of sinusoidal components. If a is a constant, a waveform data point calculation requires a phase pointer advance, two $[\sin(x), \cos(x)]$ calculations, nine multiplies, five additions, and one divide.

We can use Equation 4 to directly compute waveform data points for a subtractive synthesis system. Several issues arise in a practical implementation, which we discuss next.

3.1 Aliasing

In a typical real-time computer music application, audio output samples are sent to a digital-to-analog converter at a fixed audio sample rate (for example the compact disc sampling rate of 44,100 Hz). To avoid unpleasant audio artifacts due to aliasing (see Burk's article "Band Limited Oscillators Using Wave Table Synthesis" (page 37) for more details on aliasing), the output samples should not have frequency components higher than one half the audio sample rate (for the compact disc sampling rate, frequency components above 22,050 Hz should not be generated).

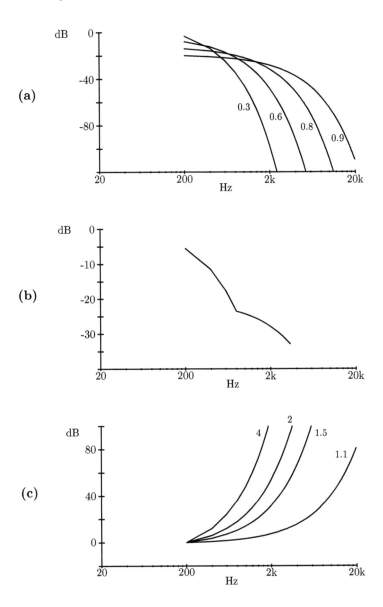

Figure 4. (a) Spectral shapes for a 200 Hz waveform produced using Equation 3, marked with its a value. (b) Spectral shape for a 200 Hz waveform produced using Equation 7. (c) Spectral shapes for a 200 Hz waveform produced using Equation 3, for values of $a > 1$ (as marked), with spectra shifted to start at 0 dB.

Examining Equation 3, we see that the highest frequency component of the generated waveform is $\cos(2\pi(H+1)p)$. In a typical computer music application, we are sweeping the phase pointer p over the range $0.0 < a < 1.0$, at a bounded rate. For example, in a MIDI application, a maximum frequency for a note may be estimated by considering the MIDI note number value and the maximum depth of all pitch modulations. Given this maximum frequency, and the output sampling rate of the system, we can choose the integral value of H that ensures aliasing can not occur.

3.2   Numerical Issues

To produce clean waveforms over a range of a values, Equation 4 must be computed using at least single precision (32-bit) IEEE floating point arithmetic or equivalent. In addition, values of a around unity should be handled with care, as the denominator evaluates to zero for $a = 1$, causing a divide-by-zero error. A simple solution is to detect all a values within an empirically determined $a = 1 \pm \varepsilon$ "dangerous regime," and replace these values with the nearest safe value.

3.3   Trigonometric Computations

The simplest (and slowest) way to compute the sine and cosine functions in Equation 4 is to use the math library functions. A much faster alternative is to use a table look-up approach. We have implemented a table-driven system that uses a single 2560 element floating-point table to represent one and one quarter cycles of the sinusoid. We directly address into this table for sine evaluations, and apply a quarter-cycle offset for cosine evaluations; no interpolation is done.

The lack of interpolation only results in significant artifacts when the denominator of Equation 4 is very close to zero. We have found it most efficient to check for this rare condition, and recompute the values using the library sine and cosine functions.

4   Cascading Multiple Functions

In more advanced synthesis applications, we may wish to cascade several copies of the function shown in Equation 3, to build up a complex spectral shape. The function shown below simplifies this task, by adding a new parameter L to specify the lowest frequency component in the signal:

$$B(p,a) = \frac{1 - |a|}{1 - |a^{H+1}|} \sum_{k=L}^{L+H} a^{k-L} \cos(2\pi(k+1)p). \qquad (5)$$

Like Equation 3, this function can also be expressed in closed form, as

$$B(p,a) = \frac{(1 - a\cos(\theta))(S_1 \cos(Q\theta) - S_2 \cos(N\theta))}{1 - 2a\cos(\theta) + a^2}$$
$$+ \frac{-a\sin(\theta)(S_2 \sin(N\theta) - S_1 \sin(Q\theta))}{1 - 2a\cos(\theta) + a^2}, \qquad (6)$$

where

$$\theta = 2\pi p$$

$$N = L + H + 2$$

$$Q = L + 1$$

$$S_1 = \frac{1 - |a|}{1 - |a^{H+1}|}$$

$$S_2 = \frac{1 - |a|}{(1/a^{H+1}) - (|a^{H+1}|/a^{H+1})}.$$

Note that if L has a value of zero, Equation 6 reduces to Equation 4, as expected. When notating a cascade of functions, we use the notation $B(p, H, L, a)$. For example, the equation

$$f(p) = B(p, 3, 0, 0.5) + 0.5073\, B(p, 12, 4, 0.92) \qquad (7)$$

describes a spectrum with a spectrum whose partials fall in amplitude quickly for lower frequencies, and more gradually for higher frequencies. The weighting value 0.5073 was chosen to match the spectral amplitudes at the crossover point. Figure 4(b) shows the spectrum produced by this function.

When we introduced Equation 3 as a stand-alone equation in Section 3, we noted that the parameter a should lie in the range $0.0 < a < 1.0$. We chose this limit because a^k grows very quickly with k if $a > 1$. This fast-growing function would be difficult to control in a musically useful way.

However, in cascaded configurations, one function in the cascade might only be active for a small range of k values. In this case, functions with $a > 1$ may be useful, in order to generate small spectral regions with positive slope. Figure 4(c) shows the positive-slope spectral shapes for the $a > 1$ condition.

5 Conclusion

The technique we describe in this article generates an interesting sound in an efficient way, without the sonic grunge of aliasing artifacts. We hope you find a use for it in your work.

6 Acknowledgements

Thanks to Eric Scheirer, Robin Davies, Perry Cook, Ronen Barzel, and Ken Greenebaum.

Annotated Bibliography

[1] ISO (International Standards Organization). International Standard ISO 14496 (MPEG-4), Part 3 (Audio), Subpart 5 (Structured Audio). Geneva, CH: ISO, 1999.

To learn more about Structured Audio, consult this comprehensive MPEG document.

[2] J. Lane, D. Hoory, E. Martinez, and P. Wang. "Modeling Analog Synthesis with DSPs." *Computer Music Journal* 21:4(1977), 23–41.

[3] R. F. Moore. *Elements of Computer Music.* Englewood Cliffs, NJ: Prentice Hall, 1990.

[4] J. A. Moorer. "The Synthesis of Complex Audio Spectra by Means of Discrete Summation Formulae." *Journal of the Audio Engineering Society* 24(1976), 717–727.

[5] E. D. Scheirer and B. L. Vercoe. "SAOL: The MPEG-4 Structured Audio Orchestra Language." *Computer Music Journal* 23:2(1999), 31–51.

[6] T. Stilson and J. O. Smith. "Alias-Free Digital Synthesis of Classic Analog Waveforms." *1996 International Computer Music Conference,* 1996.

A review comparing series summation technique for pulse generation with other approaches.

[7] G. Winham and K. Steiglitz. "Input Generators for Digital Sound Synthesis." *Journal of the Acoustical Society of America* 47:2(1970), 665–666.

Introduction of the series summation technique.

Signal Processing

Finite Impulse Response Filters

Stuart Allman

When designing applications requiring digital signal processing functionality, it is desirable to be able to use one filter that is both simple to implement and can scale with system resources. A finite impulse response filter offers the designer tradeoffs based on system constraints such as ALU word length, memory footprints, and processor performance.

The finite impulse response filter may just hold the key to fulfilling your desire for such a simple filter. The Finite Impulse Response filter, or FIR filter as it is more casually referred to, uses the inherently simple attributes of convolution to shape the frequency response of an input signal. Unlike an infinite impulse response filter, the calculations involved in an FIR filter do not employ feedback so oscillations based on ALU quantization error are not an issue.

This article begins with a "far view" explanation of how the filter works and then progresses into a bit of theory on the filter. The goal of this article is to provide enough resources to enable the reader to implement a filter in half an hour, or analyze the filter attributes in more detail over several hours. To this end, an example FIR filter implementation coded in C will be presented which is available on the CD-ROM accompanying this book.

1   A Simple Explanation

The finite impulse response filter is one of the most elegant and basic signal processing algorithms. If you are already acquainted with the concept of convolution, from perhaps a college signal processing class, then the finite impulse response filter will seem quite familiar, otherwise the basic concepts are quite straightforward as we will shortly see.

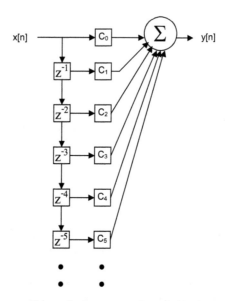

Figure 1. Structure of a FIR filter.

A graphical depiction of the signal process is shown in Figure 1. The z^{-n} elements of the drawing represent discrete time single sample delay elements. As we will see later, z^{-n} represents a delay of n samples in general. Each of the $C_0 \ldots C_n$ elements represent the filter coefficients that are multiplied by the current input and the delay chain. Since the filter does not employ feedback and the number of coefficients is finite, so is the impulse response, thus the name holds true. In all, the filter delays the input signal 0 to $n-1$ time samples, weights each sample by a coefficient, and sums the multiplication results into an output signal. The calculation of the coefficients will be explained later in this article. The number of coefficients in the filter determines the frequency selectivity of the filter.

The property of convolution that makes a FIR filter a special case of convolution is that convolution in the time domain is equivalent to multiplication in the frequency domain. In other words, you are essentially taking the frequency response of the incoming signal and multiplying it by the desired frequency response curve given from the coefficients of the filter, however, the finite impulse response filter keeps this operation in the time domain.

Now if we carry forward the idea of multiplying by the frequency response, then you can easily deduce that the more coefficients (shown as

Using MATLAB commands, let's create an order 64 FIR band pass filter with the bands from 0.2*Nyquist to 0.3*Nyquist.

```
C = fir1( 64, [0.2,0.3] );
```

Then let's transform the coefficients to take a look at the frequency response of the filter.

```
T = fft(C);
Plot(abs(T));
```

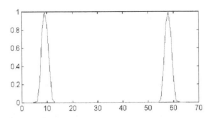

Now create a square waveform with fundamental frequency at 0.125*Nyquist and plot its FFT. This will have a third harmonic at 0.375*Nyquist that we want to filter out and keep.

```
X = [1 1 1 1 -1 -1 -1 -1......];
Plot(abs(fft(x))/64);
```

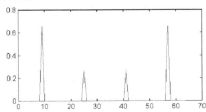

We create the output of the filter by convolution of the C coefficients and the X square wave input. You will see that the first harmonic has been completely removed, leaving the 0.375*sample rate harmonic plus side lobes from the FIR coefficient windowing (hamming in this case).

```
Y=conv(X, C);
Plot( abs( fft(Y) ) / 64);
```

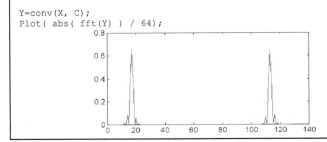

Figure 2. An example FIR filter using a simple square wave input.

$C_0 \ldots C_n$) are in the filter, the more frequency selectivity you can get. If you just think about performing a discrete Fourier transform on any set of numbers, then you will remember that the number of frequency bins produced in the output is directly proportional to the number of input samples. For a larger number of coefficients, you get more and smaller frequency bins, and thus more control over the frequency response of the output. (Chamberlin's articles, on pages 101 and 127, provide much more information about the Fourier transform.)

To illustrate this point further, let's take a look at Figure 2. In this example, I created a 64 coefficient FIR band pass filter with cutoff at 0.2 to 0.3 times the Nyquist frequency (the Nyquist frequency is half the sample rate). Filter response is always relative to the sample rate. If you double the sample rate, then you have doubled the response curve frequencies. In the first picture, I plotted the FFT of the coefficients. As you can see, the FFT shows a band pass filter response around 0.2 to 0.3 times the Nyquist frequency. Next, I created a waveform that I knew would have a strong third harmonic, in this case a square waveform with a fundamental frequency of 0.125 times the Nyquist frequency. Our goal here is to remove the fundamental and leave the third harmonic intact. To do this, I simply used convolution (i.e., finite impulse response filter) of the square wave and the filter coefficients to eliminate the fundamental.

These figures are also handy to see how if you laid the FFT of the square wave over the FFT of the coefficients and simply multiplied each point for point, you could get the output waveform Y. The exception is the side lobes of the frequency response that are created by the windowing of the finite impulse response filter coefficients. The specifics of window properties are beyond the scope of this article and will not be discussed further.

2   A Bit of Theory

First, since we know that an FIR filter is simply convolution, a good place to start is with the definition of convolution:

$$y[i] = \sum_{k=0}^{n} C_k x[i - k].$$

As you can see, the C_k terms correspond to the coefficients of the FIR filter.

For the purpose of illustration I will begin by showing an example of a first-order, low-pass filter with cutoff at $\pi/2$, or one-half of the Nyquist frequency. Remember that when we are working in the mathematical domain, the input frequencies range from $-\pi < \omega < \pi$. Placing the filter coefficients into the convolution formula results in the following linear difference equation:

$$y[n] = 0.5x[n] + 0.5x[n-1].$$

Translating this to the discrete time domain (z domain) results in the equation

$$h(z) = 0.5z^0 + 0.5z^{-1}.$$

Now we will take the filter and translate it to the standard format. You will see why this is necessary for the analysis of the filter a little further on. In general, the standard format we want to put the filter in for analysis is

$$h(z) = K(\alpha - az^{-1})(\beta - bz^{-1})(\chi - cz^{-1})\ldots$$

So our filter fits into the standard format as

$$h(z) = 0.5(1 - (-1)z^{-1}).$$

Note that this function has a zero at $z = -1$ and a pole at $z = 0$. This single zero creates the necessary rolloff at high frequencies. Because of the definition of convolution, a finite impulse response filter can only implement zeroes. The poles of the system are always at the origin, so they never affect the response of the filter.

Figure 3 shows the pole-zero plot for this filter. The zero forms a vector from the origin out to $z = -1$. Now we simply place a complex sinusoid input vector $e^{j\omega}$ on the plot starting from $z = 1$ which corresponds to $\omega = 0$ and rotating to $z = -1$ which corresponds to $\omega = \pi$. The magnitude of the output is determined by the transfer function $|h[z]| = |0.5| \cdot |(1 + e^{-j\omega})|$. To form the output vector, we place a $|1|$ vector along the zero vector, but in the opposite direction, then add this vector to the vector created by the complex sinusoid $e^{-j\omega}$. The result is the output vector shown in the figure with the magnitude of the vector times 0.5 equaling the magnitude of the output of the filter and phase equal to ϕ. Visually you can realize that at $\omega = 0$ the vector is 2 units long and gets smaller and smaller as ω approaches π, thus creating a low-pass filter.

The phase of the output is determined by the transfer function $h[z] = (1 - (-1)z^{-1})$ with z equal to $e^{j\omega}$. So effectively the formula for phase

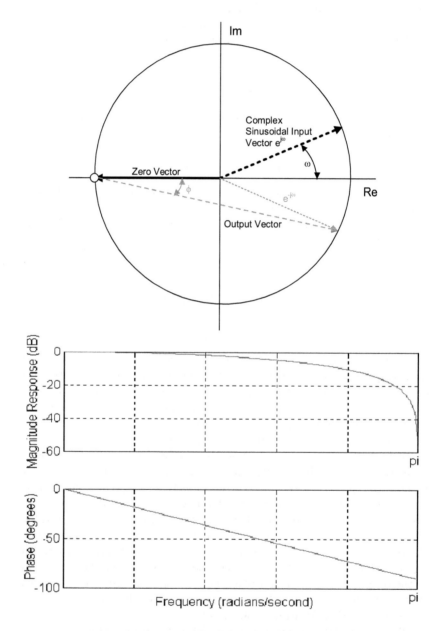

Figure 3. Pole-Zero plot for first-order FIR filter example.

becomes $\phi = \angle(1 + e^{-j\omega})$ or $\phi = -\omega/2$. In Figure 3, you can see how as the input frequency goes toward π, the angle ϕ goes toward -90 degrees.

The group delay (the delay of each frequency) of the FIR filter is calculated by taking the derivative of the phase with respect to frequency. In this case the group delay can be characterized by the formula $d/d\omega\angle(1 + e^{-j\omega})$ or -0.5 and is measured in time relative to the sample rate. For instance, if we were using a 44.1kHz sample rate, the group delay of this filter would be $0.5/44100 =\sim 11.3\mu s$. Because the group delay is a constant in this case, all frequencies passed through this filter will be delayed an equal amount. This is equivalent to claiming that this filter has a linear phase as the $\phi = -\omega/2$ expression shows.

3 Coefficients

With the previous illustration, you probably found the fundamental basis of the finite impulse response filter easy to understand. Now how do you generate the coefficients of the filter? This article could go into many more details about phase, frequency response, and poles and zeros of a system, but for practical reasons, it won't.

The simple answer is—you don't. Generating filter coefficients by hand is purely an academic exercise in the professional world. A number of commercial and freeware programs can save you a vast number of hours and can perform this task for you. Unless you are the type of person who times your microwave with a stopwatch, then you shouldn't feel compelled to generate filter coefficients by hand except in rare and special cases. The example shown in Figure 2 was generated by simple commands in a mathematics software package called MATLAB (The Mathworks). Some of the other packages I have personally used or have heard about success with include Ptolemy (freeware for Linux), QEDesign (Momentum Data Systems), and DSPlay (freeware). A demo version of QEDesign is provided on the CD-ROM accompanying this book (see Bore's article "The QEDesign Filter Design Package" (page 255)). Octave, a MATLAB-like open-source signal processing package is included on the accompanying CD-ROM. A simple search on an Internet search engine will return dozens of useful links to shareware or freeware filter design software that will generate the filter coefficients for you.

Some of the freeware filter design packages out there will even generate C or assembly output for common DSP processors. I have not always found the code output incredibly efficient, but at least it provides some degree of quick functionality to perform algorithm scratchpad testing.

4 Possible Sources of Error

As simple as the finite impulse response filter first appears, there are some basic anomalies of which to be aware.

Often designers implementing their first FIR filter quickly run into problems with frequency resolution versus filter order. The example in Figure 2 demonstrated how the two frequency domains are overlapped and multiplied. Taking a step back and looking at the frequency response of the C coefficients, we see that the frequency selectivity of the filter is highly dependent on the number of coefficients.

For example, if we have three coefficients, then the frequency response of the C_{n+1} coefficients will be very rough indeed. However, if we use 1024 coefficients, then we can pretty well pick and place how we want the filter to look because we have very high resolution and selectivity in the frequency domain.

The resulting anomaly is that if you want the filter to respond correctly at frequencies much, much lower than the Nyquist frequency, then you need to have enough frequency resolution at those lower frequencies to adequately approximate the desired frequency response. This generally requires a large number of coefficients. In some instances it may be better to choose an infinite impulse response filter topology to correctly operate in the lower audio octaves (as described in my article "Infinite Impulse Response Filters," page 8).

A second anomaly that tends to occur with long finite impulse response filters is quantization error. This is especially true for fixed-point implementations of this filter. Keep in mind that each coefficient is probably a rounded off approximation of the true coefficient. Each time the input is multiplied by the coefficient, a roundoff error is introduced. If the ALU being used does not have a register for the mantissa, then the summation operation also induces roundoff error. This roundoff error, or quantization error, as it's generally referred to, will cause noise and distortion at the output. All FIR filters have this problem with limited resolution, but the problem is usually not noticeable except with higher order filters. If the distortion introduced becomes a problem, then one of the common noise shaping techniques should be considered.

The last anomaly that you may experience is filter length versus group delay. The larger the number of coefficients in your finite impulse response filter, the greater the group delay induced by the convolution operation. Depending on the coefficients you use, this may create an undesirable delay path in your signal processing system. Luckily, this is usually easy to determine in the design process and simple to provide a delay in the other paths of your processing to compensate for the filter group delay.

5 A C Software Example

The C listing in Figure 4 implements a function that calculates the next output of a FIR filter. This function may be called in a loop that performs a DSP algorithm. Alternately the function may be modified to block filter a set of samples. The finite impulse response filter coefficients can be calculated with the aforementioned DSP software.

```c
/***********************************************************
//
//     DSP example function - FIR filter
//
***********************************************************/

#include <stdio.h>              /* printf debug info */
#include <stdlib.h>             /* EXIT_SUCCESS return value */

/* function prototype */
float FIR_filter(float*,float*,int);

int main()
{

float seq[3]      = {0.5, 1.0,-2.0};
float samples[3]    = {0.0, 0.0, 0.0};
float coeff[3]     = {0.5, 1.0, 0.5};
float output     = 0.0;
int no_coeff     = 3;

/* calls to FIR filter NOTE: 2n-1 calls to complete filtering
   normally this function would be called in a processing
   loop
*/
    samples[0] = seq[0];                    /* load new sample */
    output = FIR_filter(samples, coeff, no_coeff);
                                            /* perform filter  */
```

Figure 4. A C software listing of an FIR filter implementation.

```
        printf("output 0:\t%1.2f\n", output); /* print result   */
        samples[0] = seq[1];
        output = FIR_filter(samples, coeff, no_coeff);
        printf("output 1:\t%1.2f\n", output);
        samples[0] = seq[2];
        output = FIR_filter(samples, coeff, no_coeff);
        printf("output 2:\t%1.2f\n", output);
        samples[0] = 0.0;
        output = FIR_filter(samples, coeff, no_coeff);
        printf("output 3:\t%1.2f\n", output);
        samples[0] = 0.0;
        output = FIR_filter(samples, coeff, no_coeff);
        printf("output 4:\t%1.2f\n", output);

        return EXIT_SUCCESS;
}


/**************************************************************
//
//      Function: FIR_filter
//      Purpose: performs an FIR filter on a new sample, then
//               returns
//      Parameters:     samples - pointer to an array of floats
//                      containing data to be filtered including
//                      the current sample at [0] and the
//                      longest delayed sample at [no_coeff].
//                      coeff - pointer to an array containing
//                      time reversed filter coefficients
//                      no_coeff - number of coefficients, also
//                      the size of the samples delay line
//      Returns: output - output of convolution operation
//      Note:  The input samples will be delayed by one when
//             this routine exits so that another sample can be
//             loaded into the [0] position next time the routine
//             is called
**************************************************************/

float FIR_filter(float* samples, float *coeff, int no_coeff)
{
```

Figure 4. cont'd.

```
      static float output;      /* output of the FIR filter */
      static int i;             /* loop counter             */
      output = 0.0;             /* clear summing variable    */

/* DEBUG: comment this part out if you do not wish to see
   the filtered data each time the function is called
*/
      for(i = 0; i < no_coeff; i++)
          printf("sample: %1.2f\tcoeff: %1.2f\n",
                  samples[i],coeff[i]);
/* END DEBUG */

for (i = no_coeff-1; i >= 0; i--)
      {
      output += samples[i] * coeff[i];
      if (i < no_coeff-1)
          {
          samples[i+1] = samples[i];
          }
      }

return output;
}
```

Figure 4. cont'd.

6 In Conclusion

By using simple convolution, a finite impulse response filter shapes the
frequency response of the input signal. This filter can only implement
zeroes in the transfer function because of the definition of convolution.
Since the finite impulse response filter only implements zeroes, the filter
can achieve linear phase output, which may be more desirable in some
solutions.

Since the finite impulse response filter is simple in structure and applies no feedback, this filter topology is not plagued by oscillation. This
fact also allows the finite impulse response filter to be implemented on
processors with less mathematical precision, however, with the drawback
of increased output noise due to quantization error.

See "Infinite Impulse Response Filters" (page 79), and "Replacing
Analog Filters with DSP by Using the Bilinear Transform" (page 93) for

descriptions of filters with unique properties that might make them better
suited for your application.

Annotated Bibliography

[1] Berner Fachhochschule University of Applied Sciences, Computer Perception Group. Available from World Wide Web (http://www.hta-bi.bfh.ch/CPG).

Among the many valuable resources available on this web site is the DSPlay software which allows you to interactively experiment with signal processing. The software is distributed as freeware.

[2] The MathWorks. Available from World Wide Web (http://www.mathworks.com/).

Developers of the ubiquitous MATLAB application.

[3] Momentum Data Designs. Available from World Wide Web (http://www.mds.com).

Momentum Data Designs distributes the highly regarded QED filter design package. The web site provides much information on Momentum's signal processing hardware, software, and courses. Free demo versions of MDS software are also available.

[4] Alan Oppenheim and Ronald Shafer. *Discrete-Time Signal Processing.* Prentice Hall, 1989.

This is the standard workhorse text of the DSP processing community. It contains an in-depth discussion of the theory and applications of the bilinear transform. This book also goes into more depth on the nonlinear mapping of the bilinear transform, and how to apply the bilinear transform to IIR filters.

[5] University of California Berkeley EECS Department's Ptolemy Project. Available from World Wide Web (http://ptolemy.berkeley.edu/).

This is the homepage for Berkeley's Ptolemy Project studying modeling, simulation, and design of concurrent, real-time embedded systems. The web site includes a wealth of information as well as a host of math, signal processing, visualization, and control systems software available under the Berkeley Public License.

Infinite Impulse Response Filters

Stuart Allman

There are often times when a signal processing application is constrained by a platform's CPU speed or memory capacity. In these cases, we have to look for ways to save that last clock cycle, or that last byte. In these situations, you may want to look at a method of filtering called an Infinite Impulse Response (IIR) filter. This type of filter has very low memory and processing horsepower requirements, yet provides a fair amount of control in all octaves.

Because the infinite impulse response filter employs feedback, it generally requires greater precision than a Finite Impulse Response (FIR) filter in the intermediate value calculations to avoid oscillation. Typically, a 20- to 32-bit precision ALU is required to faultlessly perform this filtering operation in real time, making an 8-bit microcontroller nearly out of the question for most audio applications.

This article explores IIR filter theory, design, and implementation providing both MATLAB simulations and actual C code.

1 The Filter Structure

The block diagrams of two typical infinite impulse response (second order, i.e. two poles, two zeros) filters are shown in Figure 1. An IIR filter works by multiplying both the incoming signal and the output signal by a set of coefficients. The input and output signals are sent down separate delay chains to be multiplied by coefficients. As shown in the diagram, the multiplication results are summed together to create the output signal. The first structure is generally referred to as *biquad*. This structure is the most common one used in audio processing algorithms for reasons we will discuss later.

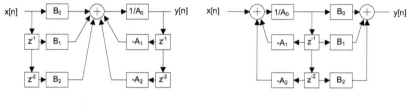

Form I: "The biquad"   *Form II: Alternative form*

Figure 1. Two topologies of IIR filters.

Processors with a high-precision ALU, such as a 32- or 64-bit floating point unit, can use the second topology, but with increased noise and chance of oscillation. Form II should only be considered for audio processing applications where you absolutely must save two words of memory.

To implement a first-order filter, you simply remove the bottom delay elements (z^{-1}) and filter coefficients (B_2, A_2) from either form. However, to increase filter order, rather than adding delay elements and coefficients, instead cascade several copies of Form I, to avoid quantization error and oscillation. On some high-precision processors, you may be able to get away with single structure third- or fourth-order filters, but the use of these are highly discouraged.

Figure 2 shows an example of a second-order IIR stop band filter with cutoff frequencies at 0.4 and 0.5*Nyquist. Keep in mind that the filter response scales with sample rate. For instance, if the sample rate were 44.1 kHz then the cutoff frequencies would be at 8.82 kHz and 11.025 kHz. Then if the sample rate was increased to 48 kHz, the cutoff frequencies would move up to 9.6 kHz and 12 kHz, respectively.

In this example, I created a multifrequency waveform with three sine waves placed within the stop band. Each of the sine elements has amplitude of 1, so that we can see that the output has conformed to the frequency response of the stop band filter after the filtering operation is complete. The output of Figure 2 demonstrates that the middle frequency, clearly placed in the 0.45*Nyquist stop band, is removed from the output. The remaining frequency components are attenuated by 3 dB because these components are at the assigned cutoff frequencies of the stop band filter.

The infinite impulse response filter implements both zeroes, like a finite impulse response filter, and poles via feedback. In contrast to the FIR filter, the IIR filter has very high-frequency selectivity and resolution with lower order and lower computational complexity. This is of great

Using MATLAB commands, let's create a second-order IIR stop band filter with the bands from 0.4 - 0.5*Nyquist.

```
[B,A] = butter(2, [0.4 0.5], 'stop');
```

Then take a look at the response in the frequency domain.

```
freqz(B,A);
```

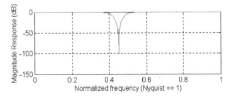

Next, let's create a multitone waveform with tones at steady intervals from 0.4 to 0.5*Nyquist and plot its frequency response.

```
for i = 1:720, x(i) = sin(0.4*pi*(i-1)) + sin(0.45*pi*(i-1)) + sin(0.5*pi*(i-1)); end
plot(abs(fft(x))/360);
```

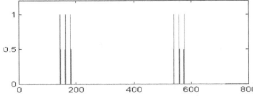

The frequency components revealed by the FFT show the three sine waves with the same amplitude. We will now filter the input and remove the middle spike representing 0.45*Nyquist.

```
y = filter(B, A, x);
plot(abs(fft(y))/360);
```

As you can see, the 0.45*Nyquist sine wave is completely removed. You may also noticed that the 0.4 and 0.5*Nyquist components that are at the designated cutoff frequencies have been attenuated by 3 dB. In practical application, this type of filter could be used to remove 60 Hz hum from professional audio electronics.

Figure 2. An example IIR filter using a multitone input.

importance for audio processing because usually cost constraints lead to CPU horsepower constraints, and an IIR filter can usually get the job done with less system resources. The drawback is that you can never achieve a system with linear phase because of the way that the zeros affect the phase response (see description later in this article). Linear phase is the property of delaying all frequencies by the same time delay.

Because the infinite impulse response filter implements feedback to achieve the desired response, we also have to worry about oscillation. If the filter is designed or computed incorrectly, then oscillation can occur during sharp transients or start and just continue ringing forever. If you are familiar with designing analog filters with feedback, then this anomaly should seem familiar to you. The possible sources of this oscillation will be discussed later in this article.

2 Theory Behind the IIR Filter

The theory behind the operation of the IIR filter starts with the general definition of a linear time-invariant system:

$$\sum_{k=0}^{A} a_k y(n - k) = \sum_{k=0}^{B} b_k x(n - k).$$

As you would expect, x represents the input waveform and y represents the output waveform of the filter. The a_k and b_k coefficients represent the coefficients of the infinite impulse response filter. However, it is not quite clear yet why this important formula allows us to change the frequency and/or phase response of a signal. The following example should shed some light on this subject.

For the purposes of demonstration, I will create a first-order IIR 0.4*Nyquist cutoff low-pass filter. The filter coefficients were generated by MATLAB and they conform to a Butterworth frequency response for a low-pass filter. For the purposes of brevity, the formula will only display the coefficients to 4 digits, however, the real coefficients have much more precision than 4 decimal places:

$$y[n] - 0.1584\, y[n - 1] = 0.4208\, x[n] + 0.4208\, x[n - 1].$$

As you can see from the formula, the y[n-1] element provides feedback from the last output sample after a one-sample delay. Now we take this linear difference equation and transform it to the discrete time domain transfer function. Note that z^{-n} represents an n sample unit delay in this domain.

$$y(z)\,z^0 - 0.1584\,y(z)\,z^{-1} = 0.4208\,x(z)\,z^0 + 0.4208\,x(z)\,z^{-1}$$

Expressing this as a transfer function $h(z) = y(z)/x(z)$:

$$h(z) = \frac{0.4208 + 0.4208z^{-1}}{1 - 0.1584z^{-1}}.$$

Now we will take the transfer function and place it into standard form as shown by the next equation:

$$h(z) = K\frac{(\alpha - az^{-1})(\beta - bz^{-1})..}{(\chi - cz^{-1})(\delta - dz^{-1})..}$$

$$h(z) = \frac{0.4208(1 - (-1)z^{-1})}{1 - 0.1584z^{-1}}.$$

The numerator has a zero at $z = -1$ and a pole at $z = 0$. The denominator has a zero at $z = 0$ and a pole at $z = 0.1584$. Since the poles of the numerator are always at $z = 0$ and do have any impact on the frequency or phase response, you can think of the numerator as only having zeroes. Likewise, the denominator only represents poles of the system because the zeroes of the denominator are always at $z = 0$ and have no impact on filter response.

Figure 3 shows a graphical representation of the input vector $(e^{j\omega})$ and the resulting transfer function numerator and denominator. Note here that the input frequency of the filter really spans from $-\pi$ to π. At $\omega = 0$, the numerator vector stretches from the zero at $z = -1$ to $z = 1$ will have a length of 2 and be multiplied by the constant K to equal $2*0.4208 = 0.8416$. Likewise, at $\omega = 0$, you can see that the denominator vector will have a length of $1 - 0.1584 = 0.8416$. So, overall, the transfer will equal 1 at $\omega = 0$ as we would expect from a low-pass filter.

At the cutoff frequency $\omega = 0.4\pi$, the magnitude of the transfer function will equal

$$\frac{0.4208|(1 + 0.3090 - j0.9511)|}{|(1 - 0.1584(0.3090 - j0.9511)|} = 0.707 = -3dB,$$

which shows us that the filter responds as we would think it should.

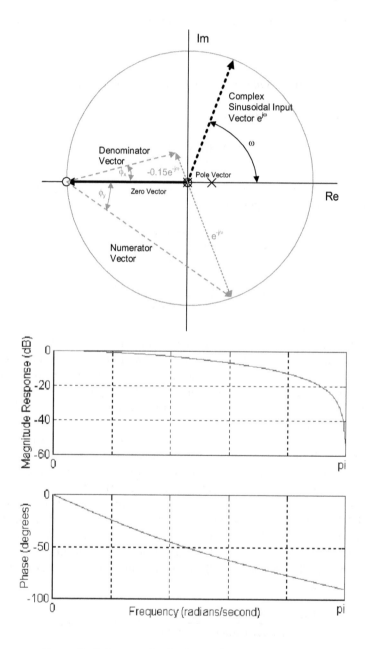

Figure 3. Pole-zero plot for first-order IIR filter example.

The phase (ϕ) response of an IIR filter, defined as the change in phase from the input to the output, i.e., $\angle y(z) - \angle x(z)$, can be described in terms of the following formulas:

$$\angle((1 - ae^{-j\omega})(1 - be^{-j\omega})) = \angle(1 - ae^{-j\omega}) + \angle(1 - be^{-j\omega})$$

and likewise

$$\angle((1 - ae^{-j\omega})/(1 - be^{-j\omega})) = \angle(1 - ae^{-j\omega}) - \angle(1 - be^{-j\omega}),$$

so

$$\phi = \angle y(z) - \angle x(z) = \angle h(z)$$

since $h(z) = y(z)/x(z)$ by definition. Therefore, to find the phase of the output, we can ignore the K factor because it is almost always a real ($\angle K = 0$) number and simply subtract the angles of the numerator and denominator to get $\angle h(z)$:

$$\phi = \angle(1 + e^{-j\omega}) - \angle(1 - 0.1584e^{-j\omega}).$$

If we have multiple zeroes in the numerator, then we can simply sum the individual angles as the previous formula shows. This is also true if we have multiple poles in the system for the denominator.

The group delay of the filter is the time delay that is induced by the filter. The group delay is calculated as the derivative of the phase with respect to frequency. The formula for group delay for our example filter is

$$\frac{d}{d\omega}\angle(1 + e^{-j\omega}) - \frac{d}{d\omega}\angle(1 - 0.1584e^{-j\omega}).$$

The calculated time of the group delay is measured relative to the sample rate period. For instance, if we have a group delay of –0.65 at a specific frequency and a sample rate of 48 kHz, then the delay of the filter is $0.65/48kHz =\sim 13.5\mu s$. Note that the negative sign on the group delay indicates a delay in the output.

3   Filter Coefficients

Now that we have performed a short filter analysis, it's time to tell you the truth about filter coefficients. Similar to FIR filter design, most DSP professionals rely on software design packages to compute and analyze IIR filter coefficients and associated frequesncy response. Please see my preceding article "Finite Impulse Response Filters" (page 67) for an exploration of filter design and analysis packages.

4   Possible Sources of Error

The most common problem that you will likely encounter is filter instability and oscillation. This is due to one of four factors:

(1) The ALU has overflowed and is not using saturation logic to set the calculated result to a maximum or minimum value.

(2) Due to quantization error, the poles and zeroes of the filter are not where you designed them to be. This generally happens on low-precision ALUs (<20 bits). Some software packages can design to these precision constraints.

(3) The result of the summation shown in Figure 1 does not have enough mantissa precision to calculate the correct output. This can happen if there is too much rounding in the intermediate calculations.

(4) The filter was designed wrong. Try to use filter design software to analyze and fix this problem. It will save you hours in the end.

From the preceding list, you probably gathered that precision is a large concern in the calculation of an IIR filter. The quantization errors of Form I and II shown in Figure 1 comes from two places in the filter: the summing junctions and the multiplication of the coefficients. Form II will have more error by design because it uses two summing junctions instead of one. This is the reason why most audio professionals choose to use Form I in their designs. It has lower THD+N and is inherently more stable than the same filter coefficients used in Form II.

5   IIR Filter Code Example

The C listing calculates the next output of an IIR filter. You can call this function in a loop that performs a DSP algorithm, or modify the routine to block filter a set of samples. The IIR filter coefficients can be generated with any of the previously mentioned programs.

```
/************************************************************
//
//    DSP example function - IIR filter
//************************************************************/
#include <stdio.h>          /* printf debug info */
#include <stdlib.h>         /* EXIT_SUCCESS return value */
```

```
/* function prototype */
float IIR_filter(float*, float*, float*, short);

int main()
{

    float delayline[4] =        /* x[-1] x[-2] y[-1] y[-2] */
        {0.0, 0.0, 0.0, 0.0};
    float samples[5] =          /* input samples          */
        {0.500, 1.000, -0.200, -1.000, 0.500};
    float coeff[5] =            /* filter coefficients    */
        {0.22019470027296, 0.44038940054592, 0.22019470027296,
         0.30756635979221, 0.18834516088404};
    short sections = 1; /* number of second order sections */
    float output;               /* current output         */

/* normally this function would be called in a processing
 * loop
 */

    output =                            /* perform filter  */
        IIR_filter(&samples[0], coeff, delayline, sections);
    printf("output 0:\t%1.3f\n", output); /* print result  */

    output =
        IIR_filter(&samples[1], coeff, delayline, sections);
    printf("output 1:\t%1.3f\n", output);

    output =
        IIR_filter(&samples[2], coeff, delayline, sections);
    printf("output 2:\t%1.3f\n", output);

    output =
        IIR_filter(&samples[3], coeff, delayline, sections);
    printf("output 3:\t%1.3f\n", output);

    output =
        IIR_filter(&samples[4], coeff, delayline, sections);
    printf("output 4:\t%1.3f\n", output);
```

```
    return EXIT_SUCCESS;
}


/*************************************************************
//
//      Function: IIR_filter
//      Purpose: performs an IIR filter on a new sample, then
//               returns
//      Parameters:    input - current input sample
//             coeff - filter coefficients
//                   [b0,b1,b2,a1,a2,b0,b1....]
//             delayline - delayed input and output samples
//                       [x[-1],x[-2],y[-1],y[-2],x[-1]....]
//             sections - number of 2nd order filters to
//                        perform. normally a filter with a
//                        larger order than two is split into
//                        a cascade of filters.  To perform a
//                        filter operation on an odd order
//                        filter you need to make b[2] and
//                        a[2] equal to zero.
//      Returns: output - output of filter operation
//      Note: The value of the input sample is changed during
//            this routine to the value of the output
//*************************************************************/

float IIR_filter(float* input, float *coeff,
                 float *delayline, short sections)
{
    /* filter output */
    static float output;

    /* loop counter for filter order > 2 */
    static int i;

    /* coeff offset for filter order > 2 */
    static unsigned int coeff_offset;

    /* delay offset for filter order > 2 */
    static unsigned int delay_offset;

    /* clear filter output value */
```

```
    output = 0.0;

    /* loop for filter order > 2 */
    for (i = 0; i < sections; i++)
    {
        /* calculate new coeff offset for filter order > 2 */
        coeff_offset = 5*i;

        /* calculate new delay offset for filter order > 2 */
        delay_offset = 4*i;

/*BEGIN DEBUG
        printf("input:\t%1.3f\n",input[0]);
        printf("x[-1]:\t%1.3f\n",delayline[0+delay_offset]);
        printf("x[-2]:\t%1.3f\n",delayline[1+delay_offset]);
        printf("y[-1]:\t%1.3f\n",delayline[2+delay_offset]);
        printf("y[-2]:\t%1.3f\n",delayline[3+delay_offset]);
        printf("   B0:\t%1.3f\n",coeff[0+coeff_offset]);
        printf("   B1:\t%1.3f\n",coeff[1+coeff_offset]);
        printf("   B2:\t%1.3f\n",coeff[2+coeff_offset]);
        printf("   A1:\t%1.3f\n",coeff[3+coeff_offset]);
        printf("   A2:\t%1.3f\n",coeff[4+coeff_offset]);
END DEBUG*/

        output = coeff[0+coeff_offset]*input[0]
                                        /* B0 * x[0]   */
          + coeff[1+coeff_offset]*delayline[0+delay_offset]
                                        /* B1 * x[-1]  */
          + coeff[2+coeff_offset]*delayline[1+delay_offset]
                                        /* B2 * x[-2]  */
          - coeff[3+coeff_offset]*delayline[2+delay_offset]
                                        /* -A1 * y[-1] */
          - coeff[4+coeff_offset]*delayline[3+delay_offset];
                                        /* -A2 * y[-2] */

        /* increment output delay line */
        delayline[3+delay_offset] =
          delayline[2+delay_offset];
        delayline[2+delay_offset] = output;

        /* increment input delay line */
```

```
        delayline[1+delay_offset] =
          delayline[0+delay_offset];
        delayline[0+delay_offset] = input[0];

        /* store new input in case filter order > 2 */
        input[0] = output;
    }
    return output;
}
```

6   Conclusion

Although the chance of oscillation due to quantization error is increased
by choosing an IIR filter, in most cases, an IIR filter requires less memory
and CPU horsepower than an FIR filter. Also, unlike an FIR filter, an IIR
filter can implement frequency gain and can be more frequency-selective
with fewer coefficients. The IIR filter is but one technique. Please refer to my other articles in this book, "Finite Impulse Response Filters"
(page 67) and "Replacing Analog Filters with DSP by Using the Bilinear Transform" (page 93), to compare the IIR filter to the FIR filter and
bilinear transform to determine what may be most appropriate for your
application. Also see "The QEDesign Filter Design Package" (page 255)
for a description of a software package for designing FIR and IIR filters.

Annotated Bibliography

[1] Berner Fachhochschule University of Applied Sciences, Com-
    puter Perception Group. Available from World Wide Web
    (http://www.hta-bi.bfh.ch/CPG).

    *Among the many valuable resources available on this web site is the
    DSPlay software which allows you to interactively experiment with
    signal processing. The software is distributed as freeware.*

[2] The MathWorks. Available from World Wide Web
    (http://www.mathworks.com/).

    Developers of the ubiquitous MATLAB application.

[3] Momentum Data Designs. Available from World Wide Web
    (http://www.mds.com).

Momentum Data Designs distributes the highly regarded QED filter design package. The web site provides much information on Momentum's signal processing hardware, software, and courses. Free demo versions of MDS software are also available.

[4] Alan Oppenheim and Ronald Shafer. *Discrete-Time Signal Processing.* Prentice Hall, 1989.

This is the standard workhorse text of the DSP processing community. It contains an in-depth discussion of the theory and applications of the bilinear transform. This book also goes into more depth on the nonlinear mapping of the bilinear transform, and how to apply the bilinear transform to IIR filters.

[5] University of California Berkeley EECS Department's Ptolemy Project. Available from World Wide Web (http://ptolemy.berkeley.edu/).

This is the homepage for Berkeley's Ptolemy Project studying modeling, simulation, and design of concurrent, real-time embedded systems. The web site includes a wealth of information as well as a host of math, signal processing, visualization, and control systems software available under the Berkeley Public License.

Replacing Analog Filters with DSP by Using the Bilinear Transform

Stuart Allman

1 Introduction

Since the late 1980s many inexpensive processors with enough processing power to perform real-time signal processing have been made available. Functions once implemented by necessity as analog circuits have been converted to digital signal processing. Cost savings from limiting the need for extremely precise analog components, the corresponding elimination of temperature induced drift, the ease of design and modification, and the ability to implement functions difficult or impossible to achieve in the analog domain are just some of the factors that motivated the digital revolution. This article explores one technique for making the conversion from analog to digitally implemented filters.

The *bilinear transform* is a useful method of converting a continuous (*Laplace domain*) system response described by *poles* and *zeros* to a discrete (*Z domain*) system response. Most often, this is used to convert analog filters to *IIR filters* when converting an analog signal processing system over to a DSP. This transform is usually not a real-time DSP operation, but rather is a method for designing DSP systems. The reader might wish to consult my article exploring the IIR filter.

One of the best aspects of using the bilinear transform is that there are software packages such as MATLAB or Octave (provided on the accompanying CD-ROM) that automatically perform this operation once you provide the desired Laplace *transfer function*. This article explores how to use the *bilinear transform* to quickly convert analog systems to DSP systems and consequently doesn't concentrate on deriving the transformation itself. While most of this article is focused on the conversion process itself, a bilinear transformation will be demonstrated for completeness.

The *bilinear transform* is an amazingly quick way to convert an analog system to a digital system, but like any algorithm, the bilinear transform has limitations which the user should understand. The bilinear transformation has the following issues. The transformation process from continuous time to discrete time is not linear. The infinite bandwidth of the analog domain maps to the frequency band from 0 Hz up to the Nyquist frequency in the discrete time domain when using the bilinear transform. The equations remain linear differential and linear difference equations, but the frequency response after conversion is warped as the frequency response approaches the *Nyquist frequency*. An example of this is shown later in this article.

2 The Mathematics

This section will explore the mathematics of the *bilinear transform*. Remember that what we want to do is transform the frequency response of an analog filter to an approximate digital equivalent. The formula on the left is the result of transforming the analog design using the Laplace transform. The digital approximation is formed by placing the Laplace transform result into the bilinear transform. The *bilinear transform* transfers the *poles* and *zeros* of an analog system to *poles* and *zeros* in a digital system. The formula for the transform is shown in Figure 1.

The transform is the substitution of the equation shown on the left into the *laplace transform* of the *transfer function*. T represents the sampling period, H_z is the Z transfer function, and H_s is the laplace transfer function. To perform a *bilinear transform*, you must first convert the physical system into its Laplace equivalent, then substitute the equation on the left for each s in the Laplace *transfer function*, and finally algebraically manipulate the equation into standard transfer function form. An example of exactly how to do this is shown in the next section.

$$s = \frac{2(1 - z^{-1})}{T(1 + z^{-1})} \quad H_z = H_s \frac{2(1 - z^{-1})}{T(1 + z^{-1})}$$

Figure 1. The bilinear transform.

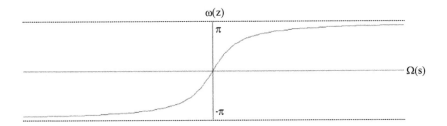

Figure 2. Nonlinear mapping of the frequency response from s to z domain.

The frequency warping effect of the transform is shown in Figure 2. As you can see, transforming from the continuous time domain to the discrete time domain is a nonlinear mapping of the *frequency response*. The real mapping is given by $\omega = 2\arctan(\Omega T/2)$, hardly a linear mapping. ω is the discrete time frequency from 0 Hz to Nyquist, Ω is the continuous time frequency from 0 Hz to infinity, and T is the sampling rate. Now you will probably understand why the frequency response goes towards $-\infty$ after transforming a low-pass filter and looking at the frequency response near the Nyquist frequency. Figure 2 clearly shows how the $\pm\infty$ in the *s domain* map to the *Nyquist frequency* in the *z domain*. The perhaps surprising consequence is that an analog filter's characteristics at $\Omega = \infty$ show up in the bilinear transformed equivalent, despite being well beyond the Nyquist frequency.

Not visually shown here, but mentioned for completeness is the fact that the phase response also maps in a nonlinear fashion from the s to z domains. The phase mapping is given by the equation $\angle(z) = 2\alpha/T \tan(\omega/2)$ where α is the continuous time linear phase factor (from $e^{-s\alpha}$ with $\angle(s) = -\alpha\omega/T$ which has constant slope a.k.a. linear phase), T is the sampling period, and ω is the frequency in radians/sec. This mapping is a tangential function also and maps $\pm\pi\alpha/T$ in the continuous time domain to $\pm\infty$ phase in the discrete time domain.

This appears quite messy; why do we want to use this nonlinear (mapping) transform? Looking more closely, the transform is relatively linear in the region from 0ω to $0.4 - 0.5\omega$, depending on your tolerance. The bilinear transform allows us to quickly transform low-frequency systems using software tools such as MATLAB or Octave. For instance, in the case of a 1 kHz low-pass filter with a sampling rate of 48 kHz, the cutoff is at 0.042ω, so frequencies above 9.6 kHz (0.4ω) really aren't that critical because we are trying to get rid of all frequencies above 1 kHz anyway.

3   An Analog-to-Digital Conversion Using the Bilinear Transform

This section will show you how to convert any analog circuit to an *IIR digital filter* using the *bilinear transform*. First, we will start a derivation of the Laplace transfer function of an analog low-pass filter. You may recall from *Bode plots* or signal processing courses that the analog components are replaced by a Laplace equivalent impedance ($R = R$, $C = 1/(Cs)$, $L = Ls$).

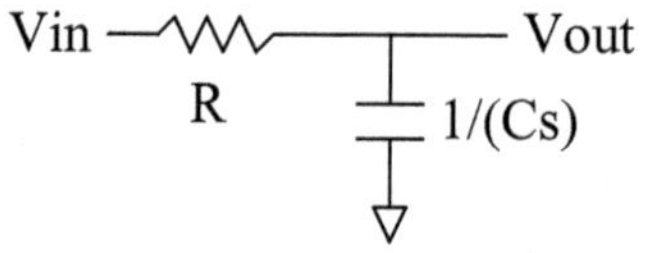

$$\text{Vin} \!-\!\!\bigwedge\!\!\!-\!\!\!\!\!-\!\!\! \text{Vout}$$
$$R \qquad 1/(Cs) \qquad H(s) = \text{Vout/Vin} = \frac{1}{RCs + 1}$$

Figure 3. An analog low-pass filter and its Laplace transfer function.

The next step is to apply the *bilinear transform* to the Laplace *transfer function*.

$$H(z) = \frac{1}{RC\dfrac{2(1 - z^{-1})}{T(1 + z^{-1})} + 1}$$

$$H(z) = \frac{(1 + z^{-1})}{(RC\dfrac{2}{T})(1 - z^{-1}) + (1 + z^{-1})}$$

$$H(z) = \frac{(1 + z^{-1})}{(1 + RC\dfrac{2}{T}) + (1 - RC\dfrac{2}{T})z^{-1}}$$

$$H(z) = \frac{\dfrac{1}{(1 + RC\dfrac{2}{T})} + \dfrac{z^{-1}}{(1 + RC\dfrac{2}{T})}}{1 + \dfrac{(1 - RC\dfrac{2}{T})z^{-1}}{(1 + RC\dfrac{2}{T})}}$$

Now that the transfer is in standard form, we can easily extract the *IIR filter* coefficients for this filter:

$$B_0 = \frac{1}{(1 + RC\frac{2}{T})} \qquad B_1 = \frac{1}{(1 + RC\frac{2}{T})}$$

$$A_0 = 1 \text{ (standard form)} \quad A_1 = \frac{(1 - RC\frac{2}{T})}{(1 + RC\frac{2}{T})}$$

Now you can specify any R and C, along with any sampling rate and transfer an analog filter to the digital domain. You can also make a library of transforms and have your signal processing program select any filter parameters you wish.

4 A Practical Design Example Using MATLAB

Now that we have explored the long mathematical way of performing a *bilinear transform*, it's time to demonstrate a more practical way to use the *bilinear transform*. The *Laplace transform* of the analog system must still be performed by hand, unless you know the *poles* and *zeros* of the system. Most real world systems are second order or greater, unfortunately making the algebra of a *bilinear transform* done by hand accident-prone. To solve this problem, a software package, such as MATLAB, provides a bilinear() command. For this example we will choose a 1 kHz analog filter and a sampling rate of 48000 in the digital domain. We will realistically choose $R = 10k\Omega$, making $C = 16nF$.

$$H(s) = \frac{1}{(0.00016s + 1)}$$

The following MATLAB commands convert the analog filter coefficients to IIR filter coefficients:

```
>> Z=[0 1];                        ⇐ analog zeros
>> P=[0.00016 1];                  ⇐ analog poles
>> [B,A] = bilinear(Z,P,48000)     ⇐ bilinear transform
B =                                ⇐ IIR filter coefficients
   0.06112469437653 0.06112469437653
A =
   1.00000000000000 -0.87775061124694
>> freqz(B,A);                     ⇐ display the filter response
```

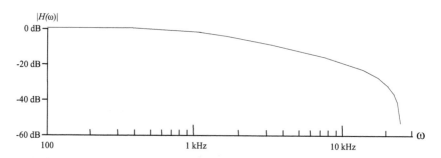

Figure 4. Frequency response of the digital 1 kHz low-pass filter.

As you can see, the software approach is much less algebraically accident-prone and gives us the same results with little or no work. In Figure 4, you will find the frequency response of the filter after transformation. Notice the frequency response warping near the *Nyquist frequency*.

5   Conclusion

The bilinear transform is a shorthand tool for converting analog systems to digital systems. Understanding the bilinear transform's limitations and characteristics will allow you to successfully transfer analog systems to digital systems in a short amount of time. Often the frequency and phase warping due to the transform's nonlinear mapping can be ignored. Software tools, such as MATLAB® or Octave, can be used to shorten the design time further by automating long algebraic steps.

Annotated Bibliography

[1] Berner Fachhochschule University of Applied Sciences, Computer Perception Group. Available from World Wide Web (http://www.hta-bi.bfh.ch/CPG).

Among the many valuable resources available on this web site is the DSPlay software which allows you to interactively experiment with signal processing. The software is distributed as freeware.

[2] The MathWorks. Available from World Wide Web (http://www.mathworks.com/).

Developers of the ubiquitous MATLAB application.

[3] Momentum Data Designs. Available from World Wide Web (http://www.mds.com).

   Momentum Data Designs distributes the highly regarded QED filter design package. The web site provides much information on Momentum's signal processing hardware, software, and courses. Free demo versions of MDS software are also available.

[4] Alan Oppenheim and Ronald Shafer. *Discrete-Time Signal Processing.* Prentice Hall, 1989.

   This is the standard workhorse text of the DSP processing community. It contains an in-depth discussion of the theory and applications of the bilinear transform. This book also goes into more depth on the nonlinear mapping of the bilinear transform, and how to apply the bilinear transform to IIR filters.

[5] University of California Berkeley EECS Department's Ptolemy Project. Available from World Wide Web (http://ptolemy.berkeley.edu/).

   This is the homepage for Berkeley's Ptolemy Project studying modeling, simulation, and design of concurrent, real-time embedded systems. The web site includes a wealth of information as well as a host of math, signal processing, visualization, and control systems software available under the Berkeley Public License.

Floating Point Fast Fourier Transform

Hal Chamberlin

Fourier transforms are the basis of many of the most important signal processing techniques in use today. Audio spectral analysis, some types of synthesis, and the very successful MP3 audio compression format are all at their core, applications of Fourier transforms. Even correlation and statistical analysis of time series data are aided tremendously by the ability to do Fourier transformation quickly.

Detailed examples of these and other applications of Fourier transforms may be found throughout this book. In this article, however, the transform itself, its properties, and its "fast" implementation as a C function will be described. The code is available on the CD-ROM accompanying this book.

This article will describe implementation of the fast Fourier transform with floating point arithmetic which allows one to focus on the algorithm and applications without worrying about machine-specific arithmetic details. My article "Fast Fourier Transform Using Integer Math" (page 127) describes conversion to integer math which extends Fourier transform applications to much smaller processors.

1   What is Fourier Transformation?

Simply put, the Fourier transform is a bridge between the *time domain*, which is concerned with waveforms and sample values, and the *frequency domain*, which is concerned with the amplitudes and phases of frequency components (harmonics). The *forward* transform begins with a block of samples assumed to represent one period of a sound waveform and converts it into a set of harmonic amplitudes and phases. The *inverse* transform begins with a set of harmonic amplitudes and phases and calculates a block of time samples representing one period of the waveform. In fact, the forward and inverse transforms are perfectly complementary; one followed by the other recreates the data block exactly (within round-off error).

Analysis typically begins with forward transforms to determine the frequency components present, then processes these further for display and other uses. Synthesis would begin with a spectral description of the sound to be produced, process that into the required format, then use inverse transforms to produce the waveform. Sound modification including filtering involves a forward transform followed by modification of the spectral data, then finally an inverse transform to produce the modified waveform. Data compression is similar except that the spectral data are coded into fewer bits for transmission. In all of these cases, one is allowed to think and work in the frequency domain which directly reflects what a listener will actually perceive.

2   Forward Discrete Fourier Transform

Fourier transforms applied to sampled data are called *discrete* Fourier transforms, since the time domain data are at discrete instants of time and the frequency data are likewise at discrete frequencies. One very important property of the discrete transform is that the waveform data are specific-sized chunks called *records*, each consisting of a specific number of samples.

The discrete transform *assumes* that the samples in the record represent exactly one cycle of a *periodic* waveform. This assumption must be made regardless of whether or not it is actually true. The transform then gives all of the harmonic amplitudes and phases of the assumed periodic waveform. One challenge in any analysis application using Fourier transforms is how to break up a continuous sample stream into records so that the artifacts resulting from this mismatch between assumption and reality are minimized.

Let's take an example. Assume a record size of 500 samples from a sound that was sampled at 25 KS/s (KiloSamples per second) which is 20 milliseconds of sound. The transform then assumes that 20 milliseconds represents one cycle of a 50 Hz fundamental waveform. Therefore, coming out of the transform will be the amplitude and phase of the fundamental (50 Hz) and all of its possible harmonics.

How many harmonics will there be? Invoking Nyquist[1], the highest frequency present in 25 KS/s data is half that or 12.5 KHz. So the highest harmonic would be 12500/50 or the 250th. The transform will also report the DC component making a total of 251 frequency components. Of course, if the sound was properly low-pass-filtered to remove frequencies near and above half the sampling frequency prior to sampling, the energy in the highest few harmonics should be very low. DC also isn't of much interest and usually is near zero as well.

For the first through the 249th harmonics, there will be an amplitude and phase angle for each. DC, of course, doesn't have a phase and, as it turns out, the Nyquist frequency doesn't either. So the total quantity of numbers from the transform (2*249 + 1 + 1) is the same as the number of samples going into the transform! Generalizing, a record of N (500) samples taken at a rate of R (25,000) samples per second will transform into N/2 + 1 (251) harmonics or "bins" evenly spaced between 0 and R/2 (12,500) Hertz inclusive. For an analysis application, the bin width (space between harmonics or frequency resolution) would be R/N (50) Hertz.

3 Inverse Discrete Fourier Transform

The inverse transform is easier to understand. One starts with a complete set of harmonic amplitudes and phases, runs the transform, and obtains a record of samples. A complete set is the same as before: amplitudes and phases of the first N/2 harmonics where N is the record size to be produced plus the DC component which is typically zero. As will be shown later, the programming algorithm difference between forward and inverse transform is very slight, so typically one C function can do the job of both.

4 Using Discrete Transforms

The record oriented property of the Discrete Fourier Transform (DFT) has several important ramifications when constantly changing arbitrary sounds are to be analyzed. In most cases, the record size is fixed or restricted to powers of two so even if a periodic waveform was being analyzed, it is unlikely that a record would exactly span a single cycle. In order to reduce the resulting error and make sense of the spectrum, the record size is usually chosen to span *several* cycles of the lowest frequency

---

[1]The Nyquist theorem states that a sample stream of F samples per second can represent any waveform having only frequencies up to F/2 Hertz without error.

expected. Then the discontinuity where the end of the record wraps back to the beginning is of less consequence.

When a large number of cycles of a truly periodic waveform is transformed, each harmonic of the actual waveform becomes a small *group* of the DFT harmonics. A demonstration of this is shown in Figure 1(a) in which 5.31 cycles of a waveform containing fundamental, second, and third harmonics in equal proportion were made into a record and transformed. The three clusters of transform harmonics correspond to the individual harmonics of the actual waveform. Energy between the clusters and above the third waveform harmonic is called *leakage* and is due to the discontinuity caused by the nonintegral number of cycles in the record.

A *time window* can be applied to the waveform data record before transformation to greatly reduce the effect of the discontinuity at the beginning and end of the record. A window is simply a carefully shaped amplitude envelope that is zero at the beginning and end and unity in the middle. This forces continuity from end to beginning regardless of what the original data was like. Window shaping and selection is a sizable discipline itself, but one shape that works well is the *raised cosine* which is one cycle of a cosine wave flipped, shifted up, and normalized to make a bell-shaped window. Figure 2(a) shows this shape and the same 5.31 cycle wave windowed, and its transform. The actual waveform harmonics are now much better defined and the high-frequency leakage above the third harmonic is practically nonexistent.

In reducing leakage, the window tends to broaden the signal frequency range that each DFT harmonic "responds" to thus reducing the final frequency resolution of the analysis. The simple raised cosine window shown here has a 2.5 bin width leakage level of about 30 dB and 5 bin width leakage of 55 dB which is good enough for most musical timbre analysis work. More complex windows can improve this; the often used Blackman-Harris window achieves almost 90 dB in 5 bin widths.

5   Phase Representation

It is natural to think of the phase of a frequency component as an angle that runs between -180 and +180 degrees (or between -pi and +pi radians) and the amplitude as an unsigned magnitude. This is called the *polar form* and subsequent discussion will use "A" for the amplitude and "P" for the phase.

DFT algorithms are simplified dramatically, however, if the frequency components are given in *rectangular form* instead. Each component is

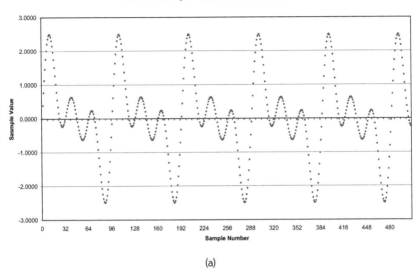

(a)

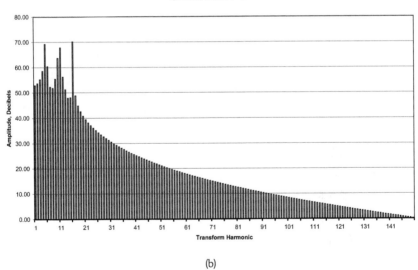

(b)

Figure 1.

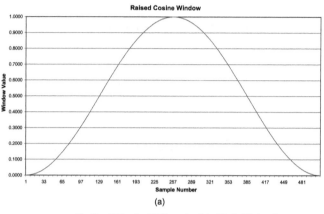

(a)

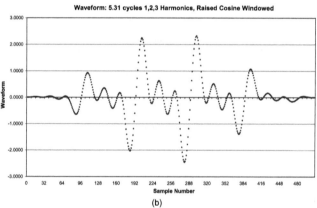

(b)

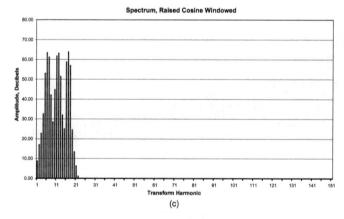

(c)

Figure 2.

considered to be the sum of *two* waves 90 degrees apart in phase, that is, cosine and sine. These two waves, combined in varying proportions (including negative), will sum to produce a single wave with any desired amplitude and phase. Subsequent discussion will use "C" for the amplitude of the cosine component and "S" for amplitude of the sine component. The rectangular form may also be called the *complex form* with C being the real part and S being the imaginary part.

Conversion between the two forms is simple trigonometry:

```
C = A*Cos(P)
S = A*Sin(P)


A = sqrt(S^2+C^2)
P = atan2(S,C)
```

The function for calculating P, `atan2`, is available in most C math libraries and calculates the angle of a vector from the origin to the point $X = C, Y = S$.

6   The Slow Fourier Transform

Before one can appreciate the beauty of the "fast" Fourier transform and indeed understand it all, it is instructive to review the straightforward, but slow, version (SFT).

7   Inverse SFT

Let's begin with the inverse slow transform first since it is more intuitive. Recall that the inverse transform begins with a complete set of harmonic amplitudes and phases, then calculates the time waveform. Expressed using the rectangular form, we begin with a complete set of cosine amplitudes, C[], and sine amplitudes, S[]. A complete set was defined as all of the harmonics from 0 through N/2 where N is the record size of the waveform to be produced.

In words, the procedure can be summarized as follows:

(1) N is the record size to be produced. Should be even.

(2) C[] is the array of cosine amplitudes; S[] is the sine amplitudes, indexed from 0 through N/2.

(3) T[] is the sample record itself, indexed from 0 through N - 1.

(4) T[] is assumed to be initialized to all zeroes.

(5) For each harmonic from 0 through N/2, we calculate a cosine wave of the correct frequency and specified amplitude and add it to T[].

(6) Repeat Step 5 for the harmonic's sine wave and sine amplitude.

(7) Repeat Steps 5 and 6 for all N/2 + 1 harmonics.

When all of the above has been done, the T[] array will have the waveform stored in it.

Function 1 is a C function implementing the above procedure with some slight alterations to improve speed. The outer loop steps through the harmonics and the inner loop steps through the sample record adding samples from each harmonic's cosine and sine components.

```
1    void ISFT(float T[], float C[], float S[], int N)
2    /* T[] is the output time sample array, N elements,
            initially zeros
3       C[] is the input array of cosine amplitudes, (N/2)+1
            elements
4       S[] is the input array of sine amplitudes, (N/2)+1
            elements
5       N   is number of samples in the output record
6    */
7    {   float ang, angstep;
8        float cval, sval;
9        int   i,j;
10       angstep=6.2831853/N;
11       for(i=0; i<=N/2; i++)
12       {   cval=C[i];
13           sval=S[i];
14           for(j=0; j<N; j++)
15           {   ang = angstep*i*j;
16               T[j] +=  cval*cos(ang)+sval*sin(ang);
17           }
18       }
19       return;
20   }
```

Function 1. Slow inverse Fourier transform.

8 Forward SFT

The forward slow transform is not as intuitive, but actually is very similar in form. It's good to improve one's intuition, however.

The basic approach for determining the amplitude of a component with a particular frequency and phase is to *generate* samples of the sought component, *multiply* them by corresponding samples of the signal to be analyzed, and then *add* up the products. The sum, after being divided by one-half the record size for averaging is the amplitude of the signal component having that frequency and phase!

This fact can be understood by remembering that multiplying two sinusoidial signals is equivalent to balanced modulation and produces a signal having only sum and difference frequency components. Recall also that any sinusoidial wave averaged over an integral number of periods is zero. It is easily seen then that if the two signals being multiplied have *different* frequencies that the product consists of two sinusoidial waves that when averaged over a duration having an integral number of periods of both, gives zero. If the frequencies being multiplied are the same, the difference frequency is zero, which is DC and results in an average value equal to the product of the signal amplitudes if they are perfectly in phase. When not in phase, the average is proportional to the cosine of the phase difference.

Fortunately, this procedure works even when one of the signals has many frequency components; if one component matches, it will contribute a DC component to the product samples. Thus by using two "probe" waves 90 degrees apart in phase at all possible harmonic frequencies of the data record, one may determine its complete harmonic amplitude and phase makeup.

In words, the forward transform procedure can be summarized as follows:

(1) N is the record size to be analyzed. Should be even.

(2) C[] is the result array of cosine amplitudes, S[] is the sine amplitudes, indexed from 0 through N/2.

(3) T[] is the input sample record itself, indexed from 0 through N - 1.

(4) For each harmonic from 0 through N/2, calculate a cosine wave of the correct frequency, multiply it by all samples in T[], add up the products, and store the sum divided by N/2 in C[].

(5) Repeat Step 4 using a sine wave and store the result in S[].

(6) Repeat Steps 4 and 5 for all N/2 + 1 harmonics.

The C function in Function 2 implements the above procedure. The outer loop steps through the harmonics and the inner loop generates the probe waves and adds up the products.

```
1    void FSFT(float T[], float C[], float S[], int N)
2    /* T[] is the input time sample array, N elements
3        C[] is the output array of cosine amplitudes, (N/2)+1
             elements
4        S[] is output array of sine amplitudes, (N/2)+1
             elements
5        N   is number of samples in the input record
6    */
7    {   float ang, angstep;
8        float Nover2;
9        float csum, ssum;
10       int   i,j;
11       angstep=6.2831853/N;
12       Nover2=N/2.;
13       for(i=0; i<=N/2; i++)
14       {   csum=0;
15           ssum=0;
16           for(j=0; j<N; j++)
17           {   ang = angstep*i*j;
18               csum += T[j]*cos(ang);
19               ssum += T[j]*sin(ang);
20           }
21           C[i]=csum/Nover2;        /* Correct the amplitude */
22           S[i]=ssum/Nover2;
23       }
24       C[0] /= 2.;                  /* Further correct the DC
                                         amplitude */
25       C[N/2] /= 2.;                /* Further correct the
                                         Nyquist amplitude */
26       return;
27   }
```

Function 2. Slow forward Fourier transform.

The division by $N/2$ in Lines 21 and 22 is necessary to report the true amplitudes of harmonics such that a subsequent inverse transform would yield the original signal data record. The DC and Nyquist components are still twice their true value which is corrected in Lines 24 and 25. The sine part of DC and Nyquist will always be zero within roundoff error.

Examination of the preceding two functions reveals that $N^2 + N$ *useful* multiplications and additions are required for the transformation. Useful is emphasized because a well-thought-out implementation could eliminate multiplications within the cosine and sine arguments by proper indexing through a cosine table. In the case of the inverse transform, half of the multiplications could be replaced by additions by using the polar form of the harmonics rather than the rectangular form.

Even with a painstakingly coded assembly language version of these functions, a tremendous amount of computation is needed for even a moderate number of samples. For example, 20 msec records taken at 25 KS/s would be 500 samples per record that, when squared, implies a quarter million multiply-adds for the transform. Upping the sample rate to 50 KS/s to fully cover the audio band quadruples the work to a million operations. Some Fourier transform applications, like SETI research, need to use million sample records. The author's 333 MHz Celeron processor takes about one second for a 500 point forward transform using the above C function. Even a gigahertz processor and assembly language would probably only improve that by a factor of 10 to 20. Without the dramatic efficiency improvement about to be described, most current applications for Fourier transforms would not be practical.

9   The Fast Fourier Transform

Like many topics in computer science, the real key to speed lies in an efficient algorithm rather than an efficient program. In the case of the DFT, such an algorithm was first publicized in 1965 and results in an enormous reduction in computation at the expense of a longer and rather difficult to understand procedure. The *fast* Fourier transform requires approximately $N\log_2 N$ multiplications and additions instead of N^2. This means that 512 samples need only about 4,600 operations while 1024 samples need about 10,200. The work for a million point transform is reduced by a factor of 50,000!

Space prohibits all but a very cursory description of the FFT algorithm here. The interested reader can check out a nonmathematical description in [1] or the original Cooley-Tukey paper in [2].

ORDER	RECORD SIZE	OPERATIONS	SAVINGS FACTOR
4	16	64	4
5	32	160	6
6	64	384	11
7	128	896	18
8	256	2048	32
9	512	4608	57
10	1024	10240	102
11	2048	22528	186
12	4096	49152	341
13	8192	106496	630
14	16384	229376	1170
15	32768	491520	2185
16	65536	1048576	4096
17	131072	2228224	7710
18	262144	4718592	14563
19	524288	9961472	27594
20	1048576	20971520	52428

Table 1. Radix 2 FFT record sizes.

One way to understand the algorithm involves the concept of *decimation*. Consider a sample record of size N where N is even. Using the SFT, one could perform N^2 operations and wind up with the spectrum. Now consider splitting the record into two smaller records with N/2 samples in each such that the even numbered samples go to one record and the odd numbered ones go to the other. If an SFT is performed on each record, it will require $N^2/4$ operations on each for a total of only $N^2/2$ operations. The trick is to combine the two resulting spectrums into one representing the true spectrum of the original record. This can be accomplished by duplicating the even sample spectrum of N/4 harmonics and adding with a progressive phase shift the odd sample spectrum, also duplicated, to yield N/2 harmonics total. The combination requires N extra multiply-adds.

If N is divisible by 4, the decimation operation could be repeated to give four records of N/4 samples each. The SFT can be performed on each, requiring only $N^2/4$ operations total, and the four resulting spectrums combined in two stages to form the final spectrum. In fact, if N is a power of two, decimation can be repeated until there are N/2 subrecords, each having only two samples. Since the DFT of two samples[2] is trivial, all the computational work becomes combining the subspectra together

---

[2] The DFT of two samples has only a DC component (sum of the sample values) and a Nyquist component (the difference of the sample values). The inverse DFT differs from the forward DFT only in the order of the subtraction for the Nyquist component.

in stages to form the final spectrum. The number of stages (order) is $\log_2(N)$ and the number of multiply-adds per stage is N yielding the total operation count mentioned above.

The essence of the FFT, then, is complete decimation of the time samples followed by recombination of the frequency spectra to form the exact spectrum of the original sample set. Decimation by two at each stage, which imposes a requirement that the sample record be a power of 2 in length, is by far the simplest but other factors like 3, 4, 5, etc. are possible. Different decimation factors can be mixed to give more flexibility in the record size, but the resulting complexity often outweighs other methods of adjusting record size, like resampling. Consequently, this article will only consider a decimation factor of 2, known as the *radix 2* FFT algorithm. Check [3] for information about FFT algorithms using other radix values. Table 1 is a list of possible radix 2 record sizes for FFTs up to order 20 along with their theoretical multiply-add count and savings factor compared to an SFT.

10 Complex Numbers

The straight-ahead FFT is a *complex* transform using complex data and complex math. "Complex" here doesn't mean difficult; it means using numbers having a "real" and an "imaginary" part—something we all learned in high school. In this paper, complex numbers will be notated as *realpart*, *imaginarypart* without the customary "i" multiplier before the imaginary part.

Considering the forward transform, it's natural that the output data, which are cosine (real) and sine (imaginary) amplitudes for the harmonics, are complex. However, the input data are audio waveform samples which are definitely real. Conversely, the inverse transform is expected to produce real data. In the former case, the imaginary parts of the input data are simply set to zero and in the latter case, they are ignored. Later, we'll learn how to avoid wasting all that space.

11 Core Floating Point FFT Function

Now we are ready to look at a practical FFT function written in the C programming language. In technical terms, it is a "radix 2 FFT using time decomposition and input bit reversal" which is probably the simplest and one of the more efficient implementations. *Time decompositon* means that the input data is decimated first and the result will appear in natural order. *Bit reversal* refers to the method of decimating the input data array, which we will describe below. It also does its computation *in place* which means that the input data array is replaced by the result data array with no intermediate result arrays required.

The first step in the FFT algorithm is to completely decompose the input samples which means that they are scrambled in bit-reversed order. Figure 3(a) shows decimation of a 16-sample record in 3 stages using the method described earlier. In the first stage, the even-numbered samples are grouped in the left subrecord and the odd-numbered samples group to the right subrecord. Then this process is repeated for each subrecord in the second stage and then again in the third stage. The procedure is complete when the subrecords are two samples each. Remember that the samples are complex so each one consists of two numbers: a real part and a complex part.

A key observation made many years ago is that after decimation, the samples are in bit-reversed order. Take a look at the four-bit binary representation of the sample numbers at the top of Figure 3(a) and compare with the ones at the bottom after decimation. It's as if the bottom strings of 1s and 0s were copied from the top using a mirror. In fact, the data record can be decimated in just one step *and* in-place by using the following procedure:

(1) Define two index counters, i1 and i2. i1 counts in a normal binary progression while i2 counts in a bit-reversed progression.

(2) Initialize i1 and i2 to zero.

(3) Compare i1 and i2. If i1 is equal or larger, skip to 5.

(4) Swap the samples pointed to by i1 and i2.

(5) Increment i1 (normal binary increment) and i2 (bit reversed increment).

(6) If i1 is less than N, go to 3, else done.

Figure 3(a) shows this procedure step by step for N = 16 and 3(b) the net effect after the procedure is complete. Using a compiled language, such as C, there are any number of creative ways to program a bit-reversed counter (the code below has one example). In assembly language, it might be faster to write a bit-reverse function that converts the value of i1 to

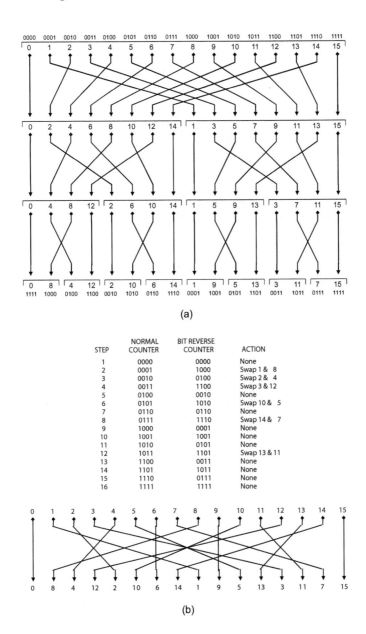

Figure 3. (a) Stages in the decimation of a 16-sample record; (b) In-place bit-reverse scrambling.

its bit-reversed equivalent. In dedicated hardware, such a function is a trivial data path rewiring.

The next step in the FFT procedure takes the scrambled sample set, massages it using a complex function called W, and produces the spectrum in natural ascending order. The computation is done *in place* which means the spectrum replaces the sample data with no intermediate storage required.

"W" is a complex function of a real angle, i/N:

$$W(i) = \cos(2\pi \frac{i}{N}), \sin(2\pi \frac{i}{N}).$$

The FFT algorithm will use arguments, i, running between 0 and $N-1$ and the resulting complex function value will be used as a multiplier. Note that

$$W(i + \frac{N}{2}) = -W(i).$$

This property will be used in the algorithm to cut the number of sine and cosine evaluations and multiplications in half.

The massaging is best described using a special flowchart called a *butterfly diagram* because of its appearance. The fundamental element of a butterfly diagram is the *node* which is illustrated in Figure 4(a). There are always two inputs to the node. One goes straight in, while the other is multiplied by the W function of a specified argument before entering. In the node, the two inputs are added together to form a single complex number, which may then become the source for further computations. A node therefore implies one *complex* multiplication and one *complex* addition. In a program, this would be accomplished with four real multiplications and four real additions as shown.

Figure 4(b) shows the butterfly diagram for an N = 16 FFT. Note that there are N rows and log₂N columns of nodes. The rows correspond to storage locations that are initially filled with the scrambled time samples and later become loaded with the spectrum harmonics. The computation proceeds one column at a time starting from the time samples at the left.

In order to realize in-place computation, the nodes are evaluated in *pairs*. Each member of the pair uses the same inputs and produces outputs on the same rows as the inputs. Furthermore, these inputs are not used by any of the other nodes in the column. Thus, after the node pair is evaluated, the node outputs can be stored in place of the values used as their inputs. Careful examination reveals that the two arguments of W used in a node pair always differ by N/2 which, as shown above, means

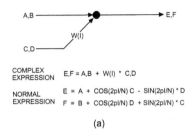

(a)

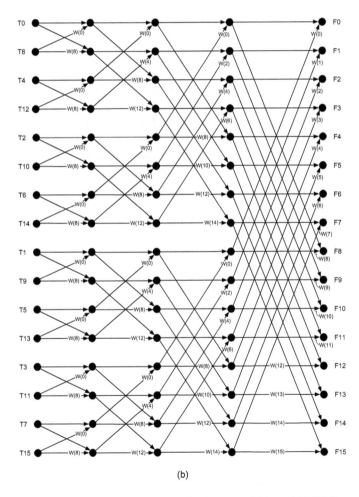

(b)

Figure 4. (a) Nodes used in FFT butterfly diagram; (b) N = 16 FFT Butterfly.

that W need be evaluated only once. Additionally, only four of the eight real multiplications for the node pair need actually be performed.

After the first column of nodes has been processed, everything is back in storage in a partially transformed state, and processing of the next column of nodes can begin. When the right-most column has been evaluated, the array contains the N complex harmonics. Note that for the first column, the modes that should be paired for calculation are adjacent. In the next column, the pair members are two apart, in the third column four apart, and so forth. Also note that the mass of crossing lines forms a group of two nodes in the first column, four nodes in the next column and so forth until there is only one mass in the final column. These and other symmetries discovered by examining the diagram should make the progression sufficiently clear so that generalization for other values of N can be understood. Since the progression is consistent from column to column, it is clear that a general FFT function can be written for any value of N that is a power of two.

Function 3 is the actual complex FFT code for forward and inverse transforms. The array of complex input samples is actually stored and handled as two arrays of normal numbers; D1 being the real part and D2 being the imaginary part. As usual, the array subscript starts at zero and goes through N − 1. When the transform is complete, the spectrum is stored in the same two arrays. The record size is specified by giving the transform order, K, which is $\log_2(N)$ and must be a positive integer. DIR specifies whether a forward (+1) or inverse (−1) transform is to be performed.

To minimize clutter, Function 3 and all other C code in this article assumes an integer size of 16 bits and long integer size of 32 bits. In the rare case of a 12/24 bit or 18/36 bit machine, such as some DSP processors, it may be possible to reduce or necessary to increase the size declarations of index variables. Comments in the code indicate when this is necessary for the usual case of 16/32 bit machines and extension to other word sizes will be obvious.

```
1    void CFFT(int K, int DIR, float D1[], float D2[])
2    /* K   is the FFT order = log2(<size of Dx[] arrays>)
3             Range is 2 to 15 inclusive.  Change declarations
             for N and i1-i8 to
4             long if you wish to transform records longer
             than 32768 complex
5             samples.
```

```
6      DIR  is +1 for forward transform (time->freq), -1 for
       inverse transform
7      D1[] is the real parts of the input and output array,
       2^K elements
8      D2[] is the imaginary parts of the input and output
       array, 2^K elements
9   */
10  {  float ang;       /* Temporary angle */
11     float t1,t2;     /* Temporary D1, D2, array readout */
12     float c,s;       /* cosine & sine multipliers */
13     unsigned int N; /* Size of D1, D2 arrays */
14     unsigned int i1,i2,i3,i4,i6,i7,i8; /* Temp indices */
15
16     N = 1<<K;  /* Calculate complex record size from K */
17     i1=0; /* Bit reverse scramble the input data order */
18     i2=N-1;
19     for(i3=1; i3<N; i3++) /* i3 is normal counter, i1 is
       bit rev counter */
20     {  i4=N;
21        while(i1+i4 > i2)  i4 >>= 1;
22        i1 = (i1%i4)+i4;
23        if(i1 > i3)
24        {  t1=D1[i3];
25           D1[i3]=D1[i1];
26           D1[i1]=t1;
27           t2=D2[i3];
28           D2[i3]=D2[i1];
29           D2[i1]=t2;
30        }
31     }
32     i4=1;                   /* Perform the complex transform */
33     while(i4<N)
34     {  i6=i4<<1;
35        for(i3=0; i3<i4; i3++)
36        {  ang=i3*3.1415927/i4;
37           c=cos(ang);
38           if (DIR>=0) s=sin(ang);
39           else s=-sin(ang);
40           for(i7=i3; i7<N; i7+=i6)
41           {  i8=i7+i4;
42              t1=c*D1[i8]-s*D2[i8];
```

```
43                        t2=c*D2[i8]+s*D1[i8];
44                        D1[i8]=D1[i7]-t1;
45                        D2[i8]=D2[i7]-t2;
46                        D1[i7]+=t1;
47                        D2[i7]+=t2;
48                   }
49               }
50           i4=i6;
51       }
52    return;
53 }
```

Function 3. Complex fast Fourier transform.

In the function itself, Lines 17–31 scramble the naturally ordered time samples into fully decimated *bit reversed* order. i3 being the "for" loop index counts naturally from 1 to N. i1 in conjunction with Lines 20–22 acts like a bit-reversed counter taking on successive values of 0, 8, 4, 12, 2, etc. (for the $K=4$, $N=16$ case). Whenever i1 is greater than i3, the samples pointed to by i1 and i3 are swapped.

Lines 32–51 implement the FFT itself and consist of three nested loops. The outer loop, which spans Lines 33–51, is iterated K times, once for each stage in the recombination. The next loop starts in line 35 and is iterated for each cosine, sine value used in the computation. Note that here is the only place where there is a difference between forward and inverse transform: the conditional negation of the sine look-up. The innermost loop starting at Line 40 covers all of the 2-point mini transforms using a particular cosine, sine value. For N = 16, the outer loop is iterated 4 times. The middle loop is executed 1, 2, 4, and 8 time(s) for each iteration of the outer loop, and the inner loop is iterated 8, 4, 2, and 1 time(s) for each iteration of the middle loop.

Innermost in the nest of loops at Lines 42–47 is the useful calculation. A count of useful operations for these lines gives 4 multiplications and 6 additions. These lines are evaluated $(N\log_2 N)/2$ times which gives a total of $2N\log_2 N$ multiplications and $3N\log_2 N$ additions.

12 Using CFFT

As mentioned earlier, the core FFT algorithm takes complex data and produces complex results. For the forward transform (DIR = 1) the real-time samples should be placed in the D1 array in natural time order and the D2 array should be zeroed. As declared, these are single precision floating point arrays but of course recompilation could change that to double which might be advisable for record lengths longer than 64K samples. There is no preset limit on K but the "memory model" used by the compiler may have to be changed when array sizes exceed 16384 float samples ($K = 14$). The int declarations may also require changing to long if K is to be greater than 15 ($N = 32768$).

The spectrum result will be returned with cosine amplitudes in D1 and sine amplitudes in D2. The $N/2 - 1$ harmonics are in Dx[1 to $N/2$ - 1] and will need to be divided by $N/2$ to be correct. The DC component is in D1[0] and the Nyquist component is in D1[N/2]; both need to be divided by N.

The upper halves of the Dx arrays contain the *complex conjugate* of the spectrum. Thus D1[N-1] = D1[1], D1[N-2] = D1[2] ... and D2[N-1] = -D2[1], D2[N-2] = -D2[2] .... For the forward transform and real data, the conjugate spectrum can be ignored.

For the inverse transform, the desired spectrum must be stored in the lower halves of D1 and D2 just as described above. For harmonics 1 through N - 1, the amplitudes should be divided by 2. Next D2[0] and D2[N/2] should be zeroed. Finally, the conjugate spectrum must be installed in the upper halves of the D1 and D2 arrays. Following this data preparation, CFFT is called with DIR = -1. It will return with the time samples in natural order in the D1 array and the D2 array will contain zeroes. Well, not really zeroes but the values, which represent computational noise, should be several orders of magnitude less than the signal in the D1 array. The time sample values returned in D1 do not need any amplitude correction.

13   Making It Real

It is possible to double the storage efficiency of the core FFT function by rearranging the data somewhat and utilizing complementary real/complex conversion functions. These functions act as a final stage in the forward transform or an initial stage in the inverse transform.

For the forward case, one first stores the real time data *alternately* in the D1 and D2 arrays. Thus T(0)->D1[0], T(1)->D2[0], T(2)->D1[1], T(3)->D2[1] ... T(2N-2)->D1[N-1], and T(2N-1)->D2[N-1] which doubles the number of time samples stored. Then CFFT is called with $K = \log_2 N$. The spectrum that emerges is no longer redundant and typically looks like a list of random numbers. At this point, a *complex-to-real* conversion is performed on the spectrum that results in a complete, conventional spectrum of N + 1 harmonics for the 2N time samples. For convenience, the Nyquist component is stored as the sine part of the DC component which would otherwise always be zero.

For an inverse transform, the spectrum is first entered into the D1 and D2 arrays normally with no conjugate duplication required. Next, a *real-to-complex* conversion is performed that transforms the set of real harmonics into a complex set. Finally, CFFT with DIR = -1 is called to generate a list of 2N time samples stored alternately in the D1 and D2 arrays as before.

Functions 4 and 5 implement complex-to-real (RealT) and real-to-complex (CplxT) conversion, respectively. RealT also scales the spectrum output so that all of the harmonics, including DC, are of the correct amplitude. Except for scaling, CplxT undoes what RealT does.

```
1     void RealT(int K, float D1[], float D2[])
2     /* This function is to be used after calling CFFT when
        performing a
3        forward transform of real data.
4        K is the FFT order = log2(<size of Dx[] arrays>).
5           Range is 2 to 15 inclusive.  Change declarations for
              N, Nover2, i1, i2
6           to long if you wish to transform records longer than
              65536 real samples.
7        The number of real samples transformed is 2*2^K.
8        D1[], D2[] is the complex spectrum result from CFFT
           that is input to
9        this function.  On return, D1 is the cosine amplitudes
           of the
10       spectrum and D2 is the sine amplitudes.  D1[0]
           contains the DC
11       component and D2[0] contains the Nyquist component.
12       The function also does amplitude correction so that
           the final
13       spectrum output is the true spectrum of the input to
           CFFT.
14    */
15    {   float t1,t2,t3,t4,t5,t6;  /* Temps for efficient
                                        calculation */
16        float ang;               /* Temporary angle */
17        float c,s;               /* cosine & sine multipliers */
18        float Ntimes2;           /* =N*2 */
```

```
19        unsigned int Nover2;  /* =N/2 */
20        unsigned int N;       /* Size of D1 and D2 arrays */
21        unsigned int i1,i2;   /* Temporary indices */
22
23        N = 1<<K;  /* Calcualte complex record size from K */
24        Ntimes2=N*2.;
25        Nover2=N/2;
26
27        t1=D1[0]; /* Compute, correct, & place DC component */
28        t2=D2[0]; /* Compute, correct, and place Nyquist */
29        D1[0]=(t1+t2)/Ntimes2;
30        D2[0]=(t1-t2)/Ntimes2;
31
32        for(i1=1; i1<=Nover2; i1++) /* Compute remainder of
                                         frequency components */
33        {   i2=N-i1;
34            ang=3.1415927*i1/N;
35            c=cos(ang);
36            s=-sin(ang);
37            t1=D1[i1]+D1[i2];
38            t2=D1[i1]-D1[i2];
39            t3=D2[i1]+D2[i2];
40            t4=D2[i1]-D2[i2];
41            t5=t2*s-t3*c;
42            t6=t2*c+t3*s;
43            D1[i1]=(t1-t5)/Ntimes2;
44            D1[i2]=(t1+t5)/Ntimes2;
45            D2[i1]=(t4-t6)/Ntimes2;
46            D2[i2]=(-t4-t6)/Ntimes2;
47        }
48        return;
49  }
```

Function 4. Complex-to-real conversion for forward real transform.

```
1   void CplxT(int K, float D1[], float D2[])
2   /* This function is to be used before calling CFFT when
       performing
3      an inverse transform to produce real data.
4      K is the FFT order = log2(<size of Dx[] arrays>).
5        Range is 2 to 15 inclusive.  Change declarations for
```

```
          N, Nover2, i1, i2
6          to long if you wish to transform records longer than
           65536 real samples.
7      The number of real samples produced is 2*2^K.
8      D1[] and D2[] is the input spectrum to this function.
9      D1 is the cosine amplitudes and D2 is the sine
       amplitudes.
10     D1[0] should contain the DC component and D2[0] the
       Nyquist component.
11     The complex spectrum produced is then processed by
       CFFT to produce
12     real samples stored alternately in D1 and D2.
13  */
14  {   float t1,t2,t3,t4,t5,t6;  /* Temps for efficient
                                      calculation */
15      float ang;                /* Temporary angle */
16      float c,s;                /* cosine & sine multipliers */
17      unsigned int N;           /* Size of D1 and D2 arrays */
18      unsigned int Nover2;      /* =N/2 */
19      unsigned int i1,i2;       /* Temporary indices */
20
21      N = ldexp(1.,K);  /* Calcualte complex record size
                             from K */
22      t1=D1[0];              /* Restore DC and Nyquist components */
23      t2=D2[0];
24      D1[0]=t1+t2;
25      D2[0]=t1-t2;
26
27      Nover2=N/2;           /* restore remainder of frequency
                                 components */
28      for(i1=1; i1<=Nover2; i1++)
29      {   i2=N-i1;
30          ang=-3.1415927*i1/N;
31          c=cos(ang);
32          s=sin(ang);
33          t1=D1[i1]+D1[i2];
34          t4=D2[i1]-D2[i2];
35          t5=D1[i2]-D1[i1];
36          t6=-D2[i1]-D2[i2];
37          t2=t5*s+t6*c;
38          t3=t6*s-t5*c;
```

```
39          D1[i1]=(t1+t2)/2.;
40          D1[i2]=(t1-t2)/2.;
41          D2[i1]=(t3+t4)/2.;
42          D2[i2]=(t3-t4)/2.;
43      }
44      return;
45  }
```

Function 5. Real-to-complex conversion for inverse real transform.

14 Testing

The accompanying CD-ROM contains all five of the functions described above. It also contains several simple, interactive test programs to illustrate usage and confirm that compilation for a particular platform is accurate. Additionally, it can be used for execution time measurement with accuracy depending on the platform's system clock implementation. There are three versions, one for CFFT alone, one for testing the CFFT, RealT, CplxT suite, and the last for FSFT and ISFT for the reader's amusement. Besides testing the transform functions, these also illustrate proper data preparation, interpretation, and function usage.

All the test programs work by asking the user to specify a record size then the frequency, sine amplitude, and cosine amplitude of as many frequency components as desired. As each component is specified, the program adds it to the data record. When all of the test frequencies have been entered, the data record is forward transformed and the complete spectrum is printed to the screen. Then the spectrum is inverse transformed and the resulting time data compared against the original. If all is well, the computed spectrum should match the reader's input and there should be very little difference between the retransformed and original data.

Annotated Bibliography

[1] Hal A. Chamberlin. *Musical Applications of Microprocessors*. Indianapolis, IN: Hayden Books, 1980, revised 1985.

The author's original description of the fast Fourier transform and its implementation in BASIC and Motorola 68000 assembly language.

[2] J. W. Cooley and J. W. Tukey. "An Algorithm for the Machine Calculation of Complex Fourier Series", *Mathematics of Computation* 19 (1965), 297–301.

Original classic paper describing the fast Fourier tansform.

The Internet is also an outstanding resource. Following are some links that, at the time of writing, the author found to be particularly informative. However, simply typing "Cooley Tukey" or "fast Fourier transform" into an Internet search engine will bring up a wealth of other links.

[3] http://aurora.phys.utk.edu/~forrest/papers/fourier/index.html.

Mathematical discussion of Fourier transform theory, plus a link to Cooley and Tukey's classic paper and many more bibliographic references.

[4] http://www.fftw.org/benchfft/.

Benchmarking fast Fourier transform implementations and other practical considerations. Includes variations that are not limited to powers of two.

[5] http://ourworld.compuserve.com/homepages/steve_kifowit/fft.htm.

General information, source code, and more links for fast Fourier transforms.

Fast Fourier Transform Using Integer Math

Hal Chamberlin

Compiled and run on today's PCs, Macs, and workstations, the Fast Fourier Transform (FFT) suite mentioned in "Floating Point Fast Fourier Transform" (page 101) is efficient and compact even though written in a straightforward manner using floating point arithmetic. Embedded systems, like measuring instruments, portable devices, and musical instruments, however, often lack floating point hardware and often even the space to contain a floating point math library. Most DSP processors, especially cores embedded into custom VLSI, are also fixed point. Even an 8-bit processor lacking hardware multiply may be called upon to execute an FFT, say, for distortion measurements in self diagnostics. In all of these cases an FFT implementation using only integer math can be a necessity.

In this article, the three FFT functions (CFFT, RealT, and CplxT) will be rewritten for integer math. If the target system has a good compiler, the functions can be compiled and used as-is with good efficiency. Alternatively, they can be hand-translated into assembly language with little difficulty even by an engineer not very familiar with signal processing.

What about accuracy when using integer math? As a general rule, if the sum of the sample's bit precision and the transform order is equal or less than the integer size, there can be little, if any, difference between integer math accuracy and floating point accuracy. Thus, a compiler with 32-bit integers can perform transforms on 16-bit data up to 64 K samples long with results as accurate as the original data. Likewise, 20-bit data and up to 4 K samples. Even using 16-bit integers, one can process 256 sample records of 8-bit data with no accuracy loss.

1   Scaling

The primary challenge in converting any algorithm to integer math is proper *scaling* of the data so that during calculation, intermediate results neither overflow nor become so small that precision is lost. Whereas floating point numbers carry around their own individual scale factors (the exponent part), the scale factors for integer data are determined by the programmer and embedded in the program logic.

For data representing signals, it is usually advantageous to select a scale factor that scales the data to be between -1 and +1, that is, fractions. Thus, for signed 16-bit ints, the scale factor would be 32768 or 2^{15}; 8-bit shorts, $2^7 = 128$, and 32-bit longs, $2^{31} = 2,147,483,648$. For unsigned data, the scale factors could be twice as large.

When adding scaled data, the scale factors of the addends must be the same and the resulting scale factor will be the same as well. For avoiding overflow, the *range* of values must be considered. When adding, the range of the result is the sum of the ranges of the addends. Thus, if the addends are fractions between -1 and +1, the sum, with a range of -2 to +2, is no longer a fraction. A one-bit right shift of the sum, which amounts to doubling the scale factor, can correct this, but of course, must be accounted for in subsequent calculations.

When multiplying, the scale factors may be different and the product scale factor will the product of the two scale factors. So, when multiplying 16-bit signed fractions, the product must be divided by 32768, which amounts to a 15-bit right shift.

For signed fractions, the full range of possible data values is -1.000... through +0.999... There can be complications though if -1.000... ever occurs in the data. One of these is the overflow that occurs when -1.000 is complemented. Another is the incorrect result when -1.000... is multiplied by -1.000... and the product adjusted by a 15-bit right shift. Although operand values of -1.000... can be tested for before every arithmetic operation, it is far more efficient to purge these values at the source and replace them by -0.999....

Now let's examine the FFT algorithm (Function 3 of "Floating Point Fast Fourier Transform" (page 101)) and see what considerations are necessary when converting to integer math. Referring to the CFFT function, also from "Floating Point Fast Fourier Transform," we see that floating point operations are confined to Lines 36–39 where the W function is evaluated and Lines 42–48 where the butterfly column is evaluated. The following discussion will assume 16-bit ints and 32-bit longs although the principles apply to any basic word length and corresponding double length.

The first task is evaluating sine and cosine for the W function. The usual library functions, of course, use heavy duty floating point math to evaluate polynomial approximations of these functions. Restricted to integer math, interpolating in sine and cosine tables comes to mind, but unless memory space is *very* limited, just straight look-up in a surprisingly small table is sufficient. Study of Line 36 reveals that the range of angles is 0 to a tad less than pi. For table look-up, we can just drop the pi factor and interpret line 36 as addressing the i3-rd entry of sine and cosine tables having i4 entries each. The largest value of i4 is N/2. Using very simple trigonometry, a single cosine table half as long as that, N/4 entries, is sufficient. Thus, for 1024 complex-point FFTs, a 256-entry cosine table suffices.

The table would hold N/4+1 cosine values covering angles from 0 to pi/2. For the cosine of angles from 0 to pi/2, just look in the table. For pi/2 to pi, the cosine's odd symmetry around pi/2 would be exploited by accessing the same table in the reverse direction and negating what is read. For the sine of angles from 0 to pi/2, access the same table in the reverse direction and for angles from pi/2 to pi, exploit the even symmetry around pi/2 by subtracting pi from the angle and accessing the table normally.

Encoding signed values of -1.00000 to +1.00000 into signed 16-bit integer entries implies a scale factor of 16384 or 14 bits of precision. The fifteenth bit is needed to accurately encode values of +1.00000 and -1.00000 and the sixteenth bit is the sign. We can get those bits back by employing a couple of tricks. First, we can utilize the aforementioned symmetry logic to "know" the sign and adjust subsequent calculations accordingly using just the magnitude from the table. Second, a magnitude of 1.00000 can be encoded as an otherwise nonoccurring value in the table data that can be recognized later when the sine and cosine values are used in Lines 42 and 43. If the code for magnitude 1.00000 is recognized, multiplication in these lines is simply skipped. If simplicity is important, 1.00000 can simply be stored as 0.99998 with just a small penalty in speed and accuracy.

The remaining butterfly computations in Lines 44–47 simply form sums and differences and store them back into the data array. Examination of these lines reveals that values stored back into the array are sums of three terms:

```
47  D2[i7] = cos(ang)*D2[i8} + sin(ang)*D1[i8] + D2[i7]
```

Worst case then, the value stored back seems like it could be three times larger than the values originally there. Actually, the largest combined value of the first two terms is 1.414 times larger which occurs when ang is pi/4 and 3*pi/4. Thus, the worst possible increase is really only 2.414 times larger.

Since the butterfly is repeated $K = \log_2(N)$ times, it would seem that, worst case, the final result values could be 2.414^K times larger than the original data values. In fact, for the forward transform, the worst case is only 2.000^K times larger. Additionally, at no point in the series of butterflies will the data values stored back be larger than 2^I times the original where I is the butterfly column number being evaluated. Thus, for scaling purposes, the range of data values can be considered to *double* with each butterfly in the forward transform.

An exception is inverse transformation of real data. If one inverse transforms a spectrum having one prominent frequency near full amplitude, then intermediate values approaching $(2.414/2)(2^I)$ can be produced and cause an overflow. Restricting the amplitude of individual frequencies to less than 82% of full scale would avoid this problem.

There are at least three ways to deal with this tendency of the data to increase in size with each butterfly calculation. The most accurate is to use long integers in the complex data arrays. Sufficient headroom to avoid overflow is assured if the product of the maximum data value and N is less than the capacity of a long integer. Best accuracy is secured if the data arrays are *prescaled* according to N such that this constraint is just satisfied. For example, if the original data is 16-bit ints and the transform size is 2048 points, the data values can be multiplied by $2^{31}/(2048 \cdot 2^{15})$ = 32 while being moved into the long int arrays for transforming.

If one can't afford the space for double size data arrays and some accuracy can be sacrificed, then a simple strategy is to simply divide the results of each butterfly calculation by two before storing back into the array. This is called *unconditional array scaling* and will positively avoid overflow for forward transforms. It can theoretically be used for any transform size regardless of wordlength. A bonus for the forward transform is that the final result will already be scaled. DC and Nyquist will still need a final division by 2, however.

Better accuracy for low signal levels can be effected by *conditionally* scaling the data arrays. As each butterfly is performed, the values stored back into the array are monitored. If any exceed a magnitude of 0.414 of the maximum positive integer (13572 for 16-bit ints), a flag is set. The flag indicates that calculations during the next butterfly could possibly overflow. When the next butterfly is performed, the result would be divided by 2 before being stored back into the array if the flag is set, else the result is stored as is. Alternatively, for the maximum possible accuracy, a dry run butterfly can be performed first to see if any result overflows. If so, the live run can divide its results by 2 before storing back into the array. This would provide approximately 1 more bit of precision at the expense of nearly doubled execution time.

In either case, a practical routine would need two flags to work properly in cases where consecutive butterflies need scaling. A counter is also needed to keep track of the number of times the data is divided by 2. Its value would be used when the final transform result is scaled.

2   Practical Integer FFT Routines

Now a practical suite of FFT functions using integer arithmetic will be described. These will use the unconditional array scaling method and clipped cosine table described above which trades some accuracy for simplicity and speed. The accompanying CD-ROM also contains a suite using the long integers and coded 1.00000 table method, plus a test program that compares speed and accuracy of the two.

Before the `ICFFT`, `IRealT`, and `ICplxT` functions can be used, a suitable cosine table must be present. The simple function below will generate such a table. The first argument, Kmax, specifies how large a table to generate. `ICFFT` can then use the table to perform transforms of any size up to that value of Kmax. The output of the function is a pair of data statements written to a file that can be compiled and linked with the target integers-only program. The first simply defines Kmax to programs using the table. The number of values generated for the second will be $2^{\text{Kmax}}/4 + 1$.

Typically, one would run this function on the platform used for development and then compile the table produced into the fixed point target program. For convenience, the CD-ROM contains an interactive calling program and tables for Kmax = 9 (up to 1024 real points), Kmax = 11 (up to 4096 real points), and Kmax = 14 (up to 32,768 real points).

```
void MakeICT(int Kmax, FILE *output_file)
/* Function to create an integer cosine table for ICFFT,
   IRealT, and ICplxT. Kmax specifies the table length to
   allow transforms up to 2^Kmax complex points.  Two data
   statements will be written to the file which can then be
   compiled into the user's application.  The first defines
```

Kmax. The second defines the table, IcosT. Its length
is 2^Kmax/4+1. Maximum Kmax is 18, minimum is 5 for a
valid table to be generated. This version creates a table
with a maximum value of 65535.
*/

```c
{   long N;                 /* Table size is N = 2^Kmax/4 +1 */
    long t;                 /* Table entry */
    long i,j;               /* Counters */

    N = 1<<(Kmax-2);        /* Calculate table size from Kmax */

    fprintf(output_file,
        "/* Cosine table for 0 - PI/2 for FFTs up to %lu ",
        N*4);
    fprintf(output_file,"complex points. */\r\n");
    fprintf(output_file,"int Kmax=%i;\r\n",Kmax);
    fprintf(output_file,
        "unsigned int IcosT[%i] = {\r\n",N+1);
    for (i=0; i<N; i+=8)
    {   /* Leading spaces at beginning of a line */
        fprintf(output_file," ");

        for (j=0; j<8; j++)
        {   t=65535*cos((i+j)*1.570796327/N)+0.5;
            fprintf(output_file,"%lu,",t);
        }

        /* End of line of 8 values */
        fprintf(output_file,"\r\n");
    }
    /* Last entry is zero then end of table */
    fprintf(output_file,"  0};\r\n");

    return;
}
```

Function 1. Cosine table creator for ICFFT, IRealT, and ICplxT.

The ICFFT function in Function 2 is very much like its floating point
counterpart, CFFT. Added arguments, Kmax and IcosT, specify the cosine

2. Practical Integer FFT Routines   133

table. As described above, division of the data arrays by 2 after every
butterfly results in the forward transform spectrum being the correct amplitude without any further adjustment. The DC component at ID1[0]
and Nyquist component at ID1[N/2] need to be divided by 2, however.

While converting an earlier assembly language version of this routine
to C, one important limitation of the C language for signal processing
work became apparent. Lines 58, 59, 61, and 62 perform the useful multiplications of the transform. What is desired is a 16-bit by 16-bit integer
multiply producing a 32-bit product to be stored in a 32-bit temp for later
use. Most integer multiply hardware (or software routine) does this by
default in one operation, but there is no way to express this in standard C.
Instead, the compiler extends each factor to 32 bits, then multiplies them
as a 32-bit by 32-bit operation. Hardware to do this directly is far less
common and so a much slower subroutine that does three or four 16-bit
by 16-bit multiplies is invoked by the compiler. If speed is important at
all, these four statements are prime candidates for rewriting as assembly
code. Alternatively, a compiler with extensions to support efficient signal
processing may offer a "C" way to do this.

```
1   void ICFFT(unsigned int IcosT[], int Kmax, int K, int DIR,
    int D1[], int D2[])
2   /* Complex fast Fourier transform using only integer math
3    IcosT is cos table for 0->pi/2; unsigned entries 0-65535
4    Kmax  is length of the cosine table: (2^Kmax/4+1) entries
5    K     is the FFT order = log2<size of Dx[] arrays>
6          Range is 2 to Kmax inclusive.
7    DIR   +1 if forward transform (time->freq), -1 if inverse
8    D1[]  real parts of input and output arrays, 2^K elements
9    D2[]  imaginary parts of input and output arrays,
10         2^K elements */
11  { unsigned int N, Nover2; /* Size of Dx arrays,1/2 that */
12    int Tish;               /* Cosine table index shift */
13    unsigned int i1,i2,i3,i4,i6,i7,i8;   /* Temp indices */
14    unsigned int ang;       /* Temps for cosine */
15    unsigned long angtemp;  /* and sine lookup */
16    unsigned int c,s;       /* cosine & sine magnitudes */
17    int cs,ss;              /* cosine & sine signs (1=negative) */
18    int td1,td2;            /* Temporary D1, D2, array readout */
19    long t1,t2,t3,t4;       /* Long temporaries */
20
21    N = 1<<K;       /* Calculate complex record size from K */
```

```
22    Nover2 = N>>1; /* N/2 */
23    Tish = Kmax-K; /* Index shift amount for cosine table */
24    i1=0;    /* Scramble input data into bit reverse order */
25    i2=N-1;
26    for(i3=1; i3<N; i3++) /* i3 is normal counter, i1 is bit
                                reverse counter */
27    { i4=N;
28      while(i1+i4 > i2)  i4 >>= 1;
29      i1 = (i1%i4)+i4;
30      if(i1 > i3)
31      { td1=D1[i3];
32        D1[i3]=D1[i1];
33        D1[i1]=td1;
34        td2=D2[i3];
35        D2[i3]=D2[i1];
36        D2[i1]=td2;
37      }
38    }
39    i4=1;                      /* Perform the complex transform */
40    while(i4<N)
41    { i6=i4<<1;
42      for(i3=0; i3<i4; i3++) /* For W function evaluation:*/
43      { angtemp=(long)i3*(long)N; /* Express angle range of
                                        0 - pi  */
44        ang=angtemp/i4;          /* as index range of 0 - N */
45        if(ang<=Nover2)          /* For 0 <= ang <= pi/2 :  */
46        { c=IcosT[ang<<Tish>>1];  /* Use ang for cosine */
47          cs=0;                   /* Sign of cosine is + */
48          s=IcosT[(Nover2-ang)<<Tish>>1]; /* Use complement
                                              ang for sin */
49        }
50        else                     /* For pi/2 < ang <= pi :  */
51        { c=IcosT[(N-ang)<<Tish>>1];    /* for cosine,
                                            complement ang */
52          cs=1;                        /* and sign is - */
53          s=IcosT[(ang-Nover2)<<Tish>>1];/* Shift ang for
                                            sine     */
54        }
55        if(DIR<0) ss=1; else ss=0; /* sine is + for forward,
                                        - for inv */
56        for(i7=i3; i7<N; i7+=i6)
```

```
57        { i8=i7+i4;
58          t1=(long)c*(long)D1[i8]; /* Cos multiplications */
59          t3=(long)c*(long)D2[i8];
60          if(cs) { t1=-t1; t3=-t3; }
61          t2=(long)s*(long)D1[i8]; /* Sin multiplications */
62          t4=(long)s*(long)D2[i8];
63          if(ss) { t2=-t2; t4=-t4; }
64          t1=((t1>>1)-(t4>>1))>>15;/* Final recombinations*/
65          t2=((t3>>1)+(t2>>1))>>15;
66
67          if(DIR>=0)
68          { t3=D1[i7]-t1;    /* Forward transform requires */
69            D1[i8]=t3>>1;    /* scaling by 1/2 every        */
70            t3=D2[i7]-t2;    /* butterfly                   */
71            D2[i8]=t3>>1;
72            t3=D1[i7]+t1;
73            D1[i7]=t3>>1;
74            t3=D2[i7]+t2;
75            D2[i7]=t3>>1;
76          }
77          else
78          { t3=D1[i7]-t1;    /* Inverse transform does not */
79            D1[i8]=t3;       /* require scaling            */
80            t3=D2[i7]-t2;
81            D2[i8]=t3;
82            t3=D1[i7]+t1;
83            D1[i7]=t3;
84            t3=D2[i7]+t2;
85            D2[i7]=t3;
86          }
87        }
88      }
89      i4=i6;
90    }
91    return;
92 }
```

Function 2. Complex fast Fourier transform using integer arithmetic.

IRealT is also very much like its floating point relative. It uses the cosine table slightly differently from ICFFT, however. If K is less than

Kmax, direct look-up in the table is performed. However, if K equals
Kmax, the table size is effectively doubled by interpolating midway between the entries. For Kmax of 10 or greater, the error incurred by doing
this is less than the LSB of the 16-bit table entries.

```
1   void IRealT(unsigned int IcosT[], int Kmax, int K, int
    D1[], int D2[])
2   /* IRealT is used after calling ICFFT when performing a
3    forward transform of real data.  Uses only integer math.
4    IcosT is cos table for 0->pi/2; unsigned entries 0-65535
5    Kmax  is length of the cosine table: (2^Kmax/4+1) entries
6    K     is the FFT order = log2(<size of Dx[] arrays>).
7          Range is 2 to Kmax inclusive.
8          The number of real samples transformed is 2*2^K.
9    D1[], D2[] are the complex spectrum results from ICFFT
10   passed as input.  On return, D1 is the cos amplitudes of
11   the spectrum & D2 is the sin amplitudes.  D1[0] holds the
12   DC component and D2[0] contains the Nyquist component.
13   The function also does amplitude correction so that the
14   final spectrum output is the true spectrum of the input
15   to CFFT. */
16  { long t1,t2,t3,t4,t5,t6;   /* Temps for efficient calcs */
17    int          Tish;        /* Cosine table index shift */
18    unsigned int c,s;         /* cosine & sine magnitudes */
19    unsigned int N;           /* Size of D1 and D2 arrays */
20    unsigned int Nover2;      /* =N/2 */
21    unsigned int i1,i2;       /* Temporary indices */
22
23    N = 1<<K;     /* Calcualte complex record size from K */
24    Nover2=N/2;
25    Tish = Kmax-K-1; /* Index shift amount for cos table */
26    t1=D1[0]; /* Compute, correct, and place DC component */
27    t2=D2[0];       /* Compute, correct, and place Nyquist */
28    D1[0]=(t1+t2)>>1;
29    D2[0]=(t1-t2)>>1;
30    for(i1=1; i1<=Nover2; i1++) /* Compute remainder of
                                     frequency components */
31    { i2=N-i1;
32      if(Tish >= 0)            /* Standard case for K<Kmax */
33      { c=IcosT[i1<<Tish];     /* Direct table lookup since*/
```

```
34          s=IcosT[(Nover2-i1)<<Tish]; /* 0 < angle <= pi/2 */
35      }
36      else                     /* Special case for K=Kmax   */
37      { if(i1%2)         /* For i1 is odd, must interpolate */
38        { t1=IcosT[i1>>1];            /* Cosine */
39          t2=IcosT[(i1>>1)+1];
40          t3=(t1+t2)>>1;
41          c=t3;
42          t1=IcosT[(Nover2-i1)>>1];    /* Sine */
43          t2=IcosT[((Nover2-i1)>>1)+1];
44          t3=(t1+t2)>>1;
45          s=t3;
46        }
47        else                      /* For even, just lookup */
48        { c=IcosT[i1>>1];
49          s=IcosT[(Nover2-i1)>>1];
50        }
51      }
52      t1=((long)D1[i1]+(long)D1[i2])>>1; /* 1st combos */
53      t2=((long)D1[i1]-(long)D1[i2])>>1;
54      t3=((long)D2[i1]+(long)D2[i2])>>1;
55      t4=((long)D2[i1]-(long)D2[i2])>>1;
56      t5=-t3*c;                  /* Cosine multiplications */
57      t6=t2*c;
58      t5-=t2*s;                  /* Sine multiplications */
59      t6-=t3*s;
60      D1[i1]=((t1<<16)-t5)>>16; /* Final combinations */
61      D1[i2]=((t1<<16)+t5)>>16;
62      D2[i1]=((t4<<16)-t6)>>16;
63      D2[i2]=((-t4<<16)-t6)>>16;
64    }
65    return;
66 }
```

Function 3. Complex to real conversion using integer arithmetic.

A real to complex function for inverse transformation of real data is also possible and is included on the CD-ROM for completeness. However, the accuracy with 16-bit data arrays is relatively poor compared with the forward case. Also, as indicated earlier, overflow is possible when synthesizing tones greater than 82% of full scale. For these reasons, it is recommended that either `ICFFT` alone be used (which wastes half of the array space for real data), or the long integers suite (`LCFFT`, `LRealT`, `LCplxT` on the CD-ROM) be used for inverse transformation.

3   Testing and Usage

Interactive test programs for the integer math FFT functions are also on the CD-ROM. These illustrate proper data preparation, scaling, and interpretation. They also give an idea of the accuracy and computational noise level that can be expected with various combinations of algorithm and transform size.

4   Summary and Conclusion

The fast Fourier transform algorithm is one of the most important discoveries in applied mathematics and makes practical a number of modern signal processing techniques. Although more complex than straightforward "slow" methods, the algorithm can be readily understood with the right approach and translates into remarkably compact code using almost any procedural computer language. Coding for fixed-point (integer) math makes the FFT practical on very constrained platforms and is key to implementation on DSP processors and dedicated hardware.

Annotated Bibliography

[1] Hal A. Chamberlin. *Musical Applications of Microprocessors*. Indianapolis, IN: Hayden Books, 1980, revised 1985.

The author's original description of the fast Fourier transform and its implementation in BASIC and Motorola 68000 assembly language.

[2] J. W. Cooley and J. W. Tukey. "An Algorithm for the Machine Calculation of Complex Fourier Series", *Mathematics of Computation* 19 (1965), 297–301.

Original classic paper describing the fast Fourier tansform.

The Internet is also an outstanding resource. Following are some links that, at the time of writing, the author found to be particularly informative. However, simply typing "Cooley Tukey" or "fast Fourier transform" into an Internet search engine will bring up a wealth of other links.

[3] http://aurora.phys.utk.edu/~forrest/papers/fourier/index.html.

Mathematical discussion of Fourier transform theory, plus a link to Cooley and Tukey's classic paper and many more bibliographic references.

[4] http://www.fftw.org/benchfft/.

Benchmarking fast Fourier transform implementations and other practical considerations. Includes variations that are not limited to powers of two.

[5] http://ourworld.compuserve.com/homepages/steve_kifowit/fft.htm.

General information, source code, and more links for fast Fourier transforms.

Spatialization

Spatialization with Stereo Loudspeakers: Understanding Balance, Panning, and Distance Attenuation

Hesham Fouad

1 Introduction

The subtleties of balance and panning are unfortunately often misunderstood. Our stereos have a knob labeled balance. Our mixers have a pot-labeled pan. The audio library we use might have a control called constant intensity panning. All of these terms apply to slightly different methods of moving audio energy between a pair of channels ultimately intended to be played through left and right loudspeakers to locate or spatialize a sound between the physical speakers.

With spatialization, we recreate the spatial characteristics of sound within a virtual acoustic environment. Current spatialization techniques utilize empirical approaches that fall into two general categories: One is the recreation of the Head-Related Transfer Function (HRTF) cues through filter convolution (explored in Haferkorns article "Head-Related Transfer Functions and the Physics of Spatial Hearing" (see *Audio Anecdotes III*), and the other is the recreation of the sound field using free field loudspeakers. In this article, we discuss the two loudspeaker panning techniques utilized in the latter approach, exploring the relevant physics, mathematics, and sample code implementations. (Ville Pulkki's article, "Spatialization with Multiple Loudspeakers" (page 159), further explores this concept by considering the more complicated multispeaker case.)

In this approach, loudspeakers are strategically located around a listener in order to simulate the effect of angular location and distance of a virtual sound source. The amplitude of the sound emanating from each loudspeaker is scaled in such a way that the resultant sound appears to be emanating from a particular location in the virtual acoustic environment. This, in effect, creates a virtual sound source at a specified direction and distance relative to the listener.

Spatialization systems utilizing loudspeaker panning can create fairly large virtual acoustic spaces able to accommodate multiple participants in a shared environment. Also, because the listener is unencumbered by headphones or head-tracking devices, a greater degree of motion is afforded to the participant. These two features make loudspeaker panning a good choice for large-scale training, simulation, or entertainment systems. Finally, the computational overhead of this approach is relatively minimal, making it ideal for instances where computational resources are at a premium.

2   The Balance Control

We can start our examination of loudspeaker panning by looking at how it is used in stereo recordings to recreate the position of musical instruments in a live musical performance. The listening field created by a stereo recording is one-dimensional, extending along an axis connecting the left and right speakers. A balance control is used during the mix-down process that allows the sound engineer to place an instrument along the interspeaker axis simply by turning a rotary knob to the left or right. The balance control manipulates the amplitude of the signal sent to each of the left and right channels placing a sound along the interspeaker axis. The control can also be changed dynamically during the mix-down giving the impression of a moving object.

We can easily simulate this type of panning in software by multiplying an input waveform directly by a left and right gain value and writing the resultant waveforms to the left and right channels of an audio output device. Assuming a balance value of –1 corresponds to hard left and +1 to hard right, we calculate the left and right gain values as follows:

$$R = \frac{Balance + 1}{2}$$
$$L = 1 - R \tag{1}$$

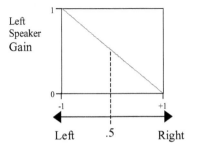
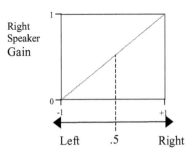

Figure 1. Left and right speaker gain for the balance control.

The gain values and corresponding source position are shown in Figure 1.

The **Balance** subroutine below implements the balance control by multiplying an input waveform by the gain value calculated for a given control position. The arguments to balance consists of a pointer to a buffer containing the input waveform that we wish to pan, the size of the buffer in samples, a balance value ranging from -1 to 1, and a pointer to a buffer where balance will write the resultant stereo output in an interleaved format commonly used by audio devices. The algorithm is fairly straightforward with the exception of the use of static variables for the gain values; in any audio processing application where a waveform is being directly modified, it is crucial that the parameters modifying the waveform change in a continuous manner, otherwise artifacts such as clicking noises result. Techniques for avoiding such artifacts are commonly referred to as dezippering techniques.

In the **Balance** subroutine, the gain values calculated from a previous invocation of the algorithm are stored in the static variables lGain and rGain. Instead of calculating gain values directly, the algorithm calculates per-sample delta values that are stored in lDeltaGain and rDeltaGain. Upon each iteration of the **for** loop that processes the samples, the delta values are added to the existing gain values resulting, at the end of the loop, in the desired gain values for the input balance position. This insures that when the balance control is dynamically modified, the gain values will change smoothly across the input sample block avoiding artifacts.

The balance subroutine follows; for the sake of brevity, error checking is not performed in the algorithms presented here.

```
// Balance pans a source along an axis connecting left and
// right speakers using a linear gain curve.

void Balance(float *mono, int size, float bal, float *stereo)
{
    static float lGain=0.0, rGain=0.0;
    float lDeltaGain;
    float rDeltaGain;
    float lgTemp;
    int i,j=0;

    // Calculate gain for the left speaker
    lgTemp = (bal + 1.0)/2.0;
    // Calculate delta values for the left gain
    lDeltaGain = (lgTemp - lGain) / size;
    // Calculate delta values for the right gain
    rDeltaGain = ((1.0 - lgTemp)- rGain) / size;

    // Apply gain values and generate 2 channels of audio
    for (i=0; i$<$size; i++)
    {
        stereo[j++] = mono[i]*lGain;
        stereo[j++] = mono[i]*rGain;
        lGain += lDeltaGain;
        rGain += rDeltaGain;
    }
}
```

We now examine how balance can be modified to simulate a virtual acoustic environment with positional sound sources and a listener. In its present form, balance is not very useful for simulating such an environment because there is not an intuitive mapping from sound source positions to a balance control value. A more appropriate specification, sound source positions as shown in Figure 2, will be used to substitute the balance control value. Source and also loudspeaker positions are specified using heading vectors with azimuth, elevation, and range values. Azimuth angles specify the angular position of an object lying on the listener's plane. Elevation angles measure the angular displacement off of that plane and finally, range specifies distance. We will use the heading vector to substitute the balance control values and in a following discussion, we will see how a heading vector specification can be used to derive gain values. First, however, we'll examine intensity and gain issues related to loudspeaker panning.

3 Maintaining Constant Intensity

The use of the linear gain curve (see Figure 1) in the balance subroutine results in an undesirable phenomenon called the "hole in the middle" effect, which has disturbing implications when simulating a virtual acoustic environment. The "hole in the middle" is a marked dip in the intensity of a virtual sound source as it moves across the stereo field between two speakers. Because the perceived distance of a sound source is largely dependent on its intensity, a source moving at a constant distance to the listener will appear to move further away as it is panned between two speakers. In order to examine why this occurs we note that by multiplying a waveform by a gain factor, we are manipulating the amplitude of the sound. The perceived distance of a sound, however, is dependent on its intensity, not amplitude. The intensity of a sound is proportional to the square of its amplitude, so we have

$$I \alpha A^2. \tag{2}$$

In our linear panning scheme above, when a sound source is midway between two speakers, the amplitude of the waveform is half that of the extreme left or right positions. The total intensity of the sound at the midpoint, summing the intensity from each side, is therefore

$$I = \frac{1}{2}^2 + \frac{1}{2}^2 = .5. \tag{3}$$

In terms of intensity, the sound is 3 dB quieter at the midpoint than at the two extremes and therefore appears to move further away as it is panned between the two speakers (see my article, "Understanding the Decibel" (see *Audio Anecdotes I*), describes the definition and use of the decibel as a measure of a sound's level).

In order to counteract this effect, we must use a panning curve that will maintain a constant intensity along the gain curve. This is called *constant intensity panning*, or sometimes *constant energy panning*. If our gain values for the left and right speakers are G_l and G_r, respectively, then we want a gain curve such that

$$G_l^2 + G_r^2 = 1. \tag{4}$$

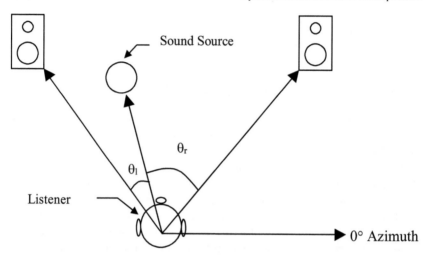

Figure 2. Measuring the azimuth angle between sound source and loudspeaker.

As it turns out, we can make use of trigonometric functions to produce the desired constant power curve. The trigonometric identity

$$\sin^2(\theta) + \cos^2(\theta) = 1 \tag{5}$$

is a good starting point as it satisfies the requirement expressed in Equation 4 above.

We consider the angles θ_l and θ_r in Figure 2, measured between the sound source and each of the left and right speakers, respectively. If we restrict the speaker placement such that any two adjacent speakers are orthogonal, then we have

$$\theta_l + \theta_r = 90^\circ$$
$$\theta_l = 90^\circ - \theta_r. \tag{6}$$

Substituting into Equation 5 above, we have

$$\sin^2(90^\circ - \theta_r) + \cos^2(\theta_l) = 1. \tag{7}$$

Making use of the identity $\sin(\theta) = \cos(\theta + 90^\circ)$, we can rewrite Equation 7 as

$$\cos^2(90^\circ - \theta_r + 90^\circ) + \cos^2(\theta_l) = 1$$
$$\cos^2(-\theta_r + 180^\circ) + \cos^2(\theta_l) = 1 \tag{8}$$
$$\cos^2(\theta_r) + \cos^2(\theta_l) = 1.$$

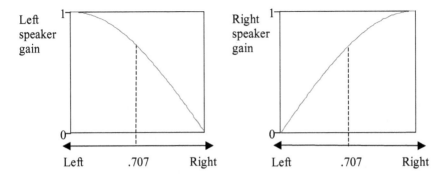

Figure 3. Constant-intensity gain curve.

The magnitude of the measured angle between the speaker and source will vary from $0°$ to $90°$ as the source moves across the listener's horizon. In the one-dimensional case, with two speakers, we will restrict the position of the sound source to lie within the arc formed by the two speakers. At the midpoint, the angles θ_l and θ_r will be 45 ° and the cosines of both angles will be .707. The intensity at the midpoint is

$$I = \cos^2(45) + \cos^2(45) = .707^2 + .707^2 = 1. \qquad (9)$$

We can formulate a general equation for a constant intensity gain curve as

$$Gi = \cos(|\theta i|)\ 0 \geq \theta i \leq 90, \qquad (10)$$

where θ_i is the angle between a sound source and loudspeaker i and $|\theta_i|$ denotes the absolute value of the angle θ_i. For angles greater than $90°$, the gain is zero. The new gain curves are shown in Figure 3.

Utilizing the constant intensity gain curve will enable us to pan a sound source between two loudspeakers while maintaining the virtual sound source at a constant distance from the listener.

In some instances, it may be necessary to mix spatialized with non-spatialized sounds. With two speakers, nonspatialized sound is the same as spatialized sound placed at the midpoint; to maintain the intensities, one must use a gain of .707. In a multispeaker installation, nonspatialized means presenting the sound over all the loudspeakers. Here the gain will depend on the number of loudspeakers used to present nonspatialized sounds and can be expressed as

$$G = \sqrt{\frac{1}{n}}, \qquad (11)$$

where n is the number of loudspeakers used to present a nonspatial-ized sound.

4   Modeling Distance

Locating a sound source in the virtual acoustic environment requires sim-ulating both the direction of a sound source as well as its distance from the listener. The auditory cues we use to judge the distance of a source include its intensity, the attenuation of the high frequency components due to absorption, the ratio between direct and reflected sound energy, and our familiarity with the sound. How we perceive the distance of a sound source is a complex topic that is not completely understood and a comprehensive treatment of the subject is well beyond the scope of this article. We will restrict our consideration here to the use of sound in-tensity as a cue for modeling the distance of a sound source from the listener.

Assuming a uniformly radiating source and free field conditions (a homogenous medium with no reflections), sound radiates outwardly as a spherical wavefront emanating equally in all directions from the source. The rate of energy being produced by the source is referred to as the sound's power. The intensity of the sound is the power per unit area at some distance from the source. By virtue of the law of conservation of energy, the power produced at the source is spread over the surface area of the expanding spherical wavefront. Because the surface area of that wavefront at distance d from the source is $4\pi d^2$, the power per unit area, and hence, the intensity at that distance will be

$$I = \frac{P}{4\pi d^2}, \tag{12}$$

where P is the power at the source measured in watts. This simply means that as the wavefront propagates farther away from the source, the intensity of sound falls off at a rate that is inversely proportional to the square of the distance. This property of sound wave propagation is referred to as the inverse square law.

The situation changes considerably in the presence of reflecting sur-faces. A sound source on or near a ground plane, for example, will only radiate into the upper hemisphere. Sound radiating towards the ground will be reflected upwards so that the sound's intensity will be twice that of the free field condition. If a reflecting wall is now placed behind that source, as would occur in an amphitheater, for example, the intensity is doubled again as the energy will only radiate into a quarter of the space.

When the sound source and listener are inside an enclosed space, free field conditions no longer hold because the intensity of the sound reaching the listener no longer depends solely on the direct path sound wave. Sound radiates from the source and repeatedly bounces off of the surfaces of the enclosure. With each reflection, some amount of energy is absorbed by the surface, the degree of which depends on the surface material's absorption coefficient. The reflections continue until the energy of the sound dissipates completely due to absorption, dissipation, and air particle friction. The net effect of all the reflected sound waves is to fill the space with a reverberant sound field whose intensity depends on the power being generated by the source and the surface area and absorption coefficients of the reflecting surfaces. The intensity of the sound reaching the listener is the sum of the intensity of the direct path sound and the intensity of the reverberant sound field. We can approximate the intensity of the reverberant sound field as

$$I_r = \frac{4P}{R_c}$$

$$R_c = \frac{\alpha S}{(1 - \alpha)},$$

(13)

where R_c is referred to as the room constant, P is the power emitted from the source, α is the average absorption coefficient of the surfaces in the enclosure, and S is the total area of the reflecting surfaces (Table 1 lists R_c values for some typical listening spaces). The total intensity of the sound reaching the listener is the sum of the intensities of the direct path sound, which obeys the inverse square law, and that of the reverberant field,

$$I = P\left(\frac{4}{R_c} + \frac{1}{4\pi d^2}\right).$$

(14)

We can see from Equation 14 that in free field conditions where R_c approaches ∞, the intensity of the reverberant field goes to zero. In a small highly reverberant enclosure, on the other hand, R_c gets small and the intensity of the reverberant sound field dominates.[1] In such conditions, the intensity of the sound reaching the listener is independent of the distance from source to listener.

Recalling that sound intensity is equivalent to the square of the amplitude, we can simulate the distance of a sound source from the listener by multiplying the waveform directly by a gain factor that is the square root

---

[1]If R_c were to approach $<=4$, the simplified model would fall apart, but as per Table 1, however, typical R_c values don't get that small.

Space Characteristics	R_c
Small Room	600
Large Room	1700
Concert Hall	9000
Free Field	∞

Table 1. A selection of typical R_c values.

of the intensity. The choice of intensity calculations (Equation 12 or 14) will depend on whether free field or enclosed spaces are being simulated. In the case of free field conditions, we simply multiply the waveform by a factor of

$$D = \sqrt{\frac{1}{4\pi d^2}} = \frac{1}{3.55d}. \tag{15}$$

In practice, we usually drop the constant multiplier in the denominator and simply multiply the waveform by a $1/d$ scale factor. For reverberant enclosures, the waveform is scaled by a factor of

$$D = \sqrt{\frac{4}{Rc} + \frac{1}{4\pi d^2}}. \tag{16}$$

It should be noted that if one uses spatialization software that models reflections, Equation 15 can be used. The distance model need not account for the reverberant sound field as that component of the sound's intensity will be accounted for by the addition of delayed versions of the waveform to the final output by the reverberation model.

It is important to note that the distance model presented here only considers attenuation due to the inverse square law. A complete treatment of sound propagation should take into consideration a number of additional factors affecting a sound wave travelling in free field conditions. High frequency rolloff, for example, causes distant sounds to loose much of their high frequency components. Because sound propagates through the atmosphere by displacing air molecules, some of the energy present in the propagating wave is consumed by frictional losses that occur when air molecules are moved. Such losses are more pronounced in the higher frequency components since they are moving air molecules at a higher rate, resulting in higher frictional losses.

Atmospheric effects also have a large impact on the propagation of sound. Temperature gradients in the atmosphere cause sound waves to refract either upwards or downwards depending on atmospheric conditions. During daylight hours, air temperatures decrease with altitude, causing sound waves to refract upwards towards the atmosphere. The opposite happens during night time, or cloudy conditions where air temperatures increase with altitude and sound waves are refracted down towards the earth. This results in sound travelling considerably farther during night time or cloudy conditions than during daylight hours.

A similar effect occurs during windy conditions. Wind velocity decreases close to the ground due to frictional drag against the earth. This difference in wind velocity causes sound to refract upwards when it is travelling against the wind and downwards when it is travelling with the wind. Sound therefore propagates farther when it is traveling in the direction of the wind.

5   Pan1D: Panning in One Dimension

The Pan1D subroutine will replace the Balance control parameter with the azimuth angle and range of the sound source. The algorithm will assume the left and right speakers will reside at 135° and 45° azimuth, respectively, which corresponds to the speaker positions depicted in Figure 2. In the interest of generality, we split off the portion of balance that multiplies the gain values with the waveform and formats the output into a separate subroutine called gain. Pan1D calculates the gain values and invokes the gain subroutine, which applies the gain to the input waveform and formats the output. In this subroutine, the free field model was used for simplicity.

```
// Pan1D pans a source along an axis connecting two speakers
// using a constant intensity gain curve.
#define PI 3.14159265
#define PI_2 PI/2.0
#define TWO_PI 2.0*PI
#define TORAD PI/180.0

void Pan1D(float *in, int size, float azim, float range,
        float *out)
{
    float gain[2];
    float lazim, razim;
    float distFact = 1.0/range;
    float lspeaker = 135.0 * TORAD;
    float rspeaker = 45.0 * TORAD;
```

```
    // Wrap the azimuth angle to the -PI to PI range and
    // reflect sources in the rear to their mirror positions
    // in the front.
    azim = fabs(azim);
    while (azim > PI)
        azim -= TWO_PI;
    azim = fabs(azim);
    // Limit the azimuth angle to lie within the arc formed
    // between the listener and the two speakers.
    if (azim > lspeaker)
        azim = lspeaker;
    else if (azim < rspeaker)
        azim = rspeaker;
    // Find the angle between the source and the left and
    // right speakers and calculate the gain for each speaker.
    lazim = lspeaker - azim;
    if (lazim > PI_2)
        gain[0] = 0.0;
    else
        gain[0] = cos(lazim)*distFact;
    razim = rspeaker - azim;
    if (razim > PI_2)
        gain[1] = 0.0;
    else
        gain[1] = cos(razim)*distFact;
    // Apply gain values to the input waveform and generate
    // interleaved audio

    Gain(in, size, gain, 2, out);
}


// Gain applies up to 8 gain values to an input waveform
// generating between 1 and 8 channels of output audio.
void Gain(float *in, int size, float *gain, int nch,
          float *out)
{
    static float storeGains[8] = { 0.0, 0.0, 0.0, 0.0,
                                   0.0, 0.0, 0.0, 0.0};
    float deltaGains[8];
    float *outptr = out;
```

```
int i,j;

for (i=0; i<nch; i++)
    deltaGains[i] = (gain[i] - storeGains[i]) / size;

for (i=0; i<size; i++)
    for (j=0; j<nch; j++)
    {
        *outptr++ = in[i] * storeGains[j];
        storeGains[j] += deltaGains[j];
    }
}
```

The reader will note the *while* loop at beginning of the subroutine; it functions to map any input azimuth angle to the legal range of $-90°$ to $90°$ and also reflects any sound source in the listener's rear half-plane to the front. Because Pan1D is a one-dimensional panning algorithm, it can only manage sounds that lie in the listener's frontal half-plane within a wedge extending from the listener and bisecting the two speakers. Sounds that lie behind the listener in the rear half-plane must be reflected to their mirror images in the front half-plane. Angles θ_l and θ_r are clamped such that positions outside the arc formed by the two speakers are not allowed.

6 Pan2D: Panning in Two Dimensions

The next step is to extend our algorithm to two dimensions utilizing an additional pair of speakers behind the listener. The two additional speakers will be placed at $-45°$ and $-135°$ azimuth for the left-rear and right-rear speakers, respectively. The subroutine applies the generalized gain equation (Equation 10) to the additional loudspeakers, generating a total of four gain values. One should note that two of the four gain values generated by Pan2D will always be zero as two of the four loudspeaker will always form an angle larger than $90°$ for any source position.

```
// Pan2D pans a source to a location on the listener's plane
// using a constant power gain curve.
#define PI 3.14159265
#define PI_2 PI/2.0
#define TWO_PI 2.0*PI
#define TORAD PI/180.0
```

```
void Pan2D(float *in, int size, float azim, float range,
           float *out)
{
    static float speakers[4] = {  45.0*TORAD,   135.0*TORAD,
                                  -45*TORAD,    -135.0*TORAD};
    float gains[4];
    float distFact = 1.0/range;
    float theta;
    int i;

    // Wrap azimuth angles to the range -PI to PI
    while (azim > PI)
        azim -= TWO_PI;
    while (azim < -PI)
        azim += TWO_PI;
    // Calculate gain values for each speaker
    for (i=0; i<4; i++)
    {
        theta = fabs(speakers[i] - azim);
        // Make sure that the angle measured between source
        // and speaker is acute.
        if (theta > PI)
            theta = TWO_PI - theta;
        // Final gain values are formed as the product of
        // azimuth gains and distance attenuation factor 1/D
        if (theta $>$ PI{\_}2)
            gains[i] = 0.0;
        else
            gains[i] = cos(theta)*distFact;
    }
    // Apply gain values to the input waveform and generate
    // interleaved audio.
    Gain(in, size, gains, 4, out);
}
```

Pan2D is functionally very similar to Pan1D, with the exception of the process used to wrap the input azimuth angle. Because we can now manage sound source positions anywhere in the listener's plane, we no longer need to reflect sounds behind the listener to positions in the front half-plane.

7 Conclusion

In this article, we presented a technique for spatializing sounds using loudspeaker panning in one and two dimensions. Constant intensity panning was discussed and techniques were presented whereby sounds are panned between loudspeakers while a constant intensity is maintained. In order to model the distance of a sound from the listener, the sound's intensity is attenuated based on its distance from the listener. Models for distance-based attenuation were presented for free field as well as reverberant enclosure conditions.

The speaker panning technique presented here is in some ways restrictive because the number of loudspeakers must be either 2, 4, or 8 (the 4-loudspeaker case can be easily extended to 8 speakers, 4 above and 4 below) and loudspeakers must be positioned orthogonal to each other. Ville Pulke's Vector Base Amplitude Panning (VBAP) technique (described in his aforementioned article) removes such restrictions allowing any number of speakers and positions. In practice, we've found that VBAP generally produces better results than the technique presented here. However, in a limited number of cases where a planer loudspeaker configuration (2 or 4) is used or where 8 loudspeakers must be placed orthogonal to each other (at the eight corners of a cube) the technique presented here performs better.

There are other factors affecting the results produced by any loudspeaker panning technique. A very important factor is loudspeaker matching. All loudspeakers color the timbre of the sounds they produce. If different kinds of loudspeakers are used in an installation, the differing coloration of the sounds are quite noticeable and distracting. Even if all the loudspeakers used are of the same type, care must be taken to ensure that they're all producing the same level of output. Even small variations in the level of one speaker will have the effect of biasing source positions towards that loudspeaker. In practice, we use active (self-amplified) loudspeakers for our installations. Active loudspeakers have a number of advantages over passive loudspeakers: The active circuitry in the loudspeaker is matched to the frequency response of the loudspeaker so that they produce a relatively flat frequency response. Also, active loudspeakers have a gain control on the loudspeaker so that one can easily match the loudspeaker gains in an installation by measuring the level of each loudspeaker using a level meter and adjusting the gain control accordingly.

Finally, in loudspeaker panning installation, one is usually limited to using fairly small loudspeakers with limited low frequency response.

The use of a subwoofer, placed outside of the speaker installation, can compensate for that without cluttering the space inside the installation.

The code presented in this article may be found on the CD-ROM accompanying this book along with examples to allow experimentation with these techniques.

Annotated Bibliography

[1] D.R. Begault. *3-D Sound for Virtual Reality and Multimedia*. Boston, MA: AP Professional, 1994.

A good general reference for spatial audio.

[2] J. M. Chowning. "The Simulation of Moving Sound Sources." *Journal of the Audio Engineering Society* 19:1(1971), 2–6.

Possibly the first article describing loudspeaker panning.

[3] S. Handel. *Listening: An Introduction to the Perception of Auditory Events*. Cambridge, MA: MIT Press, 1989.

[4] W. M. Hartmann. *Signals, Sound, and Sensation*. New York, NY: Springer Verlag, 1998.

Good reference for auditory perception.

[5] R. Moore. *Elements of Computer Music*. Englewood Cliffs, NJ: Prentice Hall, 1990.

Excellent coverage of many topics in sound synthesis and spatial listening. Includes code listings.

[6] V. Pulkki. "Virtual Source Positioning Using Vector Base Amplitude Panning." *Journal of the Audio Engineering Society* 45:6(1997), 456–466.

A technique for three-dimensional speaker panning.

[7] C. Roads. *The Computer Music Tutorial*. Cambridge, MA: The MIT Press, 1998.

Contains a wealth of information concerning many aspects of audio processing.

Spatialization with Multiple Loudspeakers

Ville Pulkki

1 Introduction

Sound spatialization is becoming more common. It can be loosely defined as making sound audible to a listener as he/she would perceive it in a natural environment (such as a room or a hall).

The fundamental issues in spatialization are 1) creating illusions of sounds coming from arbitrary directions and distances, and 2) simulation of early reflections and reverberation of rooms. More advanced spatialization techniques attempt to model higher order acoustic phenomena such as the Doppler effect, atmospheric attenuation, and surface effects including diffraction.

This article explores the use of a computationally inexpensive algorithm and multiple loudspeakers for the creation of directional illusions, limiting itself to the fundamental spatialization phenomena. A perceived sound object with the illusion of direction is called a virtual source.

Many modern sound cards offer the capability to create three-dimensional sound with headphones or with two near-field loudspeakers. The techniques are based on simulating the effects of pinna, head, and torso, using digital filters implementing measured Head-Related Transfer Functions (HRTFs) [1] as explored by Haferkorn in "Head-Related Transfer Functions and the Physics of Spatial Hearing" (see *Audio Anecdotes III*). Unfortunately, these techniques have some shortcomings: The methods are computationally complicated; in loudspeaker reproduction the effect can be heard only in a very small listening area (called the sweet spot); and, with headphone reproduction, the virtual sources are confused if movements of the listener's head are not tracked and the virtual sources moved accordingly. See Gehring's article "Interactive Entertainment with Three-Dimensional Sound" (see *Audio Anecdotes III*) for an entertainment application using HRTF spatialization effects in less than optimal loudspeaker environments.

Virtual source positioning can be implemented using multiple loudspeakers. When the loudspeakers are located on the horizontal plane, a virtual source can be positioned to any direction on the plane by panning the sound signal to two adjacent loudspeakers, between which the virtual source direction points. This method is called pair-wise panning paradigm [4] and the loudspeaker configuration is called two-dimensional loudspeaker setup (see Fouad's article "Spatialization with Stereo Loudspeakers: Understanding Balance, Panning, and Distance Attenuation" (page 143) to review panning basics). Pair-wise panning creates robust virtual sources that are perceived similarly on a large listening area. However, there are some restrictions in loudspeaker positioning to produce stable virtual sources, which will be discussed later. Pair-wise paradigm is not sufficient if set-ups also include elevated or descended loudspeakers. Such setups are denoted as three-dimensional loudspeaker setups.

Ambisonics [5] is a microphone technique that was presented in the 1970s, which attempts to reproduce spatial audio over multiple loudspeakers. For Ambisonics reproduction, sound is recorded with a specific multichannel microphone. Simulation of Ambisonics allows sound source positioning for certain three-dimensional loudspeaker setups. However, there are some drawbacks with Ambisonics; it is best suited only for symmetric loudspeaker setups, and the sound signal appears virtually in all loudspeakers making the optimal listening area small. Outside the best listening area, the virtual sources are perceived from the loudspeaker that is nearest a listener, due to the precedence effect [7]. The precedence effect is active when a sound arrives to the listener from multiple directions with short time delays. Only the direction of first arrival is perceived as direction of the sound object. In addition, in best listening position, the directional cues produced by the Ambisonics technique are unnatural [9]. The directional cues consist of binaural and monaural cues that humans use in decoding sound source direction; a review of them can be found in [6].

Vector Base Amplitude Panning (VBAP) [12] is a recently published method for virtual source positioning to two-dimensional or three-dimensional loudspeaker setups with an arbitrary number of loudspeakers. There are no requirements for loudspeaker setup symmetry. VBAP is computationally very efficient, and produces good spatial impression to a large listening area if a sufficient number of loudspeakers is provided. In this article, the VBAP method is presented briefly and an efficient implementation is explored.

2 Vector Base Amplitude Panning

Amplitude panning presents an audio signal to a number of loudspeakers with different amplitudes [3].

A listener perceives a virtual source at a direction that can be controlled by gain factors that control amplitudes of loudspeakers. Amplitude panning is most often applied to two loudspeakers in front of the listener in a horizontal plane. This allows positioning of virtual sources to a line between the loudspeakers. When the listener is surrounded by loudspeakers, pair-wise panning can be applied, which is illustrated in Figure 1. The sound signal is applied to one pair at a time. The pairs are formed naturally by adjacent loudspeakers.

Three-dimensional loudspeaker setups can be formulated as a set of non-overlapping triangles (loudspeaker triplets), to one of which the signal is panned at one time. As a three-dimensional generalization of pair-wise panning, this is called triplet-wise panning, which is illustrated in

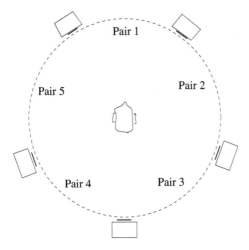

Figure 1. A two-dimensional loudspeaker setup is divided to loudspeaker pairs.

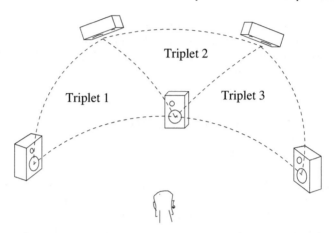

Figure 2. A three-dimensional loudspeaker setup is divided to loudspeaker triplets.

Figure 2. The division to triplets is not as apparent as it is with two-dimensional panning. A loudspeaker setups can be divided to a set of triangles using greedy triangulation [8], its application for triplet-wise panning is presented in [13]. For triangulation, all loudspeakers are projected to the surface of the unit sphere. All possible loudspeaker triangles are formed, the sides of triangles run on the surface of unit sphere. All crossings of triangle sides are searched and the triangles that have longer sides are deleted. Triangles that include loudspeakers are also deleted. The greedy triangulation method selects the triangles in a way that the distances between loudspeakers in selected triangles are minimized. This is favorable since increasing distances between loudspeakers decreases virtual source quality.

VBAP can be used to calculate the gain factors for pair- or triplet-wise panning. The calculation is performed using vector bases formed by the listener and the loudspeaker pairs or triplets. In a three-dimensional case, the base is defined by unit-length vectors $\mathbf{l}_m = [l_{m1} \ l_{m2} \ l_{m3}]^T$, $\mathbf{l}_n = [l_{n1} \ l_{n2} \ l_{n3}]^T$ and $\mathbf{l}_k = [l_{k1} \ l_{k2} \ l_{k3}]^T$, which are pointing towards loudspeakers m, n, and k, respectively, as seen in Figure 3.

Given a desired panning direction expressed as a unit-length vector $\mathbf{p}$, it can be treated as a linear combination of loudspeaker vectors:

$$\mathbf{p} = g_m \mathbf{l}_m + g_n \mathbf{l}_n + g_k \mathbf{l}_k. \tag{1}$$

Here, g_m, g_n, and g_k are called gain factors of respective loudspeakers. This equation defines the barycentric coordinates of vector $\mathbf{p}$ in a vector

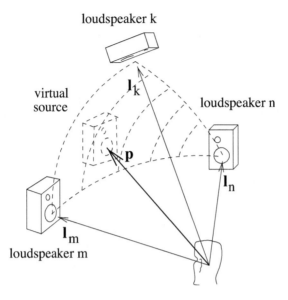

Figure 3. A loudspeaker triplet being formulated with three-dimensional VBAP.

base defined by $\mathbf{L}_{mnk}$. Barycentric coordinates were originally proposed by Moebius in 1885. They are used in various fields, e.g., in algebraic topology and in computational geometry.

The gain factors can be solved as:

$$\mathbf{g} = \mathbf{p}^T \mathbf{L}_{mnk}^{-1}, \tag{2}$$

where $\mathbf{g} = [g_m \ g_n \ g_k]^T$ and $\mathbf{L}_{mnk} = [\mathbf{l}_m \ \mathbf{l}_n \ \mathbf{l}_k]$. The calculated factors are used in amplitude panning as gain factors of the signals applied to respective loudspeakers after suitable normalization, e.g., $\|\mathbf{g}\| = 1$. In normal room acoustics, a suitable normalization is constant-energy normalization, i.e., the sum of gain squares should be one. In very dry acoustics, instead of sum of squares, direct sum of gains should be set to unity. The selection of normalization affects only the loudness of virtual source; the direction of it is not affected. These equations can be easily formulated for two-dimensional setups by reducing the vector dimensionalities to two and forming the bases from two vectors.

VBAP has three important properties: 1) if the virtual source is located in the same direction with any of the loudspeakers, the signal emanates only from that particular loudspeaker, which provides maximal sharpness of the virtual source; 2) if the virtual source is located on a line connecting two loudspeakers, the sound is applied only to that pair; and, 3) if the virtual source is located to the center of gravity of the triplet, the gain factors of the loudspeakers are equal. These features ensure that virtual sources created with VBAP are as sharp as possible with the current loudspeaker setups and amplitude panning technique. Also, if the virtual sources are moved in the sound stage, there will be no disturbing clicks or other artifacts since the loudspeakers are faded in and out smoothly when the triplet used in panning is changed.

3   Using VBAP

While the quality of the spatial sound scape increases with the number of loudspeakers available, typically, a realistic horizontal sound stage can be created with five or six loudspeakers placed evenly around the listener. Panning can be performed with fairly good accuracy to the upper hemisphere if three or more loudspeakers are added to elevated positions and also to the lower hemisphere with three or more loudspeakers at descended positions, as in Figure 4. The loudspeakers should be equidistant and their levels should be equal at the listening point. However, if the loudspeakers are on different distances, the loudspeaker signals should be delayed individually in order to set equal the arrival time to the best listening point. The levels should then also be measured and adjusted individually. Level adjustment can be done by comparing levels of loudspeakers perceptually by ear, or with a sound pressure level meter. A sufficient signal type for

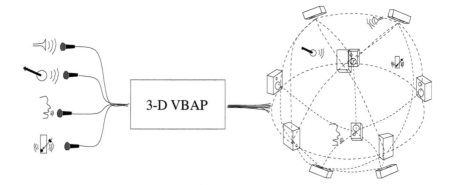

Figure 4. Three-dimensional VBAP being used to position virtual sources to an arbitrary loudspeaker configuration.

level setting depends on the acoustics of the room; the author has used one-octave, band-passed noise with center frequency near 1 kHz, to avoid room modes at low frequencies and directional effects of loudspeakers at high frequencies.

A drawback with pair- or triplet-wise panning is that the perceived spread of the virtual sources is dependent on panning direction. When a virtual source is panned between loudspeakers, it will be spread to some extent, and when it is panned towards a loudspeaker, it is point-like. If a virtual source is moved in a sound scape, the movement may be perceived as jumping between loudspeakers. We can get around this issue by using multiple panning directions simultaneously for one virtual source [11]. A set of panning directions closely around the actual panning direction is chosen, and the sound signal is applied to each direction. The spread of the virtual source can be thus controlled. If a sufficient set of panning directions is applied, the virtual source spread is no longer dependent on panning direction. The virtual source can be also spread to all loudspeakers if a large amount of panning directions are used, and if they are pointed evenly to all directions. This is similar to Fouad's idea of nonspatialized audio (see his aforementioned article), in which sound is applied to all loudspeakers with equal gains. However, in such an approach, the loudspeaker setup should be symmetric, otherwise the sound energy is distributed unevenly in space. For example, if there are more loudspeakers on the left than the right, more sound energy will arrive to a listener from the left. With the multiple-panning-directions approach, a loudspeaker setup can also be asymmetric, since the sound energy distribution is automatically symmetric.

VBAP is computationally efficient. During a sample period, a virtual source sample is multiplied with a gain factor, and is written to a corresponding output. This is repeated for each loudspeaker whose gain factor is nonzero for each virtual source. This can be regarded as efficient when compared with HRTF techniques in which tens of multiplications are needed for each sound sample. The gain factor calculation with VBAP requires approximately less than 1000 operation cycles. However, the gain factors must be updated only when a new virtual source is created. Additionally, if a virtual source is moving, or the virtual source spread is changed, the gain factors have to be updated with 1-20 Hz frequency depending on the speed of the movement. This update rate is very low when compared to a typical sampling rate of 44100 Hz. The update rate is highly dependent on the speed of each virtual source. If the movement is slow enough, 1 Hz may be enough. The human perception ability of auditory movement is limited. For example, if a sound source rotates three times in a second around the listener, most sound sources are perceived to be diffuse. Therefore, the update rate of 20 Hz should be enough for any virtual source movement speed.

The new gain factors cannot be changed immediately in the panning process, audible clicks might occur in such cases. A cross-fade should be performed. The best method, in principle, for cross fade would be to use constant energy fading (keep the sum-of-squares of gain factors constant during fading). However, since the update speed is very low, linear cross-fading normally does not produce audible artifacts.

The area where the direction of virtual source is perceived most correctly is quite small. In pair-wise panning, the effect can be heard on a line, each point of which is equidistant to both speakers. Moving about 30 cm away from the line makes a virtual source panned between the loudspeakers with equal gains to move to the closest speaker that is emanating sound, which means maximally 50°–60° error in perception. However, this is valid when loudspeaker aperture is about 60°. When aperture is smaller, a virtual source is less sensitive to movement. With triplet-wise panning, the effect is similar—the sound is never perceived outside a loudspeaker triplet. The maximum error is thus proportional to the size of pair or triplet, which can be decreased by adding more loudspeakers. When compared to panning methods that apply the sound to virtually all of the speakers, the angular error can be even 180°, and it does not decrease when the number of loudspeakers is increased.

In a normal room, the accuracy of directional hearing is a few degrees at best, and it can be as bad as about 20°[2], depending on source direction. If there are many spatialized virtual sources (or reflections and reverberation) present in a produced sound scape, directional errors of 10° to 20° can be tolerated easily.

We may list some phenomena that affect choosing the loudspeaker directions in horizontal setups. It is widely known that when the aperture between loudspeakers is wider, the localization accuracy is worse. It is also known that there should be loudspeakers at lateral directions to be able to create virtual sources there [14]. If most of the loudspeakers are in the horizontal plane and elevated virtual sources are desired, the author has found in informal tests that at least three elevated loudspeakers are needed. With fewer loudspeakers, the perception of elevation is vague. With triplet-wise panning, the number of loudspeakers in relatively small rooms should be about ten (5–6 horizontal and 3–4 elevated loudspeakers) to get convincing surrounding effects to listening positions in a large listening area, excluding positions less than about one meter from each loudspeaker. In larger theatres, the loudspeaker amount should be higher.

However, the author believes that more than 30 loudspeakers are needed very seldomly. The perception of amplitude-panned virtual sources is a complicated topic. The author has studied it with psychoacoustic tests and with simulations of human directional hearing. The results can be found in [10], which is available on the Internet.

4 Programming VBAP

The following C code is a simple example of how to implement VBAP. The example printed in this book presents the parts that have to be ported to different environments. The subprograms for loudspeaker data initialization (define_loudspeakers) and for gain factor calculation (vbap) are fairly long and are not presented in the text of this article, but are provided on the CD-ROM accompanying this book. The subprograms are written using standard C code and there should be no difficulties porting them to different environments.

The audio to be panned is stored to array in and the resulting multichannel audio to array out. The example can be extended easily to distribute multiple sound signals. The signals are loaded and one gain factor set is calculated with VBAP for each signal with different panning directions. The only difference is that the result of multiplication between input signal sample and gain factor would be added to the previous value of array out instead of direct substitution.

If the moving virtual sources are to be implemented, the gain factors have to be updated constantly. As previously mentioned, typically 20 Hz is a sufficient update rate to accomodate even very rapid virtual sound source movements. When new gain factors are calculated, the old ones have to be cross-faded to new ones to avoid clicks.

The example program can be also modified to spread out the virtual sources with multiple-direction panning. For one audio signal multiple gain factor sets are calculated with multiple panning directions. The gain factor for each loudspeaker is computed as a sum of gain factors of the corresponding loudspeaker over different panning directions. The norm of resulting gains should be normalized to one to retain the loudness of the virtual source.

```
/* defining loudspeaker data */
define_loudspeakers(&ls_data, ls_set_dim, ls_num, ls_dirs);
/*
ls_data
```

```
      is a struct containing data specific to
      loudspeaker setups
  ls_set_dim
      is 2 if loudspeakers are on a (horizontal) plane
  ls_set_dim
      is 3 if also elevated or descended loudspeakers exist
  ls_num
      is the number of loudspeakers
  ls_dirs
      is an array containing the angular directions of
      loudspeakers
  */


  /* calculate gain factors for virtual source
  in direction (int azimuth, int elevation) */
vbap(gains, &ls_data, azimuth, elevation);

  /* panning monophonic audio to multiple outputs*/
for(j=0;j<num_of_buffers;j++){
  gainptr=gains;
  for (k=0; k<numchannels; k++){
    /* outptr points to current output channel */
    outptr= out[k];
    /* inptr points to audio to be panned  */
    inptr = in;
    /* gain factor for this channel (loudspeaker)*/
    gain = *gainptr++;
    if(gain != 0.0)
      for (i=0; i<BUFFER_LENGTH; ++i)    /* panning */
        *outptr++ = *inptr++ * gain;
    else                 /* no output to this channel */
      for (i=0; i<BUFFER_LENGTH; ++i)
        *outptr++ = 0.0;
    }
  /* to be added: buffer "out" is written to your
    multi-channel audio device */
}
```

5 Conclusions

As demonstrated above, VBAP is a generic, easy to implement, and computationally efficient method to position virtual sources when multiple output channels and loudspeaker arrays are available. The technique scales to setups with an arbitrary number of loudspeakers in any physical configuration. The spreading and apparent location of virtual sources can be controlled with multiple-direction amplitude panning. The author hopes the reader will be able to experiment with these techniques using the provided VBAP example implementation found on the CD-ROM accompanying this book.

6 Acknowledgements

Ville Pulkki has received funding from the Academy of Finland (#101339).

Annotated Bibliography

[1] D. R. Begault. *3-D Sound For Virtual Reality and Multimedia*. Cambridge, MA: AP Professional, 1994.

  This is a classic book about HRTF-processed three-dimensional sound.

[2] J. Blauert. *Spatial Hearing, revised edition*. Cambridge, MA: MIT Press, 1997.

  This is a large collection of psychoacoustic facts in spatial hearing.

[3] A. D. Blumlein. U.K. patent 394,325. 1931. Reprinted in Stereophonic Techniques, New York, Audio Eng. Soc., 1986.

  This patent covers different topics on sound technology, one of which is using coincident velocity microphones, that is equivalent to amplitude panning.

[4] J. Chowning. "The Simulation of Moving Sound Sources." *J. Audio Eng. Soc.* 19:1 (1971), 2–6.

  Pair-wise panning is used first in this paper.

[5] M. A. Gerzon. "Periphony: With-Height Sound Reproduction." *J. Audio Eng. Soc.* 21:1 (1972), 2–10.

  Various theories to record three-dimensional audio for loudspeaker reproduction are presented.

[6] R. H. Gilkey and T. R. Anderson, editors. *Binaural and Spatial Hearing in Real and Virtual Environments.* Mahwah, NJ: Lawrence Erlbaum Assoc., 1997.

This is a nice collection of papers describing basics and recent findings on spatial hearing.

[7] R. Y. Litovsky, H. S. Colburn, W. A. Yost, and S. J. Gutman. "The Precedence Effect." *J. Acoust. Soc. Am.* 106:4 (1999) 1633–1654.

[8] F. Preparata and M. Shamos. *Computational Geometry: An Introduction.* New York: Springer-Verlag, 1985.

A basic textbook on computational geometry. Also covers different triangulation methods.

[9] V. Pulkki. "Microphone Techniques and Directional Quality of Sound Reproduction." Convention Paper 5500 presented at the 112th Convention Munich, Germany, 2002.

Directional qualities produced with different microphone techniques and loudspeaker positioning are studied using binaural auditory model simulations.

[10] V. Pulkki. "Spatial Sound Generation and Perception by Amplitude Panning Techniques." Ph.D. diss., Helsinki University of Technology, 2001. Available from World Wide Web (http://www.acoustics.hut.fi/~ville/references.html).

The Ph.D. dissertation book of the author. VBAP and related techniques are introduced. The directional quality of virtual sources are studied using listening tests and modeling of binaural auditory system.

[11] V. Pulkki. "Uniform Spreading of Amplitude Panned Virtual Sources." In *Proceedings of the 1999 IEEE Workshop on Applications of Signal Processing to Audio and Acoustics.* New Paltz, NJ: Mohonk Mountain House, 1999.

A method to control the spread of amplitude-panned virtual sources is introduced.

[12] V. Pulkki. "Virtual Source Positioning Using Vector Base Amplitude Panning." *J. Audio Eng. Soc.*, 45:6 (1997), 456–466.

The theory of VBAP is introduced here.

[13] V. Pulkki and Tapio Lokki. "Creating Auditory Displays to Multiple Loudspeakers Using VBAP: A Case Study with DIVA Project." In *International Conference on Auditory Display*, Glasgow, Scotland: ICAD, 1998.

In this paper, VBAP is used in creation of virtual acoustics. An automatic loudspeaker setup triangularization is introduced.

[14] G. Theile and G. Plenge. "Localization of Lateral Phantom Sources." *J. Audio Eng. Soc.*, 25:4 (1977) 196–200.

Listening test results are reported. A virtual source cannot be positioned between two loudspeakers if they are placed symmetrically left-front and left-back (or right-front and right-back).

Computer Techniques

No Need to Shout: Volume Controls and the Digital Sound Convergence

Ken Greenebaum

1 Motivation

While the ubiquitous and inexpensive personal computer now provides many audio applications and services, for many years the PC audio subsystem was not highly considered. Audio was mainly included to provide informational clicks and beeps or to support games or other noncritical applications. Apple's first Macintosh (released in 1984) was bundled with low fidelity, but innovative (for the time) 8-bit PCM-audio. However, the original IBM PC and its *Wintel* descendents came bundled with only a simple square wave generator suitable for making beeps. On the PC platform digital PCM sound capable of playing arbitrary sounds was available only as an add-on. As a result, audio reproduction on the early PCs was of inconsistent quality, the audio subsystem wasn't well integrated into the system software, and the user interface made little if any use of sound.

Today, most users consider sound a fundamental capability of the PC, and the significant amount of audio hardware and software shipped with computers reflect this expectation. Users commonly play high-quality DVD movies, copy music from CDs, *burn* their own compilation CDs, compress music in the popular MP3 format and listen to the results on their computers or on portable MP3 players. Internet streaming audio and video services are becoming increasingly popular with the availability of high bandwidth Internet connections for home users. Even video editing is becoming commonplace partly due to the availability of inexpensive digital video camcorders and the FireWire interface.

These new audio capabilities have been added to the PC environment in an ad-hoc manner resulting in an awkward situation where audio applications do not interact well with each other or with the informational sounds produced by the desktop environment. System sounds, such as the *bell* that rings to announce the arrival of new mail or an instant message, will blare if the user has turned up the volume to listen to the latest MP3 music file (legally) downloaded off the Internet. Or, the informational system tone may not be heard at all if the user has turned down the master volume level while playing background music. The volume has to be adjusted again to make a game's explosions sound impressive because the system gain was last set to make the system bell a reasonable level.

This article explores the history leading to the present situation where applications don't moderate their volume always outputting the maximum audio level; effectively they shout. This situation forces the end-user to make the only intervention possible, changing the master volume level. Continuing, this article suggests some ways application developers and system designers can use straightforward, but not often used, techniques to improve the shouting situation for their users. In particular, I explore how to control sound levels on a per application basis in software, an approach similar to how a PC soundcard's analog mixer hardware provides independent audio levels for each hardware audio source.

2   An Evolving Sound Capacity

The PC's sound system is an ad-hoc collection of parts. The average PC has a vestigial soundcard that has probably been integrated onto the motherboard, and external amplified speakers often supplied by the user. Multiple "volume" control knobs and sliders bedevil the user, some physical (like those on the amplifier) and some software-based sliders that control a mixer on the soundcard.

Soundcard designers originally addressed the problem of establishing different sound levels for different applications by incorporating a hardware mixer that provided a separate, computer-controlled attenuator for each distinct source of sound the soundcard accepted. Microsoft Windows' "volume control" application in turn exposed these controls to the user.

For example, my Sony laptop's sound capabilities are provided by Yamaha's DS-XG chipset. The Windows Volume Control application provides a mixer interface to the chipset that exposes level controls for the following audio channels: Master, Wave, PC Beep, Telephony, Microphone, Line, CD Audio, MIDI Out, PC Beep(Ext), Line(Ext), and

3D-Wide. This allows me to independently set the audio levels for each of the laptop's hardware audio sources. The volume level for CD playback may be set relative to the volume of the modem's connection tones, relative to the hardware PC Beep, and so on ...

This clever approach worked as long every sound application was implemented in hardware and had its own channel in the mixer: a music sequencer using the hardware MIDI synthesizer, CD playback using an analog connection between the CD drive and soundcard, telephony via the analog connection to the modem, and the PC beep being generated by an integrated square wave generator. The volume of each sound hardware application could be set appropriately and independently of each other and the master level all controlled by the same analog mixer. The digital convergence of hardware and software has changed the situation for designers and users alike.

3   The Digital Convergence

As general purpose processors have increased in speed and power, more and more applications formerly implemented by necessity in hardware are now implemented far more flexibly and inexpensively in software. This convergence makes sound economic sense, too, with seldom used hardware left out of the machine and replaced by programs that, when required, use a small percentage of the CPU's resources. More and more of the audio functionality once using dedicated hardware with its own dedicated mixer channel and level control is now managed by the CPU and shares the Wave channel of the mixer.

The squarewave PC beep hardware should be relegated to the past, not only does it produce unpleasant tones, but if the functionality is desired for backwards compatibility it can easily be emulated in software. The desktop and modern applications no longer use this device, but rather play back digital recordings of the desired beeps and trills. Hopefully sometime soon, applications will begin synthesizing appropriate sounds instead of playing sampled sounds. (Please see the chapters on synthesis techniques.)

Similarly, the FM and sampling MIDI hardware synthesizers are also being replaced by more flexible software solutions. FM synthesis has fallen out of favor since digital sampling techniques produce much more accurate musical sounds. Software-based sampling synthesizers are relatively lightweight to implement and don't impose hard limits like the number of voices, amount of sample memory available, and the availability of signal processing that the hardware-based synthesizers do.

The CD Digital Audio Extraction (DAE) capability, originally pioneered by SGI and Toshiba, has found great popularity with users who demand the ability to copy and share digital music. DAE has eliminated the need for an analog connection to exist between the CD-ROM player soundcard for audio CDs to be played back though the computer. Applications that pull audio digitally from a CD may easily provide all manner of new features such as the ability to record to the hard disk, or apply signal processing algorithms such as speeding up or slowing down the rate of the music without affecting its pitch, or removing the vocal tract.

While this digital sound convergence is a positive phenomenon, it nonetheless breaks the *status quo* of the hardware-mixer model. Users can no longer use the soundcard's analog attenuators to adjust the relative sound level of applications because most sound is being produced in software and played by the wave device, with the other analog inputs to the soundcard's mixer increasingly unused. Thus, the move toward software-based audio devices has eliminated the per application volume control functionality that the soundcard mixer once provided.

4   Digital Audio Screams

Most audio developers ignore PC *legacy* devices like the FM synthesizers, squarewave generators, and even MIDI synthesizers still included in PCs for backward compatibility, in favor of more flexible software-based solutions. CPUs easily handle the extra burden imposed by these audio tasks in a small fraction of their available cycles; however, a problem has been created.

The new digital audio applications often play back unattenuated, fully normalized digitized sound. Playing unattenuated sound seems to be reasonable since attenuating the signal implies voluntarily throwing away some of the 96-dB dynamic range that 16-bit digital audio systems provide and users used to CD players expect. (Please see Ballas and Fouad's article "Auditory Psyhophysics: Basic Concepts and Implications for DAC Quantization" (see *Audio Anecdotes III*) for a full exploration.)

Unfortunately, playing unattenuated sound is tantamount to screaming! All of the sound is played through the wave channel of the sound mixer, with every application also playing its sound as loud as it can. Without separate volume controls, the user must constantly adjust the master level to make one application play at an appropriate level while simultaneously making the other applications play at inappropriate, sometimes painful, levels.

5 Simple, Short-Term Solutions

An easy solution to significantly improve the present situation is for developers to add user-controllable attenuation to each application (but even when an application provides a volume control, the user never knows if the control attenuates the output of the application or merely adjusts the master volume control). Games, typically very sophisticated applications, have included these kinds of controls for a while. Audio system designers can go one step further and provide a centralized software-based mixer control that allows the end-user to set the relative volume level for every audio application on the system. In this way, users could receive the benefit immediately without requiring existing audio applications to add individual controls.

Software audio attenuation is an extremely inexpensive operation on today's CPUs, accomplished by a single multiplication per sample. Less than 100,000 multiplies are required for each high-quality stereo sound stream per second. Easier yet, system sound services such as Microsoft's DirectSound already support per stream sound attenuation.

Providing per-application attenuation controls is only part of the solution. Applications must default to a sensible level. Defaulting to shouting (no attenuation) is not acceptable. Since many users never discover the more sophisticated controls, applications should default to a reasonable audio output level. (My article "Sound Pressure: Mine Goes to 11!" (see *Audio Anecdotes I*) describes the potential for explicitly setting levels in terms of dB sound pressure level) As the most ubiquitous source of sound on the computer, it is especially important for the system's desktop sounds to default to an attenuated level since these unexpected sounds frequently make users reach to turn down the master volume level.

6 Issues and a Long-Term Hardware Solution

Most consumer PC's audio systems today include 16-bit Digitial-to-Analog converters which provide the same theoretical 96 dB dynamic range as the CD. To play a sound at the highest fidelity requires using all the available bits. Digital attenuation effectively throws low order bits away, and will degrade the quality of the sound being reproduced. Every time the sound's level is cut in half, we use one less bit of quantization. In an extreme case, a 16-bit audio stream might be reduced to only a few bits. The resulting sound would be highly distorted, but also probably barely audible at the very low sound level it would be reduced to. The implication is that if we, as suggested, by default attenuate all the sound produced on the PC, then all the sound will be compromised; no sound or application can use the full dynamic range provided by the hardware.

A long-term solution to this problem is to provide additional "headroom" in the audio system. Commercial digital mixers commonly use a similar solution. For instance, our present 16-bit sounds should be mixed and attenuated in a digital system of greater dynamic range, perhaps 20 or 24 bits. In this way, the full 16-bit sound may be preserved while still having plenty of headroom to mix many streams together. The results would be played back through the 20- or 24-bit DACs. Ultimately, this solution will also run into trouble as consumers begin to manipulate 20- or 24-bit sound, thereby requiring digital mixers to provide even more headroom in the future.

7 Summary

Users expect computer environments to act like enhancements of the real world, and real-world devices such as televisions, stereos, and telephones come with independent volume controls. Turning up the stereo doesn't make the telephone blare as is the situation on today's PC, where turning up the MP3 player can make system sounds blare.

To satisfy users' expectations, we need to design applications that allow the user to individually set each application's sound output level. Audio libraries should facilitate volume control by providing per audio stream attenuation. Applications should default to an attenuated output level. Operating system designers can and should provide centralized control of setting the relative output levels of individual applications. Finally, hardware designers must begin building audio systems with extra headroom to facilitate high-quality mixing.

No fancy algorithms need to be created; we just need to start working together, to stop our applications from shouting!

Annotated Bibliography

[1] PC Design Guides. Intel and Microsoft. Available from World Wide Web (http://pcdesguide.org).

This web site publishes the latest versions of the PC Design Guides, which are maintained by Intel and Microsoft with contributions from the entire industry. The guides specify categories of machines (i.e., basic PC, legacy free PC, workstation, server, or entertainment) and their constituent hardware and features down to the color coding scheme for connectors. Digital media specifications are provided in detail. While not every recommendation becomes reality these are the guides according to which PC manufacturers around the world design their new computers.

Count in Frames!
(Not Samples or Bytes)

Ken Greenebaum

1 Motivation

Through the years, I have developed many digital media applications as well as the libraries, drivers, and operating system services on which they rely. Even after spending considerable time and effort debugging and testing, I receive too many "bugs" reported against this code. Helping customers and colleagues troubleshoot their applications which use my services, I often find the problems result from the same core problem, the inconsistent maintenance of sound buffer attributes such as the buffer size and stream quantization.

I have found that standardizing on using the *audio frame* as the unit of data in application programming interfaces (APIs) greatly reduces uncertainty, confusion, and bugs. An *audio frame* is a bundle of one or more audio samples intended to be presented at the same time. For example, a single audio frame has one sample for a mono stream and two samples for a stereo stream. Furthermore, designing a C++ class to record buffer parameters and provide unit conversions has made my own code more robust by removing a class of error caused by inconsistently tracking this information.

This article quickly explores the problem of maintaining audio parameter consistency, then provides a C++ class implementation that makes tracking and converting these parameters safe and easy.

2   Poor Code Hygiene

While modern coding practice stresses the merits of data hiding and code re-use, all too many media applications are full of single use data structures and scratch pad variables cobbled together to keep track of audio buffer specifications or to pass this information between functions.

Media libraries themselves specify this information in confusing or inconsistent ways. For instance Microsoft's WaveIO specifies an audio stream using the waveformatex structure and the ping-pong buffers associated with that stream as a wavehdr structure (see Figure 1).

WAVEFORMATEX seems to encode redundant information. For instance, the nAvgBytesPerSec seems redundant provided nSamplesPerSec, nChannels, nBlockAlign, and wBitsPerSample are already known. Does nSamplesPerSec really encode the number of samples per second, a value that would be twice as great for a stereo stream than for a mono stream (as well as being somewhat redundant with nChannels)? What unit does WAVEHDR's dwBufferLength parameter encode length in? Bytes?

Most media libraries track the information describing a buffer or stream differently and an application which uses multiple libraries (perhaps one to parse audio data from a media file, another to apply signal processing, and a third to output the resulting audio) needs to constantly convert between these representations.

Compounding the problem, media applications tend to be littered with constants or magic values often used when calculating simple values on the fly such as the size of an audio buffer in bytes, or its duration in seconds. These simple calculations are explicitly recoded each time they are needed.

```
typedef struct {                    typedef struct {
    WORD   wFormatTag;                  LPSTR      lpData;
    WORD   nChannels;                   DWORD      dwBufferLength;
    DWORD  nSamplesPerSec;              DWORD      dwBytesRecorded;
    DWORD  nAvgBytesPerSec;             DWORD_PTR  dwUser;
    WORD   nBlockAlign;                 DWORD      dwFlags;
    WORD   wBitsPerSample;              DWORD      dwLoops;
    WORD   cbSize;                      struct wavehdr_tag * lpNext;
} WAVEFORMATEX;                         DWORD_PTR  reserved;
                                    } WAVEHDR;
          (a)                                      (b)
```

Figure 1. (a) WAVEFORMATEX structure; (b) WAVEHDR structure.

A common example of an on-the-fly calculation is the act of allocating a block of memory for an audio buffer (values in caps are constants):

```
void *sampleBuffer = (void *)malloc(numSeconds * SAMPLE_RATE
                      * BYTES_PER_SAMPLE * SAMPLES_PER_FRAME);
```

Being mature programmers, our code comes close to working correctly the first time. The behavior of the program likely only diverges from what is desired in a small way; perhaps the audio is played too slowly: one half the rate it should be, only the first half of a sound is played, or the sound is mono instead of stereo.

Quickly, we realize that the math is off by a factor of two. These problems are of a type similar to the all too common "off by one" problems which plague beginning programmers. Often the urge to quickly fix the problem and experience the program in all of its glory often outweighs our desire to fully understand the root cause of the problem, and we quickly drop in a multiply by two somewhere or other until the application plays correctly and the problem is seemingly resolved.

Unfortunately, all too often the quick fix really only masked the actual problem by balancing the math in one situation, but leaving the more subtle, and difficult to debug, problem buried. Even worse, the situation could now cause new, correctly written code to malfunction, forcing more "fixes."

3   The Solution

After battling such a simple but prevalent problem once too often, I adopted a strategy that limits these types of issues and has worked well for me in the media code I develop. The system also seems to reduce the problems developers experience when using my libraries, both making them happy that their code works the first time and making me happy that I don't have to debug an issue that turns out to be in their code. An added benefit is that this strategy creates code that is aesthetically cleaner, rendering the code easier to write, understand, debug, and maintain.

Fundamentally, I standardize on one unit, audio frame count, as a measure of size. I define all of my programmatic interfaces in terms of audio frames instead of the unit most commonly used for this purpose, byte count, or the well meaning but confusing unit, audio samples.

As previously mentioned, an audio frame is one or more audio samples that are intended to be presented at the same time. A mono stream contains one sample per frame, stereo, two samples per frame, and of course, n samples per frame in an n-way multiplexed stream.

Since the reader and writer of any stream have already agreed upon sample rate (number of samples per second), quantization (number of bits per sample), multiplexing (number of channels), and perhaps packing, all the intermediate code really needs to concern itself with is the number of frames of this audio data it is shuttling from place to place. In ordinary circumstances, all transactions would be in whole frame units since you wouldn't want to deliver incomplete audio frames.

Programming interfaces that use bytes cause applications to constantly convert between the unit they most likely conceptually use internally, the audio frame, and the unit the computer tends to use internally, the byte. Newer media interfaces tend to be defined in terms of the audio sample, an improvement over use of bytes, but unfortunately using samples still results in confusion regarding multiplexing.

Last of all, I create a library, or better yet object, in object-oriented environments, which encapsulates all of the simple but sometimes error prone mathematics involved with audio formats and timing. For example, when I create a sound buffer class, I have the methods that specify buffer size take the integer number of frames as a parameter, and those that query buffer return the number of frames similarly. Use of my buffer class ensures that the math is correct and always applied consistently. Constants and magic numbers are not scattered throughout the code where they can cause inconsistency.

In many media programs, conversions such as the following contain constants and are used throughout the application:

```
time = bufferBytes * sampleRate * 2;
```

This practice is tempting since the math is so simple. This implementation works great until the sound is changed in some way, perhaps from mono to stereo or from 16 to 8 bits. Then we have to track down every last inlined calculation and fix it.

Finally, the object allows audio format parameters which are tediously tracked and passed to many interfaces to be contained in a single place; here they are easily kept or passed as parameters. In an Object Oriented environment, audio objects may inherit from this class so that all audio objects consistently track and allow audio format information to be queried, returning the results in any unit the caller desired.

4 Implementation

The following is a base class for sound buffers; it keeps track of the size and quantization parameters of buffers. Buffer size may be set or queried in terms of bytes, frames, or seconds. Additional methods provide convenience conversion between these units based on the quantization parameters of the buffer. The class internally uses these same conversion routines. This class is written for clarity and has not addressed potential complications like data packing (see "Audio File Formats: A Formal Description-Based Approach" (see *Audio Anecdotes I*), by Eleftheriadis, Hresko, and Greenebaum, for more information on data packing).

```
class PCMsound {
  public:
    PCMsound(unsigned int framesPerSecond,
             unsigned char bytesPerSample,
             unsigned char samplesPerFrame);

    // set buffer size by various methods
    void SetBytes(unsigned long bytes);
    void SetFrames(unsigned long frames);
    void SetSeconds(double seconds);

    // conversions
    unsigned long SecondsToFrames(double seconds);
    unsigned long FramesToBytes(unsigned long frames);
    unsigned long SecondsToBytes(double seconds);
           double FramesToSeconds(unsigned long frames);
    unsigned long BytesToFrames(unsigned long bytes)
           double BytesToSeconds(unsigned long bytes);

    // get stream info
    unsigned char GetBytesPerSample();
    unsigned char GetSamplesPerFrame();
    unsigned int  GetFramesPerSecond();

    // get buffer size in various formats
    unsigned long GetBytes();
    unsigned long GetFrames();
    double        GetSeconds();
```

```
private:
  // describe the PCM stream quantization
  unsigned char _bytesPerSample;   // both quantization
                                   //   and packing
  unsigned char _samplesPerFrame;  // multiplexing (1 mono,
                                   //   2 stereo, etc.)
  unsigned int  _framesPerSecond;  // confusingly referred
                                   //   to (in other APIs)
                                   //   as samplerate

  // describe the buffer
  unsigned long _bytes;            // size of buffer in bytes
};
```

The public interface does not expose the internal representation, however, examining the private members you will notice that we track the
PCM stream's quantization by: bytes per sample (which may differ from
bits per sample due to packing, for instance, 20-bit samples are often
packaged, unpacked, into the upper 20 of 32 bits of 4 bytes), samples per
frame which encodes the degree of multiplexing (1 sample per frame is
mono, 2 stereo, 4 quad), and frames per second; stream quantization is
set at creation time. Internally, the size of the buffer is maintained in
bytes, however, this value may be set by specifying the buffer's size in
frames or seconds as well as bytes. Using accessors, the buffers size may
be queried as bytes, frames, or seconds.

The conversions, as simple as they are, are implemented, inline, in
four of the six conversion routines:

```
inline unsigned long PCMsound::SecondsToFrames(double seconds)
  { return((unsigned long)(seconds * _framesPerSecond)); }

inline unsigned long PCMsound::FramesToBytes(unsigned long frames)
  { return(frames * _samplesPerFrame * _bytesPerSample); }

inline double  PCMsound::FramesToSeconds(unsigned long frames)
  { return((double)frames/(double)_framesPerSecond); }

inline unsigned long PCMsound::BytesToFrames(unsigned long bytes)
  { return(bytes/_bytesPerSample/_samplesPerFrame); }
```

These conversions are used internally by the class itself such as for:

```
unsigned long SecondsToBytes(double seconds)
          { return(FramesToBytes(SecondsToFrames(seconds)) ); }
```

or:

```
unsigned long GetFrames()  { return( BytesToFrames(_bytes)); }
      double GetSeconds() { return(BytesToSeconds(_bytes)); }
```

The conversions are also exposed as public members so these conversions may be used by the application and thus not have to be redefined, potentially inconsistently, outside of this class.

5   Example

The following is an example of a class derived from PCMsound used to create and maintain a sound buffer:

```
class pablioBuffer: public PCMsound {
  public:
    // constructor, specifying stream and buffer size in seconds
    pablioBuffer(
      unsigned  int framesPerSecond,
      unsigned char bytesPerSample,
      unsigned char samplesPerFrame,
            double seconds) :
        _buffer(0),PCMsound(framesPerSecond, bytesPerSample,
                            samplesPerFrame) {
      SetSeconds(seconds);
      _reallocateBuffer();
      }

    // constructor, specifying stream and buffer size in bytes
    pablioBuffer(
      unsigned  int framesPerSecond,
      unsigned char bytesPerSample,
      unsigned char samplesPerFrame,
      unsigned long frames) :
        _buffer(0),PCMsound(framesPerSecond, bytesPerSample,
                            samplesPerFrame) {
      SetFrames(frames);
      _reallocateBuffer();
      }

    void SetSeconds(double seconds) {
      PCMsound::SetSeconds(seconds);
      _reallocateBuffer();
      }
```

```
    void SetFrames(unsigned long frames) {
     PCMsound::SetFrames(frames);
     _reallocateBuffer();
    }

    void SetBytes(unsigned long bytes) {
     PCMsound::SetFrames(bytes);
     _reallocateBuffer();
    }


    ~pablioBuffer() { if(_buffer) free(_buffer); }

    void *getBuffer() {return(_buffer);}

  private:
    void _reallocateBuffer() {
     if(_buffer) free(_buffer);
     _buffer = (void *)malloc(GetBytes());
    }
    void *_buffer;
};
```

The class relies on PCMsound to track stream and buffer size parameters. Examining the implementation of the private member, _reallocateBuffer(), all calculations also derive from PCMsound. This affords the class great flexibility. Not only can the class be constructed specifying the buffer in terms of seconds:

```
pablioBuffer pBuffer(44100, 2, 1, 10.0);
```

or frames:

```
pablioBuffer pBuffer(44100, 2, 1, 10000);
```

additionaly any of the PCMsound base classes' accessors, GetBytes, GetFrames, GetSeconds are available as well as the conversion routines, SecondsToFrames, FramesToBytes, SecondsToBytes (in terms of the current buffer's parameters).

6   Conclusion

Counting in frames and tracking buffer parameters using the class provided are very simple techniques, however, I have found them effective in saving me and my clients time and grief. I hope these techniques may make your code a little more robust and easy to comprehend. Please see my article "Simple Interfaces: Small (Hello) World" (see *Audio Anecdotes I*) for a deeper exploration of sound interface design.

Introduction to the Ring Buffer FIFO Queue

Ken Greenebaum

1 Motivation

The First In First Out (FIFO) Queue, also known as Silo, performs a fundamental role in digital streaming media. The FIFO provides the *elasticity* needed to allow data to flow smoothly between media producers and consumers each with different characteristics. The FIFO can connect the inherently *bursty* output of a computer application to the methodically isochronous requirements of an audio hardware digital-to-analog converter (DAC). For example, consider the fable of the farmer's stove.

The farmer must keep his family warm in the dead of winter using a simple coal stove. The farmer's need for coal is modest, but steady; the coal stove will keep the family warm if he adds one piece of coal every six hours. However if he fails to put a fresh piece of coal in at the end of the sixth hour (when the previous coal is completely consumed), the stove will go out and his family will freeze (it is very difficult to relight a stove). The coal delivery service can deliver massive amounts of coal however their delivery schedule is both erratic and infrequent and thus cannot not be counted on to deliver one piece of coal every six hours (and even if they could, the frequent delivery fees would be prohibitive). The farmer (being a wise engineer) realizes that he needs a coal silo (See Figure 1).

Now the farmer can accept irregularly timed deliveries of economically large quantities of coal that are added to the top of the silo. The farmer keeps the stove burning by taking a piece of coal from the bottom of the silo every six hours. (The farmer takes coal from the bottom so that the

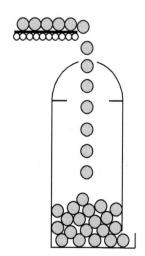

Figure 1. Coal silo accepting a delivery. Coal is consumed from the bottom in the order it was delivered.

oldest coal gets used first, so none of it can sit too long and become too damp and difficult to light.)

The audio scenario we will be exploring is similar to that of the farmer's stove. In this scenario we have a producer, the software process (coal delivery service), which synthesizes audio samples (coal). The software can produce audio at a very fast rate, however, for many reasons, including running on a multitasking operating system, the producer can only deliver audio on an irregular basis.

The consumer, a DAC, is similar to the coal stove in that it regularly needs the next item or there will be the dire consequence of glitched audio (frozen family). Finally, a FIFO queue (coal silo) is used as a buffer, but in this scenario the precise order of the audio samples (coal) must be maintained.

The software process can likely synthesize audio at rates that are orders of magnitude faster than real time; that is, the rate that they are consumed by the DAC. For indefinitely continuous audio output to be possible at all, the synthesizer must be able to create audio at least as fast as the DAC can consume it, and in practice, at least a little faster, since an application on a multitasking system must share system resources with other applications. CPUs are fast (and getting faster), and are already orders of magnitude more powerful than what is required to run many audio algorithms. The typical software synthesizer can produce audio very quickly, but there is no guarantee when the operating system will next allow the synthesizer's process to run and produce the next *batch* of audio.

The DAC converts a stream of digital audio frames to create a corresponding analog signal that is amplified and placed on the computer's analog audio outputs. The DAC accepts one audio frame at a time (44,100 times a seconds for CD-quality audio). This timing is controlled by a crystal-oscillator-based time source.

While a software synthesizer can produce millions of audio frames a second, there is no guarantee it will be there to hand a new frame to the DAC every time the DAC needs one (approximately every $23\mu s$ or $\frac{1}{44100}$ second). It is inefficient for the audio process to wait to deliver each sample to the DAC, especially on a typical multitasking operating system like UNIX or Windows which runs for perhaps a 20-ms quantum before being preempted by the OS kernel so that another process can have its own run. The audio synthesis process might not run again for an indeterminate amount of time. (see [4] for more information on process scheduling.)

The FIFO (coal silo) acts as a buffer allowing the synthesis process to infrequently create a large number of audio frames in an efficient burst and for the DAC to receive its frames one at a time in a relative dribble.

This article explores the ring buffer FIFO queue and its implementation. An algebra is also presented for making the most effective use of the buffer. My article, "Wrapped I/O" (page 209), further explores how to provide added value by wrapping a FIFO in a function call.

2   FIFO Implementations

The linked list implementation is typically demonstrated when the FIFO data structure is studied in school. This implementation is flexible and may be modified to explore a wide range of variations. It also has convenient characteristics such as being able to contain arbitrary-sized pieces of data or to grow indefinitely but this flexibility comes at the cost of requiring frequent memory management calls. Much of the flexibility afforded by the linked list implementation is unnecessary for our audio application, where the data (audio samples) are of a fixed, small size. Additionally, the linked list's memory allocation requirements become onerous for audio streams, where almost 200,000 audio samples are *pushed* and *popped* from the FIFO every second (2 I/O × 2 Stereo × 48000 Frames/Second). The memory indirection and fragmentation in the linked list implementation causes inefficient cache utilization in the CPU which in turn can lead to an order of magnitude slowdown as the algorithm must wait for data to be read from (slow) main memory instead of the (very fast) memory cache.

Array-based cyclic buffers are often taught, too. They allocate an array of a fixed size used to store the data and use a pair of indexes to determine where data is to be added to the array by the producer, or removed by the consumer. Semaphores are used to guarantee that the structure is always in a consistent state since the producer and consumer attempt to access the FIFO at the same. The semaphores enforce mutual exclusion (*mutex*) making sure that, for instance, the consumer will have to wait for the producer to finish adding samples and modifying the FIFO's metadata indices before the consumer may gain access to the FIFO and remove samples. This implementation addresses many of the problems with pumping large amounts of audio data through linked-list-based FIFOs. Most notably, the array implementation eliminates the memory allocation needed to add a new value to the list and the freedom to remove it. The array also offers a linear address space where values need not be added individually, but rather a contiguous block may be added at once. Data stored in contiguous memory is necessary for hardware Direct Memory Access (DMA) to copy data to or from the buffer with minimal CPU intervention.

The ring buffer implementation we explore in this article is very similar to the array-based FIFO with two small, but critical, distinctions. First, an array and indices aren't used but rather a pool of contiguous memory and pointers. Second by having the producer and consumer individually only modify a single, atomic, pointer producer and consumer may simultaneously modify the data structure without requiring a mutual exclusion. Both of these differences will be discussed in more detail.

Using a block of memory and pointers instead of an array and indices can be more efficient when data is only incrementally accessed such as the case with the FIFO's producer and consumer. Naïve compilers use a multiply to dereference each index-based array access. Pointers also make it easier to maintain a ring buffer in memory, such as a soundcard's shared memory, that is not on the stack or heap. Many DSPs have built-in features, like modulo addressing modes, which are designed to make ring buffers even more efficient to implement.

Perhaps most importantly, by combining the use of word length pointers to track the status of the buffer with an algebra specifying the logic of the buffer, the producer and consumer can manipulate the buffer simultaneously without requiring mutex. CPUs guarantee that word-sized writes are atomic (are uninterruptible), which means that it is impossible for

one process to be preempted by the operating system and allow another
process to read the incorrect, partially updated value.

Removing the necessity for a mutex makes buffer access lightweight
and avoids the classic lockout, priority inversion and deadlock issues associated with mutual exclusion. (This technique can be applied to array
based FIFO implementations but isn't in many algorithm textbooks)

3   Buffering in Digital Media

While the ring buffer FIFO is both easy to implement and efficient, it
has had only moderate acceptance outside of the signal processing field.
When compared to other FIFO buffer implementations, the ring buffer
has many attractive characteristics such as allowing reads and writes of
flexible size, simultaneous access by the producer and consumer without requiring mutual exclusion, and allowing for continuously variable
latency (dynamically changing the length of the FIFO). Surprisingly the
ring buffer is not more frequently used or described.

Many audio systems (such as Microsoft's WaveIO) have used double
buffers, also known as ping pong buffers, to read or write audio (my article "Simple Interfaces, Small (Hello) World" (see *Audio Anecdotes I*)
includes an example WaveIO application). For example, for a process to
output audio using ping pong buffers, it must first create a pool of two or
more fixed-sized buffers. These buffers are then filled with audio frames
and added to the output queue. The application must either poll, block on
a signal, or receive a call back when one buffer empties, and must then be
refilled with samples and returned to the system. PortAudio, the portable
audio library described in "PortAudio: An API for Portable Real-Time
Audio" (see *Audio Anecdotes I*), also uses fixed-sized buffers with a callback to implement buffering. PortAudio, in turn, serves as the portability
layer for PABLIO, the blocking I/O library in which *Audio Anecdotes* example programs are written. More information on blocking I/O may be
found in my articles "Wrapped I/O" (page 209) and "PABLIO: A Simple
Audio I/O Library" (see *Audio Anecdotes I*).

One difficulty with double buffers is that it forces a process into writing fixed-sized numbers of audio frames corresponding to the size of the
predefined fixed buffers. This potentially requires the application writer
to devise their own rebuffering techniques to be able to precisely fill the
buffer. For instance, a teleconferencing system may receive audio data
from the network in unevenly sized chunks. To play this audio, the application would have to store up enough audio samples to fill the audio

system's buffer while keeping the remaining *crumbs* for next time. An application writing directly to a ring buffer may write any number of audio frames so long as enough space is available in the buffer. If accessing the buffer through a *wrapped* interface, arbitrarily large writes are possible at any time; the call will just block as necessary if there is not enough room in the buffer for the write to complete.

4   The Anatomy of a Ring Buffer

There are many different, but self-consistent, schemes for annotating and operating a ring buffer. Described below is a common scheme with naming consistent with [1], albeit with some extensions.

The structure of the ring buffer is simple, being comprised of a linear region of memory, two pointers (head and tail), and three scalar values (size of the buffer, and the high and low water marks). The head points to the next available sample in the buffer that is to be removed by the consumer. The tail points to the next available location to be filled by the producer. Pointers always increase. (I like to remember, "The head chases the tail.") When a pointer is incremented past the end of the buffer, it wraps back around to the beginning to form the ring. Figure 2 shows a partially filled ring buffer.

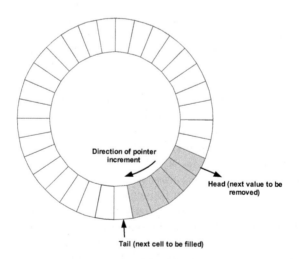

Figure 2. Basic ring buffer.

The ring buffer's ability to allow producer and consumer to simultaneously access and modify the buffer without requiring any form of locking derives from its careful construction and manipulation. Pointers fit into single words. CPUs guarantee that single word reads and writes are executed atomically. For instance, if the process performing a word write was interrupted, and another process attempted to read the memory location being written, the reading process will either read the value which was there before the write, or the value written, but not a combination of the two, a situation which would be possible if each byte of the word was written separately without the guarantee of atomicity.

In our scheme, the producer only modifies the tail, and the consumer only modifies the head. Since no element of the control structure is written by more than one party, there is no potential read-modify-write scenario to protect. At worst, one party might read a pointer to be used in a space calculation that is then changed before the results of the calculation can be used. As we will see, these calculations are designed to be conservative. Even if the other party changes the data structure, the now inaccurately calculated number of samples available (or the number of locations available) may only (safely) increase as a size calculation becomes outdated.

Two scalar values are used to control latency. For the purposes of this article, the producer and consumer must factor these values into their

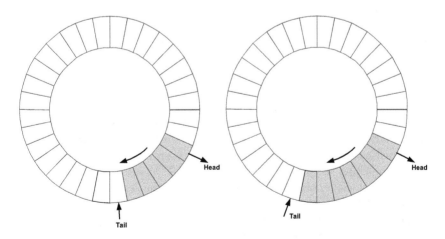

Figure 3. Buffer fills by producer after consumer determines the number of available samples (consumer may still safely remove the five of samples originally calculated).

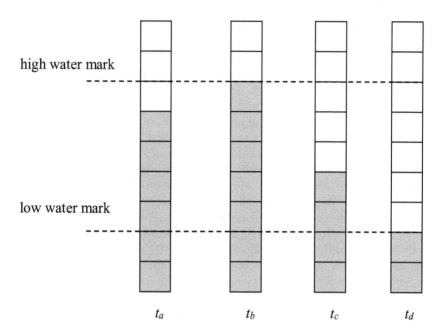

high water mark

low water mark

t_a t_b t_c t_d

Figure 4. High and low water marks: t_a, producer filling FIFO; t_b, FIFO fills to high water mark blocking producer; t_c, consumer draining FIFO; t_d, FIFO emptied to low water mark unblocking producer.

calculations when deciding how much data to exchange with the buffer. In the wrapped I/O case presented in my article "Wrapped I/O" (page 209), the functions wrapping the data structure manage these calculations.

Whether wrapped or not, the high water mark controls how far the ring buffer may be filled before the producer must stop writing to the buffer. Once the producer fills the ring buffer to the high water mark, it may not write to the buffer again until the buffer has drained to the low water mark. The following illustration shows a FIFO filling to the high water mark causing the producer to block, then drain to the low water mark unblocking the producer again (linear FIFO's are used to make this concept more clear, samples are removed from the bottom of the FIFO and added from the top).

The high water mark sets the maximum latency of the system by controlling how far ahead the producer may precompute audio. For instance, if a synthesis application allowed human interaction—perhaps to control volume via a Graphic User Interface (GUI)—the result of the user's interaction with the application wouldn't be heard until all the audio frames

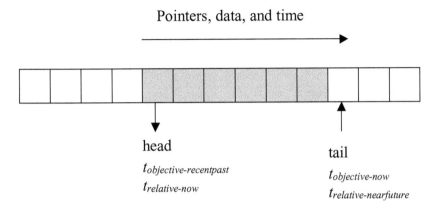

Figure 5. Knowing the future by living in the past. In the objective time frame, current data are being inserted at the tail; however, from the relative perspective of the application now is the data at the head and by snooping ahead in the buffer, the application can perfectly *predict* the near future!

calculated before the interaction were played first. The lower the frame count the high water mark is set to, the fewer samples the producer is allowed to precompute, and the lower the latency of the system.

Small, but predictable, latencies, known as preroll times in the professional video world, are actually beneficial. Among other things, latencies allow digital systems to operate in the recent past where the system can have complete knowledge of the near "future."

The low water mark is used to overcome the worst-case scheduling jitter, plus the length of time needed to synthesize the next burst of audio for the ring buffer. If the producer could instantaneously refill the ring buffer, then the low water mark could be set at zero. This is impossible since even a real-time operating system would take time to reschedule and run the producer and the algorithm the producer used to synthesize audio also takes time. The low water mark controls the lower bound on the latency of the system.

The producer could be unblocked and allowed to write the buffer anytime room is available for it to write (the low water mark set to one position below the high water mark); however, this setting would provide little hysteresis and likely be inefficient. Similarly, it is very inefficient, and damaging, for your home furnace to cycle on and off constantly trying to maintain a temperature of precisely 68 ° F. High and low water marks may be set to provide desired characteristics, and additionally may be dynamically tuned while the system is running.

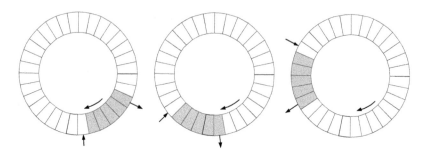

Figure 6. The utilized area of the ring buffer will spin around the buffer (high water mark set to 5).

Typically, the high water mark and ring buffer size are selected in such a way that the high water mark is much smaller than the ring buffer capacity. This allows the effective size of the ring buffer to be elastic. The latency of the buffer may be dynamically grown by merely changing the high water mark.

Figure 6 shows a ring buffer with a high water mark considerably below its maximum size, but with plenty of room to dynamically *grow* the buffer and the corresponding latency of the system. Notice how the filled region of the buffer will spin around the buffer.

Dynamic latency is desirable in instances where the characteristics of the system change over time, such as if the graphics frame rate changes due to scene complexity, or if network congestion increases in a streaming media application. Where worst-case figures aren't known, or performance is considered more important than quality, a system may dynamically tune itself by increasing buffering by increasing the high water mark until underflows are infrequent.

5   Ring Buffer Algebra

A virtue of this system is that there exists a way to inexpensively compute the exact state of the system at any given time using a small number of subtractions. No expensive or dangerous locks are needed to *snapshot* the critical data structures, nor do they need to be maintained to complete critical operations. Without locking for purposes of mutual exclusion, there is no chance for deadlock, priority inversion, or many of the other issues that can plague multithreaded real-time applications. The results of the calculations will become less accurate the longer they are held, but since the system is designed to be conservative, this is of little worry.

Samples Available	(Tail - Head - 1) mod Size
Space Available	min((Head - Tail -1) mod Size, high water mark)
Empty Buffer when	Head = Tail
Buffer full when	(Head - Tail) Mod Size = 1

Table 1. Ring buffer calculations.

For example, it is not a problem if the ring buffer emptied a bit in the time since the producer last queried the pointers and calculated the space available in the buffer to fill. It just means that the buffer won't be completely full (up to the high-water mark). The buffer would quickly drain after the fill was made anyway.

Table 1 shows the basic calculations that can be made on the ring buffer.

These calculations are based on the understanding that the ring buffer can only be filled to one less than the total size of the buffer, but that the buffer can be completely emptied. As previously mentioned, there are a variety of valid combinations of rules to define a ring buffer algebra; this set has worked well for me. As long as the producer and consumer share a consistent understanding of the ring buffer, any algebra will work well.

Figure 7 shows an empty ring buffer, a ring buffer with one value, and the logically full ring buffer.

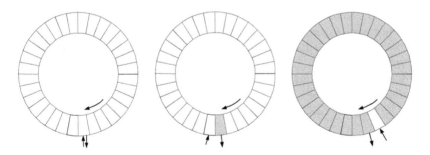

Figure 7. Empty buffer, buffer with one element, full buffer.

6 Implementation

This section includes a simple C++ class which implements many of the concepts described in this article. Significant code fragments are described in the text and the full implementation is available on the CD-ROM accompanying this book. For clarity, the implementation is simplified in a number of ways.

Because our target platforms' threading models are so inconsistent, this version doesn't support blocking I/O. Instead, the comments indicate where the producer or consumer threads could be blocked or unblocked in a more sophisticated implementation (however, ultimately, a blocking model would also use a low water mark not considered in this implementation).

Additionally, this version manages a buffer implemented as an array allocated on the heap instead of a block of memory perhaps located on the soundcard instead of main memory. A managed memory implementation is better suited for DMA (Direct Memory Access) transfers which can accelerate copying blocks of memory by not requiring PIO (programmed I/O). PIO requires the CPU to read and write each memory word individually, perhaps stalling on a cache miss, instead of leaving memory copies to dedicated hardware, leaving the CPU free to accomplish other tasks. The push and pop methods access one sample at a time instead of more efficiently allowing contiguous blocks of samples to be added or removed in a single call.

The `RingBuffer` is implemented as an array of 16-bit audio samples created at instantiation time. The size of the `RingBuffer` and array is specified when the `RingBuffer` is created. In the constructor, the specified `highWaterMark` is recorded and the head and tail pointers are set to point to the same value (zero). Setting the head and tail to point to the same sample causes the buffer to be considered empty. The contents of the buffer do not have to be initialized unless quiescent underflow (see "Wrapped I/O" (page 209)) is implemented. The constructor does write to both the head and tail pointers, but is still threadsafe since other methods may not be called until the constructor completes.

The `RingBuffer` constructor:

```
RingBuffer::RingBuffer(unsigned int size, unsigned int
highWaterMark) :
_size(size),_highWaterMark(highWaterMark),_head(0),_tail(0)
{
    _buffer = new short[_size]; // allocate buffer

    // ensure legal size
    _highWaterMark =
        (_highWaterMark>_size)?_size:_highWaterMark;
}
```

Next, the Samples Available and Space Available calculations (from Table 1) are implemented. Notice that the implementation is slightly different from that described in the text. The implementation adds the size of the buffer to the calculation because the C++ modulo operator, "%," doesn't work as required with negative values.

First, the SamplesAvailable calculation:

```
unsigned int RingBuffer::getSamplesAvailable()
{
    return((_tail - _head + _size) % _size);
}
```

The Space Available calculation is slightly more complicated due to consideration of the highWaterMark. Basically, we use the lower of two calculations: 1) how many samples are available in the RingBuffer; or 2) how many empty samples are available "under" the highWaterMark. The second calculation will be used for any setting of the highWaterMark smaller than one less than the size of the buffer (the buffer, when full, can only contain one less than the size of the buffer):

```
unsigned int RingBuffer::getSpaceAvailable()
{
    int free = (_head - _tail + _size - 1)%_size;
    int underMark = _highWaterMark - getSamplesAvailable();
    return(min(underMark, free));
}
```

As mentioned above, the push and pop methods are not blocking in this implementation; instead, they return zero if the operation cannot complete because the buffer is full, or at the highWaterMark for the push operation, or empty for the pop.

The push method adds a single value to the RingBuffer. Note that while it performs a calculation requiring access to the head and tail, it only modifies the _tail, thus, it doesn't require a mutex in a multithreaded environment (as described in the text, the calculation is conservative; if the consumer were to update the head pointer after the getSpaceAvailable calculation was performed, then the number of empty samples available to fill would only be greater).

Push method:

```
int RingBuffer::push(short value)
{
    int status = 1;

    if(getSpaceAvailable()) {
        _buffer[_tail] = value;     // store value
        _tail = ++_tail % _size;    // increment tail
    } else {
    // if blocking I/O: block the calling thread (the
    // producer) and unblock the consumer thread
        status = 0;
    }

    return(status);
}
```

Pop works in a similar way:

```
int RingBuffer::pop(short *value)
{
    int status = 1;

    if(getSamplesAvailable()) {
        *value = _buffer[_head];    // retrieve the value
        _head = ++_head % _size;    // increment head
    } else {
    // if blocking I/O: block the calling thread (the
    // consumer) and unblock the producer
        status = 0;
    }

    return(status);
}
```

The next example shows samples pushed and popped from the buffer with the position of the head (h), tail (t), and the calculated number of samples full and fillable:

Initial empty buffer (head==tail) of size 5 with highwater mark set to 3:

```
status: h( 0), t( 0), full( 0), fillable( 3)
```

Push a bunch of samples until full:

```
pushed 1: h( 0), t( 1), full( 1), fillable( 2)
pushed 2: h( 0), t( 2), full( 2), fillable( 1)
pushed 3: h( 0), t( 3), full( 3), fillable( 0)
pushed 4: h( 0), t( 3), full( 3), fillable( 0)
push(4) failed, buffer full
```

Pop values back off:

```
popped 1: h( 1), t( 3), full( 2), fillable( 1)
popped 2: h( 2), t( 3), full( 1), fillable( 2)
popped 3: h( 3), t( 3), full( 0), fillable( 3)
pop failed, buffer empty
```

Push some more to watch the pointers wrap around the buffer:

```
pushed 1: h( 3), t( 4), full( 1), fillable( 2)
pushed 2: h( 3), t( 0), full( 2), fillable( 1)
pushed 3: h( 3), t( 1), full( 3), fillable( 0)
pushed 4: h( 3), t( 1), full( 3), fillable( 0)
push(4) failed, buffer full
```

7   Conclusion

The ring buffer implementation of the FIFO queue offers a lightweight mechanism to stream data between a producer and consumer allowing for simultaneous access without requiring expensive and potentially danger-ous locks. Having the producer and consumer share a common algebra for understanding ring buffer status makes the technique even more powerful. In "Wrapped I/O" (page 209), we explore more sophisticated opportuni-ties for managing audio data streams when the ring buffer is wrapped by a library interface.

Annotated Bibliography

[1] Thomas H. Cormen, Charles E. Leiserson and Ronald L. Rivest. *Introduction to Algorithms*. Cambridge, MA: MIT Press, 1999.

An excellent undergraduate-level algorithms text.

[2] Digital Signal Processor User's Manual. DSP56000/DSP56001. Motorola, 1990.

The 56000 is a DSP which is very popular in audio applications. The user's manual contains examples of the ring buffer and other signal processing algorithms, as well as implementations using the special DSP modulo addressing mode.

[3] Donald Knuth . *The Art of Computer Programming: Fundamental Algorithms*. Reading, MA: Addison-Wesley, 1973.

This is one volume of perhaps the most classic text in computer science. The author illustrates algorithms, including some of the data structures mentioned in this article, using MIX, an idealized machine instruction set.

[4] Andrew S. Tanenbaum. *Operating Systems Design and Implementation*. Upper Saddle River, NJ: Prentice Hall, 1987.

A fun undergraduate-level operating systems text which illustrates its concepts by providing source code to a small, fully functional, operating system.

Wrapped I/O

Ken Greenebaum

1 Motivation

In "Introduction to the Ring Buffer FIFO" (page 193), we introduced
the ring buffer FIFO queue and described its structure and some of its
virtues. In this article, we explore more advanced functionality enabled
by wrapping the data structure accesses in function calls, thereby creating
a library.

Some of the benefits of this approach are straightforward: enforcing
uniform access to the structure (for instance, so one application doesn't
implement full as (`head == tail`) and another as (`head== tail+1`)), hiding the data structure implementation (to allow the system designers to
change the implementation in the future without forcing the application
code to be rewritten) and code reuse (not forcing every application to
recreate the same code to access the structure which includes the potential for creating bugs).

Wrapping I/O offers other more subtle benefits as well. Having a library providing library calls which *touch* every audio sample provides a
convenient framework to implement advanced signal processing features
such as level attenuation, equalization, and format conversion. The library can also manage the stream providing blocking flow control, underflow detection, and policy.

A concrete example of a ring-buffer-based output application will
help demonstrate the trade-offs and subtleties inherent in such a system.
For the purposes of this article we will explore a simple audio output
interface which wraps ring buffer access behind library calls to provide

automatic blocking writes, format conversion, and consistent buffer management policy.

2 Underflow

It is not always obvious which is the correct way for an application to handle a buffer problem such as an overflowing output buffer or an underflowing input buffer. Most PC based audio interfaces, like Microsoft's Direct Sound and WaveIO, don't notify the application if a buffer overrun has occurred. These libraries tend not to expose enough information for their applications to determine buffer overrun problems for themselves. The previous statement isn't completely true, for the intrepid developer can find ways to extract more information from these libraries.

When I created the digital media framework for Microsoft's Direct Animation, I used Direct Sound for audio I/O. Unfortunately, Direct Sound doesn't provide explicit buffer underflow information (Direct Sound doesn't monitor the producer's use of the buffer and, hence, doesn't *know* if underflow has occurred). Additionally, Direct Sound doesn't provide a counter that may be queried to determine how many audio samples it has output. Consequently, I developed a mechanism to monitor buffers and determine if my application's Direct Sound buffer ever underflowed due to my application's high-priority audio thread not being run by the operating system.

Underflow can't be deduced directly by monitoring the Direct Sound output buffer because of sampling theory. It is unclear if the buffer pointer has underflowed, since it will just wrap back around to a legal value again (this is called aliasing) and is illustrated in Figure 1.

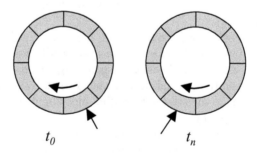

t_0 t_n

Figure 1. Aliasing. Did the pointer move one position between t_0 and t_n? How many times did the pointer spin around the buffer between these two snapshots?

If the buffer pointer has wrapped, there is no way to tell how many times it has. To avoid aliasing, my method employed creating an extra, very large, silent, streaming buffer to use as a time reference. If between writes, more *time* had expired on the clock buffer than the size of the output buffer, then the output buffer had surely underflowed by an amount that may then be calculated. In Figure 2 it becomes obvious that the smaller buffer underflowed by noticing the nine position pointer movement in the larger buffers.

For this mechanism to work, the large, clock buffer must be large enough to *ride out* the largest anticipated scheduling lapse during which the monitoring process might not be run. Otherwise, observation of the clock buffer would be subject to aliasing, too. The high-resolution CPU clock could also be used for this purpose with the added complication that

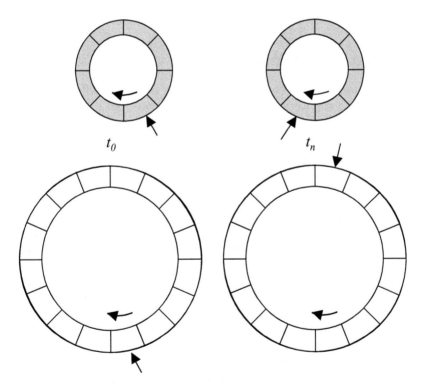

Figure 2. With more information, we can determine that underflow did occur in the Figure 1 (the pointers advanced by nine (or more!) positions between t_0 and t_n.

the CPU clock and DAC clock are not locked and will drift with respect to each other.

Due to the seeming inevitability of buffer errors, and the complexity of even determining when an error has occurred, most designers of PC audio applications don't even concern themselves with detecting or attempting to recover from buffer problems. They instead weigh how amenable their application and users are to buffer errors versus the added buffer size and resulting latency they use to mitigate errors.

A test such as `RampTest`, described in "RampTest: Quantifying Audio Performance" (see Audio Anecdotes I), could be adapted to determine if applications were experiencing buffer errors. Most often, designers take a more heuristic approach to tuning their applications. If audio glitches are noticed, perhaps on slower machines, the designer will increase the buffer size until the errors go away or the degree of latency is determined to be too great.

3   Detecting Underflow

After examining the issues involved in trying to detect buffer underflow issues from the application side, it becomes obvious that it is valuable for the audio system software to detect underflow *and* overflow events.

Unfortunately, it is difficult for a system like Direct Sound to monitor buffer underflow. Direct Sound only tracks one of the pair of ring buffer pointers described in the aforementioned ring buffer article. For the case of an output buffer, Direct Sound uses, and provides to the application, what we refer to as the consumer's head pointer. Direct Sound keeps track of the location in the buffer from where it is reading and provides this information to the application so the application can be sure to keep writing fresh audio in front of the Direct Sound pointer. It is up to the application itself to manage its own tail pointer to keep track of where the application is writing data to the buffer.

Since Direct Sound doesn't have access to both the head and tail pointers, it can't perform the ring buffer algebra described in the previous article. Direct Sound has no knowledge of the state of the buffer, or the number of samples stored in the buffer, and consequently can't detect that a buffer has overflowed or underflowed.

Fortunately, it is straightforward for an audio system to keep track of both the position of the head and tail pointers, and detect buffer problems. Our hypothetical system tracks and even manages the read and write pointer positions when calls are made to *push* or *pop* information from the queue. Thus, it can determine if a producer has *pushed* too many audio samples onto the queue causing it to overflow, or if the consumer has *popped* the queue into an underflow situation. These buffer error states are simple to detect. What's not so obvious is what the audio library should do when this occurs. I call the way a library or application manages buffer issues *underflow policy*.

4 Underflow Policy

There isn't one correct policy for managing buffer issues. Every application (and user) has unique characteristics and requirements that need to be considered when designing policy. In some cases, the design is obvious; elsewhere, the trade-offs may need to be weighed before deciding on a policy.

I favor designing audio systems so that they provide a reasonable default behavior while providing flexibility for the application to select the policy that is most appropriate for the circumstance. The following video game, karaoke, transcription, and CD-mastering audio application scenarios demonstrate some of the breadth of policy requirements.

Video games are designed to provide interactive, immersive experiences stimulating all of our senses. As described DiFilippo's article "Perceivable Auditory Latencies" (see *Audio Anecdotes I*) low latencies are critical to maintaining the illusion of reality. Game designers consequently tune their applications toward low-latency responsiveness at the potential expense of generating audio glitches. These tradeoffs are the most appropriate to make it feel as if pulling the game controller's trigger actually shot the gun your character is holding. The game designer doesn't care if a sound effect didn't *fire* correctly as long as the next one does; the mistake probably wasn't noticed in the heat of the battle anyway.

The karaoke application is quite different. It isn't interactive once a song is selected; consequently, the designer would likely have favored designing additional audio buffering and robustness into the system over providing ultra low, interactive, latencies. This scenario becomes more interesting when we consider an output buffer underflow. Perhaps an email arrived while the song was playing, stealing the CPU from the karaoke application for five seconds, much longer than needed to starve its output buffer of samples, causing an underflow.

On many audio systems, this five-second lapse would be filled with the annoying sound of the last contents of the buffer playing over and over again in rapid succession. Fortunately our hypothetical audio system performs quiescent underflow, yielding only a silent pause. Our hypothetical audio system also will inform the karaoke application of the five-second underflow, but what should the karaoke application do with this information? On most audio systems the application wouldn't know that there was any interruption, and it would continue where it left off on the song with the lip-syncing singer now five seconds further into the song and suddenly very confused when the music resumed in the wrong place from his perspective.

In this scenario, it would be best for the application to actively skip ahead the missing five seconds and resume the music in synchrony with the unamused singer (fuming that his accompaniment disappeared for five seconds).

The designer of the transcription machine would likely arrive at the opposite design decision when faced with a similar scenario. The typist would want to wait for the voice playback to resume and certainly wouldn't want to miss any of the material.

The decision of what the CD mastering application should do in a similar situation might be influenced by the user of the application. Many professional applications have a *rehearsal* mode which is very much like a dress rehearsal; everything is supposed to be like the *real* performance, but it is not critical that everything go perfectly. In rehearsal mode, a glitch might be detected and a warning provided for the user. In an actual mastering situation, the operation would likely be terminated immediately if an error of any size was detected. I have been mastering CDs since the days when CD recorders were rack mount devices costing thousands of dollars. Those recorders recorded at less than real time. A professional disappointed that a mastering session failed would become downright angry if it took hours to find out that the recording glitch occurred in the first seconds.

5 What is an Audio System to Do?

Since there isn't a one-size-fits-all solution to audio policy, in keeping with the principles introduced in my article "Simple Interfaces, Small (Hello) World" (see *Audio Anecdotes I*), there may be some reasonable default behaviors. Provided that there are ways for applications to alter the default behaviors to suit their unique requirements, I suggest the following as useful defaults that have worked well for systems I have helped design. These decisions are interrelated; making one change in policy will likely affect the other decisions.

6 Must Be Alike to Mix

Modern operating systems are multitasking, which means that they run more than one application at the same time. It is only reasonable that these operating systems should allow more than one audio application to run at the same time, somehow *sharing* the audio resource. In the real world, sounds mix.

We can hear the phone ring while the radio is playing. Users expect the same from their computers. They would like to be able to hear the teleconferencing system's ring while playing an MP3 music file. Consequently audio systems like SGI's Audio Library (AL) and Microsoft's Direct Sound provide mixers.

Many audio systems will allow applications to output audio in its native format, usually 8- or 16-bit samples, mono or stereo interleaved, sampled at a given rate, 48,000 Hz in much professional audio. Some systems like the AL or PABLIO will allow floating point samples to be written as well, which is a great convenience for floating point signal processing applications.

In order to efficiently mix streams of audio together, they should already be in a uniform format. The wrapped I/O interface provides a convenient place to provide this format conversion. The format conversion can be performed in user space in the audio library's write audio frame call where extremely fast floating point math is available instead of in protected kernel space where only less efficient integer operations may be used. (Operating systems typically reduce context switch overhead by avoiding saving the floating point register's context during interrupts. Consequently, floating point is often not available in the operating system kernel or in drivers.)

I like to convert all streams to a common, canonical format corresponding to the highest quality output format supported by the hardware. Since this decision is abstracted from the application, the audio system designer is free to change the canonical format at any time. A more sophisticated system might allow a single audio stream to be output using its native audio format, perhaps 8-bit, 8-KHz, mono, voice grade audio. At the time a second stream was to start, both the streams could be dynamically converted to the canonical format and mixed. In this way, the expense of conversion would only be incurred if needed.

Converting quantization formats is an easy operation usually involving shifts, masks, and copies. For instance converting our voice quality, 8-bit, mono stream to 16-bit stereo involves left-shifting each sample, then replicating it to provide equivalent, mono, left, and right values. The dynamic sample rate conversion that would be required to convert the 8 kHz voice quality stream to a 48 kHz canonical stream is more complicated. Microsoft's Direct Sound implements a simple fractional pointer algorithm which is very efficient but also causes highly undesirable artifacts in the resulting signal especially when converting to a lower sampling rate. Theoretically, there is no reason a higher quality algorithm can't be provided, perhaps as an option to the application developer or even end-user who could control the quality versus CPU load trade-off. Ramstad's article "Rate Conversion" (see *Audio Anecdotes I*) provides much more information on rate conversion including an efficient high-quality algorithm.

Providing per-stream attenuation is another operation possible in the same code that performs the format conversion. Attenuation is analogous to the fader controls on a mixer (but without being able to provide gain) and is necessary for setting the relative levels of inputs to the mix. See my article "No Need to Shout: Volume Controls and the Digital Sound Convergence" (page 175) for further motivation. Signal processing operations like equalization, echo cancellation, and others may be performed at the same time.

Performing these operations at the same time as the copy operation is highly efficient since the copy will have already filled the CPU's cache lines with the audio data.

7   Quiescent Underflow

The sound system designer must decide on an underflow policy for mixing. What should occur if one of a group of applications whose output are being mixed fails to receive enough CPU time to keep its output buffer filled and allows it to underflow?

It doesn't seem reasonable to stop all the successful audio applications, interrupting their performances because one failed. However, this policy would keep the streams synchronized. Perhaps this doesn't feel right because it doesn't happen in the real world. A skipping CD doesn't cause the radio or TV to skip as well.

As previously mentioned, in Direct Sound, underflow is not detected. The output buffer for the underflowing application will loop annoyingly on whatever was last in its buffer. The other applications will continue to play on, which does seem reasonable.

Also previously referred to, audio systems like SGI's AL and this book's PABLIO quiescently underflow. If an application outputting an audio stream cannot fulfill its obligation to keep the output buffer from underflowing, the audio system will emit silence and keep track of how long the underflow lasted so that the application can perform its own underflow policy as appropriate.

Not only does quiescent underflow make the inevitable underflow more pleasant than annoyingly continuing to play the contents of the output buffer (especially in the event of a crash, or when running an audio application in a debugger), but it also affords unexpected benefits. For instance, quiescent underflow allows an application to very simply play short duration sounds like an application's notifiers (bell, click) or a game's sound effect footstep or gunshot.

The application desiring to play these short sounds could leave the audio stream open, and underflowing in silence, then *drop* samples into the stream when appropriate. Contrast this to the similar operation using Direct Sound where the application, instead of just outputting its samples and moving on, needs to explicitly wait for the sound to finish, flushing the buffer with silence so the stream may be left unattended and silent.

This technique may be extended allowing sounds to be played at very precise times, even frame accurately, in the near future using a concept similar to the silent, black leader on a movie film. This technique is explored in my article "Sample Accurate Synchronization Using Pipelines: Put a Sample In and We Know When It Will Come Out" (see *Audio Anecdotes III*).

One last benefit of allowing output buffer underflow situations to produce silence is that the consumer code can be as simple and lightweight as possible. The consumer (or the library on it's behalf) doesn't have to make comparisons or perform math on each sample consumed to determine whether underflow has occurred or to perform a special operation in that circumstance. Rather, all the consumer needs to do to support quiescent underflow is to obliviously zero the samples as they are fetched from the buffer.

Keeping the consumer code as simple and lightweight as possible allows it to be run more often on fewer samples potentially helping the audio system to support very low latencies. For instance, the SGI AL's implementation is run 1000 times a second and can reliably provide less than 2 ms of audio latency (The latency of the audio system is only one component of achievable latency. The second involves how long a process has to wait to be scheduled by the operating system. On a multiprocessor machine with a CPU dedicated to the audio process, sub 2-ms latencies are achievable. Five-ms latencies are achievable on single processor machines with the audio process running at a high, nondegrading priority, and with the process *pinned* to memory.)

8   Blocking I/O

Wrapping the I/O data structure in a library interface provides an excellent opportunity to support blocking I/O. Blocking logic is often incorporated into ring buffer read or write calls. Blocking I/O is not appropriate for all situations, but works remarkably well for the most common cases providing automatic flow-control which greatly simplifies the task of writing an application that reads or writes audio.

Consider how simple the main loop for a process writing audio is when implemented using a blocking I/O scheme:

```
while(1){
    // synthesize a buffer
    synthesize(  audioBuffer, NUMSAMPLES);

    // output w/blocking
    writeSamples(audioBuffer, NUMSAMPLES);
}
```

As long as the **synthesize** call can produce samples faster than real time, the loop will function perfectly without consuming undue CPU cycles polling, requiring the author to write complicated buffer sniffing logic, or callback functions.

The logic works as follows:

- Writing process blocks when the buffer fills (past high-water mark).

- Writing process unblocks when the buffer empties (past low-water mark).

- Reading process blocks when the buffer empties (past low-water mark).

- Reading process unblocks when the buffer fills (past high-water mark).

If the ring buffer blocking scheme utilizes thread-blocking facilities provided by the operating system (such as UNIX's selectable semaphore, or Windows' **WaitForSingleObject**), then the blocking operation can be very efficient.

The naive polling and sleeping schemes often implemented by programmers unfamiliar with threaded code are inefficient or radically increase scheduling latency depending on the length of time they sleep between polling (See Figure 3).

```
while(1) {
    // read a variable sized block from a network stream
    ReadSamples(netStream, audioBuffer, &numSamples);

    samplesAvailable = getSamplesAvailable();

    // poll until there exists enough space
    while(samplesAvailable < numSamples {
        sleep(1); // nap so we don't burn too much cpu polling
            samplesAvailable = getSamplesAvailable();
    }

    // output buffer
    writeSamplesNonBlocking(audioBuffer, numSamples);
}
```

Figure 3. Naïve implementation not benefiting from blocking ring buffer writes.

9 Write Nonfixed-Sized Chunks

Another benefit of using blocking I/O on top of a flexible ring buffer implementation is the ability to read and write variable-sized buffers. Various synthesizers might find it most convenient to output different length buffers. Perhaps a collision synthesizer would produce collision impulses of varying lengths depending on energy and resonance parameters. Perhaps, as in our example, the synthesizer is merely receiving or decoding chunks of audio from a stream and those are arriving in different sizes perhaps as a result of a fixed bitrate compression scheme. See Figure 4.

```
while(1){
    // read a variable sized block from a network stream
    readSamples(netStream, audioBuffer, &numSamples);
    writeSamples(audioBuffer, numSamples);    // output buffer
}
```

Figure 4. Inner loop not requiring rebuffering by using variable-sized writes.

The example in Figure 4 would require awkward rebuffering logic if a double-buffered, fixed-buffer-sized streaming scheme similar to Microsoft's WaveIO was used. The code in Figure 5 is complicated and difficult to debug.

```
while(1) {
    while(outputBufferIndex < BUFFERSIZE) {
        // read a variable sized block from a network stream
        readSamples(netStream, netBuffer, &numSamples);

        // copy as much as can fit into output buffer from
        samples = min((BUFFERSIZE-outputBufferIndex),
                      (numSamples netbuffer))
    }

    swapBuffer(outputBuffer); // output buffer

}
```

Figure 5. Using double buffer requiring complicated rebuffering logic.

Blocking I/O automatically accommodates extreme cases. For instance, writes much larger than the underlying FIFO size may be passed to the write call with impunity. The audio system will automatically cause the thread to remain blocked in the write call for multiple cycles of writing, blocking, and waiting till the buffer drains to the low-water mark, until all the audio frames are committed to the buffer followed by the call returning to the application like normal. At the other extreme, an audio producer may easily make single audio frame writes to the buffer simplifying the application's own buffering requirements while incurring some degree of unnecessary call overhead.

10   Blocking I/O Encourages Multithreaded Design

Blocking I/O schemes encourage compound tasks to be broken into multiple threads. For instance DirectAnimation, the animation engine I helped design for Microsoft, attempts to render computer graphics at the monitor refresh rate (often 60 to 80 Hz); decode video at video frame rate (often 30 Hz); synthesize audio samples at the sampling rate (often 24 KHz to 48 KHz) in bursts small enough to both provide low latency and update synthesis parameters often enough to make the changes imperceptible.

Instead of having one loop with many difficult-to-reconcile goals requiring problematic polling and snooping, the problem may be factored into much simpler pieces, each being implemented in its own thread using straightforward logic and blocking I/O for timing and flow control. Indeed, Presto/Changeo, DirectAnimation's second generation engine decoupled frame buffer composition, video stream decoding, audio synthesis, and dynamic behavior evaluation into separate lightweight threads with impressive results.

11 Schedulers Optimized for Bursty Computing

A less understood benefit of using system-blocking facilities is that the scheduler in many operating systems was written with an understanding that computing is bursty and many processes spend most of their time blocked on I/O. Consider that a word processor spends most of its time blocked waiting for the slow human to press a key! In an effort to make these I/O bound processes feel more responsive to interaction, the scheduler boosts the effective priority of recently unblocked processes, allowing them to run very soon after unblocking; this factor alone can greatly reduce scheduling latency and allow audio synthesis at far lower latencies than would be possible without.

Figure 6 demonstrates that a process only runs for a brief period of time after it becomes unblocked by receiving input, like a key being hit in a word processor. The smaller the scheduling delay, the time between when the event occurred and the time the operating system scheduled the process to run, the more responsive the system will feel. Some operating systems will temporarily boost the priority of a process to attempt to cause it to run as soon after the event as possible. Notice that the process spends the majority of the time blocked waiting for I/O.

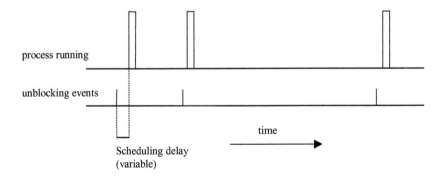

Figure 6. Graph correlating unblocking event arrival to process running.

12   Summary/Conclusion

The ring buffer FIFO queue provides a flexible mechanism to implement audio I/O, however, it is difficult to use the full potential of such an interface without guaranteeing consistent access semantics. Having applications make calls on a library wrapping the data structure is a convenient way to enforce uniformity and provides a wonderful place to provide a host of advanced features.

In this article, we explored some of the basics like format conversion, signal processing, buffer management, underflow policy, and blocking I/O. Space did not permit mention of more advanced topics like sample-accurate time stamping and synchronization.

The PABLIO implementation provided on the accompanying CD-ROM provides a nice opportunity to experiment with the topics presented in this article since the entire system runs in user space. This makes PABLIO easy to experiment on and debug without concerning oneself with device drivers. I suggest first writing an application making use of the existing blocking I/O scheme, then digging in and adding new capabilities to PABLIO.

Annotated Bibliography

[1] *IRIS Media Libraries.* Silicon Graphics.

   This manual describes the SGI Audio Library interface in detail.

[2] John Lions. *Lions' Commentary on UNIX Sixth Edition.* Menlo Park, CA: Peer-to-Peer Communications, 1996.

   John Lions annotated an early UNIX kernel circa 1977. Because of restrictions on distributing UNIX kernel source, the material was never published, but it instead was passed from one hacker to the next. Finally published, this book provides an incredible view of a time when operating systems were simple, elegant, and easy to grasp. I encourage the reader to review the scheduler and notice how blocking I/O is implemented. It might also be interesting to examine how interrupts call assembly language code that affects a context switch.

[3] Microsoft Developer's Network. Available from World Wide Web (http://msdn.microsoft.com).

   The web site to search for all Microsoft documentation. I encourage the reader to review Microsoft's Direct Sound and Direct Animation.

[4] Andrew S. Tanenbaum. *Operating Systems Design and Implementation*. Upper Saddle River, NJ: Prentice Hall, 1987.

This operating system text provides the source code to a simple UNIX-like operating system, MINIX, to illustrate operating system principals. This text provides more hand holding than Lions. Incidentally, LINUX grew out of the MINIX user community which Linus Torvalds was a participant in.

Computer Tools

SoX Sound Exchange Library

Chris Bagwell

1 SoX and libst

SoX is an audio format conversion utility written to be portable and as a result runs on most popular operating systems and platforms, including Windows, Macs, and UNIX variants.

An incomplete list of file formats that SoX can read and write includes .raw audio data, Apple/SGI's .aiff files, SUN/NeXT's .au files, CD audio, NIST SPHERE files, Sound Blaster .voc files, Microsoft .wav files, and Psion .wve files.

While SoX is copying the audio data from an input file to an output file, it is capable of modifying the audio data. It does this by passing the audio data through an "effects" engine. This effects engine is cable of applying filters, changing the sample rate, adding echoes, trimming the size of the data, and much more.

SoX is a command line program which means it has no graphical interface and can be used in scripts to process multiple audio files at once. It is distributed in source code form and uses the Open Source license LGPL so that you are free to modify it and distribute it with your own programs. You can read more about the LGPL license at http://www.gnu.org/. SoX works on low-end 16-bit computers up to high-end 64-bit computers and works on both little endian and big endian machines.

SoX is distributed along with its source code so that people are able to easily add new features and so that it can be modified to run under new OSs as they are released. The preferred method of compiling SoX is to use a UNIX-like environment. Under UNIX and Mac OS X, the needed tools are almost always available. Under Windows it requires installing the free

Cygwin package which includes the GNU C compiler and standard UNIX compiler support programs. While Cygwin is distributed with this book (on the accompanying CD-ROM) the latest version of the Cygwin package is always available at http://sources.redhat.com/cygwin. SoX provides some support for compiling using Microsoft Visual C++; additionally pre-compiled versions are available on the Internet for those not interested in rolling their own from the source code.

The source code to SoX is also included on the CD-ROM accompanying this book. There is a script included with SoX that can determine everything required to compile it on most computer systems. It is known to work with Linux, BSD-based systems, Solaris, AIX, Mac OS X, and Windows with the Cygwin compiler suite. All that is needed to compile SoX is to run the following commands:

```
cd sox
./configure
make
```

This will result in an executable being created called sox. You may test it by performing some file format conversions on the included sample audio file called "monkey.au," which is a short monkey screech. To convert audio files from one format to another, you run SoX using command line options of the form:

```
sox [input options] [input filename] [output options]
[output file name] [effects]
```

To convert the sample AU file to a WAV file you would run:

```
sox monkey.au monkey.wav
```

SoX keys off the file extension and creates a file using the standard WAV (.wav) format. During the conversion process, you can inform SoX of specific format information of the input or output file. You would want to specify input options if SoX does not correctly determine the format of the audio data. This can happen if you have a corrupt audio file or if it is raw audio data with no header information. You would want to specify output options if you want the output file to save the audio data in a different format than the input file. Input and output options are actually the same set of options, but they just apply to either the input or output file.

SoX understands audio data types that are stored in 8-bit, 16-bit, or 32-bits. SoX uses the options -d, -w, and –l, respectively, to be informed of this fact.

Once you specify the size of the data type, you need to also specify how the data is encoded within these bits. 8-bit data is usually unsigned (meaning the combinations of 1s and 0s represent a number from 0 to 255). The -u flag is used to indicate this. 16-bit and 32-bit data are usually stored using signed encoding (half the possible values are positive and half are negative) and use the -s option. Other valid options include 8-bit data that is encoded using u-law, a-law, or ADPCM compression. These are represented by the options -U, -A, and -a, respectively.

Audio data can contain one or more channels. In the case of stereo files, there will be two channels of audio data. This can be specified using the -c option followed by the number of channels. Audio data also has a sample rate associated with it. This can be specified using the -r option followed by the sample rate in Hertz.

During the conversion process, you can request several modifications to be made. Suppose you want to save the audio data in monkey.au to a CD-ROM so that you can listen to it in your CD player. CD audio data is required to be 2-channel, 16-bit signed data that is recorded at 44100 Hz. The monkey.au file was recorded as monochannel 8-bit u-law at 8000 Hz. By specifying the appropriate output options, SoX will convert the data:

```
sox monkey.au -c 2 -s -w -r 44100 monkey.wav
```

The options specified before the output file name tell SoX that you want the output file to contain two channels, data stored using signed words, and a sample rate of 44100 Hz. When creating a new file that contains more channels than the input file, SoX will duplicate the audio data from the preexisting channel into the new channel. The new audio file is now ready to be written to your CD-ROM using standard CD burning software.

Next, suppose that you are not happy with the sound quality of monkey.au. Perhaps the screech of the monkey is too high a pitch for your liking. The high-pitched sounds can be removed by making use of SoX's effects engine. The low-pass filter effect can be specified and told to remove all audio data that is above 3000 Hz.

```
sox monkey.au -c 2 -s -w -r 441000 monkey.wav lowpass 3000
```

SoX can read and write most common audio file formats and can apply a wide range of different effects to the audio file. For more advanced usage of SoX, you will need to read the sox.txt and soxexam.txt files that are included with the source files and precompiled executables on the CD-ROM.

2   Using the libst Library

The command line program SoX is actually making use of an included library called libst. libst was designed to make it very easy for people to add new file handlers and effects.

The file handler library defines an API that must be used when creating new file handlers that can read and write a specific audio file format. A specific file handler must be able to read in an audio file containing audio data of various data types and convert the audio data into 32-bit signed data. It must also be able to take 32-bit signed audio data and create an audio file with audio data of various data types. Since all audio file handlers use an intermediate format of 32-bit signed data, you can mix and match handlers to read in one format and write out to another.

libst also has an effects engine that defines an API for effects that will read in 32-bit signed audio data and write 32-bit signed data back out. This effects engine can be used in between the reading and writing stages of the file handlers to modify the audio data. By using only 32-bit audio data, effects writers can concentrate on the effects algorithm instead of worrying about reading and writing various audio data types.

The following is a very simple program that makes use of libst to read in a .wav file using stdin and write back out a .wav audio file to stdout. It also forces the output audio data type to always be 8-bit unsigned data to show how this is specified to libst. It can be compiled and run on most systems by using the following commands from within the SoX build directory:

```
cc -I. -L. -o convert convert.c -lst -lm
convert < input.wav > output.wav
```

Some systems will not need the -lm flag. You can copy the following text to a file or obtain it from the CD-ROM accompanying this book.

```
#include "st.h"
/* Required to be defined for libst to be called
 * during severe failures
```

```
 */
void cleanup()
{
    return;
}
int main()
{
    struct st_soundstream in_file;
    struct st_soundstream out_file;
    long len;
    signed long buf[1024];
    /* String that tells libst what type of file format
     * we are working with.  The string is the same as
     * the standardized file extension when one exists.
     */
    in_file.filetype = "wav";
    /* Set some basic information on the actual file
     * based on standard information obtained with the C
     * FILE type, fopen() and related functions.
     */
    in_file.filename = "stdin";
    in_file.fp = stdin;
    in_file.seekable = 0;
    /* The info fields must be set up with either a known
     * set of default values or overridden to force libst
     * to process data as if it were in a specific data type.
     */
    in_file.info.rate = 0;
    in_file.info.size = -1;
    in_file.info.encoding = -1;
    in_file.info.channels = -1;
    /* Some audio files contain comment data inside the
     * file.  libst will store those comments as a
     * string.  Initialize to NULL so that we can test
     * for non-NULL to see if a comment was found.
     */
    in_file.comment = NULL;
    /* When working with RAW audio files, this flag can
     * be set to non-zero to swap bytes when read in,
     * thereby fixing endian problems.
     */
```

```
in_file.swap = 0;
/* Fill in some other structure data based on the
 * filetype field.
 */
st_gettype(&in_file);
out_file.filetype = "wav";
out_file.filename = "stdout";
out_file.fp = stdout;
out_file.seekable = 0;
/* Known default values are needed for output file
 * as well unless you want to the output file to
 * be saved using different data types then the
 * input file.
 */
out_file.info.rate = 0;
out_file.info.size = -1;
out_file.info.encoding = -1;
out_file.info.channels = -1;
/* Here is an example of not using the default values
 * for the info fields and forcing the output file
 * to use 8000Hz sample rate, unsigned 8-bit
 * data.  Channels and Rate are left at -1 because
 * they require the effects engine to do that
 * conversion.
 */
out_file.info.size = ST_SIZE_BYTE;
out_file.info.encoding = ST_ENCODING_UNSIGNED;
out_file.comment = NULL;
out_file.swap = 0;

st_gettype(&out_file);
/* Open the input file for reading and verify
 * that its really a file that is "filetype".
 * Returns ST_EOF on failure so a useful program
 * would check for that.  This function
 * will overwrite all the default values in the
 * info fields with values based on the audio
 * file's header.
 */
in_file.h->startread(&in_file);
/* This function makes sure that no default
```

```
 * values are remaining. Files like RAW can not
 * always determine the data types and so we must
 * check for this.
 * Calls exit() on failure.
 */
st_checkformat(&in_file);
/* We need to replace default values in the output
 * info fields with the values from the input file.
 * st_copyformat() will do this for us.
 */
st_copyformat(&in_file, &out_file);
out_file.h->startwrite(&out_file);
/* Typical file I/O is performed for the rest of
 * the file.  The way you call the read and write
 * routines look a little strange but it works
 * the same no matter what the underlying audio
 * file data format looks like.
 * Buffer data is always in signed 32-bit format
 * no matter what the input and output formats
 * are.
 */
while((len=(*in_file.h->read)(&in_file, buf, 1024)) > 0)
{
    (*out_file.h->write)(&out_file, buf, len);
}
(*in_file.h->stopread)(&in_file);
(*out_file.h->stopwrite)(&out_file);
return 0;
}
```

This sample program can make use of any other file format handler inside of libst by changing the `filetype` variable. A more complicated program could attempt to guess the file format type by looking at the filename's extension. You can refer to the file SoX.c included with sox for examples of more complicated usages of libst. Sox.c is really just an enhanced version of the above example program.

Any new file format handler added to SoX must implement all of the functions that are defined in structure **st_format_t** that is located in st.h. You can tell from the example convert program how they are used in a real program.

```
typedef struct st_format {
```

```
    char    **names;          /* file type names */
    int     flags;            /* details about file type */
    int     (*startread)(ft_t ft);
    LONG    (*read)(ft_t ft, LONG *buf, LONG len);
    int     (*stopread)(ft_t ft);
    int     (*startwrite)(ft_t ft);
    LONG    (*write)(ft_t ft, LONG *buf, LONG len);
    int     (*stopwrite)(ft_t ft);
} st_format_t;
```

Below is an example taken from the handlers.c file of the file handler for .wav files. Refer to the file wav.c for the actual implementation of the functions.

```
static char *wavnames[] = {
        "wav",
        (char *) 0
};
{ wavnames, ST_FILE_STEREO,                  /* Microsoftt RIFF */
  st_wavstartread, st_wavread, st_nothing,
  st_wavstartwrite, st_wavwrite, st_wavstopwrite},
```

Names is an array of filename extensions that are used to detect this format; in the case of .wav files the only valid extension is .wav. This corresponds to the filetype field in the example program.

The flags field contains a flag if this format can support one or more channels; which the .wav format does.

The function startread() is a function that will be called to open up an audio file for reading. Read() should return a buffer of 32-bit signed audio data of the specified length. Stopread() is called when closing the file to do any clean-up work required.

The function startwrite() is a function that will be called to open up an audio file for writing. Write() should take the buffer of 32-bit signed audio data and write out the specified length of data. Stopwrite() is called when closing the file and should do any needed clean-up work, such as updating a length field inside the file.

You can create a new file format handler by implementing just six new functions as described above. There is a skeleton C file that defines examples of these six functions included with SoX. Refer to the file skel.c for an example of implementing a new file handler.

Implementing new effects requires implementing similar functions. The structure st_effect_t needs to be defined for each new effect.

```
typedef struct {
        char  *name;                    /* effect name */
        int   flags;                    /* this and that */
                                        /* process arguments */
        int   (*getopts)(eff_t effp, int argc, char **argv);
                                        /* start off effect */
        int   (*start)(eff_t effp);
                                        /* do a buffer */
        int   (*flow)(eff_t effp, LONG *ibuf, LONG *obuf,
                      LONG *isamp, LONG *osamp);
                                        /* drain out at end */
        int   (*drain)(eff_t effp, LONG *obuf, LONG *osamp);
        int   (*stop)(eff_t effp);      /* finish up effect */
} st_effect_t;
```

An example of this structure for the low-pass filter is shown below. Refer to the file lowp.c for the actual implementation of these functions.

```
{"lowp", 0,
 st_lowp_getopts, st_lowp_start, st_lowp_flow,
 st_null_drain, st_lowp_stop},
```

The name field contains a string that the user will specify on the command line to invoke this effect. In this case, it is the string lowp.

The flags field contains flags for special features of this effect. This includes the ST_EFF_CHAN flag if the effect can cause the number of channels on the output side to be different than the number on the input side. ST_EFF_RATE is specified when the sample rate on the output side can differ from the input side. ST_EFF_MCHAN is used if your effect can handle audio data with more then one channel. If the ST_EFF_MCHAN is not specified, SoX will split your audio data into separate channels and run each channel through the effects engine separately.

The function getopts() will be passed through all command line options that the user passed in. This function must parse those options and store them in a reserved memory area.

The start() function will be called to let the effect set up any initial variables.

The flow() function will be called to pass in audio data to the effect from the input audio file. The flow effect should read in audio data from the ibuf and output audio data in to the obuf. It should also modify the ilen and olen variable to reflect the amount of data it read in and how much it placed into the obuf. The `flow()` function is not required to read any data or write any data, but it must inform the library when it does using the `ilen` and `olen` variables.

Once all the audio data has been read in, SoX will begin to call the `drain()` function to let the effect drain out any extra audio data it has been buffering up. SoX will continue to call the `drain()` function until the effect stops returning data. Not many effects need to make use of this function. In that case, you can just use the predefined function `st_null_drain` which does nothing.

The `stop()` function will be called last so that any clean-up work can be done.

There is a C file called skeleff.c that implements the minimum functions required to create a new effect and can be used as a template.

`libst` is a great tool for doing quick prototypes of new filters and effects for audio data. It allows you to worry about your algorithms and not worry about implementing user interfaces. It also allows you to work with just the audio data of any standard audio file format without having to understand how the data is stored.

The Synthesis ToolKit (STK) in C++

Perry R. Cook and Gary Scavone

1 Motivations

The Synthesis ToolKit (STK) in C++ was motivated in part by the desire to bring together numerous sound synthesis algorithms that we had developed over the course of three decades in such diverse environments and languages as SmallTalk, Lisp, real-time synthesis in Motorola DSP56001 assembler (and connected using the NeXTStep MusicKit), Objective C, and ANSI C code. STK was designed to provide a portable, object-oriented, user-extensible environment for real-time audio and sound synthesis development by exploiting the increasing efficiency and power of modern host processors, as well as performance improvements of optimizing C compilers. There was also a desire to establish a better framework for implementing many of the "intelligent player" objects as discussed in [17], [18], and [13], and a motivation to make rapid experimentation with custom controllers coupled to new synthesis algorithms [10], [36].

Finally, for future research, teaching, and music composition and performance, there was a desire to create a set of examples of different synthesis techniques which wherever possible share a common interface, but allow the unique features of each particular synthesis algorithm to be exploited. By sharing a common interface, algorithms can be rapidly compared. In addition, synthesis can be accomplished in a scaleable fashion, by selecting the algorithm that accomplishes a desired task in the most efficient and/or expressive manner.

The Synthesis ToolKit is made available freely for academic and research uses and is provided on the CD-ROM accompanying this book.

The latest version is available via various FTP servers, including Princeton Computer Science, the Princeton Sound Kitchen, and the Stanford Center for Computer Research in Music and Acoustics (CCRMA). Numerous algorithms from STK have been ported to other sound synthesis systems such as the Vanilla Sound Server from NCSA, Csound, MSP, and SuperCollider.

2 Overview

Specific design goals have included cross-platform functionality, ease of use, instructional code examples, and real-time control. Classes can be divided into three categories:

(1) basic audio sample sources and manipulators called *unit generators*,

(2) sound synthesis and audio signal processing algorithms built from unit generators, and

(3) control signal and system-dependent handlers.

Sound synthesis algorithms include additive (Fourier) synthesis, subtractive synthesis, frequency modulation synthesis of various topologies, modal (resonant filter) synthesis, a variety of physical models including stringed and wind instruments, and physically inspired stochastic event models for the synthesis of particle sounds.

Nearly all of STK is written in generic C and C++ and can be compiled on any system with a C++ compiler. Cross-platform functionality is further aided by encapsulating operating system dependencies, such as real-time sound and MIDI input/output, within just a few classes.

Complete class documentation, a tutorial, and usage information are provided in HTML and PDF formats with the STK distribution, as well as from the STK website: http://www-ccrma.stanford.edu/software/stk/.

3 Unit Generators

Nearly all Synthesis ToolKit classes inherit from a master class called *Stk*. The *Stk* class provides a variety of common functionality, including error handling, sample rate control, and byte-swapping. In addition, it offers a convenient place to centralize machine-specific #defines, switches, and global parameters. For example, distinct operating system and architecture definitions in *Stk* allow appropriate byte-swapping, socket and thread control, and audio/MIDI Application Programming Interface (API) selection to occur for all STK classes during program compilation and linking. The Synthesis ToolKit currently includes real-time audio input/output and MIDI input support for the Windows, Linux, Macintosh OS X, and IRIX operating systems.

The complementary base classes, *WvIn* and *WvOut*, handle audio data input and output in .wav, .snd, .aiff, .mat (MATLAB MAT-file), and .raw (STK raw) file formats. Protected subclasses provide real-time audio input/output from sound hardware and internet *streaming* TCP/IP connections. *WvIn* provides interpolating services and the subclass *WaveLoop* allows for file looping.

Audio and control signals throughout STK are stored and passed using a floating point data type, the exact precision of which can be controlled using the MY_FLOAT #define statement in the *Stk* class. Thus, the toolkit can use any normalization scheme desired. The base instruments and algorithms are implemented with a general audio sample dynamic maximum of approximately +/-1.0, and the *WvIn* and *WvOut* classes and subclasses scale appropriately for DAC or soundfile input and output.

All audio-sample-based unit generators implement a `tick()` method in which their fundamental sample calculations are performed. Some unit generators are only sample sources, such as the simple envelope generator *Envelope*, the noise generator *Noise*, or any of the *WvIn* objects. These source-only objects return MY_FLOAT values, but take no input arguments to their `tick()` function. Consumer-only objects like the *WvOut* classes take a MY_FLOAT argument and return void. Objects like filters, delay lines, etc., both take and yield a MY_FLOAT sample in their `tick()` function. All objects which are sources of audio samples implement a method `lastOut()`, which returns the last computed sample. This allows a single source to feed multiple sample consuming objects without necessitating an interim storage variable. Further, since each object saves its output state in an internally protected variable, bugs arising from the use of shared, nonprotected *patchpoints* are avoided. As a simple example, an algorithm can be constructed which reads a one-channel input stream from a file, filters it, multiplies it by a time-varying envelope, and writes the output to a signed 16-bit WAV formatted file. Only the constructor (function which creates and initializes unit generators and object variables), and the `tick()` functions are shown below. For a good introductory reference on C++, consult [43].

```
ExampleClass :: ExampleClass() {
envelope = new Envelope;
```

```
input = new WvIn("infile.snd");
filter = new OnePole;
output = new WvOut("outfile.wav", 1, WVOUT_WAV, STK_SINT16);
}


void ExampleClass :: tick(void) {
output->tick(envelope->tick() * filter->tick(input->tick()));
return;
}
```

The calculations necessary to implement the Karplus-Strong [20] plucked string algorithm (provided by the STK *Plucked* class) can be implemented as in the following tick() function:

```
MY_FLOAT Plucked :: tick(void) {
  output = delay->tick(filter->tick(delay->lastOut() * gain));
  return output;
}
```

The Synthesis ToolKit unit generator classes take and/or yield single sample values via their `tick()` function. This allows for minimum memory usage, the ability to modularly build short (one sample) recursive loops, and guaranteed minimum latency through the system. In addition, all unit generators provide an overloaded `tick()` function which allows for vector-based calculations. Vectorized unit generators take and/or yield pointers to arrays of sample values, and improve performance significantly depending on the processor type and vector size. Multichannel processing in the *WvIn* and *WvOut* classes is handled by `tickFrame()` functions, including overloaded vector-based variants.

4   Music Synthesis Algorithms

Algorithms supported in the Synthesis ToolKit include simple oscillator-based additive synthesis, subtractive synthesis, frequency modulation nonlinear synthesis, modal synthesis, PCM sampling synthesis, and physical models of many types. Consult [27], [34], and [39] for more information on digital audio processing and music synthesis (also see the other articles in this chapter). Additive analysis/synthesis, also called Fourier synthesis, is covered in [29], [38]. In subtractive synthesis, a complex sound is filtered to shape the spectrum into a desired pattern. The most popular historical forms of subtractive synthesis involve the phase and channel VoCoder (voice coder) [16], [30], [15], and Linear Predictive Coding (LPC) [2], [26], [31], [39]. Frequency modulation synthesis [4], [5] and WaveShaping [24] employ nonlinear warping of basic functions (like sine waves) to create a complex spectrum. Modal synthesis models individual physical resonances of an instrument using resonant filters, excited by parametric or analyzed excitations [1], [41], [23]. Physical models endeavor to solve the physics of instruments in the time-domain, typically by numerical solution of the differential traveling-wave equation, to synthesize sound [37], [19], [8], [10], [28], [6], [35], and [36]. STK contains physical models for flute, clarinet, saxophone, brass, plucked string, and bowed string instruments. (See Cook's article "Introduction to Physical Modeling" (see *Audio Anecdotes I*)).

The Synthesis ToolKit provides multiple models of the voice, and more vocal synthesis models are planned for the future. References on voice synthesis using subtractive, FM, and physical modeling include [21], [33], [22], [5], [3], [9], [11], [12], and [25].

Particle-models based on statistical/physical models [14] are also implemented in STK. These models, combined with modal and PCM wavetable techniques, provide the framework for parametric synthesis of a large variety of real-world sounds and sound effects.

5 Audio Effects Algorithms

The Synthesis ToolKit includes a few simple delay-based effects classes such as reverberation (modeling of sound reflections in rooms), chorus (simulating the effect of multiple sound sources from a single sound), and pitch shifting. See [32] and the book by [34] for more details on reverberation and effects processing.

6 SKINI: Yet Another "Better" MIDI?

A simple, though extensible, control protocol called SKINI was developed for the Synthesis ToolKit. SKINI (Synthesis toolKit Instrument Network Interface) extends MIDI in incremental ways, specifically in representation accuracy by allowing floating point note numbers (enabling microtuning for example), floating point control values, and double-precision time stamps and delta-time values. Further, a text message basis for the control stream is used to allow for easy creation of SKINI files (anything that can produce and manipulate formatted text) and debugging of SKINI control consumers and providers. Finally, SKINI goes beyond MIDI in that it allows for parametric control curves and functions to be specified and used. This allows continuous control streams to be potentially lower in bandwidth than MIDI (hence, part of the name SKINI), yet higher in resolution and quality because the control functions are *rendered* in the instrument and/or in a performer-expert class which controls the instrument. Expressive figures like trills, drum rolls, characteristic pitch bends, heavy-metal guitar hammer-ons, etc., can all be specified and called up using text messages. More sophisticated protocols for music control have been proposed and implemented [7], but SKINI provides a simple solution by which STK can support a unified control interface across multiple platforms, multiple control signal sources such as GUIs of various flavors, MIDI controllers and score files, and simple text-based connections between processes on a single machine and across networks.

To support SKINI control messages, the ToolKit provides a SKINI parsing class, *SKINI*. See Appendix 4 of this document, and the ToolKit documentation, for information on the SKINI format and new features as they develop. An input control handling class, *Messager*, is provided with STK in order to simplify the acquisition and distribution of control messages from a variety of sources. *Messager* can accept and parse simultaneous SKINI control input streams via pipe, socket, and/or MIDI connections, as well as SKINI scorefiles.

7   GUI Support

In keeping with cross-platform support and compatibility, simple Graphical User Interfaces (GUIs) for Synthesis ToolKit instruments have been implemented in Tcl/Tk [42]. These allow simple real-time editing of the important control parameters of each synthesis algorithm using standard MIDI control messages, so MIDI controllers can be exchanged for GUI control enabling real-time expressive synthesis control. The GUI used to demonstrate nearly all of the STK synthesis algorithms is shown in Figure 1.

Acknowledgments

Many ideas for the Synthesis ToolKit and the algorithms came from people at CCRMA, specifically Julius Smith, John Chowning, and Max Mathews. Dexter Morrill and Chris Chafe were instrumental in forming opinions on controllers and protocols for real-time synthesis. The NeXT

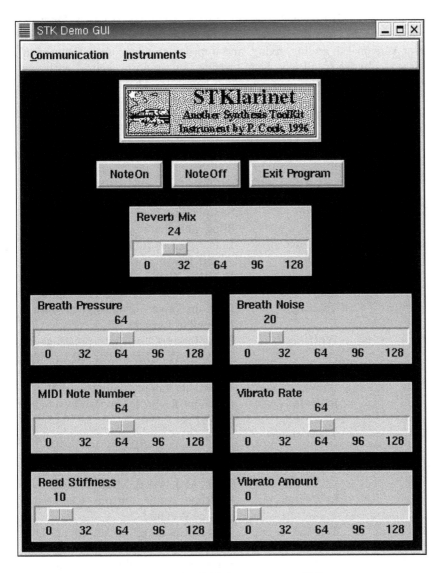

Figure 1. The STK demonstration GUI.

MusicKit and ZIPI have also been inspirational and instructive. Perry especially thanks Gary for taking over lots of the maintenance of the ToolKit after Version 1.0, adding, fixing, and improving greatly upon the original release. Thanks to all who have provided bug reports, helped with new sound I/O capabilities, and provided support. Thanks to Tim Stilson for porting the first ToolKit classes to Linux, Bill Putnam for providing help on Windows real-time classes, and Dave Chisholm for updating the DirectSound code.

Appendix A: Unit Generators

Master Class:	Stk.cpp	Sample rate, byte-swapping, error handling, and shared global functionality
Sources:	Envelope.cpp	Linearly Goes to Target by Rate
	ADSR.cpp	ADSR Flavor of Envelope
	Noise.cpp	Random Number Generator
	SubNoise.cpp	Random Numbers each N samples
	Table.cpp	Look-up Table (assumes given data in big-endian format)
	WvIn.cpp	Data Input Class (interpolating) for RAW, WAV, SND (AU), AIFF, MAT-file files
	WaveLoop.cpp	Wavetable looping (subclass of WvIn)
	RtWvIn.cpp	Realtime Audio Input Class (subclass of WvIn)
	TcpWvIn.cpp	Audio Streaming (socket server) Input Class (subclass of WvIn)
Sinks:	WvOut.cpp	Output Master Class for RAW, WAV, SND (AU), AIFF, MAT-file files
	RtWvOut.cpp	Realtime Audio Output Class (subclass of WvOut)
	TcpWvOut.cpp	Audio Streaming (socket client) Output Class (subclass of WvOut)
Duplex:	RtDuplex.cpp	Synchronous Real-time Audio Input/Output Class
Filters:	Filter.cpp	Filter Master Class
	OneZero.cpp	One Zero Filter
	OnePole.cpp	One Pole Filter
	PoleZero.cpp	One Pole/One Zero Filter
	TwoZero.cpp	Two Zero Filter

	TwoPole.cpp	Two Pole Filter
	BiQuad.cpp	Two Pole/Two Zero Filter
	FormSwep.cpp	Sweepable BiQuad Filter (goes to target by rate)
	Delay.cpp	NonInterpolating Delay Line Class
	DelayL.cpp	Linearly Interpolating Delay Line (subclass of Delay)
	DelayA.cpp	All-Pass Interpolating Delay Line (subclass of Delay)
Non-Linear:	JetTabl.cpp	Cubic Jet Nonlinearity
	BowTabl.cpp	x^(-3) Bow Nonlinearity
	ReedTabl.cpp	One Breakpoint Saturating Reed Nonlinearity
Derived:	Modulate.cpp	Periodic and Random Vibrato: WvIn, SubNoise, OnePole
	SingWave.cpp	Looping Wavetable with: Modulate, WaveLoop, Envelope

Appendix B: Algorithms and Instruments

Each class is either listed with some of the unit generators it uses, or in terms of the algorithm it implements. All inherit from Instrmnt, which inherits from Stk.

Simple.cpp	Simple Instrument	Pulse oscillator + resonant filtered noise
Plucked.cpp	Basic Plucked String	DelayA, OneZero, OnePole, Noise
StifKarp.cpp	Plucked String with Stiffness	DelayA, DelayL, OneZero, BiQuad, Noise
PluckTwo.cpp	Not So Basic Pluck	DelayL, DlineA, OneZero
Mandolin.cpp	Commuted Mandolin	Subclass of PluckTwo, with body
Bowed.cpp	So So Bowed String	DelayL, BowTabl, OnePole, BiQuad, WaveLoop, ADSR
Brass.cpp	Not So Bad Brass Instrument	DelayA, BiQuad, PoleZero, ADSR, WaveLoop

Clarinet.cpp	Pretty Good Clarinet	DelayL, ReedTabl, OneZero, Envelope, Noise, WaveLoop
BlowHole.cpp	Clarinet with Tone/Vent Holes	DelayL, ReedTabl, OneZero, Envelope, Noise, WaveLoop
Saxofony.cpp	A Faux Saxophone	DelayL, ReedTabl, OneZero, Envelope, Noise, WaveLoop
Flute.cpp	Pretty Good Flute	JetTabl, DelayL, OnePole, PoleZero, Noise, WaveLoop
BlowBotl.cpp	Blown Bottle	JetTabl, BiQuad, PoleZero, Noise, ADSR, WaveLoop
BandedWG.cpp	Banded Waveguide Meta-Object	Delay, BowTabl, ADSR, BiQuad
Modal.cpp	N Resonances	Envelope, WaveLoop, BiQuad, OnePole
ModalBar.cpp	Various presets	4 Resonance Models
FM.cpp	N Operator FM Master	ADSR, WaveLoop, TwoZero
HevyMetl.cpp	Distorted FM Synthesizer	3 Cascade with FB Modulator
PercFlut.cpp	Percussive Flute	3 Cascade Operators
Rhodey.cpp	Rhodes-Like Electric Piano	2 Parallel Simple FMs
Wurley.cpp	Wurlitzer Electric Piano	2 Parallel Simple FMs
TubeBell.cpp	Classic FM Bell	2 Parallel Simple FMs
FMVoices.cpp	3 Formant FM Voice	3 Carriers Share 1 Modulator
VoicForm.cpp	4 Formant Voice Synthesis	FormSwep, SingWave, OnePole, OneZero, Noise
BeeThree.cpp	Cheezy Additive Organ	4 Oscillators Additive
Sampler.cpp	Sampling Synthesizer	5 each ADSR, WvIn, WaveLoop, OnePole
Moog.cpp	Swept Filter	Sampler with Swept Filter
Resonate.cpp	Filtered Noise	ADSR, BiQuad, Noise
Drummer.cpp	Drum Synthesizer	Bunch of WvIns, and OnePole
Shakers.cpp	PhISM statistical model for shakers and real-world sound effects	

Mesh2D.cpp	Two-dimensional, rectilinear digital waveguide mesh	
Whistle.cpp	Hybrid physical/spectral model of a police whistle	
Reverb.cpp	Reverberator Effects Processor	Master Class for reverberators
JCRev.cpp	Chowning Reverberator	3 series allpass units, 4 parallel combs, 2 stereo delays
NRev.cpp	Another CCRMA Reverb	8 allpass, 6 parallel comb filters
PRCRev.cpp	Dirt Cheap Reverb by Cook	2 allpass, 2 comb filters
Flanger.cpp	Flanger Effects Processor	DelayL, WaveLoop
Chorus.cpp	Chorus Effects Processor	DelayL, WaveLoop
PitShift.cpp	Cheap Pitch Shifter	DelayL

Appendix C: Other Support Classes and Files

RtAudio.cpp	Multi-OS/API audio I/O routines
RtMidi.cpp	Multi-OS/API MIDI I/O routines
Messager.cpp	Pipe, Socket, and MIDI control message handling
Voicer.cpp	Multi-instrument voice manager
demo.cpp	Demonstration program for most synthesis algorithms
effects.cpp	Effects demonstration program
ragamatic.cpp	Nirvana just waiting to happen
SKINI.cpp	SKINI file/message parser object
SKINI.msg	#defines for often used and universal MIDI/SKINI symbols
SKINI.tbl	Table of SKINI messages, see Appendix 4.

Appendix D: SKINI Message Basics

The SKINI.tbl file contains an array of structures that are accessed by the parser object SKINI.cpp. The structure is defined as:

```
struct SKINISpec {
    char messageString[32];
    long  type;
    long data2;
```

```
    long data3;
};
```

where

- *messageString* is a distinct label defined in SKINI.tbl,

- *type* is the message type sent back from the SKINI parser, and

- *data*<n> is either

  NOPE: field not used, specifically, there aren't going to be
            any more fields on this line. So if there is a NOPE in
            data2, data3 won't even be checked

  SK_INT: byte (actually scanned as 32-bit signed long int). If it's
            a MIDI data field which is required to be an integer,
            like a controller number, it's 0-127. Otherwise, get
            creative with SK_INTs.

  SK_DBL: double precision floating point. SKINI uses these in
            the MIDI context for note numbers with micro-tuning,
            velocities, controller values, etc.

  SK_STR: only valid in final field. This allows (nearly) arbitrary
            message types to be supported by simply scanning the
            string to EndOfLine and then passing it to a more in-
            telligent handler. For example, MIDI SYSEX (system
            exclusive) messages of up to 256 bytes can be read as
            space-delimited integers into the 1K SK_STR buffer.
            Longer bulk dumps, soundfiles, etc. should be han-
            dled as a new message type pointing to a FileName,
            Socket, or something else stored in the SK_STR field,
            or as a new type of multiline message.

Here are a few lines from the SKINI.tbl file:

```
{"NoteOff",      __SK_NoteOff_,        SK_DBL,           SK_DBL},
{"NoteOn",       __SK_NoteOn_,         SK_DBL,           SK_DBL},
{"ControlChange",__SK_ControlChange_,SK_INT,             SK_DBL},
{"Volume",       __SK_ControlChange_,__SK_Volume_,       SK_DBL},
{"StringDamping",__SK_ControlChange_,__SK_StringDamping_,SK_DBL},
{"StringDetune", __SK_ControlChange_,__SK_StringDetune_, SK_DBL},
```

The first three types are basic MIDI messages. The first two would
cause the parser, after recognizing a match of the string "NoteOff" or
"NoteOn," to set the message type to 128 or 144 (__SK_NoteOff_ and

_SK_NoteOn_ are #defined in the file SKINI.msg to be the MIDI byte value, without channel, of the actual MIDI messages for NoteOn and NoteOff). The parser would then set the time or delta time (this is always done and is therefore not described in the SKINI message structure). The next two fields would be scanned as double-precision floats and assigned to the byteTwo and byteThree variables of the SKINI parser. The remainder of the line is stashed in the remainderString variable.

The ControlChange line is basically the same as NoteOn and NoteOff, but the second data byte is set to an integer (for checking later as to what MIDI control is being changed). The Volume line is a SKINI / MIDI extension message, which behaves like a ControlChange message with the controller number set explicitly to the value for MIDI Volume (7). Thus, the following two lines would accomplish the same changing of MIDI volume on channel 2:

```
ControlChange    0.000000    2    7       64.1
Volume           0.000000    2    64.1
```

The StringDamping and StringDetune messages behave the same as the Volume message, but use Control Numbers which are not specifically nailed-down in MIDI. Note that these Control Numbers are carried around as long integers, and thus are not limited to the range 0–127. If, however, you want to use a MIDI controller to play an instrument, using controller numbers in the range of 0–127 might make sense.

Annotated Bibliography

[1] J. Adrien. "Etude de structures complexes vibrantes, application-la synthse par modeles physiques." Ph.D. diss., Université Paris VI, 1988.

[2] B. Alta. "Speech Analysis and Synthesis by Linear Prediction of the Speech Wave." *Journal of the Acoustical Society of America* 47.65:A (1970), 637–655.

[3] G. Carlson and L. Neovius. "Implementations of Synthesis Models for Speech and Singing." *STL-Quarterly Progress and Status Report* 2-3, pp. 63-67. Stockholm, Sweden: KTH.

[4] J. Chowning. "The Synthesis of Complex Audio Spectra by Means of Frequency Modulation." *Journal of the Audio Engineering Society* 21:7 (1973), 526-534.

[5] J. Chowning. "Computer Synthesis of the Singing Voice." In *Research Aspects on Singing*, pp. 4-13. Stockholm, Sweden: KTH, 1981.

[6] CMJ. *Computer Music Journal.* Special Issues on Physical Modeling 16:4 & 17:1 (1992-3).

[7] CMJ. *Computer Music Journal.* Special Issue on ZIPI 18:4 (1994).

[8] P. Cook. "TBone: An Interactive Waveguide Brass Instrument Synthesis Workbench for the NeXT Machine." In *Proc. International Computer Music Conference*, pp. 297–299. San Francisco, CA: ICMA, 1991.

[9] P. Cook. "LECTOR: An Ecclesiastical Latin Control Language for the SPASM/Singer Instrument." In *Proc. International Computer Music Conference*, pp. 319–321. San Francisco, CA: ICMA, 1991.

[10] P. Cook. "A Meta-Wind-Instrument Physical Model, and a Meta-Controller for Real-Time Performance Control." In *Proc. International Computer Music Conference*, pp. 273–276. San Francisco, CA: ICMA, 1992.

[11] P. Cook. "SPASM: A Real-Time Vocal Tract Physical Model Editor/Controller and Singer: The Companion Software Synthesis System." Colloque les modeles physiques dans l'analyse, la production et la creation sonore, ACROE, Grenoble, 1990. Published in *Computer Music Journal* 17:1 (1992), 30–44.

[12] P. Cook, D. Kamarotos, T. Diamantopoulos, and G. Philippis. "IGDIS: A Modern Greek Text to Speech/Singing Program for the SPASM/Singer Instrument." In *Proceedings of the International Computer Music Conference*, pp. 387–389. San Francisco, CA: ICMA, 1993.

[13] P. Cook. "A Hierarchical System for Controlling Synthesis by Physical Modeling." In *Proceedings of the International Computer Music Conference*, pp. 108–109. San Francisco, CA: ICMA, 1993.

[14] P. Cook. "Physically Informed Sonic Modeling: Synthesis of Percussive Sounds." *Computer Music Journal* 21:3 (1997), 38–49.

[15] M. Dolson. "The Phase Vocoder: A Tutorial." *Computer Music Journal* 10:4 (1986), 14–27.

[16] H. Dudley. "The Vocoder." *Bell Laboratories Record.* December (1939).

[17] B. Garton. "Virtual Performance Modeling." In *Proceedings of the International Computer Music Conference*, pp. 219–222. San Francisco, CA: ICMA, 1992.

[18] Z. Janosy, M. Karjalainen, and V. Valimaki. "Intelligent Synthesis Control with Applications to a Physical Model of the Acoustic Guitar." In *Proceedings of the International Computer Music Conference*, pp. 402–406. San Francisco, CA: ICMA, 1994.

[19] M. Karjalainen, U. Laine, T. Laakso, and V. Valimaki. "Transmission Line Modeling and Real-Time Synthesis of String and Wind Instruments." In *Proceedings of the International Computer Music Conference*, pp. 293–296. San Francisco, CA: ICMA, 1991.

[20] K. Karpus and A. Strong. "Digital Synthesis of Plucked-String and Drum Timbres." *Computer Music Journal* 7:2 (1983), 43–55.

[21] J. Kelly and C. Lochbaum. "Speech Synthesis." In *Proc. Fourth Intern. Congress Acoustics*, Paper G42, pp.1–4, ICIAM, 1962.

[22] D. Klatt. "Software for a Cascade/Parallel Formant Synthesizer." *Journal of the Acoustical Society of America* 67:3 (1980), 971–995.

[23] J. Larouche and J. Meillier. "Multichannel Excitation/Filter Modeling of Percussive Sounds with Application to the Piano." *IEEE Trans. Speech and Audio* 2:2(1994), 329–344.

[24] M. LeBrun. "Digital Waveshaping Synthesis." *Journal of the Audio Engineering Society* 27:4 (1979), 250–266.

[25] R. Maher. "Turnable Bandpass Filters in Music Synthesis." *Audio Engineering Society Conference*, Paper Number 4098(L2), 1995.

[26] J. Makhoul. "Linear Prediction: A Tutorial Review." In *Proc. of the IEEE, Volume 63*, pp. 561-580, 1975.

[27] M. Matthews and J. Pierce. *Some Current Directions in Computer Music Research.* Cambridge, MA: MIT Press, 1989.

[28] M. McIntyre, R. Schumacher, and J. Woodhouse. "On the Oscillations of Musical Instruments." *Journal of the Acoustical Society of America* 74:5 (1983), 1325–1345.

[29] R. McAulay and T. Quatieri. "Speech Analysis/Synthesis Based on a Sinusoidal Representation." *IEEE Trans. Acoust. Speech and Sig. Proc.* ASSP 34:4 (1986), 744–754.

[30] A. Moorer. "The Use of the Phase Vocoder in Computer Music Applications." *Journal of the Audio Engineering Society* 26:1–2 (1978), 42–45.

[31] A. Moorer. "The Use of Linear Prediction of Speech in Computer Music Applications." *Journal of the Audio Engineering Society* 27:3 (1979), 134–140.

[32] A. Moorer. "About this Reverberation Business." *Computer Music Journal* 3:2 (1979), 13–28.

[33] L. Rabiner. "Digital Formant Synthesizer." *Journal of the Acoustical Society of America* 43:4 (1968), 822–828.

[34] C. Roads. *The Computer Music Tutorial.* Cambridge, MA: MIT Press, 1976.

[35] G. Scavone. "An Acoustic Analysis of Single-Reed Woodwind Instruments, with an Emphasis on Design and Performance Issues and Digital Waveguide Modeling Techniques." Ph.D. diss, Stanford University, 1997.

[36] G. Scavone and P. Cook. "Real-Time Computer Modeling of Woodwind Instruments." In *Proc. of Intl. Symposium on Musical Acoustics*, 1998.

[37] J. Smith. *Musical Applications of Digital Waveguides.* Stanford University Center for Computer Research in Music and Acoustics. Report STAN-M-39, 1987.

[38] J. Smith and X. Serra. "PARSHL: An Analysis/Synthesis Program for Non-Harmonic Sounds Based on a Sinusoidal Representation." In *Proceedings of the International Computer Music Conference*, pp. 290–297. San Francisco, CA: ICMA, 1987.

[39] K. Steiglitz and P. Lansky. "Synthesis of Timbral Families by Warped Linear Prediction." *Computer Music Journal* 5:3 (1981), 45–49.

[40] K. Steiglitz. *Digital Signal Processing Primer.* New York: Addison-Wesley, 1996.

[41] J. Wawrzynek. "VSLI Models for Sound Synthesis." In *Current Directions in Computer Music Research*, edited by M. Matthews and J. Pierce, pp. 113–148. Cambridge, MA: MIT Press, 1989.

[42] B. Welch. *Practical Programming in Tcl and Tk*. Saddle River, NJ: Prentice-Hall, 1995.

[43] P. Winston. *On to C++*. New York: Addison-Wesley, 1994.

The QEDesign Filter Design Package

Chris Bore

QEDesign, by Momentum Data Systems, is a family of easy-to-use digital filter design packages for Microsoft's Windows 9x and NT. QEDesign designs FIR and IIR filters. The packages output filter coefficients as ASCII text files. Optional DSP assembler and C code generators are available as well. A demonstration copy of QEDesign is provided on the CD-ROM accompanying this book.

QEDesign supports FIR filter design by the window and Parks McLellan (equiripple) methods. Many window functions are available including Hanning, Hamming, Blackman, Harris, Kaiser, and cosine windows. FIR designs include arbitrary magnitude, hilbert, halfband, and raised cosine shapes. Window filters up to 8,192 coefficients can be designed. The Parks McLellan design has choices to allow modification of the "equiripple" characteristic and to specify rolloff. The program uses extended arithmetic—essential in the design of long filters. Parks McLellan filters can be designed with up to 4,089 coefficients.

QEDesign supports IIR filter designs using the bilinear and impulse invariant methods, based on Butterworth, Bessel, Tschbyschev, and Elliptic prototypes. IIR designs can be cascade or parallel, using either direct form I or direct form II implementation. IIR filters can be specified by band attenuations, or through direct input of z domain or s domain parameters. IIR filter orders up to 80 (low and high pass) or 160 (band and arbitrary group delay) can be designed.

Filter design requires very accurate calculations: QEDesign uses 64-bit floating point arithmetic throughout, with 128-bit for critical design areas. QEDesign handles coefficient quantization from 8 to 32 bits in fixed and floating point format, and models the effects of quantization on the filter's actual response. Filters can have nominal or maximum gain of 1, and scaling for quantization effects. For selected filter types, the transition regions can be specified.

A Windows demonstration version of QEDesign1000 is included on the CD-ROM accompanying this book. This version is fully functional except it does not allow the user to save the session. Please visit the Momentum Data Systems web site, http://www.mds.com, for information on all of our products as well as the latest evaluation copies of QEDdesign.

For background on FIR and IIR filters, see Allman's articles "Finite Impulse Response Filters," (page 67), and "Infinite Impulse Response Filters," (page 79). Readers might also be interested in visiting our free online DSP class at http://www.mds.com/training/on-line that cover the following topics:

- Basics. Sampling, aliasing, reconstruction and quantization.

- Time domain processing. Correlation and convolution.

- Frequency analysis. Fourier transforms, resolution, spectral leakage, and windowing.

- Filtering. Including FIR filters.

- IIR filters. Design, realization, and quantization effects.

- DSP processors. Real-world requirements, special features.

- Programming a DSP processor.

Music Theory

Basic Music Theory: Notation, Scales, and Chords

Benjamin Tomassetti

Fundamental to the study of music is pitch theory, which includes such topics as pitch names and definitions, music notation, intervals, scales, chords, and an introduction to diatonic harmony. In a larger and somewhat more abstract sense, pitch theory, as it applies to the majority of western European music, can be defined as the general controlling principles of *harmonic* and *melodic consonance* and *dissonance* as they apply to distinctly tuned stable frequencies.

1 Pitch Definitions: The Musical Alphabet

In the most general sense, the word *pitch* is analogous to frequency, as measured in Hertz. Audio engineers think in terms of frequencies; musicians think in terms of pitches. For example, the pitch Middle C on a tuned piano has a frequency of 261.6 Hz. The tuning standard used in the US is A below Middle C equals 440 Hz. One can purchase a tuning fork which will vibrate at 440 cycles per second. Pitch also refers to one's perception of high and low frequencies and to one's musical memory. For example, does an individual have a good sense of pitch? If so, that individual would have a good musical memory, hold a steady sense of pitch, and remember the pitch level, or tonality, of the original melody. This means that an individual with a good sense of pitch would be able to sing back musical examples of more than seven notes in one hearing, sing stable pitches that don't waver, and remain "in key" during the sing back.

The word *pitch* also means specific named pitches (or notes) in a music composition. In the United States, we use the first seven letters of the alphabet as the names of the basic pitches, or notes. The musical alphabet consists of the letter names A, B, C, D, E, F, and G. The typical order of the letters A through G would sound like a type of musical scale, ascending in seven incremental steps, when played on an instrument, such as a piano. Conversely, the reverse order of the letters A through G would sound like the same scale descending in seven steps. When we play the eighth note, the letter name repeats itself (A, for example), and the exact pitch is exactly an *octave* higher (or lower) than the first note name, where the scale began. An octave constitutes the ratio of 2:1 between two pitches. For example, if the pitch A below Middle C has a frequency of 440 Hz, then the A an octave higher (A above Middle C) has a frequency of 880 Hz

2   Pitch Notation: The Grand Staff

Pitches are notated on a musical *staff*. The plural of staff is staves. A staff is a type of grid with five horizontal lines evenly spaced. On the staff is a *clef* that identifies the exact placement of each named pitch within its grid. The *grand staff* contains two *staves*, and each *staff* has its own distinct *clef*. Looking at Figure 1, the top staff has a *treble clef* and the bottom staff has a *bass clef*. The notes written in the *treble clef* are generally higher in pitch (frequency) than the notes written in the *bass clef*.

When looking at a musical staff, one always counts the lines of the staff from the bottom up: The fifth line is the top line. The treble clef specifically identifies the note G by curving around the second line of the staff. Historically, the treble was originally printed as a floridly cursive capital letter G, and is sometimes called the *G-clef*. The bass clef identifies the note F by the placement of the two dots on both sides of the fourth line. This clef was originally written as a capital letter F, and it too has been typographically changed over time. Figure 2 shows the correct placement for the notes G and F in a grand staff.

Figure 1. The grand staff.

Figure 2. The grand staff with the guide notes, treble clef G, and bass clef F.

Figure 3. The grand staff with the guide notes and with Middle C written in both the treble and bass clefs.

By beginning on the G in the treble clef, we can systematically ascend and descend to identify the placement of the other notes from the musical alphabet. Consider that G is written on the second line of the treble staff (the staff transects the note). The next note above is A, and it is written in the space between the second and third lines of the staff. The note B is directly above A, and is written on the third line. The order of notes ascending from G is A, B, C, D, E, F, and G again. This continues, in theory, forever. If needed, we can extend the staff by the use of *leger lines*. A leger line is a short horizontal line that extends the staff, either above or below, to accommodate the notation of pitches that are either too high or too low in frequency to notate within the staff. The bass staff's system is built around F. By starting on the fourth line and systematically counting down, we can identify the other named notes. The next note down from F is E. It is written in the third space of the staff. The order of pitches down from F is E, D, C, B, A, G, and finally, F again. This continues, theoretically, forever. *Middle C* is the note where the two clefs historically come together. Start on the bass clef F in Figure 3, and systematically ascend five notes to *Middle C*. Next, start on treble G and incrementally descend five notes to *Middle C*. Notice that each Middle C is written on a *leger line*.

Notice that while Middle C is a specific pitch, it can be written in either staff, but it never is written exactly between the two staves. In fact the notes directly around Middle C, (the D and E above and the B and A below) are commonly written in either staff.

Figure 5 shows a common range of written pitches on the grand staff.

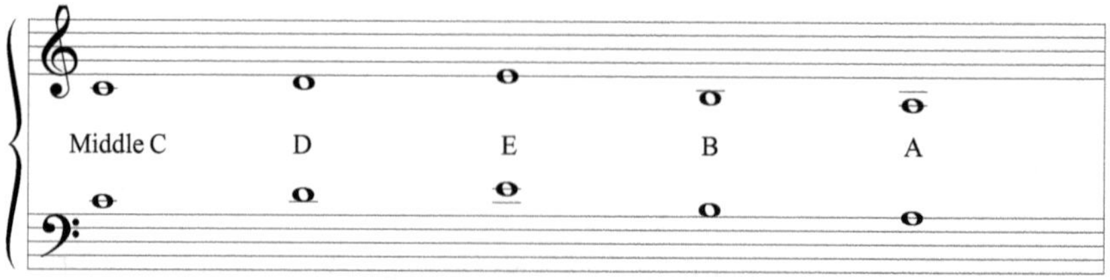

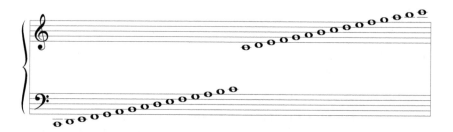

Figure 4. Middle C and the pitches directly around it written in both clefs (D and E above, and B and A below).

Figure 5. Four octaves of pitches written in the grand staff.

3   Accidentals

An *accidental* is simply a *sharp*, a *flat*, or a *natural* placed directly in front of a note in musical notation. A sharp raises the pitch of the note by one *semitone*, or *half-step*, and a *flat* lowers the pitch of the note by the same amount. A natural cancels a previously written sharp or flat, and is used to designate the plain letter-name pitch for any given note. A *semitone* can easily be identified on a piano keyboard as the distance between any two adjacent keys (either white or black). Figure 6 illustrates the pitches G, G-sharp, and G-flat, written in the treble clef, and the notes F, F-sharp, and F-flat written in the bass clef.

4   Enharmonics

When two notes are spelled differently, but are the same frequency, an *enharmonic* relationship occurs between the notes. For example, in Figure 7, there are two examples of different enharmonically spelled pitches.

Figure 6. The pitches G, G-sharp, and G-flat written in the treble clef, and the pitches F, F-sharp, and F-flat written in the bass clef.

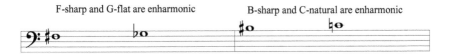

Figure 7. Enharmonics.

The first example contains the notes F# and Gb in the bass clef. Since F and G are adjacent white keys on a piano keyboard, the F# and Gb both share the same black key on the keyboard. F# and Gb are the same pitch, or frequency, but are spelled differently on the musical staff. The "rules" that dictate how to spell any given note in a musical passage are complex, and are beyond the scope of this article. The second example, also written in the bass clef, contains the notes B# and C. On a piano keyboard, the notes B and C are adjacent white keys, but there is no black key between them. By raising the pitch of the note B-natural to B#, the frequency of B# is the same as that for C-natural. Therefore, they are enharmonic.

5 Introduction to Intervals: Keyboard Steps

An interval is the musical distance between two pitches. Intervals are important to the study of theory because they are the foundation upon which all other pitch theory must reside. Without a firm understanding of intervals, how they are identified, classified, and inverted, it is difficult to discuss other musical concepts such as scales, chords, and harmony.

If we think of a semitone as a "keyboard step" (adjacent keys on a piano keyboard), it is easy to identify the two smallest intervals, *semitone* and *wholetone*. A semitone is the smallest interval used in the western European tradition, and is one keyboard step in size. For example, in

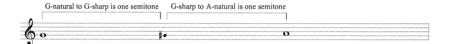

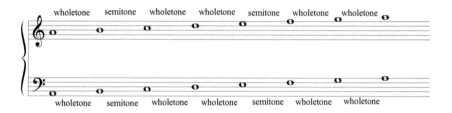

Figure 8. A wholetone is comprised of two semitones, or keyboard steps.

Figure 9. Intervals between the notes of the musical alphabet.

Figure 6, the G# is a semitone higher in pitch than the G. A *wholetone* is comprised of two keyboard steps, or two semitones. For example, in Figure 8, the written notes G and A are a wholetone, or whole step, apart. *Unison* is a special type of interval because it defines the distance between the exact same notes, or pitches. For example, the G written on the second line of the treble clef is in unison with another G written on the exact same line in the staff. Musicians often tune their instruments by comparing the frequency of a tuned standard (a piano, for example) with the frequency of their instrument. The musician then adjusts a setting on his/her instrument to make it play in *unison* with the tuning note supplied by the piano.

The way our pitch system evolved over the centuries has dictated that the musical alphabet is comprised of letter-named notes that are mostly a wholetone apart. There are two sets of letter-named notes that are only a semitone apart: E/F, and B/C.

Figure 9 shows the musical alphabet (letters A through A, an octave higher) written in the grand staff with the intervals identified between each set of adjacent notes.

6   Musical Intervals: Size and Quality

All intervals can be identified by the number of semitones (keyboard steps) contained between the two notes in question. Beyond the names *semitone* and *wholetone*, we use other names for all of the intervals. The name consists of a size (a number) and a quality (a word). To calculate the size of an interval, simply begin on the lower note, count it as *one* and count up the musical alphabet in order until you get to the correct letter-name of the higher note. For example, Figure 10(a) has two notes written in the treble clef: F and Gb. Count the F as *one*, and count up the alphabet until one gets to the letter G. G is the next letter. Therefore, the size of the interval between F and G is a *second*.

The quality of all intervals can be identified by thinking of the concept of *large versus small*. The concept of large versus small is very important to the classification of the quality of any given interval. Unfortunately, we use five different words to describe the qualities of the various intervals in music. These words are *major, minor, perfect, diminished,* and *augmented*. This system of naming intervals, while mathematically convoluted, has been handed-down through the centuries. To determine the quality of the interval in Figure 10(a), we count the semitones between the specific notes. There is one semitone (keyboard step) located between the notes F and Gb (F to Gb is one keyboard step). Because there

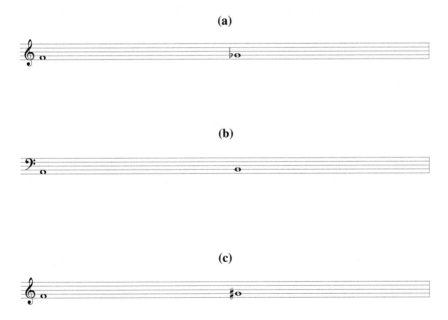

Figure 10. (a) The interval of a minor second. (b) The interval of a major second. (c) The interval of an augmented second.

is only one semitone contained within the specific *second* in Figure 10(a), this interval is called a *minor second*. A *minor second* is the same as a *semitone*.

Figure 10(b) shows two notes written in the bass clef: A and B. The size of the interval is a second, but the quality is different than in Figure 10(a). When one counts the semitones between A and B, it is determined that there are two semitones contained in this interval. The quality of this type of *second* is *major* because of the two semitones. A *major second* is the same as a *wholetone*. A major second is a larger second than a minor second (two semitones versus one semitone). The words *diminished* and *augmented*, in this example refer to seconds that are either smaller or larger than the typical minor second and major second. For example, the third example in Figure 10(c) contains the notes F and G#. When the semitone inventory is taken, it is determined that this particular second encompasses three semitones. A major second encompasses two semitones, so this is larger than a major second. This type of second is called an *augmented second;* it is one semitone larger than a *major second*. The majority of seconds used in musical scales in the western European tradition is *major seconds* and *minor seconds*. A *diminished second* is one semitone smaller than a minor second. Diminished seconds are rarely used in the majority of mainstream western European music.

7   Intervals: Thirds

Figure 11(a) has a number of musical thirds written in the treble clef, and Figure 11(b) has several intervals written in the bass clef. By counting the lower of the two notes as "one" in each example—count up the musical alphabet to the higher note—it can be easily determined that all of the intervals encompass a third. The first example uses the notes C and E. To determine the quality of this third, one must inventory the semitones (keyboard steps) between the two notes. The semitones contained within this interval are C-C#, C#-D, D-D#, D#-E. There are four semitones contained within this third. The quality of this third is *major*. This is a *major third*. It is now possible to qualify all thirds that encompass four semitones as *major thirds*.

The second example from Figure 11(a) uses the notes C and Eb. To determine the quality of this third, the same inventory procedure must be followed. The semitones contained within this third are C-C#, C#-D, D-Eb. Eb and D# are enharmonic. There are three semitones contained within this third, therefore, this is a *minor third*. All minor thirds encom-

(a)

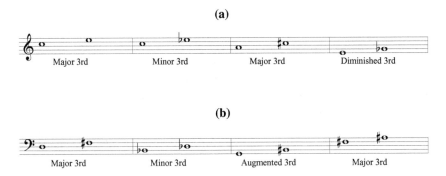

Figure 11. (a) Thirds written in the treble clef. (b) Thirds written in the bass clef.

pass three semitones, and are one semitone smaller than major thirds. The type of thirds found in the majority of scales used in the western European musical tradition are major thirds and minor thirds. An *augmented third* is one semitone larger than a *major third*, and a *diminished third* is one semitone smaller than a *minor third*.

Go through the remainder of the examples in Figures 11(a) and 11(b) and prove that the intervals are correctly identified by both size and quality.

8   Intervals: Fourths

Fourths belong to a class of intervals called *perfect consonance*. There is a long history of music theory in the western European tradition, and through the centuries, the intervals of unison, fourth, fifth, and octave have been classified as *perfect consonances*.

A *perfect fourth* is a fourth that encompasses five semitones. For example, in Figure 12, the first interval uses the notes B and E written in

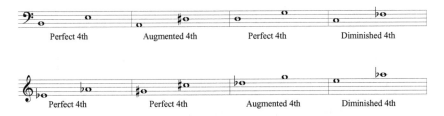

Figure 12. Fourths written in the treble and bass clefs.

the bass clef. By counting the B as "one," and counting up the musical alphabet to the note E, it is determined that the size of this interval is a fourth. By taking inventory of all of the semitones encompassed between B and E, it is further determined that there are five. A *diminished fourth* encompasses four semitones, and an *augmented fourth* encompasses six semitones. Figure 12 contains several examples of different fourths written in both the treble and bass clef.

Table 1 consists of a chart listing all of the intervals contained within one octave, their sizes, their qualities, and the number of semitones encompassed within.

Size	Quality	Encompassed Semitones
Unison	Perfect	0
2nd	Diminished	0
2nd	Minor	1
2nd	Major	2
2nd	Augmented	3
3rd	Diminished	2
3rd	Minor	3
3rd	Major	4
3rd	Augmented	5
4th	Diminished	4
4th	Perfect	5
4th	Augmented	6
5th	Diminished	6
5th	Perfect	7
5th	Augmented	8
6th	Diminished	7
6th	Minor	8
6th	Major	9
6th	Augmented	10
7th	Diminished	9
7th	Minor	10
7th	Major	11
7th	Augmented	12
Octave (8th)	Perfect	12

Table 1. Intervals contained within the octave.

9   Inversion of Intervals

Inversion of intervals means to simply take the bottom note of an interval and play it an octave higher to make it the top note of a new interval. The letter names of the notes don't change, just the position (top note is now the bottom note). When an interval is inverted, a new interval is formed. For example, the interval formed by the notes C up to G (C-G) is a perfect fifth. When this interval is inverted (G-C), it becomes a perfect fourth. Fortunately, a pattern exists which makes this easy to remember, and more importantly, demonstrates an element of the subtle beauty of western harmony. The pattern is illustrated in Table 2.

Original Interval	Inversion (New Interval)
Perfect Unison	Perfect Octave
Diminished 2nd	Augmented 7th
Minor 2nd	Major 7th
Major 2nd	Minor 7th
Augmented 2nd	Diminished 7th
Diminished 3rd	Augmented 6th
Minor 3rd	Major 6th
Major 3rd	Minor 6th
Augmented 3rd	Diminished 6th
Diminished 4th	Augmented 5th
Perfect 4th	Perfect 5th
Augmented 4th	Diminished 5th
Diminished 5th	Augmented 4th
Perfect 5th	Perfect 4th
Augmented 5th	Diminished 4th
Diminished 6th	Augmented 3rd
Minor 6th	Major 3rd
Major 6th	Minor 3rd
Augmented 6th	Diminished 3rd
Diminished 7th	Augmented 2nd
Minor 7th	Major 2nd
Major 7th	Minor 2nd
Augmented 7th	Diminished 2nd
Perfect Octave	Perfect Unison

Table 2. Inversion of intervals.

When inverting intervals, notice that all perfect intervals remain perfect in the inversion. Also notice that all minor intervals become major intervals in the inversion, all major intervals become minor intervals in the inversion, all diminished intervals become augmented in the inversion, and all augmented intervals become diminished intervals in the inversion. Another part of the pattern is the size of the intervals. Unisons become octaves, seconds become sevenths, thirds become sixths, fourths become fifths, fifths become fourths, sixths become thirds, sevenths become seconds, and octaves become unisons. A simple way to verify an interval inversion is to add the numeric values for the interval sizes together: They should always total nine.

10   Consonance versus Dissonance

When two notes are sounding together, they form either a consonance or a dissonance of varying degrees. *Consonance* can be defined as a pleasant human response to at least two musical tones that are sounding together. Consonant sounds tend to be pleasing to listen to, and *dissonant* sounds tend to be less so. All of the musical intervals contained within the octave have been categorized as to their relative consonant and dissonant properties. Table 3 shows the classification of all of the intervals contained within the octave in terms of *consonance* and *dissonance*.

In traditional western classical music, dissonance produces harmonic tension. This tension can be resolved when the interval changes to consonance. This movement from dissonance to consonance is called a *resolution*: dissonance resolves to consonance.

Perfect Consonances	Imperfect Consonances	Dissonances
Unison, perfect fourth, perfect fifth, and octave	Major and minor thirds, major and minor sixths	All augmented and diminished intervals, major and minor seconds, major and minor sevenths

Table 3. Consonant and dissonant intervals.

11 Scales

A musical scale, in the simplest sense, is a collection of pitches organized in a hierarchical order. The *major scale* and the *minor scale* are the two most common scales used in western music, and their structure is well documented.

12 The Major Scale

The *major scale* consists of eight notes, typically arranged from low to high, with the first note being repeated an octave higher. The first note is, in many ways, the most important note of the scale, and is called the *tonic* note of the scale. Each letter-named note is used once, and only once, within an octave of the scale. Figure 13 is the C major scale written in the grand staff.

Let us examine the scale by identifying each interval between the adjacent notes of the scale. Between the C and the D (notes 1 and 2), there is a major second, or a wholetone. Between the D and the E (notes 2 and 3), there is another major second.

By continuing this process, it can be determined that the scale consists of wholetones (major seconds) between all of its adjacent notes except between notes 3 and 4 (E and F) and notes 7 and 8 (B and C). Between notes 3 and 4 and between notes 7 and 8 are semitones (minor seconds). This is true for all major scales.

With this information in mind, it is now possible to construct a major scale that uses any named pitch as its first note. For example, Figure 14 illustrates all of the standard major scales written in the grand staff. Notice that some of the scales are enharmonic equivalents for another scale, C# and Db, for example.

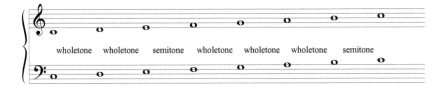

Figure 13. The C major scale written in the grand staff with the intervals identified.

Figure 14. The major scales.

13 Key Signatures

A *key signature* is simply a shorthand system to quickly communicate the key (or scale) in which a musical composition is composed. By placing the appropriate pattern of sharps or flats on the staff at the beginning of the music, the musicians can instantly determine the scale from which most of the notes will be derived. The pattern of sharps and flats has been standardized, and written music that uses key signatures should conform to the pattern. When a key signature is used, it implies those accidentals be used throughout the composition, unless a natural is used

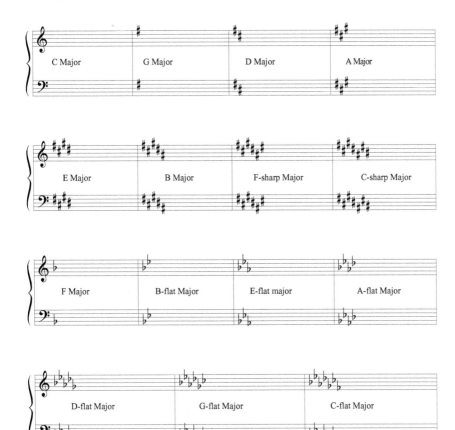

Figure 15. The major key signatures.

to momentarily cancel the key signature just for that note. Figure 15 illustrates the standard key signatures for major keys/scales in both the treble and bass clefs.

14 Cycle of Fifths

The *cycle of fifths* is a theoretical concept that makes it easier to re-member the order of major (and minor) scales and their key signatures. By constructing a grid similar in design to a clock face, it is possible to systematically arrange the names of the scales around the outside of the

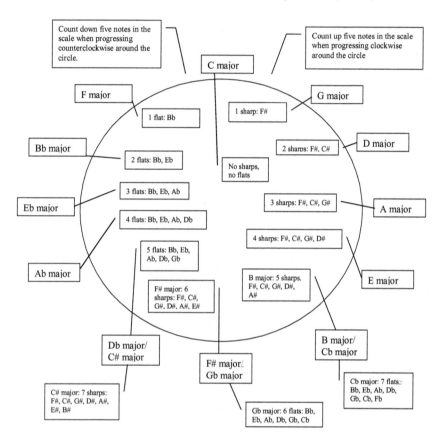

Figure 16. The cycle of fifths: major scales.

clock while simultaneously arranging the order of sharps and flats around the inside of the circle. The guiding principle is everything is arranged in perfect fifths. Figure 16 is a complete cycle of fifths.

Begin at the top of the circle (12 o'clock position) and progress clockwise around the circle. Notice the C major scale is at the top of the circle. It has neither sharps nor flats in its key signature. By counting the C as "one" and counting up five notes in the C major scale, we can identify the name of the scale that has one sharp in its key signature. Using this process, it is determined that G is the major scale with one sharp (C up to G is a perfect fifth). The sharp in the key of G major is F#. Notice it is written on the inside of the circle. In the key of G major, count the

G as "one," and count up five notes to find the name of the scale with two sharps in its key signature. This is the D major scale. To find the name of the new sharp in D major (the F# carries over), go to the inside of the circle, count the F# as "one" and count up five letter names. This identifies the note C# as the new sharp in the key of D major. By continuing this process, it is possible to identify each major scale with sharps in the key signature until we come to the scale that has all sharps in its signature, C# major.

Begin again at the top of the circle with C major and progress counterclockwise around the circle. Count down five notes in the key of C major. This will identify the name of the major scale that has one flat in its key signature. F major is this scale, and the one flat is a B-flat (Bb). In the key of F major, count the F as "one," and count down five notes to determine the name of the major scale that has two flats in its key signature. This is the B-flat major scale. To identify the new flat in the key of Bb, go to the inside of the circle and count down from the last known flat which was the Bb in the key of F major. Counting down five notes from Bb leads us to the note Eb. Eb is a perfect fifth lower in pitch than Bb. By continuing this process, it is possible to identify each major scale with flats in the key signature until we come to the scale that has all flats in its signature, Cb major.

The circle of fifths is a very useful conceptual tool for remembering the key signatures of all of the standard major scales, and for reinforcing the importance of the interval of a perfect fifth in the western European harmonic tradition. When chords and chord progressions are introduced, the importance of the perfect fifth will become more evident.

15 Minor Scales

There are a number of ways to derive a minor scale. Some musicians construct minor scales by determining their interval content, similar to the method we used to derive the major scale. However, once the major scale has been comfortably studied, this author thinks it best to derive the minor scale directly from the major scale.

The minor scale can be derived from any given major scale simply by finding the sixth note of the major scale. Once this note has been identified, build a new scale beginning with the sixth note, and progress through the exact same collection of notes from the original major scale. For example, beginning with the C major scale, it is evident that the sixth note is the pitch A. Use the notes from the C major scale, but build

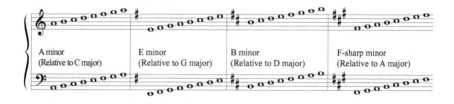

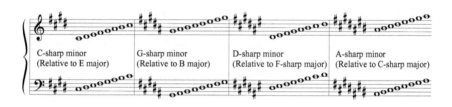

Figure 17. Natural minor scales, minor key signatures, and relative major names.

it beginning on A: A, B, C, D, E, F, G, A. This is the A *natural minor scale*. The key signature for A minor is the same as the key signature for C major, no sharps and no flats.

By using a known major scale to derive the natural minor scale, it is possible to say that a relationship between the scales exists. This relationship is called *relative minor*. In other words, the major scale and the derived natural minor scale are related to each other. They share the same collection of pitches, which is indicated by the key signature. They share the same key signature. With this in mind, it is now possible to construct any relative natural minor scale from any given major scale. Figure 17 shows all of the standard natural minor scales, their related major scale names, and their key signatures written in the grand staff.

It is also possible to conceive of a natural minor scale as an altered form of a major scale with the same name. Using the relative minor approach from above (C major and A minor are related), we discover that the collection of pitches remains constant (C, D, E, F, G, A, B, C is related to A, B, C, D, E, F, G, A), but the names of the scales change (C major and A minor). What if we could turn a C major scale into a C minor scale? In this case, the names of some of the pitches within the major scale will change, but the name C will remain a constant. To convert a C major scale into a C minor scale, simply lower by one semitone the third, sixth, and seventh notes of the major scale. For example, the C major scale (C, D, E, F, G, A, B, C) will be altered to become the C minor scale (C, D, E-flat, F, G, A-flat, B-flat, C). This concept is referred to as *parallel minor*.

16   Harmonic Minor Scales

Historically, western European classical composers exploited different aspects of the minor scale to create music that they considered beautiful. As a result, the natural minor scale has evolved to include two other forms of minor scale: the *harmonic minor scale* and the *melodic minor scale*.

The harmonic minor scale has one *chromatic* alteration from the natural minor scale. That is, the harmonic minor scale uses an accidental to alter the pitch of one note from the minor scale's key signature. This note is the seventh note of the scale, and it is chromatically raised one semitone in the harmonic minor scale. This "raised seventh" is called the *leading tone* of the scale. Figure 18 shows all of the standard harmonic minor scales written in the grand staff.

17   Melodic Minor Scales

The melodic minor scale is another chromatically altered version of the natural minor scale. To construct a melodic minor scale, begin with the

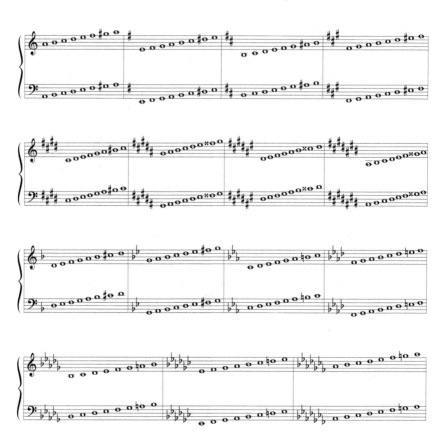

Figure 18. Harmonic minor scales.

natural minor scale, and chromatically raise the sixth and seventh notes a
semitone when writing the ascending scale. The descending version of the
melodic minor scale is exactly the same as the descending version of the
natural minor scale. In other words, there are two "flavors" of melodic
minor: ascending and descending.

Historically, melodic music that chromatically changes the sixth and
seventh notes of the minor scale during ascending passages is typically
Baroque *contrapuntal* compositions, such as a *fugue* by J. S. Bach. Figure 19 shows all of the standard melodic minor scales written in the
grand staff.

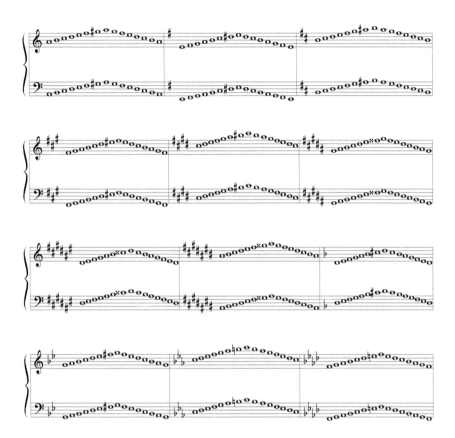

Figure 19. Melodic minor scales.

18   Modes from the Major Scale

If it is possible to derive the natural minor scale simply by rewriting the major scale beginning and ending on the sixth notes, it is possible to derive other scales, called *modes*, by rewriting the major scale beginning and ending on the other notes of the scale. For example, if one were to rewrite the C major scale (no sharps and no flats in the key signature) beginning and ending on the second note of the scale, one would have constructed the *D dorian* mode from the C major scale. When deriving the other modes from a major scale, the major scale is often called the *parent scale*. It is possible to derive seven other modes from any given

Name of the Mode	How It is Derived from the Parent Major Scale
Ionian (same as the major scale)	Begin on the first note of the major scale and progress up one octave (notes 1–8 of the major scale)
Dorian	Begin on the second note of the major scale and progress up one octave (notes 2–9 of the major scale)
Phrygian	Begin on the third note of the major scale and progress up one octave (notes 3–10 of the major scale)
Lydian	Begin on the fourth note of the major scale and progress up one octave (notes 4–11 of the major scale)
Mixolydian	Begin on the fifth note of the major scale and progress up one octave (notes 5–12 of the major scale)
Aeolian (same as natural minor)	Begin on the sixth note of the major scale and progress up one octave (notes 6–13 of the major scale)
Locrian	Begin on the seventh note of the major scale and progress up one octave (notes 7–14 of the major scale)

Table 4. Modes derived from the major scale.

parent major scale. Table 4 shows the names and the constructions of these modes.

19   Chords and Triads

A *chord* can be defined as being a vertical construction of at least three different *pitch classes*. A pitch class is simply an exact note name. For example, C and C# are two different pitch classes. A chord can be constructed by sounding any three different pitch classes at the same time. A *triad* is a specific type of chord. There are four types of triads: major, minor, diminished, and augmented. Triads are built in thirds above a *root*. For example, the Bb *major triad* consists of the notes Bb, D, and F.

Bb is the root of the chord. The D is a third higher than Bb, and the F is a third higher than the D. By comparing this triad to the notes of the Bb major scale, it is determined that the notes of the Bb major triad are the same as the first, third, and fifth notes of the Bb major scale. Therefore, we can now say that the notes of any major triad are the same as the first, third, and fifth notes from the corresponding major scale.

Another way to identify the notes of a major triad is to analyze the interval content. For example, with a Bb major triad, there is a root (Bb), major third (D), and perfect fifth (F). Therefore, it is possible to conclude that all major triads consist of a root, major third, and perfect fifth when the intervals are analyzed in relation to the root of the chord.

Minor triads consist of a root, minor third, and perfect fifth when the intervals are analyzed in relation to the root of the chord. The Bb minor triad, then, consists of Bb, Db, and F. It is also possible to identify the notes of a minor triad by comparing the triad to the corresponding natural minor scale. Using this method, it is possible to identify the notes of a minor triad as being the first, third, and fifth notes from the natural minor scale with the same name (Bb minor triad = Bb natural minor scale in this scenario).

A third way to conceive of a minor triad is to compare it to the corresponding major triad. For example, the Bb major triad consists of the notes Bb, D, and F. The Bb minor triad consists of the notes Bb, Db, and F. By comparing the minor triad to the major triad, we can conclude that the minor triad has the same notes as the major triad except the minor triad has a third that is a semitone lower in pitch than the major triad.

The last common way to conceive of a minor triad is to compare it to the correspondingly named major scale. In this scenario, the Bb minor triad consists of the first, lowered third, and fifth notes from the Bb major scale (first, flatted-third, and fifth from the major scale).

The *diminished triad* consists of a root, a minor third, and a diminished fifth. For example, the Bb diminished triad is spelled Bb, Db, and Fb. When comparing the diminished triad to the minor triad, it is evident that the root and third are common to both, but the fifth is a semitone smaller in the diminished triad than that in the minor triad. Diminished triads are universally treated as a dissonance in harmonic music, and they serve an important function in terms of *diatonic harmony*.

Another way to conceive of the diminished triad is to think of it in comparison to the major triad. The Bb major triad is spelled as Bb, D, and F. When comparing the Bb diminished triad to the Bb major triad, it is determined that the diminished triad contains a root, a lowered third from the major triad, and a lowered fifth from the major triad. Using

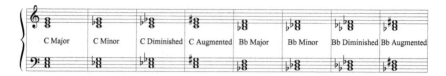

Figure 20. The four basic triad types written with C and Bb as the root.

this system it is fairly simple to derive the Bb diminished triad and to determine the correct spelling: Bb, Db, and Fb.

The *augmented triad* consists of a root, a major third, and an augmented fifth. Augmented triads are also considered dissonant, but do not possess the same level of harmonic function and flexibility as do diminished triads. The Bb augmented triad is spelled Bb, D, and F#. By comparing the augmented to the major triad, it is evident that both share the same root and major third, but the fifth is different. In the Bb major triad (Bb, D, and F), the fifth is a perfect fifth above the root, whereas in the augmented triad (Bb, D, and F#), the fifth is an augmented fifth above the root. This means that the fifth of the chord in an augmented triad is a semitone larger than the fifth of the correspondingly named major triad. Figure 20 shows different triads (major, minor, diminished, and augmented) all built above the same root notes of Bb and C.

20   Seventh Chords

Seventh chords four-note are chords that contain another note above the fifth of the triad. All of these chords are built in thirds (a vertical stack of thirds), so the new note is the interval of a seventh above the root. There are five families of seventh chords: major seventh, minor seventh, dominant seventh (sometimes called major-minor seventh), half-diminished seventh, and diminished-seventh (sometimes called fully diminished seventh). The primary point to remember is that while a triad is a three-note stack of thirds, all seventh chords are four-note stacks of thirds.

The *major seventh* chords consist of a major triad with the new note being a major seventh above the root (major triad + major seventh). For example, the D major seventh chord is spelled D, F#, A, C#. The D major triad (D, F#, A) is completed in this case by the addition of the note (C#) that lies a major seventh above the root. One easy way to determine the correct notes in a major seventh chord is to compare our example (D major seventh chord) to the notes of the D major scale. The notes of the chord are the first, third, fifth, and seventh notes from the D major scale. By simply thinking of the major scale that has the same name as the root of the chord in question.

Dominant seventh (*major-minor seventh*) chords consist of a major triad with the new note being a minor seventh above the root (major triad + minor seventh). This distinction of major triad with a minor seventh is the reason these chords are often called major-minor seventh chords. Most musicians refer to them as dominant seventh chords, because of the way these chords function in the context of harmonic music. For our purposes, the name "dominant seventh" will suffice.

The D dominant seven chord is spelled D, F#, A, C. Determining the notes of any given dominant seventh chord can easily be accomplished in one of two ways. One can use the interval construction (major triad + minor seventh), or one can compare the notes to a known major scale. The D major scale, for example, contains the notes D, F#, A, and C#. The D dominant seventh chord contains three of these notes, but uses a C-natural, not a C-sharp. We can now conclude that any dominant seventh chord uses the first, third, fifth, and lowered seventh from the corresponding major scale.

The *minor seventh* chord consists of a minor triad plus a minor seventh. The D minor seventh chord is comprised of the notes D, F, A, and C. By comparing the notes of this chord to the D natural minor scale, it is determined that the notes of the chord are the same as the first, third, fifth, and seventh notes of the scale. One can also compare the notes of the minor seventh chord to the notes of the correspondingly named major scale, since most people are more familiar with major scales than with minor scales. This method brings about the conclusion that the notes from any minor seventh chord are the same as the first, lowered third, fifth, and lowered seventh notes from the major scale.

The *half-diminished seventh chord* consists of a diminished triad plus a minor seventh. The notes of the D half diminished seventh chord are D, F, Ab, and C. By using the major scale comparison method, we can discover that the notes from any half-diminished seventh chord are the same as the first, lowered third, lowered fifth, and lowered seventh notes from the major scale.

The *diminished-seventh chord* (sometimes called the *fully diminished-seventh chord*) consists of a diminished triad plus a diminished seventh. The notes of the D diminished-seventh chord are D, F, Ab, and Cb. By using the major scale comparison method, we can discover that the notes of any diminished-seventh chord are the same as the first, lowered third, lowered fifth, and doubly lowered seventh notes from the major

Figure 21. The five basic seventh chord types written with C and D as the root.

scale. The diminished seventh chord has many intrinsic properties that make it interesting for composers and theorists. Composers such as Bela Bartok, Claude Debussy, and Igor Stravinsky have used either the chord itself in interesting ways, or have exploited some structural principles from the chord to compose some of the most expressive music in the twentieth century. Figure 21 illustrates major seventh, minor seventh, half-diminished seventh, and fully diminished seventh chords all written above the roots of D and C.

21   A Note about Equal Temperament

Equal temperament, as it is currently understood, was designed to make modulation into other key centers during a single music composition easier than the previously used systems of temperament. There is a long history in western European music concerning the manner in which instruments were tuned as well as which combinations of pitches and intervals were considered consonant and dissonant.

The mathematics of equal temperament is not too complicated, and is an elegant expression of the solution to the original problem: that of tonal modulation into other (and ultimately distant) keys within the musical context of a single composition.

Equal temperament keeps the octave as the only "pure" interval, that is, the octave retains its mathematical ratio of 2:1. All other intervals are slightly increased or decreased from their "pure" states according to the formula: $f^{12} = 2$. Western European music had used 12 semitones to the

Pitch Name (given pitch equals 110 Hz for A2)	Multiplied by this Mathematical Value (rounded to the nearest thousandth)	= This Frequency (rounded to the nearest tenth of a Hertz)
A2 (110 Hz)	110 x 1.000=	110.00
A#2/Bb2	110 x 1.059=	116.5
B2	110 x 1.122=	123.4
C3	110 x 1.189=	130.8
C#3/Db3	110 x 1.260=	138.6
D3	110 x 1.335=	146.9
D#3/Eb3	110 x 1.414=	155.5
E3	110 x 1.498=	164.8
F3	110 x 1.587=	174.6
F#3/Gb3	110 x 1.682=	185.0
G3	110 x 1.782=	196.0
G#3/Ab3	110 x 1.888=	207.7
A3	110 x 2.000=	220.0

Table 5. Mathematical values used in the equally tempered scale to determine the pitch of any semitone contained within the octave. Note: The pitch A will be used as the low and high notes of the octave [1].

octave for approximately 300 years before the adoption of equal temperament as our tuning standard. Since there are 12 semitones per octave, we must find the frequency of the intervening pitches that lie between 1 (a given pitch) and 2 (an octave above the given pitch). Another way of saying this is that frequency f must be the twelfth root of 2. Therefore, the formula $f = (2)^{1/12} = 1.059$.

Through extrapolation, we can determine that the mathematical values needed to calculate any given pitch, within the octave, above a known frequency. They are shown in Table 5.

22 Conclusion

The study of pitch theory in western harmonic music is crucial to understanding the world in which musicians live. This article is intended as an introduction to the rudiments of pitch theory, and it is hoped that it will provide the reader with enough information to "wet one's whistle" and pursue a more thorough education in this fascinating subject.

Appendix A: Frequencies of the Equally Tempered Scale

Equal Temperament	Hertz
A0	27.50
A#0/Bb0	29.14
B0	30.87
C1	32.70
C#1/Db1	34.65
D1	36.71
D#1/Eb1	38.89
E1	41.20
F1	43.65
F#1/Gb1	46.25
G1	49.00
G#1/Ab1	51.91
A1	55.00
A#1/Bb1	58.27
B1	61.74
C2	65.41
C#2/Db2	69.30
D2	73.42
D#2/Eb2	77.78
E2	82.41
F2	87.31
F#2/Gb2	92.50
G2	98.00
G#2/Ab2	103.83
A2	110.00
A#2/Bb2	116.54
B2	123.47
C3	130.8
C#3/Db3	138.6
D3	146.8
D#3/Eb3	155.6
E3	164.8

Table 6.

F3	174.6
F#3/Gb3	185.0
G3	196.0
G#3/Ab3	207.7
A3	220.0
A#3/Bb3	233.1
B3	246.9
C4 (Middle C)	261.6
C#4/Db4	277.2
D4	293.7
D#4/Eb4	311.1
E4	329.6
F4	349.2
F#4/Gb4	370.0
G4	392.0
G#4/Ab4	415.3
A4 (A 440)	440.0
A#4/Bb4	466.2
B4	493.9
C5	523.3
C#5/Db5	554.4
D5	587.3
D#5/Eb5	622.3
E5	659.3
F5	698.5
F#5/Gb5	740.0
G5	784.0
G#5/Ab5	830.6
A5	880.0
A#5/Bb5	932.3
B5	937.8
C6	1046.5
C#6/Db6	1108.7
D6	1174.7
D#6/Eb6	1244.5
E6	1318.5

Table 6. (cont.'d)

F6	1397
F#6/Gb6	1480
G6	1568
G#6/Ab6	1661
A6	1760
A#6/Bb6	1865
B6	1976
C7	2093
C#7/Db7	2218
D7	2349
D#7/Eb7	2489
E7	2637
F7	2794
F#7/Gb7	2960
G7	3136
G#7/Ab7	3322
A7	3520
A#7/Bb7	3729
B7	3951
C8	4186

Table 6. (cont.'d)

Annotated Bibliography

[1] John Backus. *The Acoustical Foundations of Music*. New York: W. W. Norton and Company, 1977.

[2] Donald E. Hall. *Musical Acoustics*. Belmont, CA: Wadsworth Publishing Company, 1980.

Basic Music Theory: Rhythm and Meter

Benjamin Tomassetti

Music is a complex art that possesses an unlimited number of facets for study. This article is designed as an introduction to some basic theoretical concepts specifically in terms of rhythm and meter in traditional musical compositions. Everything in this article will be applicable to pop/rock music, jazz music, country and bluegrass music, and most classical music.

Music is often described as constituting an "unfolding." This analogy is relevant because music exists in time. All of the performing arts (music, theater/drama, and dance) share this feature. A musical unfolding consists of the order in which the sonic events (notes, pitches, chords, etc.) are presented to the audience. The areas of music that control the unfolding are rhythm and meter: the temporal domain of music.

1 The Nature of Rhythm

Rhythm can be described as the surface level details of the musical unfolding. Over the past several centuries, a highly organized system of rhythmic notation has evolved, and this system greatly influences how we conceive of musical rhythm. On the simplest level, rhythmic values consist of note-lengths that correspond to different amounts of time in relation to each other. In other words, rhythmic note-values represent ratios as they are compared to a standard. That standard is typically defined as being equal to one *beat* in a musical composition. In the vast majority of mainstream music (rock, pop, country, jazz, bluegrass, etc.), the *quarter-note* is the rhythmic value equal to one beat. Figure 1(a) consists of the

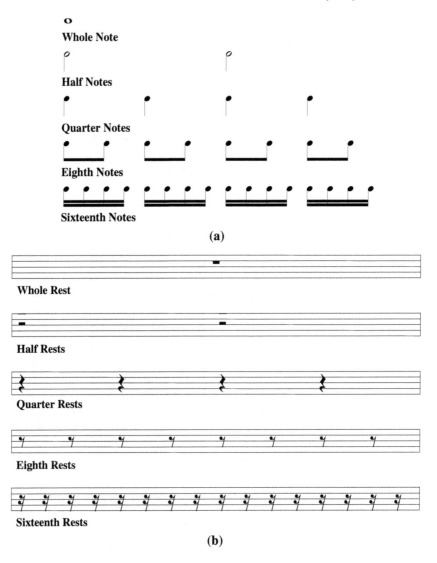

Figure 1. Common rhythmic values. (a) Simple time; (b) Rests.

basic rhythmic values used in the vast majority of popular music, and Figure 1(b) illustrates the corresponding *rests* used in musical notation.

The values have mathematical relationships to each other. Beginning with the whole-note, there are two half-notes in a whole note. There are two quarter-notes in a half-note, two eighth-notes in a quarter-note, and

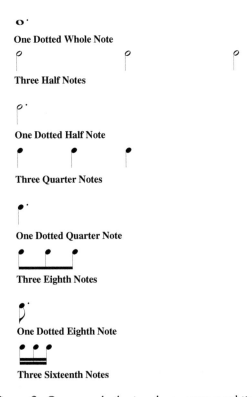

One Dotted Whole Note

Three Half Notes

One Dotted Half Note

Three Quarter Notes

One Dotted Quarter Note

Three Eighth Notes

One Dotted Eighth Note

Three Sixteenth Notes

Figure 2. Common rhythmic values: compound time.

two sixteenth-notes in an eighth-note. Another way of describing this is to say that the amount of time occupied by a whole-note can be equally filled by two half-notes. The amount of time occupied by a half-note can be equally filled by two quarter-notes, so on and so forth. Notice the relationship is a binary one. It takes two of the next faster rhythmic value (note-length) from Figure 1 to occupy the same amount of time as the next longer rhythmic value. Music that naturally has this "feel" or "sound" to it is referred to as having a *simple* rhythmic nature. Some common tunes that have this feel are "Twinkle, Twinkle Little Star," "When the Saints Go Marching In," and "Mary Had a Little Lamb."

In addition to this binary rhythmic system, there is a tertiary rhythmic system. By adding a dot to a single rhythmic value (quarter-note, for example), three of the next faster rhythmic values from Figure 1 are now required to occupy the same amount of time (eighth-notes, for example). This gives the feel of the music a very natural "three-feel." This type of rhythmic feel is referred to as *compound*. Figure 2 illustrates the rhythmic relationships in the *compound* rhythmic system.

Some common tunes that have this compound feel are "Row, Row, Row Your Boat," "Take Me Out to the Ball Game," and "Pop Goes the Weasel."

2   Beats in Music

Beats in music can be defined as a series of regularly occurring pulses upon which all of the other rhythmic relationships depend. Let's take "Mary Had a Little Lamb" as an example. If one claps his hands during every syllable (while singing this tune), we discover that the pulses occur on a regular basis. Figure 3 illustrates the beats of this tune as they occur with the lyrics.

(Lyrics)   Mar-y Had A Lit-tle Lamb, Lit-tle Lamb, Lit-tle Lamb
(Beats)   X   X X   X X X X X   X X X X X X X X

Figure 3.

Notice that the word "Lamb" has two Xs under it. This is because that word is two beats (or claps) long in the context of this tune. Also notice that the beats fall into a pattern of strong-weak, strong-weak, etc. throughout the duration of this tune. This pattern of beats is called *meter* in music.

3   Musical Meter

Meter can be defined as a hierarchical structure of beats in music. The most important beat in the regularly occurring pattern is the first beat. The first beat identifies the beginning of the next repetition of the pattern. The first beat is so important, it has a special name: *downbeat*. The downbeat of each measure in music is the first beat of the regularly occurring metric pattern.In musical notation, we define the metric pattern as being one *measure* in length. A measure consists of one instance of the regularly occurring pattern of beats in a tune, and is identified by the use of *barlines*. A *barline* is simply a vertical line drawn through the line of music to indicate the end of each measure. That is important. *Barlines* come at the end, not the beginning, of measures. Since the barline

Mar - y   Had   a   Lit - tle   Lamb,   Lit - tle   Lamb,   Lit - tle   Lamb

Figure 4. Simple meter versus compound meter.

visually defines the end of the measure (the end of the regularly occurring metric pattern), it is easy to visually identify the downbeat of each
measure. Simply look to the right of the barline.

In "Mary Had a Little Lamb," for example, the pattern is strong-
weak, strong-weak for the duration of the tune. We can now identify this
tune as having a pattern that is two beats long, and the first beat is the
stronger beat of the two. This means that the meter of this tune can
be identified as *duple* (2 beats per measure). For notational purposes, a
rhythmic value must be assigned as being equal to one beat. Since most
music in western culture uses the quarter-note as the beat unit, we should
use the quarter-note for this example. If we have two beats per measure,
and we know the quarter-note is equal to one beat, we can now identify
the meter of this tune as being in *two-four time*. This can be represented
in musical notation by the *time signature*.

Time signatures in musical notation consist of a number written directly on top of another number in the musical staff. The top number
represents the number of beats in each metric pattern, and the bottom
number represents the note-value that will be equal to one beat. Figure
4 is the first phrase of "Mary Had a Little Lamb" written in standard
rhythmic notation with the lyrics.

Earlier, we briefly discussed music that exhibits a *simple* (binary)
rhythmic feel, and music that exhibits a *compound* (tertiary) rhythmic
feel. The terms *simple* and *compound* are more commonly used to describe
the metric nature of a piece of music. "Mary Had a Little Lamb" can be
described as being in *simple-duple* time. This means there are two beats
per measure, and the beats are simple in that they divide into rhythmic
groups of two (binary system).

"Take Me Out to the Ballgame" is an example of a tune with two beats
per measure, but the beats have the "three feel:" they are compound
beats. We can therefore describe the meter of "Take Me Out to the
Ballgame" as being *Compound-Duple* (two beats per measure, and the
beats are compound in nature).

4   Time Signatures (Meter Signatures)

Time signatures (also called *meter signatures*), as mentioned earlier, are shorthand notations to briefly describe the metric nature of a piece of music. The signature consists of two numbers, one placed directly on top of the other number. Sometimes in hand-written scores or musical charts, the composer writes the signature as if it were a fraction (with a line between the two numbers). This is incorrect. There should never be a line between the numbers of a time signature.

When dealing with simple metric music (the beats divide into a natural "two-feel"), the top number represents the number of beats in each measure, and the bottom number represents the type of notational rhythmic value equal to one beat. *Three-four Time*, for example, means there are three beats in each measure, and the quarter-note represents the beat. *Four-four time* means there are four beats in the measure (top four), and the quarter note represents the beat. *Four-eight time* means there are four beats in each measure, and the eighth-note represents the beat. Figure 5 illustrates the most common simple time signatures.

Compound time is another story when it comes to time signatures. Because of the "three-feel," there is no single integer that represents the correct beat value. If a tune (like "Take Me Out to the Ballgame") has two beats in each measure, we can have a "2" in the top number position of the time signature, but the beats are compound in nature. This means that the notational rhythmic value is a dotted value (dotted quarter-note, for example), and there is no single whole number/integer to represent that dotted rhythmic value. For this reason, we use a "lowest common denominator" approach to time signatures in compound time. Two dotted quarter-notes per measure is mathematically the same as six eighth-notes in each measure (If a regular quarter-note is worth two eighth-notes, then a dotted quarter-note is worth three eighth-notes. See Figures 1 and 2).

"Take Me out to the Ball Game" is in compound-duple time, but because of the mathematics of time signatures, the correct time signature is *six-eight time* (6 over 8 in the time signature). Figure 6 is "Take Me Out to the Ball Game" written in standard rhythmic notation with the lyrics printed beneath the music.

Commonly called "Cut Time"

Figure 5. Common time signatures in simple time.

Figure 7. Time signatures in compound meters. The dotted quarter notes are the correct rhythmic values for the beats in these meters.

Figure 7 illustrates the most common meter signatures in compound time.

5 Other Meters

Not all music is in duple (two beats per measure), triple (three beats per measure), or quadruple (four beats per measure) time. It is certainly possible to have any number of beats in a measure as long as the regularly occurring metric pattern is memorable. The Pink Floyd tune, "Money," for example, is in *septuple time* (seven beats per measure). If written in standard musical notation, it would probably be written in *seven-four time* (seven beats per measure, and the quarter-note is equal to one beat). The famous jazz tune by Paul Desmond, "Take Five," is in *five-four time* (five beats per measure, and the quarter-note is equal to one beat). The music of northern India (Hindustani) is often in a metric pattern consisting of 17 or more beats per metric pattern.

6 Tempo

Tempo in music is simply the speed at which the beats occur. How fast are the beats going? If one taps one's toe while listening to music, how fast do the taps occur?

Humans feel tempo in relation to our heartbeats. In general, music that is slower than an individual's heart-rate will be felt as being generally slow by that individual (and vice-versa). This subjectivity in how a given piece of music is felt is inherent in our psychological response to rhythmic stimuli. Psychological research in this field is ongoing, but the relationship between the human heart rate and the perception of musical tempo is

Figure 8. "Mary Had a Little Lamb" written with the beat notated on the quarter-note rhythmic level, and the lyrics unfolding on the eighth-note rhythmic level.

well documented. Our music notational system allows for this flexibility (or subjectivity) in human response. For example, earlier we notated "Mary Had a Little Lamb," in two-four time (Figure 4). We notated the rhythmic unfolding of that tune with the speed of the beats coinciding with the speed of the syllables from the first few words of the lyrics ("Mar-y Had a Lit-tle"). In other words, there is one syllable per notated beat in Figure 4. However, it is possible to notate this tune with the speed of the beats (the tempo of the tune) going slower than the speed/tempo of the syllables of the lyrics. The manner in which most people "feel" this tune dictates that there are two syllables ("Mar-y") occupying the amount of time of one beat (2 syllables per beat). If one taps one's toe while singing this tune, it is much more probable that one's toe will tap only on the beginning of the words "Mary," "Had," "Little," and "Lamb." Figure 8 is "Mary Had a Little Lamb" notated in *two-four time* with the beat level being equal to the *quarter-note*, but the syllables of the lyrics are progressing on the *eighth-note* level (two syllables for each notated beat).

Tempo can be mathematically identified for any piece of music by counting the number of beats that occurred over one minute of performance time and assigning that number as a tempo marking on the musical score. A *metronome* is a mechanical device (now computerized, of course) that ticks at regular intervals. The numerical scale that the musician uses to set the metronome to the correct tempo is standardized as *beats per minute* on the front of the unit. In Figure 8, the *tempo* is indicated as "quarter note equals 88 beats per minute."

7   Rhythmic Subdivision

Rhythmic *subdivision* in music is simply the act of performing rhythms that are generally faster than the pace of the beats. For example, in Figure 8, we must perform two syllables of the lyric for each beat until we get to the word "Lamb." Sing this tune while tapping one's toe on the beats (and only on the beats). There should be two syllables ("Mar-y

(Tap your foot where marked by arrows)

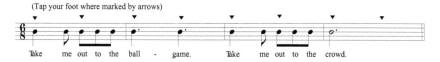

Take   me   out to the   ball -   game.   Take   me out to the crowd.

Figure 9. "Take Me Out to the Ball Game" in rhythmic notation.

Had a Lit-tle") for each tap of the toe. During this performance, you
were subdividing on a 2:1 ratio. Two syllables per beat are the same as
two eighth-notes per quarter-note in this example.

It is possible to subdivide musical beats into very fast rhythms. For
the purposes of this article, we will explore 3:1 ratios and 4:1 ratios. "Take
Me Out to the Ballgame" is an example of a tune that is in compound
time, and would typically be written in *six-eight time (compound duple)*.
Refer to Figure 9.

Sing this tune while tapping one's toe where it is indicated. Notice
that the words "out to the" occupy the entirety of the second beat of the
first measure. This is an example of subdividing a 3:1 rhythmic ratio in
the performance of a piece of music.

The tune, "Doe, a deer, a female deer," from *The Sound of Music* is
an example of a tune that uses lots of 4:1 rhythmic subdivisions. Figure
10 is the tune written in standard musical rhythmic notation.

Sing this song while tapping one's toe on the beats as indicated. The
line "Ray, a drop of golden sun" illustrates the 4:1 subdivision. Look
specifically at the words "drop of golden." These words occupy the second
beat of the third measure in Figure 10. The rhythmic unfolding consists
of four *sixteenth-notes* which occupy the same amount of time as a single
quarter-note. They are a grouped together by the way they are *beamed*.

Beaming in music notation is a common way to indicate the specific
beat to which a group of faster rhythmic values belongs. The sixteenth-
notes in question in Figure 10 are connected by the solid horizontal *beams*.
Notice the sixteenth-note directly before the group of beamed sixteenths.
This single sixteenth-note goes with the word "a" (as in "a drop of golden
sun"), and is actually a part of beat one in that measure. Notice how it

♩=72

Doe,   a deer,   a   fe - male deer.   Ray,   a drop of gol-den sun.

Figure 10.

is beamed to the dotted eighth-note that precedes it. Sing this line of the song and tap your toe on the beats as indicated in Figure 10. The word "a" should occur a split second before your toe taps on beat two of that measure. The word "drop" should coincide exactly with the toe striking the floor. Because the word "a" occurs before the second beat, it must be the last portion of the first beat in that measure. The beaming of the rhythms helps communicate this to the musician.

8   Ties and Dots, Rhythmic Addition

A *tie* in music is a curved line attached to different rhythmic values to create longer sustained notes out of shorter rhythmic values. Think of it as a form of rhythmic addition. For example, in the song "Battle Hymn of the Republic," the *chorus* of the song contains the famous line "Glory, Glory Hallelujah." Figure 11 is the chorus of this song in standard rhythmic notation. Notice that this tune is in compound-duple time (2 beats per measure, and the beats are compound in nature-they have the "three-feel").

Notice the first instance of the word "Glor-y." The first syllable is more than one beat long, but less than two beats long. The correct rhythm is a dotted quarter-note tied to a quarter-note (this leaves an eighth-note remaining for the second syllable "y"). We can now describe the rhythmic length of the first syllable of the word "Glor-y" as being one and two-thirds beats long. The *tie* allows us to easily add the rhythmic values of the two notes in question together.

As mentioned earlier, when we add a dot to a rhythmic note value (quarter-note, for example), we are making that value equal to three of the next fastest note-values (eighth-notes, for example). In compound time, the beat itself is represented exclusively by dotted values. Six-eight time, for example, has two beats in each measure, and the dotted quarter-note represents each beat. What if we have a dotted quarter-note in simple time? This means that the length of the note in question is three eighth-notes long. Figure 12 illustrates an example of this type of rhythm.

Figure 11.

Figure 12. Use of a dotted quarter note in simple time.

Notice the rhythm of the second measure of Figure 12. It consists of a dotted-quarter-note followed by a single eighth-note, followed by four more eighth-notes (beamed in groups of two). When we add together all of these rhythmic values, we discover a complete measure in *four-four time*. Measure two in Figure 12 begins with a dotted quarter-note. Using simple rhythmic analysis, we take metric inventory of every note in the measure. There are four quarter-notes worth of rhythms in this measure. This means there are also eight eighth-notes worth of rhythms in this measure. All of beat one is accounted for by the quarter-note appearing at the beginning of the measure. The beginning, or *downbeat*, of beat two is not readily apparent. The first note in this measure is a dotted quarter-note. The dot represents an extra eighth-note added to the length of the regular quarter-note. Since all of beat one is accounted for by the regular quarter-note itself, the dot represents the eighth-note that occurs on the *downbeat* of beat two in this measure. The second eighth-note of beat two, the *upbeat*, is represented by the eighth-note that is notated with

Figure 13. Rhythmic exercises to be performed.

a flag (not part of the beamed groupings). Beat three is represented by the first grouping of two eighth-notes beamed together, and beat four is represented by the second grouping of two eighth-notes beamed together. In simple time, a dot on a note is typically used as a type of shorthand instead of using a tie.

Figure 13 consists of several rhythmic exercises that are to be performed by the reader. It is recommended that one tap one's toe on the beats and vocalizes the specific rhythms using the syllable "DAH" during the vocalizations. Keep steady time with your foot, and strive for exact rhythmic accuracy. If something goes wrong, take metric inventory and discover the exact placement within the measure for each note (downbeat or upbeat). When the quarter-note is the beat, the first eighth-note for beat one is called the *downbeat* of beat one, and the second eighth-note is called the *upbeat* of beat one. The same holds true for beats two, three, and four (depending upon the number of beats in each measure—look at the time signature).

9   Conclusion

Rhythm and meter are fundamental concepts in music, and any level of study must explore these issues. This article is designed to be a mere introduction to the concepts, and it is hoped will serve as the motivation for further study in music theory.

Annotated Bibliography

[1] Bruce Benward and Barbara S. Jackson. *Practical Beginning Theory: A Fundamentals Worktext, Seventh edition.* Dubuque, IA: Brown & Benchmark, 1991.

[2] Bruce Benward and Gary C. White. *Music in Theory and Practice, Volumes 1–2,*

    Fifth edition. Dubuque, IA: Brown & Benchmark, 1992.

[3] William Duckworth. *A Creative Approach to Music Fundamentals, Sixth edition.* New York: Wadsworth Publishing Co., 1997.

[4] Tom Manoff. *The Music Kit: Workbook, Rhythm Reader, Scorebook, Third edition.* New York: W. W. Norton & Company, 1994.

[5] Marjorie Merryman. *The Music Theory Handbook*. Orlando, FL: Harcourt Brace, 1996.

[6] Harold Owen. *Music Theory Resource Book, First edition*. Oxford, UK: Oxford University Press, 2000.

[7] Peter A. Spencer. *Music Theory for Non-Music Majors, Second edition*. Upper Saddle River, NJ: Prentice Hall, 2000.

Sound Design

Designing the Auditory Narrative: A Methodology for Sound Design

Maribeth J. Back

1 Introduction

Determining the content in a good sound design is an ill-defined art. Why should a product or interactive system sound the way it does? What is the basis for choosing one particular sound over another? How does the design of sound for interactive systems differ from that for noninteractive systems? Clearly, patterns of creative, perceptual, and practical affordances are involved in sound design decisions. In practice, however, most sound design knowledge is passed along through apprenticeship or is rediscovered through trial and error. Reliable criteria for judging the effectiveness of a given sound design have not been developed, though some of the research in auditory perception and in auditory interface design offers intriguing hints [3], [5], [14], and [16].

An effective design methodology for sound can be based on recognizing, creating, and/or manipulating listeners' narrative expectations. An overtly literary design approach is an invaluable tool for imagining and creating a particular sound, as well as designing larger sound environments. Telling stories with sound has a long history in radio and cinema (and is explored in Thom's article "Designing a Movie for Sound" (see Audio Anecdotes I); it's an intrinsic part of the sound designer's vocabulary [8], [33]. Sound designers must decide what sound goes with a particular action, and why. In other words, the chosen sound must tell a plausible story. In new media and interactive systems, the sound designer must use sound to tell stories to listeners engaged in either asynchronous or real-time interaction, both of which change the narrative task in some significant ways.

Additionally, sound designers must avail themselves of current research into the perceptual and cognitive factors involved in creating the human auditory landscape. The problem of auditory scene analysis—how we distinguish between sounds, and how we extract meaning from what we hear—is of vital importance in building effective soundscapes (see Bregman and Woszczyk's article "Controlling the Perceptual Organization of Sound: Guidelines Derived from Principles of Auditory Scene Analysis (ASA)" (see Audio Anecdotes I); describing Auditory Scene Analysis principals). Other applicable research investigates the operation of sound within multimodal systems, those that use a variety of sensory modalities. How multimodal systems differ from audio-only systems varies widely according to the modalities used and the design of each element within a given mode. If the visuals are animated, for example, sound design is likely to be keyed directly to the animation. Some sensory modes are more naturally privileged by the human perceptual system than others. Leveraging this knowledge allows sound designers to craft their stories more effectively.

As a case study, we will examine the sound design for *Audio Aura*, an audio augmented reality environment built at Xerox PARC [26]. This sound design is part of a continuing research agenda focused on the application of rich, layered sound in computational environments and interfaces.

1.1   Characterizing Sound Design

The sound designer is in essence a creator of realities: a storyteller. The difference between a writer and a sound designer lies in the raw material used—alphabets or waveforms—but they share a common end: to create a scene or an impression in the mind of other humans.

Sound designers create audio content for media ranging from film, theater, and television to interactive systems like the World Wide Web and museum exhibits. To do this successfully, sound designers must first imagine, then build, and then test the sounds they make. In most cases, the sounds are designed to accompany visuals or other sensory effects. In interactive systems, sound often provides feedback for user actions or directives to new functions. In such cases, sound serves a new kind of narrative function: It creates a set of expectations—an auditory context—which helps people to understand more easily what their next choices are.

For example, one of the major pitfalls in the use of sound is "local" design, that is, using a sound that works well enough in the immediate context, but that doesn't support (or may even actively work against) an overall design structure. Arbitrary use of sound may confuse the listener and create mistrust of the auditory modality in general (e.g., "I hate computer sound"). Just as artists and writers labor to construct cohesive works, each with its own internal logic, sound designers must work within the affordances of their materials to create coherent structures. A coherent and internally logical sonic reality supports the listener's engagement with the story of an interactive environment.

Sound design rarely exists in a vacuum. Most sound designers work with a team of other people to produce a multimodal artifact, possibly including visual, tactile, or other sensory modalities. This is how sound design differs from music and sound art (though it may use either as material). A sound designer must take into account the design gestalt of the entire artifact, not just the sound.

Grammars for dynamic media such as film and video are described as formalizations of the methods developed over many years of production. Such elements as camera angle, focus, shot width, and camera motion are combined in known ways to produce certain effects. Such grammars in dynamic media are not prescriptive, that is, they do not exclude new possibilities. Rather, these lexical structures add to possible creative combinations by allowing the artist to consider as single units scenes with internal complexities, much as a writer might use a favorite phrase that is made out of individual words. An important aspect of such a grammar is that it must be understood by listeners as well as designers, because it grows from a base of shared media experience.

1.2 Rebuilding Sonic Reality

The sound design problem can be thought of as an exercise in signal flow: Design principles are used to structure a sound event (the acoustic occurrence) in order to produce the desired auditory event (the human sensory perception) in order to create the desired cognitive event (understanding the sound).

The sound designer's task is to manage the entire signal path: not just through an electronic system, but from one human brain to another. A sound design includes not only electronic signals but also cultural and perceptual signals. Sound designers are rebuilding the sonic reality of their listeners, using two primary sets of cognitive mappings. These categories are:

(1) cultural conditioning (including ability to interpret the intended meaning of sound in a medium as well as understanding of genre, the media context within which a sound design is heard), and

(2) real-life experience of the physical world.

The design materials are real or artificial acoustic events generally belonging to one of several categories: speech, music, sound effects, and ambiences (reflective qualities of apparent space).

1.3 Distinguishing Types of Sound: Speech, Music, Nonspeech Audio

Speech, music, and nonspeech audio (sound effects) are the most obvious material elements in a sound design. Speech, though often treated separately, needs to be considered as intrinsic to the design, so that the frequency content and amplitude envelopes of music and sound effects do not interfere too much or make the speech unintelligible.

Speech and music are both systems of organizing sound that have coherent internal structures. The rest of the sound we encounter, generated by natural systems or our interactions with the physical world, are sometimes called everyday sound. In design work, they are called sound effects or Foley effects (after the art of Foley sound in the film industry, named for Jack Foley, the creator of the art) or, in the computer industry, nonspeech audio (although this term would seem to include music, it actually refers to sound effects or simple sounds that are intended to convey data). Some researchers have proposed models for understanding structure in everyday sound, notably Bill Gaver, whose work includes a system for creating synthetic physical models on computers for replicating and encoding everyday sounds [7].

1.4 The Real-World Listening Environment

Artificial ambiences added by the sound designer often help to create a cohesive sound that distinguishes the sound design from real-world ambient sounds in the final listener's environment. The reproduction qualities of the sound system must be considered; a sound system for a personal computer will tend to have very different audible qualities than a theatrical system.

Finally, the physical environment will impact the sound design; not merely the acoustics of the space and competing noise elements, but also other sensory competition like visual variety, activity level, and even smell.

A small museum gallery presents very different design problems than those in a workplace, a video arcade, or an outdoor park.

1.5   Genre and Media Context

Sound design shows up in all kinds of environments and artifacts. For example: film, television, theater, radio, museums, computer games, arcades, World Wide Web, three-dimensional graphic presentations, and CD-ROMs. Even "serious" business applications like presentation programs, spreadsheets, phone systems, and word processors have increasingly sophisticated sonic displays. In research labs and universities, sound design is being applied in data visualization/sonification systems, virtual reality, augmented reality, high-end medical systems, wearable computers, and smart environments [2], [3], [13], [14], [22], [35].

Understanding the medium and the genre within the medium are essential in sound design. Bach's "Jesu Joy of Man's Desiring," heard on the radio, is simply a piece of music to be enjoyed. But if it's part of a TV commercial, the advertiser hopes that you, as listener, will associate the advertised product with the cultural standing of a beautiful classical piece of music.

Determining the right emotional tone for a sound design involves understanding relative uses of sound for affect in different media. The more complex and encompassing the type of environment, the more subtly sound designers must work to accomplish equivalent tasks. Environments with lower resolution and less immersive capability require sound to perform more strongly to generate emotional cues and sense of place.

Here's a brief examination of how music and sound effects operate differently within the following environments:

Video game. Once terrible, but now approaching television's visual resolution, noisy environment. Sound and music deliver as much information as possible, especially information mapped to overt actions (shooting) or to navigation. Caricature in sound design—a kind of sonic cartooning—is very helpful in this environment.

CD-ROM. Limited file space, usually small and inaccurate speakers, better quality graphics. Added environmental complexity is offered by interactivity beyond shooting and steering. Sound apparently generated both by the environment and by user actions, increases sense of involvement and sense of place.

Television. Less environmental complexity due to lack of interactivity is offset by more complexity in image quality (full-screen video) and sound sophistication. Music and sound seem to serve much the same function as in film; but TV is at a disadvantage due to its smaller scale, placement in competing environments (living room, bar), and time constraints (commercials, hour-long program slots). The medium must work harder to create the desired impression in the viewer; one way to do this is by increasing the evocative and emotional power of the sound and music. For this reason, TV music, when heard in other contexts, often seems overwrought, or "hammy."

Film. Environmental complexity is added due to large screen size and visual resolution as well as specialized environment. Music/sound often serves a narrative function, in addition to the sound used to add "realism" by appearing in a causal relation to physical events. Most of the sound heard in film is created months after the film is shot; a door slam is probably not really the sound of that particular door, though it's been matched for material, context, apparent force, and apparent ambience and distance.

Live theater. Environmental complexity is added due to the presence of living humans as part of the construct. Sound and music must not "take focus" or tell the audience too much; that is the actor's job. Theater music, heard in other contexts, often seems static.

Many interactive environments use combinations of media; for example, a museum installation may use video in conjunction with kinetic sculpture or a radio along with robotic actors. Tensions that arise between these genre and media types are the result of deliberate design choices, in the sonic realm no less than the visual.

1.6   Authoring the Recording: Why Real Sound Doesn't Work

Perhaps the most vital realization in sound design is this: *Real sound doesn't work.* It's tempting to believe that we hear truth, just as it's tempting to believe what we see. But people don't always interpret sound correctly when it stands alone. In real life, we use confirmatory evidence from other senses and our knowledge of context and history to help decode auditory information.

For sound designers, this fact is both a boon and a bust. People interpret what they hear in recordings according to their own ideas of what's happening; they tell themselves a story about what they're hearing. Thus, sound designers can just record the sound of pulverizing grapefruit or watermelon for sound effects in gory action flicks. The sound tells a believable story within the context.

To tell a specific story in sound, one cannot simply run out and "record the sound." *Effective storytelling* in recording differs from a*ccuracy* in recording. A good recording is an act of authoring, not capturing. Similar to the use of carefully crafted sets and artificial lighting in a film, sound must also be designed, not found.

To catch the meaning of the sound that's needed for a particular sound design, one must record the story in the sound. Most often, this means combining the right *character* with the right *behavior*. In the case of complex sounds or environments, it means capturing the right balance of elements and the characters and behaviors that are most salient to the story that is needed.

1.7   Mental Templates: The Ideal Sound

What a sound designer really needs to deliver is the ideal of a sound as it exists in the listener's mind. Therefore, a recording must match that ideal, in spite of the fact that the real sound may be wildly different. Never mind that seagulls make hundreds of sounds, many of them highly un-seagull-like; what a listener expects to hear is one of two or three "characteristic" seagull sounds. The listener's mental model of any particular sound is the key. To be effective in design work, the recording must match the story of the sound that's already in the listener's head. Of course, a designer can stretch and train a listener's expectations through manipulation of sonic context; that too is a literary task.

How does the sound designer go about imagining and creating these ideal sounds? First, by telling the story of each sound correctly; and secondly, by taking full advantage of perceptual features of the auditory system in support of this sonic storytelling. So, the sound designer's task is to imagine what the ideal instance of a given effect sounds like, given the likely audience, the media, and genre within which the sound appears, and the immediate context of the scene or the interaction. In created realities like theater or film, stories play out in a creative shorthand invented for that particular piece.

2   Narrative as Mapping Algorithm: Creating Sound Using Traditional Literary Elements

The idea of story in sound has been used as a pragmatic device by sound designers for decades and by composers for centuries before that. But overt recognition of the literary aspects of the sound design task allows application of traditional narrative structures in design methodology. Sound design for interactive systems can fruitfully draw from literary structures in nonlinear narratives. Nontraditional narrative approaches are discussed in the next section.

Here is a partial list of traditional narrative elements that can be used to help create a sonic reality. Sound design can answer many of the following questions.

Setting. Where are we? Beach, urban traffic, countryside...? Environmental sounds are often layered to include 20 or more discrete sounds. Beach sounds, for example, may include any mixture of the following: various kinds of waves and their elements (the crash, the rush inwards, the foam hissing, and the rolling of pebbles on recession); seagulls (fighting, calling in flight, close by, far away); other kinds of birds (pipers); wind (stereo, and possibly causing other sounds like sails flapping); bell buoy or foghorn or both; boat horns; children playing.

Plot. What's the storyline? What has happened up to now? Composers often use the leitmotif to signal characters or a particular theme to signify a place or an emotion; the same affordance is available to sound designers, whether through the use of music or through a sonic ambience or a sound. The recurrence of a particular sound in varying situations adds layers of richness to the meaning of the sound.

Context. How do other narrative elements affect what's going on? For example, the sound of ticking might represent an innocuous clock, a straightforward commentary on the passing of time; exactly the same sound might be used to signify the ticking of a bomb.

Dynamics. What's occurring right this moment? A swift change in sound can focus or shift attention. One very effective sound designer's trick is to cut suddenly from intense sound to silence—thereby drawing attention to the richness of the sound that had been present, and greatly heightening the effect of whatever else is happening at that moment.

Expression. How does it feel? Encoding expressiveness in sound is most noticeable in music but occurs in sound effects as well. In a recording session for sound effects, capturing the correct expressive behavior is often the most difficult task. Varying the force and sharpness of attack or making an expressive dynamic change in the sustain and delay of a sound changes how we "read" the sound: impatient or angry, sad or sleepy.

Characterization. What's the nature of this person, this object, this place? In the case of the place settings mentioned above, for example, one must ask, a French beach, or Californian? An English countryside, or a Ugandan? A 1910 horse-and-buggy Kansas City, or London at rush hour? Some layers of sound exist to provide the needed characterization: urban traffic, yes, but with the very specific sound of the London taxi layered on top. Giving the desired character to a sound includes identifying and emphasizing the physical components of the desired quality and suppressing things that detract from it, through judicious editing and the use of equalization, compression, and artificial ambiences.

Anticipation. What happens next? Presaging the plot with the sound score is a common practice in theater and film: Leitmotifs may recur, or emotive patterns.

Transition. In constructed realities, time is often compressed through presentation of one scene after another with an artificial transition between them. Sound is a vital element in transitions; in film, often the sound changes before the visual does. In theater, the sound of one scene will often be subsumed by a transition sound, which then fades into the sound of the next scene. Sound is used as a virtual time/space machine in many kinds of media.

Instruction. Providing the listener with an interpretation of some action or process through sonic commentary, especially feedback: a reassurance, an alarm, a query, and an indication of how to proceed.

Point of view. Who's telling me all this? The sonic narration takes on a point of view most strongly when the designer is given a free hand in developing the grammar and sound palette specific to the environment or artifact.

Other elements of traditional narratives like pace, style, and dramatic arc also affect and inform sound design. A surreal or overtly artistic environment allows for a much freer sound design than one constrained to realism or to strict one-to-one meaning-to-sound mappings. And, like well-made literature, sound design should be allowed to mature into a fully cohesive pattern through an iterative design process.

3   Non-Traditional Narrative Elements for Interactive Audio Environments

An interactive environment is one that changes state with the actions of a user. The simplest possible form of interaction can be likened to the flipping of a light switch; the mapping is one input (motion) to one output (change in light level) with highly predictable consequences. A more complex interaction might require some skill on the part of the user to produce the desired result: Such a complex interaction will have more than one possible result from a single action (multiple mappings), and may combine a number of possibilities depending on the mode of the environment. Where the designer's task becomes challenging is in the multiplicity of possible actions in a single environment, some simple and some complex.

Nonlinear narrative in sound means designing a set of sounds that work well especially for transitions and navigational instruction. In most interactive systems, the problem is how to get from one small narrative section to another. The content of each segment must be adjusted to link well to other segments, and some overall protocol established for manipulating the linkage. In music, some important bridge elements are key, tempo, voice, and volume. In a series of everyday sounds, not only volume but the attack and release envelopes of each sound are vital in arranging a graceful exit from one sound while another begins to play. Establishing an auditory narrative allows the listener to make the transition between sounds logically, without loss of context.

The sound design task for interaction is closely linked with the programmed capabilities of the environment. How much sound should be attached to objects or to spatial coordinates within a particular environment? How many layers of sound can co-exist before they become meaningless? How many layers of sound will a given program allow? If the sound in question is speech, usually only one source at a time can be understood; but nonspeech audio and music can become quite rich before subsuming into muddiness or unintelligibility [6], [18].

Nontraditional stories, developed for interactive media and nonlinear narrative, add a new set of elements in their construction. Applying sonic narrative in interactive environments can help people figure out where they are (history and navigation), what's going on around them (context), and what actions are appropriate at any given moment (guidance and feedback). Especially in three-dimensional graphical environments (virtual reality) and in complex hypertext environments, sound can be created to the pattern of some of these less traditional literary elements.

Navigation. Where to go, and how? Some examples of the use of sound in navigation are voice labels on doorways or gateways, alarms for unsafe or otherwise notable places, and sonic beacons, similar to bell buoys, for marking places. These kinds of sound are very useful in virtual environments, for example, where it's often easy to lose a sense of direction.

History. Where have I been (this time)? Nonlinear narratives allow people to take different pathways through a story; this changes the view of plot and context considerably. Sound can help ameliorate confusion that might arise, by creating links between different contexts and places.

Multi-user. Is there someone else here with me? How are they represented? How am I represented to them? Who are they? Can I hear how they affect the environment? That is, if they drop a virtual glass, do I hear it shatter? Can we all hear the same sounds at the same time?

Personal interaction. Can I talk to or otherwise affect other people? Can I hear them talk to me? What if more than one person is speaking at once?

Object interaction. What can I do with this thing? Does it make noise, as it would in the real world? Are the noises it makes of the same character as in the real world? Does it possess unusual qualities? If I talk to it, will it respond?

Behavior. How does this thing behave? Does it appear to know that I am present? Does my behavior affect it? Can I turn it on and off?

Artificial physics. How do things in this environment generally behave? Does sound drop off naturally as I move away from it, or does it cut off abruptly as I cross some (possibly invisible) barrier?

Geometry of story. Instead of a simple arc, an interactive story often takes the form of connected nodes arranged in varying geometries. Branching-tree is probably the best known of the nonlinear narrative geometries, but there are many others: for example, nodes arranged around the surface of a sphere; a moebius strip; a spiral or helix; or a Gaussian distribution of points. Each geometry requires a different model of cross-linking between sounds associated with the nodes or with the transitions between the nodes.

3.1 Micro-Narratives

Micro-narratives are the smallest "unit" of auditory narrative. It is useful to think of even a single sonic event possessing a narrative "microstructure." Audio engineers and Foley artists know that in making a single sound cue, what's important is that the sound "read" correctly, that is, it must tell its own miniature story accurately.

Layered, detailed manipulation of the waveform is a major part of the sound designer's work; it is also one of the most creative parts. Using sound manipulation software (analogous to a word processor), the sound designer mixes files, shapes loudness levels, adds or subtracts frequencies, lengthens or shortens or reverses the sound. All of this work serves one purpose: to match the mental template he or she has of the sound that must be built.

For example, a sound as apparently simple as the opening and closing of a car door possesses many variables, all of which must support the narrative correctly. All the sounds that make up this "simple" cue must share an ambience. They must appear to issue from the same point in space (auditory perspective), must appear to come from the right kind of car (no pairing a Volkswagen door slam with a Chevy door opening—at least, not unless it's been tuned to match). A list of sounds that make up this story might include:

(1) Footsteps toward the car (what surface? male or female? angry, hurried, sad, bouncy?),

(2) Jingle of keys (how many? from a purse or a pocket, or just held in the hand?),

(3) Scrape and possible fumble at the lock (drunk? mad? not paying attention?),

(4) Insert and turn key in lock, lock thunks open (are we close enough to hear this sound?),

(5) Open door (does door squeak? old car? what make?),

(6) Slide into car (toss bundles/purse in first?),

(7) Slam door shut (must match door-opening sound; might include emotive information: angry?).

And questions about global sounds that lie behind this sequence include:

(1) What's the dynamic context? Time of day? Other people in vicinity?

(2) What's the ambient context? Garage, driveway, or street? Background traffic?

(3) Should the context sounds reinforce the general feeling of the cue or provide contrast to it?

(4) What's the auditory perspective? Close, far away?

Each individual sound in the list should be recorded, edited, and tweaked for maximum effect in response to the salient questions. An annoyed key fumble is different than a drunk key fumble; it's got much harsher attacks in the amplitude envelope, a higher sound level overall, and should possess a feeling of impatience—a faster and more deliberate rhythm.

The final and most important question is this: Does the micro-narrative told by this set of sounds serve the purpose of the overall story and design structure as well as it can? A sound design does not live in isolation; each element of it must be honed to a precise fit.

4 Perception, Schema, and Understanding the Auditory Scene

The second basis for a story-based audio design methodology lies in the study of human auditory perception. Perceptual and cognitive psychologists have been speculating about the place of story in the construction of knowledge and memory in the human brain. It's generally agreed that narrative is a powerful cognitive mechanism, in memory [28] in knowledge construction and retention [25], [29], and in sensory perception, including auditory perception [6], [18].

If, as some perceptual psychologists argue, much of our cognitive modeling is schema-based, then using sound design to "tell a story"—that is, build a schema—is a powerful way to deliver information. Albert Bregman, a psychologist specializing in auditory perception and fellow *Audio Anecdotes* author, distinguishes between "primitive" perceptual processes (those found in infants, for example, or those employed when one hears an unfamiliar sound) and "schema-based" perceptual processes, where attention focus, prior experience, and gestalt mechanisms combine to create a mental model about a sound that is integral to the understanding of the perception. Bregman's work showed that, in fact, if the schema was strongly developed, significant portions of a sound could be completely masked or missing, yet still be perceived as present, due to the listener's schema-based perceptual processing.

Bregman defines his own use of the term *schema*:

> This word is used by cognitive psychologists to refer to some control system in the human brain that is sensitive to some frequently occurring pattern, either in the environment, in ourselves, or in how the two interact ... .When we perceptually analyze our auditory input, we can make use of schemas about recurring patterns in the world of sound. These patterns vary enormously in their degree of complexity and abstraction.... .

> Often the sound we are listening to contains more than one pattern. If each pattern activates a schema, there will be a combination or pattern of schemas active at that time. Sometimes the pattern of activated schemas will form a larger pattern that the perceiver has experienced in the past. In this case the pattern of activity can evoke a higher-order schema [6].

Bregman's description of higher-order schema built from smaller auditory patterns offers a parallel to the sound designer's conceptual process: Imagine a sound, then an accompanying sound, and then the environment within which the two sounds must occur; then other sounds will suggest themselves, as an extension of the pattern.

Schank and Abelson take the idea of the schema-based perceptual process even further:

> ...we argue that stories about one's experiences and the experiences of others are the fundamental constituents of human memory, knowledge, and social communication. This argument includes three propositions:

> (1) Virtually all human knowledge is based on stories constructed around past experiences.

> (2) New experiences are interpreted in terms of old stories.

> (3) The content of story memories depends on whether and how they are told to others, and these reconstituted memories form the basis of the individual's remembered self.

> Further, shared story memories within social groups define particular social selves, which may bolster or complete with individual remembered selves. [28].

Story as the human system for understanding experience leads naturally to the idea of the creative user often described as a collaborator in the artistic experience. Schank and Abelson would claim that, in fact, the experience is created entirely by the user, from cues provided by the designer. This view, while acknowledged even by its authors to be controversial, at least affords the designer a useful metaphor.

4.1   Leveraging the Listener's Real-World Experience

Much of our knowledge about the way our world works comes from firsthand encounters. The natural laws of our physical environment are the constraints within which we all begin learning, and they are reinforced by everyday physical experience. Our social and experiential learning combine into natural metaphoric mappings that are of great use to the multimodal designer who finds them.

As a simple example, a sound designer who knows that a sound needs to function as an alarm (the story of the sound) may look to cognitive and perceptual research to discover what auditory parameters are most effective in alerting the brain (such as envelope shape and frequency content) and how overt content might override perceptual guidelines (the voice of one's own child is a very effective alarm, whether it fits envelope parameters or not).

Many navigable environments (virtual reality, for example) include the notion that proximity is related to volume; that is, as one approaches a virtual river, its sound becomes louder, and when moving away from it, the river sound fades. Proximity-to-volume is an intuitive mapping based in physical experience. Elizabeth Wenzel, in her work for NASA, has described her perceptual experiments in using these mappings in VR environments [35], [36], [37], [38].

The Doppler shift is another example of intuitive mapping. In "flying" through a virtual environment [4], objects emitting sound should appear to drop in pitch as they pass and move away from the user. (In the real world, police sirens racing past provide a good example of the Doppler effect.) Building such capabilities into the sound systems of computational environments gives users a comfortable feeling of familiarity, of "knowing" how the environment works.

By building such copycat rules into the constructed universe inside the computer, designers can help users understand the environment on a more visceral level. Interactivity thus begins to feel natural; the environment's response is predictable enough that the user can rely on a familiar input to produce a familiar output. This is an effective design basis for physical modeling in sound synthesis.

5   Case Study: Audio Aura

Audio Aura is a prototype of an audio augmented reality system, built at Xerox PARC [26]. The basic idea of an audio augmented reality system is that the physical world can be augmented with auditory cues. Augmented realities are usually personal-technology systems, worn by individuals, and they can be active—as when the wearer deliberately explores an auditory overlay within a physical space—or passive, where the sonic environment is keyed by a person's natural movements through a physical environment. We wanted to create an aura of auditory information that mimics existing background-level auditory awareness cues.

We combined active badges [31], distributed systems, and wireless headphones to allow the movements of users through their workplace to trigger the transmission of auditory cues. These cues can summarize information about the activity of colleagues, notify the arrival of email or the start of a meeting, and remind of tasks such as retrieving a book at opportune times. People (wearing wireless headphones based from their own networked PC) can "graze" on this auditory information through their natural interactions with their workplace, like walking through the hallways or pausing near a co-worker's office door.

5.1   Telling the Story in Sound: Mapping to Processes and Actions

We explored how to provide a range of information with Audio Aura. For example, employees at PARC can use the system to augment their physical environment with information about their colleagues. At the entryway to the office of a colleague who is out for the day, they might hear an appropriate greeting (e.g., "gone fishing, stop by next week for home-smoked trout"). Or Audio Aura might use its database to create an iconic summary of a person's recent activity (again at the entryway to their office), perhaps indicating that they had left just a few minutes earlier.

The audio content could also reflect the history of the person wearing the device. Following the previous example, if I again passed a colleague's office, the summary of their activity might only reflect the time since my last visit. Since Audio Aura knows the identity of the listener, the system can deliver personalized information such as a summary of newly arrived email messages while pouring coffee in the break room or hearing a reminder for a meeting that is about to start.

Proximity to various artifacts could trigger auditory cues; for example, standing near a bookshelf may trigger a message about recent acquisitions. The longer a user lingers, the more detail he/she receives.

5.2   Cognitive Considerations and the Perceptual Palette

We deliberately designed for the auditory periphery, so the sounds had to avoid the "alarm" paradigm so frequently found in computational environments. Alarm sounds tend to have sharp attacks, high volume levels, and substantial frequency content in the same general range as the human voice (200–2,000 Hz). Most of the sound used in computer interfaces has (sometimes inadvertently) fit into this model.

Another way to avoid the alarm model is to embed cues into a continually running, low-level soundtrack, or "channel," so that the user is not startled by the sudden impingement of clearly artificial sound. In Audio Aura, the running track itself carries information about global levels of activity within the building, within a workgroup, or on the network. This "group pulse" sound forms the channel bed within which other auditory information lies.

For example, because speech tends to carry foreground information (and because humans tend to pay more attention to speech), a sound involving speech may not be heard unless the user lingers in a location for more than a few seconds. For a user who is simply walking through an area, the sounds remain at a peripheral level, both in volume and in semantic content.

5.3   Mapping Sounds to System Functionality: Creating Sonic Ecologies

We created several sets, or ecologies, of auditory cues, in order to compare their effectiveness and explore a range of use and preference. The Audio Aura system offers four different sound designs: voice only, music only, sound effects only, and a rich sound environment using all three types of sound (music, voice, and sound effects). These different types of auditory cues, though mapped to the same type of events, afford different levels of specificity and required differing levels of awareness [3], [5], [27].

One important aspect of our design approach is the construction of sonic ecologies, where the changing behavior of the Audio Aura system is interpreted through the semantic roles sounds play [15], [32]. By introducing a consistent sense of place—whether real, like a beach, or conceptual, like a musical environment—the sound designer's ability to tell sonic stories is greatly enhanced.

For example, particular sets of functionalities can be mapped to particular sets of sounds. In our current sound effects design, the amount of email is mapped to seagull cries, email from particular people or groups is mapped to the cries of other beach birds or to seal sounds, group activity level is mapped to surf, wave volume, and activity, and office occupation history is mapped to the number of buoy bells.

Within each of the four sound design models, we have tried several different types of sounds, varying the harmonic content, the pitch, the attack and decay, and the rhythms caused by simultaneously looping sounds of different lengths. For example, by looping three long, low-pitched sounds without much high harmonic content and with long, gentle attacks and decays, we create a sonic background in which we leave room for other sounds to be effectively heard. In the music environment, this sound is a low, clear vibe sound; in the sound effects environment, it is distant surf.

Another useful tool in the ecological approach to sound design is considering frequency bandwidth and human perception as limited resources. Given this design perspective, we built the sounds for Audio Aura with attention to the perceptual niche in which each sound resides. Each sound was crafted with attention to its frequency content, amplitude envelope, and possible masking interaction with other sounds.

5.4   Implementation

We modeled Audio Aura in VRML 2.0, a web-based, three-dimensional graphical scene description protocol that allows real-time interaction with multiple high-quality sound sources. The VRML design prototype (a virtual model of PARC's Computer Science Lab, where the real system was installed) allowed us to experiment easily with multiple sound designs. It also served as the interface for user personalization of the Audio Aura system. It was designed so that a user could try out various sound designs and choose functionalities in the virtual prototype; these preferences were then loaded into the real audio augmentation system.

Here is an overview of the four sonic ecologies:

Nonspeech audio. (Phrase that has come to mean "sound effects" in auditory display.) Constructing a semantic environment, using sound effects. Every sound carries meaning, mapped as well as possible to the type of data it represents.

Voice only. Speech indicating room names or numbers by default; system user-configurable to include personal messages ("I'm in Australia, be back next week") and people's names instead of numbers. Note that in the case of location, voice allows a much finer-grained location data mapping. Although it would be easy (as an example) to map pitched notes for each office, learning such a system would be fairly difficult.

Earcons, or musical icons. A system of meaning based in musical terms, using (for example) pitch, rhythm, or instrumentation to convey meaning. We use a set of related arpeggios in the key of D minor, with two or three different voices (bell, vibe, cello).

Rich. A conceptual combination of the three above-mentioned types of sound into a cohesive environment. Note that this rich environment uses sounds from each of the other three environments. This is the trickiest to design, but the most rewarding; people don't tire of it as easily. Care must be taken not to overload a particular swath of bandwidth.

Table 1 shows the types of functionality provided by the Audio Aura system, the possible messages returned, and the sound each message was mapped to in each ecology. Notice that there is a fair amount of complexity: 14 different messages available, from 5 different kinds of information. They are: amount of email, notification of other messages like voicemail and meeting alerts, a "group pulse" reflecting general activity level, office "footprints" showing office occupation data, and interior location data, which is either room-by-room (voice labels at doorways) or building-by-building (reflected in the type of sound used for the group pulse).

5.5   Designing for Privacy: Auditory Disguise

One of the primary parameters in developing the Audio Aura system's sound designs was understanding what level of privacy the system should offer. Protecting personal privacy is one very good reason to parse data about human activity through a nonspecific medium like audio. For example, unless you personally controlled the information about your office occupation history—how much time you actually spend in your office— you might feel uncomfortable about having it broadcast throughout your workplace. In this case, we used the audio design to strip clues to individual identity out of the data.

5.6   Extracting Data from Sonic Stories

In the informal user tests we ran with Audio Aura, people seemed to like the rich environment and the sound effects environment. The musical earcons, though they could understand the data well enough, were dismissed as too similar all the time (a possible solution we suggested is some algorithmic composition for each type of cue, within an overall framework).

The voice environment was found to be too intrusive, as we suspected— humans have a hard time ignoring other people's voices. Serendipitous interaction with the auditory periphery was our aim.

Amount of email	Sound effects	Voice	Earcons	Rich (combined)
None	A single high seagull cry	"No email"	A single low bell.	A single high seagull cry
A few (< 5)	A gull calling a few times	"You have *n* emails."	A two-note bell (D-A)	A gull calling a few times
Some (< 15)	A few gulls calling together	"You have *n* emails."	A four-note minor arpeggio	A few gulls calling together
Lots (> 15)	Many gulls squabbling	"You have *n* emails."	A longer bell arpeggio	Many gulls squabbling

Other messages	Sound effects	Voice	Earcons	Rich (combined)
Voicemail	Seal barking	"You have voicemail"	Descending melody	Seal barking
Meeting alerts	A group of children playing	"Time for your meeting"	Rhythmic pizzicato	A group of children playing

Office footprints	Sound effects	Voice	Earcons	Rich (combined)
Just stepped out	One buoy bell	"voice file by office occupant"	One high bell	One buoy bell
Not in today	Two buoy bells	e.g., "at the dentist"	Two high bells	Two buoy bells
On vacation	Three buoy bells	"gone fishing"	Three high bells	Three buoy bells

Interior location	Sound effects	Voice	Earcons	Rich (combined)
Two types: area textures (per building) vs. specific door-by-door labeling	Group pulse voice texture; Bldg. 2-1 was ocean surf, Bldg. 2-2 was also surf, but sand not rock	e.g., "Room 2120" "The CSL Commons" "Joe Smith"	Group pulse voice texture: Bldg. 2-1's is a long low vibe; Bldg. 2-2 is a cello	e.g., "Room 2120" "The CSL Commons" "Joe Smith"

Table 1.

We found that our cohesive sets of nonvocal sounds carried data well, as long as the listener felt that he/she understood the story that the sounds were trying to communicate. The audio design created a scenario for the listener to interpret, allowing the sounds within the augmented reality system to be read correctly.

6   Conclusion and Acknowledgments

The methods and examples discussed in this article barely scratch the surface of the possibilities in describing a sound design methodology. They are offered as a way to begin to think creatively about the set of tasks involved in any sound design, and especially about the subset of tasks that are specific to interactive systems. As we understand interactivity better, as our understanding of our perceptual and cognitive abilities develops, and as our technical ability to manipulate sound improves, the methods discussed here should become stronger and more useful. It requires continual attention and self-education on the part of sound designers (who, luckily, are already accustomed to this) and ways to distribute and disseminate new knowledge as it becomes available.

This book is one such way; many thanks to Ken Greenebaum, editor. Thanks also to the many colleagues whose work has influenced mine, and collaborators with whom Audio Aura was built: Beth Mynatt, Roy Want, Keith Edwards, Ron Frederick, Jason Ellis and Michael Baer. Finally, much appreciation to Rich Gold and my colleagues in the RED group at Xerox PARC, for myriad enlightening discussions on new genres (including audio genres), interactive systems, and multimodal design.

Annotated Bibliography

[1] Maribeth Back. "Micro-Narratives in Sound Design: Context, Character, and Caricature in Waveform Manipulation." In *Proceedings of the Third International Conference on Auditory Display*, edited by Dr. Steve Frysinger, 1996.

[2] Maribeth Back. "Reconceiving the Computer Game as an Instrument for Expression: Narrative Techniques for Nonspeech Audio in the Design of Multimodal Systems." Ph.D. diss., Harvard Graduate School of Design, 1996.

[3] James A. Ballas. "Delivery of Information Through Sound." In *Auditory Display: Sonification, Audification, and Auditory Interfaces*, edited by G. Kramer, pp. 79-94, Reading, MA: Addison-Wesley, 1992.

[4] Joshua Bers and Richard A. Bolt. "Up, Up and Away... : Intuitive Flight Through Virtual Worlds." MIT Media Laboratory, 1995.

[5] M. M. Blattner, D. A. Sumikawa, and R. M. Greenberg. "Earcons and Icons: Their Structure and Common Design Principles." *Human-Computer Interaction* 4:1(1991), 11– 44.

[6] Albert Bregman. *Auditory Scene Analysis.* Cambridge, MA: MIT Press, 1990.

[7] B. Buxton, W. Gaver, and S. Bly. *Nonspeech Audio at the Interface.* Manuscript; Partially published as tutorial notes in *Nonspeech Audio, CHI '89 Conference Proceedings,* New York: ACM Press, 1989.

[8] Michel Chion. *Audio-Vision: Sound on Screen.* New York: Columbia University Press, 1993.

[9] *Communications of the ACM.* Special issue on augmented environments.36:7(1993).

[10] David Cope. "On Algorithmic Representations of Musical Style." In *Understanding Music with AI,* edited by Balaban et al., pp. 354–363, Menlo Park, CA: The AAAI Press, 1992.

[11] N.I. Durlach, A. Rigopulos, X.D. Pang, W.S. Woods, A Kulkarni, H.S. Colburn, and E.M. Wenzel. "On the Externalization of Auditory Images." *Presence* 1:2(1992): 251–257.

[12] Thomas Erickson. "Working with Interface Metaphors." In *The Art of Human-Computer Interface Design,* edited by Brenda Laurel, pp. 65—74, Reading, MA: Addison Wesley, 1990.

[13] S. Feiner, B. MacIntyre, and D. Seligmann. "Annotating the Real World with Knowledge-Based Graphics on a See-Through Head-Mounted Display." In *Proceedings, Graphics Interface 1992,* pp. 78–85, Vancouver, Canada: Canadian Human-Computer Communication Society, 1992.

[14] W. Gaver. "The Sonic Finder: An Interface that Uses Auditory Icons." *Human-Computer Interaction* 4:1(1989), 67–94.

[15] W. Gaver. "What in the World Do We Hear: An Ecological Approach to Auditory Event Perception." *Ecological Perception* 5:1(1993), 1–29.

[16] W. Gaver. "Using and Creating Auditory Icons." In *Auditory Display: The Proceedings of ICAD '92,* edited by G. Kramer, pp. 417–446, Reading, MA: Addison-Wesley, 1994.

[17] W. Gaver, R. Smith, and T. O'Shea. "Effective Sound in Complex Systems: The ARKola Simulation" *Proceedings of CHI'91*, pp. 85–90, New York: ACM Press, 1991.

[18] Stephen Handel. *Listening: An Introduction to the Perception of Auditory Events.* Cambridge, MA: MIT Press, 1989.

[19] Tomlinson Holman. *Sound for Film and Television.* Boston, MA: Focal Press, 1997.

[20] J. H. Howard, Jr. and J.A. Ballas. "Syntactic and Semantic Factors in the Classification of Nonspeech Transient Patterns." *Perception &Psychology* 28(1980): 431–439.

[21] Scott E. Hudson and Ian Smith. "Electronic Mail Previews Using Nonspeech Audio." *CHI '96 Conference Companion*, pp. 237–238, New York: ACM Press, 1996.

[22] Gregory Kramer. "An Introduction to Auditory Display." *Proceedings of the 2nd International Conference on Auditory Display*, Reading, MA: Addison-Wesley, 1992.

[23] Brenda Laurel. *Computers as Theatre.* Reading, MA: Addison-Wesley, 1991.

[24] G. A. Miller. "Dictionaries of the Mind." *23rd Meeting of the Association for Computational Linguistics*, 1985.

[25] M. Minsky. *The Society of Mind.* New York: Simon and Schuster, 1985.

[26] E. Mynatt, M. Back, and R. Want. "Designing Audio Aura." *Proceedings of CHI '98*, pp. 566–573, New York: ACM Press, 1998.

[27] E. Mynatt. "Designing with Auditory Icons." In *Proceedings of the 2nd International Conference on Auditory Display*, pp. 269–270, 1994.

[28] Roger C. Schank and Robert P. Abelson. "Knowledge and Memory: The Real Story." In *Advances in Social Cognition, Volume VIII*, edited by Robert S. Wyer, Jr., pp. 1–85, Hillsdale, NJ: Lawrence Erlbaum Associates, 1995.

[29] Mark Turner. *The Literary Mind.* Oxford, UK: Oxford University Press, 1996.

[30] Robert Walker. "The Effects of Culture, Environment, Age, and Musical training on Choices of Visual Metaphors for Sound." *Perception and Psychophysics* 42:5(1987), 491–502.

[31] R. Want, A. Hopper, V. Falcao, and J. Gibbons. "The Active Badge Location System." *ACM Transactions on Information Systems* 10:1(1992), 91–102.

[32] W. Warren and R. Vebrugge. "Auditory Perception of Breaking and Bouncing Events: A Case Study in Ecological Acoustics." *Journal of Experimental Psychology* 10(1984): 704–712.

[33] Elisabeth Weis and John Belton, Editors. *Film Sound - Theory and Practice*, New York: Columbia University Press, 1985.

[34] M. Weiser. "The Computer of the 21st Century." *Scientific American* 265:3(1991), 94–104.

[35] E. M. Wenzel and S. H. Foster. "Real-Time Digital Synthesis of Virtual Acoustic Environments." *Computer Graphics* 24:2(1990), 139–140.

[36] Wenzel, E. M., F. L. Wightman, and D. J. Kistler. "Localization with Non-individualized Virtual Acoustic Display Cues." *CHI '91 Proceedings,* pp. 351–359. Reading, MA: ACM Press/Addison-Wesley, 1991.

[37] E. M. Wenzel. "Localization in Virtual Acoustic Displays." *Presence: Teleoperators & Virtual Enviroments* 1(1992), 80–107.

[38] E. M. Wenzel. "Spatial Sound and Sonification." In *Auditory Display: Sonification, Audification, and Auditory Interfaces,* edited by G. Kramer, pp. 127–150, Reading, MA: Addison Wesley, 1994.

[39] H. Wu, M. Siegel, and P. Khosla. "Vehicle Sound Signature Recognition by Frequency Vector Principal Component Analysis." *IEEE Instrumentation and Measurement Technology Conference,* 1998.

Sound as Information: An Introduction to Auditory Display

Rob Tannen

1 Introduction

The purpose of this article to is to provide an introduction to the use of sound as a means to display information. The article will cover some of the key properties of sound that make it a unique and rich medium for communication. Various applications for the use of sound will be described, and some general guidelines about listening environments are provided to assist in the implementation of auditory display.

We are accustomed to listening to sounds for information in our daily lives. Of course, speech is our primary form of audible communication, but we also attend to a wide range of natural and manmade sounds. For example, some sounds serve to alert us or capture our attention: a telephone ring, thunder in a rainstorm, a fire truck's siren. At other times, sounds can reveal detailed information about objects or environments, although sometimes only to a trained ear. For example, a skilled mechanic might diagnose an engine problem by detecting a rattle, or a cave-explorer could judge the size of a cavern by listening to the echoes. In other cases, sounds may convey mood more so than information: the restful sound of surf on the beach, a moving string adagio, or a creepy coyote howl in the middle of the night.

Despite the powerful influence that nonspeech sound can have on us, it has not been used widely as an information display medium. The use of audio has not been exploited to the same degree as visual displays for the delivery and presentation of information. Consider, for example, that while we shop for PCs with high-resolution monitors for video display, many of us (at least until recently) have no problem settling for internal or low-end speakers for audio display. This is not surprising. Consider surfing the Internet with your monitor on and your speakers off. Now consider the reverse situation.

Early on, the use of sound in personal computers was limited to simple beeps and clicks. More recent enhancements in the sound generation and delivery capabilities of PCs, particularly digital signal processing and the Internet, have broadened the applicability and characteristics of audio presentation. Typical home PCs have sound synthesis capabilities far beyond the best synthesizers from a generation ago, and the variety of available sounds is now virtually limitless, but many developers have not made significant efforts to incorporate sound into software applications. At the same time, recent enthusiasm about PC audio has more to do with playing music than for application-oriented use of sounds. This is unfortunate, as audio is an extremely powerful and useful means of conveying information, and is particularly useful in situations where visual display is insufficient.

While advocating the use of sounds, it is important that this not be done so haphazardly. It is critical to think about sounds in terms of purpose. That is, what functions can sound serve? Sound can be used for many purposes—to provide listening enjoyment, convey information, capture someone's attention, and much more. By considering user goals and capabilities, you can better select, design, and present sound to the listener. In order to succeed, you need to understand some of the charac-teristics of sound. Making the most of auditory display requires a basic understanding of sound and how people listen.

2 Sound and Hearing

Most people think about sounds in terms of certain basic psychoacoustical (e.g., loudness, pitch) and aesthetic (e.g., pleasantness) qualities, but the physical, physiological, and psychological interactions that result in the perception of sound are more complex than one might expect. Consider the kind of information that sound delivers.

2.1 Interaction of Materials

Gaver wrote that: "a given sound provides information about an interac-tion of materials at a location in an environment" [3]. Gaver's description succinctly delineates the key components of an acoustical event. Sound, by definition, requires the movement of an object or objects. Even the quietist sounds arise out of the vibrations of air molecules as the result of some physical event: the rustling of leaves, a drip of water, the contraction of a cardiac muscle. Consequently, hearing a sound implicitly indicates that an event has occurred. The particular materials and interactions involved will determine the characteristics of the resulting sound. As any sound effects (Foley) artist can tell you, a child's light, hurried footsteps are distinctive from that of a larger adult's deliberate ones, footsteps on gravel sound different from footsteps on wood, boots are louder than moccasins, etc. Such differences in the interactions and materials that create sounds inform listeners about what is occurring. This means that the meaning of a sound will be based not only on the general type of sound (e.g., footsteps), but on the other relevant characteristics including its attack (how quickly or gradually the sound reaches its maximum intensity), loudness, and repetition.

2.2 Localization

Getting back to Gaver's description of sound, beyond the materials involved and their interactions, sound informs listeners about location. It is our ability to localize an event via its sound that enables us to react appropriately. A sound that is distant will elicit a different reaction than a sound that is nearby. Likewise a sound that occurs behind will cause a response differently than a sound that is in front of a listener. The ability to localize information via sound is arguably the greatest asset of hearing. Localizing sounds even helps us with sight. Since hearing is omnidirectional, we are able to pick up information about events that are outside the field of view of eyesight. Then we are able to precisely orient the eyes to the direction of the sound source.

To a limited extent, the location of sound sources can be determined based on the materials and interactions involved. That is, one can get a good idea of where a sound is coming from if one is familiar with the location of things in the environment. For instance, past experience would dictate a high probability that the sound of a jet airplane would be coming from above a listener. But the mechanisms of sound localization are far more sophisticated, and rooted in the way we hear. It was initially believed that our localization abilities were based on the time delay between sound reaching the near and far ears relative to a sound source. Sound travels in waves propagating out from the source. Consequently, a sound source to one's left will arrive at the left ear slightly earlier than the right ear. This intra-aural time delay allows for differentiation of a source location. The greater the delay, the greater the laterality of the sound source. In addition, depending on the frequency of the sound wave, the phase of the wave may be perceptibly different at the two ears.

While this explanation makes sense for sound sources that are closer to one ear or the other, it is insufficient for cases where a sound source is equidistant from the two ears. For example, how does one discriminate among sources that are directly in front, directly behind, or directly above, as in all of those cases the sound will arrive at the two ears simultaneously? It is now understood that localization is based upon a number of contributing factors, and has to do with the distinctive shapes of our heads and bodies. Getting back to the example of a sound arriving at one's left ear slightly before the right one, not only is there a difference in when the sounds arrive, but there are differences in the characteristics of the sounds at each ear. The sound arriving at the further ear will be slightly dampened by absorption by the listener's head and body. Similarly, sounds arriving from different positions equidistant from the two ears will be reflected and absorbed by the ears, head, and body in different ways. These patterns of frequency-dependent attenuations are known as Head-Related Transfer Functions or HRTFs. A sound arriving from in front of a listener will be reflected off of the head and body and particularly the front of the ears (pinnae), enhancing certain frequencies and resulting in a sound distinct from a sound source behind or above.

While we may not be cognizant of these acoustical differences, we clearly perceive them as localization differences. In fact, individuals with hearing in only a single ear are able to localize sounds (although not as well as those with binaural hearing[1]).

Since we each have unique heads and bodies, and consequently, hear the world in slightly different ways, it is technically complex to reproduce the effects of HRTFs specific to each and every listener. On the other hand, laterality effects can be easily reproduced with left and right placed speakers or stereophonic earphones as sound sources. The greater the degree of laterality, or panning, with respect to each speaker, the greater perceived laterality of the sound. This assumes of course that speakers are arranged reasonably with respect to the listener. A good rule of thumb is to have the two speakers and the listener as the three points of an approximately equilateral triangle. The speakers should be equidistant from each other and from the listener, although the listener may be slightly more or

---

[1]See Gehring's article "Why 3D Sound through Headphones?" (see *Audio Anecdotes III*) and Haferkorn's article "Head-Related Transfer Functions and the Physics of Spatial Hearing" (see *Audio Anecdotes III*) for more discussion of HRTFs and binaural audio.

less distant from the midpoint between the speakers. A typical desktop arrangement can accommodate these general requirements if the speakers are placed several inches away from each side of the display monitor.

2.3 Environment

The last part of Gaver's definition refers to the interaction of materials at a location in an *environment*. Sound informs the listener about an event-taking place at a certain location within a certain kind of environment. There are a number of ways in which the environment may alter the acoustical characteristics of a sound. The most obvious example is an echo, where the size and reflectivity of the environment allow for audible repetitions of a sound, with each successive repetition weaker than the previous. Any environment (with the exception of a completely open or absorptive space) will reflect sound waves and create repetitions. Only when the repetitions are audible and spaced enough apart (greater than 40 milliseconds), do we perceive echoes or delays. Audible repetitions that fall within the 40 ms interval are referred to as reverberations. Harder surfaces (concrete, metal) reflect more than softer surfaces (fiber, cloth) and larger spaces (arenas) have greater delay between reflections than smaller spaces (offices). The unique combination of materials and spaciousness are what define the acoustical signature of an environment. For example, a small space with hard surfaces will provide a lot of reverberation; hence, people like to sing in their showers. An orchestra playing in an opera house full of listeners will actually be quieter than playing to an empty house because all of the bodies absorb a significant amount of the acoustical energy.

It should be evident by now that any sound can reveal a great deal of information to a listener: the interaction of objects involved in creating the sound, the location of the sound with respect to the listener, and the spaciousness and composition of the environment. The richness of information inherent in auditory perception can be leveraged to use sound as a more effective means to communicate. To do so successfully requires a fuller understanding of how sound can and has been used to display information.

3   Sound as Information

While most of us are familiar with music and sound effects, the use of nonspeech sound as a more concrete information conveyance may be somewhat foreign. We are accustomed to using visuals to convey and understand information. For example, graphs and charts are often the tools first selected when we wish to analyze or share data. Until recently, technical constraints made visual presentation of information to a broad audience (e.g., a newspaper) much simpler than audio presentation, but the prevalence of digital technology has minimized this "sensory gap." The utilization of sound for information conveyance, or auditory display, is an area that has received some attention.

Mountford and Gaver eloquently stated that: "Sound exists in time and over space, vision exists in space and over time" [6].

In other words, sound is suited to indicate changes over time, and can be picked up over a wide range of spatial locations. Visual information is usually less transitory, but can only be perceived at specific locations in space. This is a simplification, but it points out that hearing and seeing differ in several important ways. Sound is omnidirectional and alerting, and it can be used to provide information over and above the limits of visual display and attention. Consequently, auditory displays have traditionally been used as warning signals and in situations where visual display is not feasible.

Sound has been extremely effective in conveying simple, short, and time-sensitive information, but it is also useful in other ways. Sound is effective in conveying presence, mood, and information. Conveying presence means using sound to simulate events or environments—sound effects. This encompasses everything from the collision of objects to the squeak of a mouse. The important feature is that such sounds are used to imitate the acoustical components of real-world events. Sound can also be used to evoke a mood. Music is often used to create a specific feeling (e.g., suspense) or to add richness to a situation (i.e., ambiance). While sound effects can also be used to evoke a mood, their primary purpose is to replicate an existing sound. Finally, sound communicates information. The most obvious and direct example of this is speech, but it is not necessary for the sounds themselves to have a particular meaning. Rather, the arrangement of otherwise meaningless sounds, as in Morse code, can also be informative. Keep in mind that these are not absolute distinctions and can change with time and the goals of a listener. For example, a particular sound may initially communicate information, but then as the listener turns attention elsewhere, become ambient background noise.

Experts in auditory display [4] recognize a continuum of sound display ranging from audification to sonification. *Audification*, is similar to the concept of icons in visual displays, in that the acoustical structure of the sound parallels that of the represented event. These are typically familiar, shortduration copies of realworld acoustical events, such as the use of a cash register "ca-ching" when entering a transaction in a financial application. At the other end, *sonification*, refers to the use of sound as a means of displaying information for events that do not typically have a relevant acoustic component, for example using varying durations and sequences of tones is the basis for Morse code. Here the sounds are the means of information conveyance, but are not meaningful in and of themselves (see data auralization in Section 4). Rather it is the relations among the sounds that provide information to a listener. The association of structured musical tones within user interfaces, or *earcons*, is one of the better known examples of sonification. It wouldn't matter what particular sound was used, as long as differences in duration and sequence remained intelligible. Note that "realistic" sounds could be used for the purpose of sonification, but this may be distracting and there is the problem of loss of recognition with changes in data. On the other hand, changing the sounds used in audification change the meaning of an event. In a nutshell: In audification, the specific characteristics of the sounds contains the information, and in sonification, the relation among sounds conveys information. This means that, in the case of sonification, changing the specific sounds does not change the information, and even simple tones may be used. In fact, this is often preferable.

4   Applications of Auditory Display

There are a number of ways that auditory display can be used to convey information. Here are a few of the key situations:

- **Accessibility.** Although auditory display can serve all listeners, it may be particularly beneficial to those with visual impairments. Given the emphasis on visual display, such individuals can be at a significant disadvantage when it comes to accessing information. Furthermore, adding auditory cues to supplement visual cues can increase the salience of information for everyone. For example, a visual icon may be designed to change on a rollover or mouseover. This rollover can also trigger an appropriate sound that distinguishes a change in state. Similarly, auditory display may be useful in the context of visual applications, such as a hypothetical graphic design application, where sound can provide information without interfering with visual tasks. For example, it can be difficult to keep track of which of the dozens of drawing tools one has last selected when using a design application. A potential solution to this is to map sounds to the functionality of tools so that use of each tool is associated with a unique tone. Whenever a tool was used (e.g., clicking on a part of an image to work on), a tone would immediately orient users to the current selection, and reduce the chance of, for instance, trying to draw a curve while the text editing function is active.

- **Alarms and Alerts.** This traditional use of sound typically uses high frequency, short duration, repeating pulses (think of all of those annoying cell phone rings). Alerts are designed to quickly grab someone's attention, usually to carry out some action: go to a meeting, leave the building, wake up, Alerts are commonly found on the desktop to notify users of incoming emails, chat messages, and the like. The advantage of auditory over visual display is powerful in this context, as line-of-sight is not necessary. On the other hand, sound alone would be insufficient in noisy environments (e.g., musical, industrial).

- **Data Auralization.** A recent development in the use of sound has been mapping acoustical parameters such as frequency, rate, and timbre to data, the auditory equivalent of data visualization. This can be useful in reviewing large amounts of data, for example in financial or scientific applications, or for process monitoring. One may listen to a stream of mapped data, listening for anomalies or outliers as outstandingly high- or low-pitched sounds. Moreover, because sound is well suited for displaying changes over time (e.g., musical melodies), emergent patterns of data may be perceived as tonal patterns that might not be picked up in a visual display. Reviewing large data sets can be inefficient on the limited space of a video monitor, compared with the virtually unlimited real estate of auditory display, particularly when a data range is too large to effectively scale visually. Keep in mind that as with visual presentation, mapping sounds to data requires appropriate scaling so that key differences are detectable and within a perceptible range.

- **Exploratory.** New techniques may be technologically feasible, but lacking in useful applications. For example, sound morphing is a popular technique for blending multiple sounds, but has not found a niche beyond entertainment. Consider using sound in situations where you might normally rely on visual display, graphics, and text. Ever notice how many web cams there are, but how often do you hear about a web microphone? Be creative, but keep in mind what works best, is most appropriate, and is most interesting. Validate your ideas by testing them with the users who would benefit from your developments.

- **Localization and Environment.** Auditory display can leverage our ability to localize sounds in the environment. This can be done in an analogous way, where the apparent positions of sounds are mapped to events and objects in a real or virtual environment. For example, the position of characters in a role-playing game can be reproduced by reproducing their relative positions in the lateral plane of the environment. Certain characteristics of the environment may also be reproduced, such as the spaciousness of an environment via reverberation and echo. Localization can also be used in a nonanalogous way, using position to differentiate more abstract categories. For instance, a security administration program could display public information lateralized to one side and secure information lateralized to the other, enabling clearer differentiation of information, thereby making it easier to spot errors or breaches.

- **Speech.** This is perhaps the most powerful form of auditory display, although not often recognized as such. Speech is good for conveying explanatory and descriptive information. In addition, it can convey aspects of character and personality (although synthesized speech may be received as impersonal). In comparison to simple tones, the acoustical richness can result in relatively large sound files, but note that the majority of content in speech falls below 1000–3000Hz. Know your audience—not everyone understands a particular language—and make use of different types of voices (gender, age, accent) where appropriate to add distinction or effect.

- **Visual Overload.** Often a good time to use sound is when a user will be otherwise visually occupied or overloaded. Much of the research on auditory displays has occurred in the military aviation domain, where the visual load of the cockpit demands researching other channels of information, but this can trickle down to everyday technology. Tannen [7] describes a web-browsing system in which content is displayed visually, but background processes, such as file download, are displayed aurally. For example, users could monitor the rate and completeness of an MP3 download via the speed of a familiar tune. The completion of the melody would correspond with the completion of the file download. This allows a person to browse primary content in a single window, while still being informed of concurrent processes without having to switch to another window.

5 Next Steps

Our ability to pick up information via sound has remained relatively un-
tapped in interface design in comparison to the use of visual displays for
conveying information. Sound informs listeners about the materials and
interactions involved in events at specific locations within an environment.
These characteristics can be mapped to displays that can both exceed and
augment the visual display of information, but it is necessary to consider
the appropriate use and implementation of sounds. The reader is encouraged to explore auditory display by reading Back's article "Designing the
Auditory Narrative: A Methodology for Sound Design" (page 305) and
Roberts and Sikora's article "Auditory Feedback for Computer Devices"
(page 341), as well as the references provided at the end of this article.

As with any application, when implementing auditory display, it is
important to consider the goals and capabilities of the end-users. That
means understanding and validating the display of sounds with users,
and designing for the equipment and environment in which people will be
listening. Desktop sound systems have come a long way since the internal
speaker, and are generally capable of producing the required output for
most applications. Many end-users also listen through earphones, which
are ideal for auditory display. Since there is a potential for variability,
it's a good idea to include appropriate instructions or explanations for
speaker set-up when it may significantly affect sound delivery, particularly
localization where source position is important.

Still others will not be able to hear sounds at all be it due to technological limitations, environmental constraints, or a hearing deficit. For
these situations, it is advisable to provide the best of both worlds via an
alternate or redundant means of information presentation. By allowing
an end-user to select either audio or visual (or some mixture of both), he
or she can use whatever works best.

Annotated Bibliography

[1] J. Beggs and D. Thede. *Designing Web Audio*. Sebastopol, CA:
O'Reilly & Associates, Inc, 2001.

*A recent, comprehensive overview of the practical and technical con-
siderations for capturing and implementing audio on the web in various popular formats including RealAudio, MP3, Flash, and Beatnik.*

[2] F. A. Everest and R. Streicher. *The New Stereo Soundbook*. Summit,
PA: Tab Books, 1992.

A practical resource for understanding the perceptual basis of various approaches to stereophonic sound, as well as extensive content on recording and reproduction tools and techniques.

[3] W. W. Gaver. "What in the World Do We Hear? An Ecological Approach to Auditory Event Perception." *Ecological Psychology* 5(1993), 1–29.

Gaver's work explains and explores sound in the context of the everyday world, and how sound is informative about events in the environment.

[4] G. Kramer. "An Introduction to Auditory Display." In *Auditory Display: Sonification, Audification, and Auditory Iinterfaces*, edited by G. Kramer. Reading, MA: Addison Wesley, 1994.

Kramer's opening chapter of the essential book on auditory display provides an excellent introduction to the subject. The subsequent chapters provide a background on conceptual and practical issues in the field from a range of experts.

[5] Brian C. J. Moorean. *An Introduction to the Psychology of Hearing.* London: Academic Press, 1989.

An excellent source for learning the historical and theoretical underpinnings of hearing, with an emphasis on physiological and psychology models.

[6] S. J. Mountford and W. W. Gaver. "Talking and Listening to Computers." In *The art of humancomputer interface design*, edited by B. Laurel, p. 322. Reading, MA: AddisonWesley, 1990.

Although written more than a decade ago, this chapter is a good starting point for understanding the fundamental issues relevant to both listening and speaking to computers.

[7] R. S. Tannen. "Breaking the Sound Barrier: Designing Auditory Displays for Global Usability, Fourth Edition." In *Proceedings of the Fourth Annual Conference on Human Factors and the Web.* Basking Ridge: NJ, 1998. Available from World Wide Web (http://www.research.att.com/conf/hfweb/proceedings/tannen/index.html).

This discussion demonstrates how research on the perception of sound can be used to develop perceptually intuitive desktop-based auditory displays.

Auditory Feedback for Computer Devices

Linda A. Roberts and Cynthia A. Sikora

1 Introduction and Background

The use of sound as feedback has become increasingly possible with advances in technology, the widespread availability of computer equipment, and the Internet. Moreover, sound has unique properties that make it very desirable as a mechanism for providing information, particularly when the user's attention is directed away from the primary task. Several sources of sound can be monitored simultaneously while the user is performing a task that requires both motor and visual attention [1]. For example, a person could be talking on the phone while going through their mail and the auditory feedback regarding a task on the computer would still be perceived and processed. Selective attention is often used to focus attention on one of multiple stimuli as is appropriate for the situation. The "cocktail party" effect of suddenly hearing your name across a crowded room is often given as an example of selectively attending to one background sound and not to others, even when they are of the same intensity [2].

Another benefit of sound as feedback is that the user can monitor or get feedback about an activity in the absence of visual cues. Furthermore, there is some evidence that sound can draw attention to, or reinforce, visual information [2]. If our car makes an unusual noise, we immediately tend to scan the instruments to see what is wrong. Sound can also enhance visual information. For example, there is some anecdotal evidence that players' scores on video games decrease when the sound is turned off

[1]. Sound also has the advantage of being available 360 degrees around the user. In addition, the auditory system is unique in that it has a continuously open channel. Even in sleep, the auditory modality can encode sound. These qualities of sound have led to devices like the alarm clock, the doorbell, and the ringing telephone.

On a more emotional level, well-designed sounds have the capability of engaging, motivating and influencing users. Auditory cues and auditory branding[1] have been a standard feature of radio and television for some time. It has also been shown that branding can project numerous attributes and can be as influential in conveying product awareness as a visual logo or celebrity spokesperson [3]. Masten [3] states that, "In traditional media, sound is an integral persuasive element of the branding and buying experience." In contrast, he points out that, "Online, the silence is deafening." Masten considers technology constraints to be the primary inhibitor of using sound during web interactions.

Despite the above-mentioned advantages of using sound as feedback or information, there are some disadvantages. One disadvantage of using sound is that most designers are visually oriented and have little musical or sound-design training or skills. Masten [3] claims that, if audio is to become viable online, web developers must be able to understand users' innate reactions to sound. Another major disadvantage is that some sounds may become disturbing after extended use. In addition to having musically astute sound designers, it is critical that feedback and branding sounds be well tested with users prior to their implementation so that they are less likely to be "turned off" by the user. Assuming that sounds are well designed and tested, auditory signals may ease the complexity of the user's interactions in complex environments such as PC-based applications or the Internet.

Sound can be used in computers to provide information about the system or environment. A continuous sound associated with data patterns or the state of the system is referred to as *auralisation* [4]. For example, the more users on the system, the more salient the sound might become and, the fewer users, the subtler the sound. Short, distinct sounds are used to provide auditory feedback of discrete events. These sounds are typically used for alerting the user or for confirmation. A user can receive a brief confirmation of an action or event being completed or taking place. An alert can inform the user of a condition or state of the system. The types of feedback discussed here will focus on auditory feedback signals.

---

[1]Branding refers to the emotional or cultural image associated with a company or product. Branding enables one product to be differentiated from others and this is often achieved by the repetition of persuasive messages.

(Readers are directed also to Rob Tannen's article "Sound as Information: An Introduction to Auditory Display (page 329), for an introduction to auditory display.)

Two classes of sounds have been proposed as auditory feedback signals: *auditory icons* and *earcons* [5]. The first, auditory icons, use environmental sounds that have a strong link with the object represented by the sound. An example is the sound of trash being emptied into a trash can to represent deleting a file. The use of these "real world" sounds has been widely accepted due to the strong functional mappings inherent in these sounds ([6], [7], [8]), as well as to their relatively easy access and creation. The second class of sounds, earcons [5], refers to abstract synthesized sounds that are more musical in origin, typically with well-defined pitches, rhythms, harmonies and timbres. These latter signals may be described as very short durations of "program music" that are created to steer the emotional reaction of the listener in support of the desired image. These sounds have less intuitive functional mappings [9], and their development requires expertise in music composition and sound design, which helps to explain their underutilization in computer/web applications.

Auditory icons have been equated to sound effects for computers [4]. These everyday sounds are mapped to analogous computer events to provide feedback or status. Auditory icons attempt to exploit the user's existing knowledge of everyday sounds to provide intuitive feedback. These sounds can be implemented to use different sound characteristics to provide different indications of the parameters of the event. For example, the sound used to act upon an item can be lower or higher in volume to indicate a smaller or larger size, respectively. In this way, families of sounds can be created to map to the same action for different items [7].

Earcons add a secondary modality to computer feedback without the harsh, often distracting, sounds of associated real-world noises. Although not as immediately intuitive, these short, musical snippets can be developed to provide more subtle feedback for computer functions. Earcons can also be designed as sound families. By systematically varying characteristics of the sound, multiple sounds can seem very different and yet still provide the same feel, thereby maintaining a family resemblance. The sounds can be used in a particular organization to indicate a structure, or the contour of the sound can be paired with analogous events. Certain characteristics of sound can also be varied to achieve a specific effect. Research has shown that sounds with high frequencies, changes in frequencies and amplitude, timbres that are not harmonic, and sudden onsets relay a sense of urgency [4].

2   Design and Brainstorm Process

Throughout this anecdote, we describe research designed for computer and telephony applications in which numerous auditory feedback signals were created for subsequent testing and validation. In this section, we describe the process that was utilized to define and create the various auditory signals that were tested.

First, we selected a professional sound designer/musician from the vicinity in which we lived (the New York City area). Selection criteria included significant education and experience in music composition as well as a well-equipped sound studio. Mark Barasch, of Sound Image NY, met all of our criteria: He is well-educated in music composition, has composed and designed for a variety of applications (e.g., jingles, movie soundtracks, television sound effects), and has an extensive sound studio (with digital audio capabilities, MIDI music generating systems, and a complement of traditional outboard audio processing gear).

We then determined the list of features for which we needed sounds, based on product or testing needs.[2] When we met with the sound designer, we presented him with a list of features, together with definitions and other relevant information. All sounds were required to be less than two seconds in length, normally in a pleasing pitch range (above 400 Hz). We also imparted information about likely user expectations (e.g., for the send call feature, the feedback signal needed to imply progress, similar to that currently provided by DTMF (Dual Tone Multiple Frequency) tones on a telephone, used for dialing and switching). The designer was then asked to create at least two candidates for each of the features and was encouraged to contact us with any questions.

When we next met with the designer, we listened to and critiqued the feedback signals, and he typically carried out at least one additional round of iterative (or new) design changes. When we were satisfied with the sound alternatives, he provided us with .wav files of the sounds that were then used for testing.

When deciding on the auditory icons to use as feedback for the functions to be tested, we employed brainstorming techniques. A group of people, who were representative of those who would use the functions under investigation, were asked to come up with real-world, everyday sounds that could be used as feedback for the functions. As ideas were generated, the facilitator recorded them, regardless of the quality of the idea. The

---

[2]For the initial research, he designed all sounds except auditory icons (we selected these from sound libraries), but he designed both earcons and auditory icons for subsequent research.

sound suggestions were then reviewed and discussed for appropriateness and intuitiveness.

3 Acceptability of Earcons and Auditory Icons in Business Applications

3.1 Functional Mappings and Pleasantness of Auditory Feedback Signals

One issue regarding the implementation of auditory icons and earcons concerns users' reactions to them, both functionally and aesthetically. Jones and Turner [9] observed that users preferred earcons even though they were better able to associate auditory icons to functions.

In our initial studies, we evaluated the usability and acceptability of three classes of sounds: 1) auditory icons, 2) earcons, and 3) communications sounds (i.e., relatively simple sounds derived from traditional electronic tones, used primarily in telecommunications products). Although we distinguished between earcons and communications sounds, the latter may be considered to be very simplistic earcons that vary only in pitch and timbre. In contrast, earcons tend to vary in harmonic and rhythmic dimensions as well. A more complete description of this work is provided in Sikora, Roberts, and Murray [10].

Barasch, our professional sound designer, created both the communications and the earcon signals for 11 different communications functions.[3] Real-world candidates were selected from sound libraries. The designer was asked to create one communication and one musical sound for each function. However, due to his enthusiasm, he created many more alternatives than requested. We culled these alternatives to 22 musical sounds and 14 communications sounds. The real-world sounds were selected from an initial set of 30 sounds and were subsequently reduced to 12. The ideas for the 30 real-world sounds were generated using brainstorming techniques with a group of human factors experts and student interns. Examples of real-world sounds and the intended functions include the sound of a door opening (join conference), paper crumpling (error), and applause (confirmation).

The first study was designed to find any natural mappings of the sounds to the functions and determine their feasibility in a business en-

---

[3]The functions included: confirmation, distinctive ring, drop from conference, end call, error, hold, join conference, logo, personalized ring, send call, and status indicator. These sounds are trademarked by Lucent Technologies and are available on the accompanying CD-ROM.

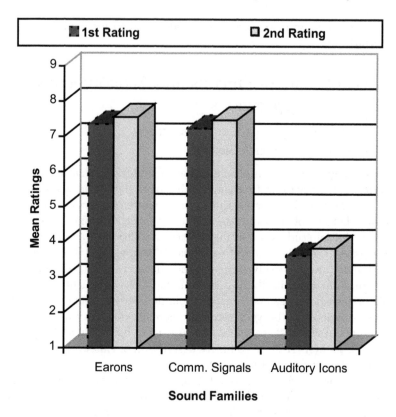

Figure 1. Pleasantness ratings for three sound classes of audibles are shown. Ratings are based on a 9-point scale where 9 is very pleasant and 1 is very unpleasant.

vironment. Thirty-eight participants were tested in groups of about four. They were familiarized with the 11 telecommunications functions and subsequently listened to 48 sounds (22 earcons, 12 auditory icons, and 14 communications signals). They were asked to map each of the sounds to one of 11 telecommunications functions and to rate the pleasantness and appropriateness of each sound. In addition, they were asked to rate their confidence in their judgments. For each of the three latter ratings, a 9-point scale was used where 9 denoted "very pleasant," "very appropriate," and "very confident." After an intermediate task, the users were presented with the sounds in a different randomized order and were asked to make the same mapping and rating judgments.

As expected, the real-world sounds mapped most predictably to the functions (i.e., strong agreement among the participants) while the vari-

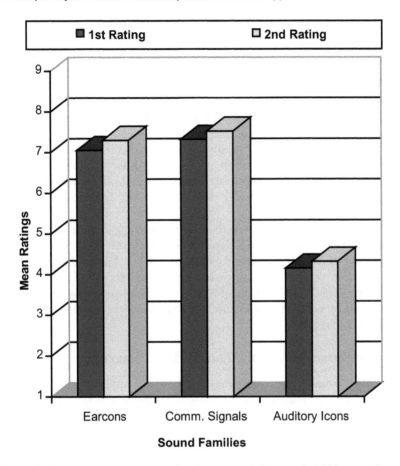

Figure 2. Appropriateness ratings for three sound classes of audibles are shown. Ratings are based on a 9-point scale where 9 is very appropriate and 1 is very inappropriate for a business environment.

ability was considerably higher for both musical and communications sounds. However, findings for pleasantness ratings demonstrated a reliable effect of sound class [$F(2,72) = 252.55$, $p <.01$], where the musical and communications sounds received significantly higher pleasantness ratings relative to the real-world sounds. These results are shown in Figure 1.

Ratings of the appropriateness for a business environment are shown in Figure 2. As occurred for pleasantness ratings, there were main effects of sound class [$F(12,72) = 168.62$, $p < .01$], where the musical and communications sounds attained reliably higher appropriateness ratings.

3.2   Replication in a Business Application

In a subsequent study, we utilized a subset of sounds selected from the work described above (the sounds with the best mappings for each of the functions—one from each of the sound classes per function). The study was designed to test the sounds further within the context of a simulated business communications PC application. Twenty-two participants, tested in groups of two to four, observed a business application simulation in which the sounds were presented during task scenarios. Within a scenario, they heard three different sounds (earcon, auditory icon and communications signal), made both pleasantness and appropriateness judgments, and then selected the best sound for that function.

Results mirrored those described above, such that both musical and communications sounds were judged to be significantly more pleasant and appropriate than the real-world sounds (p<01). Moreover, individual users seldom chose a real-world sound as the best choice for any of the functions. Indeed, of the eleven functions, seven were best represented by musical sounds and four were best represented by communications sounds.

3.3   Descriminability of the Earcon-Based Sound Family

The "best" sounds from the simulated business application study were chosen to create a family of sounds. It is important that the sounds within the family are discriminable and that they sound like they belong to the same family of sounds. This work is described in greater detail in Sikora and Roberts [11].

In this research, 38 participants rated the similarity of the 11 sounds (one for each function). Using a computer simulation, participants listened to pairs of sounds and rated the degree of similarity of each pairing. The data from the sound similarity ratings revealed that the discriminiability within the sound family was quite good, with the exception of one pair of sounds. Based on subjective reporting in conjunction with a multidimensional scaling analysis of the data, it appears that three dimensions were used to make their similarity judgments: duration, average pitch and harmonic complexity.

3.4   Global Testing of the Earcon-Based Sound Family

This research investigated the extent to which people in different countries can use abstract musical feedback signals designed and developed in the United States. These findings are described more fully in Sikora and Roberts [12]. The same stimuli were used as in the discriminability study in which 11 musical- or communications-based sounds were evaluated. The study investigated how well the sounds mapped to the 11 functions, as well as their perceived pleasantness, appropriateness, and confidence. Participants also rated the entire set in terms of how well they fit together as a family. Seventy-four participants from four different countries (India, Singapore, Turkey, and the United States) participated in the study. Based on earlier findings, it was hypothesized that users in all countries would find the sounds aesthetically appropriate, but that functional mappings would be unreliable.

The data were analyzed to determine which sounds mapped most often to which functions and how this compared to the sound/function pairings that were intended. The error function had the best performance with 32 percent of the participants selecting the function for that sound. Participants across countries were equally variable in their responses.

To evaluate how the sounds were perceived aesthetically, a "desirability rating" was devised by computing a factor analysis on the overall subjective ratings of the sounds (i.e., their pleasantness, appropriateness, confidence, and family ratings). Main desirability ratings were quite high, ranging from 6.0 to 6.54 on a 9-point scale. A multivariate analysis of variance of the difference between countries on the desirability rating of all eleven functions found a significant difference for two functions (end call and send call). No other function feedback sounds differed across countries.

In summary, it was found that participants of the four countries tested responded well to the sounds in terms of subjective reactions. However, pairing the sounds with the functions was consistently unreliable. No cultural bias due to pairing the sounds with functions based on initial testing with American participants was observed.

4 Viability of Earcons, Auditory Icons, and Speech in Business Applications

4.1 Functional Mappings and Pleasantness of Auditory Feedback Signals

Our objectives were to expand the sound family defined above, and to further investigate earlier findings that demonstrated that earcons (musical signals) are more appropriate than auditory icons (real-world signals) in business applications. We observed that, when users were asked to indicate which class of auditory signal they would prefer in their business environment, they invariably selected the musical signals. Indeed, many indicated that they would want to "turn off" the real-world sounds if they listened to them on a daily basis. Several shortcomings were noted in the earlier research [10]. First, the stimulus sets contained more musical sounds than real-world sounds, which might have led respondents to favor these sounds when making their judgments. Second, the real-world sounds may have been disadvantaged since they were selected from sound libraries and were not privy to the same treatment as the other signals, which were created by a sound designer.

Another goal of this research was to examine the role of digitized speech as an alternative to auditory icons or earcons. Speech can no doubt provide less ambiguous feedback than either real-world or musical signals. In the present research, we used explicitly the same number of sounds in the real-world, musical, and speech stimulus sets and all stimuli were created by a professional sound designer/musician. This work is described more fully in Roberts and Sikora [13].

We utilized the same process as in our earlier research [10]. The first experiment was designed to find natural mappings of the stimuli to 12 communications functions.[4] These functions were different than those examined earlier. Seventy-two sounds were evaluated, consisting of 24 sounds from each of the three sound classes. That is, for each of the 12 functions of interest, two different alternatives were selected for each of the three sound classes. The content of the speech signals was derived by brainstorming with usability engineering experts.

Thirty-three participants listened to each of the sounds, selected the function that best matched the sound as a feedback signal, and subsequently rated the sound for pleasantness and appropriateness.

The data was examined to determine the frequency with which sounds mapped to the functions. Overall, the speech stimuli mapped most predictably to the functions, where there was a clear consensus for 11 of the 12 functions. As expected, results were more ambiguous for the musical and real-world sounds; 5 of the musical stimuli mapped well to their respective functions and 7 of the real world stimuli mapped well to the given functions.

Analyses of variance and subsequent Scheffe tests demonstrated that both the speech and musical signals were judged to be reliably more pleas-

---

[4]The functions evaluated here included: mail sent, message arrived, message error, urgent message, recording, conference invitation, open file, share file, button press, exit, warning, and a new logo sound.

ant $[F(2,69) = 32.0, p<.01]$ and more appropriate $[F(2,69) = 28.5, p<.01]$ than the real-world signals.

4.2 Replication in a Business Application

This study was designed to test the "best" sounds from the previous study within the context of a simulated business communications application. Thirty-five participants were tested in the study. After hearing each sound, respondents rated its pleasantness and appropriateness. Within a scenario, participants heard three sounds (one from each of the three classes: real world, earcons, and speech) and, following individual ratings, were asked to rank their preferences for that function.

Reliable sound class differences were observed for both pleasantness and appropriateness ratings $(p<.01)$. Subsequent Scheffé tests demonstrated that, for both ratings, differences were significant among the three groups. Speech signals were judged to be more pleasant and appropriate than both musical and real-world sounds and musical sounds were judged to be more pleasant and appropriate than real-world sounds. For the ranking data, for every function, the speech signals achieved the highest mean rank.

These results corroborate earlier research in which musical sounds were judged to be more appropriate and pleasant than real-world sounds, although other results were surprising. First, we did not find the superior mapping of the real-world signals relative to the musical signals that was observed earlier. This may have been due to the more abstract nature of the functions for which we were seeking auditory feedback, which included functions involved in collaborative work. Although we anticipated that speech would provide excellent mappings to their functions, it was not expected that speech would be judged to be more pleasant or appropriate than musical sounds.

4.3 Long-Term Testing of Speech and Earcons

In addition to evaluating feedback signals for an entirely new set of features, this work was motivated by earlier findings that, for one-session testing, speech was judged to be more pleasant and appropriate as feedback than was the case for musical signals. We also wanted to observe whether speech and/or earcons would become annoying over a period of extended use.

Fifteen participants listened to either musical (earcons) or speech-based feedback for 22 functions over 8 sessions (two per week for four weeks). Participants were tested in groups of two or three. This simulated a business environment in which they would hear the auditory feedback of their own computer, as well as the sounds coming from other computers in the office. During each of the eight sessions, participants were given tasks, which included a variety of business functions related to telecommunications and administration. The type of sound feedback heard by the participants was the same for each group, such that all of the auditory feedback they heard comprised either musical or speech sounds. Participants made ratings of the sounds prior to hearing them during the tasks and made these same ratings (e.g., pleasantness, appropriateness) following the four weeks of testing. We observed that, for these ratings, speech and musical signals were found to be equally pleasant, with no degradation in preference for either class of sound over time.

These findings are particularly surprising since there is anecdotal evidence suggesting that speech may be annoying upon extended use. In fact, the experimenter of this research, who was present at all experimental sessions, found the speech feedback to be very annoying by the end of the four weeks. This observation suggests that our testing time may not have been long enough to reach tolerance levels for these users. Other concerns about using speech in multimedia devices are the costs involved in adding this capability, the inflexibility of speech in global settings, the localization difficulties inherent in speech, as well as the difficulty of using these kinds of signals for telecommunications-based tasks.

5   Using Auditory Feedback During Web Navigation

5.1   Determining Appropriate Sound Feedback for Web Navigation

An obvious extension of this work is in Internet applications. As discussed earlier, this medium currently is relatively silent, with only a few sites utilizing sound at all, and rarely for feedback. The expectation is that the same evolution will occur on the Internet as was observed in computer interfaces: from text-based, to graphic interfaces, to multimedia interfaces. We expect that auditory feedback will be popular when the Internet moves from the use of streaming audio for entertainment to multimedia for usability. Our expectation is that, appropriately done, auditory feedback during web navigation will enhance the user experience by providing more efficient navigation as well as a more pleasant experience.

In the first phase of this work, we tested two sound stimulus sets. The first used sounds developed by Leplatre and Brewster [14] to present musical sequences within a hierarchical framework as a tool for navigation in a telephone messaging system. The sounds were very musical in origin and primarily varied in their grammatic structure. Due to their long duration, they were deemed to be inappropriate as dynamic feedback during transactional interactions. These sounds, which were up to seven seconds in length, are likely more representative of music per se than earcons (i.e., very brief snippets of music). New sounds were developed by Mark Barasch of Sound Image NY based on requirements that they be pleasing and no longer than two seconds in duration. The resultant set of earcons varied in pitch, duration, rhythm, harmonic complexity, and timbre.

Forty-seven participants listened to one of the two sound sets described above (i.e., music versus earcons). Each sound set contained 24 unique stimuli. As occurred in the Leplatre and Brewster study [14], participants received fairly extensive training in which they heard one of the sets of 24 sounds while seeing a structural representation projected on a screen (either hierarchical or linear). In both cases, the nodes were numbered 1 through 24. During testing, the projector was turned off and, referring to a paper copy of the structure, participants indicated which numbered node within the structure they felt the sound represented. Results demonstrated better recall for the music set, likely due to the length of the stimuli. However, participants preferred the shorter set of earcons. It was also observed that the hierarchical structure had better recall than the linear structure for both sound sets. This work is described in greater detail in Sikora and Roberts [15].

Additional testing was conducted in which users navigated the web and either heard earcons during their search or did not. This feedback modality was paired with other navigation aides, including visual cues and the structure of the history mechanism, in a fully counterbalanced experimental design. Subjects who had auditory feedback indicated that the sounds associated with the pages were not particularly useful in assisting them in returning to the web pages. Although the subjects considered the sounds pleasant, they indicated that they would probably not use the sounds if they were available on their PC. Interestingly, particular combinations of the navigation aides led to significantly different performance and usability results for particular classes of users. Specifically, an individual difference was found that indicated that the usability of the system was improved for some people and degraded for others by providing multimodal cues. This may suggest that sound combined with other navigational aides may be beneficial for some classes of users. Additional research needs to identify the personality construct that may be associated with this individual difference.

6 Using Auditory Feedback for Web Branding

6.1 Initial Evaluation of Earcons for Web Branding

Although sound is evident in most of our interactions with our environment, there is a notable absence of sound on the Internet. Exceptions at the time of this writing include web sites such as Logo, Intel, Ford, Universal Studios, and Monkey Media. It has been reported recently that sounds associated with brand identity on the web can carry the same level of brand recognition and brand attributes as the visual brand identity alone. Cheskin Research found that "not only does sound enhance brand, it adds a more compelling level of sensory experience that keeps viewers 'stuck' on websites." They further state that "small personal devices with limited visual real estate and low resolution such as the Palm, Windows, CE devices, and cellular telephones can leverage sound to provide more information and stronger brand communication" [16].

The findings described above suggest that memory for web sites will be enhanced when auditory branding is utilized. To evaluate that hypothesis, we had 40 web-savvy users perform tasks on and then rate 12 unfamiliar web sites. Web sites were selected that had been reviewed either positively or negatively. For each user, half of the sites had earcons that were played every time they accessed a new page of the site while half of the sites had no sounds. In addition, for each user, the earcon-based sites comprised randomly assigned earcons from a pool of eight sounds. Following tasks and ratings of the 12 sites, participants were given an unexpected task— to list the web sites they had seen in the study. Results showed that memory of the sites was unaffected by whether or not the sites had an earcon associated with them. Although this finding does not support the results described above, it may be that memory effects were not observed since we did not create earcons specifically for each of the sites. Indeed, anecdotal comments from users suggested that, when earcons did not match the content of the web site, that site was negatively perceived. Cheskin Research [15] observed that poorly designed audio can actually have a negative impact on brand attributes. Thus, it is possible that any positive associations of earcons with particular sites were washed out by negative associations of earcons with other sites. It would be useful to replicate this study using earcons that represent the content of each of their corresponding sites, versus random assignment from a pool of sounds.

7 Summary and Conclusions

This work has a number of ramifications for auditory interfaces as well as for user interface design. The primary findings may be summarized as follows:

(1) Auditory icons (real-world signals) tend to provide better mappings to communications-based functions than do earcons (musical signals), particularly for concrete functions. This advantage, however, may be reduced for more abstract functions.

(2) Earcons (musical signals) are judged to be significantly more pleasant and appropriate for business environments. This result appears to be very robust since it was replicated in several environments, for a variety of features, with a large number of participants. We expect that similar findings would be observed for consumer PC or Internet environments as well. However, it must be pointed out that earcons would not be appropriate for every environment; auditory icons would clearly be preferable when rapid mapping of sound to function is needed (such as in an airplane cockpit). In addition, it is likely that a combination of auditory icons and earcons would work well in many applications.

(3) Speech as feedback may provide the optimal feedback since these stimuli have superior mapping to their functions and are judged to be at least as pleasant as earcons. However, implementing speech as feedback may be cost prohibitive, inappropriate for global applications, and may elicit localization difficulties.

(4) Based on four weeks of testing, feedback comprising either speech or earcons appears to be effective for long-term usage. Our primary concern was that these sounds would become annoying after repeated usage, but this finding was not observed. However, it may be that our testing duration was not sufficient to observe long-term patterns.

(5) Earcons can be identified with associated nodes in a sound structure. We are currently testing the utility of linking the sound structure to the search path as a way of enhancing memory during web navigation.

(6) Earcons and auditory icons would be excellent candidates for branding on the web. The effectiveness of these sounds has already been observed outside of this medium for NBC (NBC chimes), Intel (four-note audio signature), and for AT&T (sparkle tone). Earcons would be expected to provide the same impact on the Internet as well. At the time of this writing, auditory icons and musical patterns have already been used effectively on the web on sites such as http://www.logo.com and http://www.monkey.com.

8 Acknowledgments

The authors thank Mark Barasch of Sound Image NY for his creative musical contributions. We thank Bonnie Kudrick and Jennifer Dail for their help in subject testing. Thanks also go to Mary Carol Day, Darryl Moore, Ed Silver, and Brenda Wilch-Ringen for their careful review of this paper.

Annotated Bibliography

[1] W. Buxton. "Introduction to this Special Issue on Nonspeech Audio." *Human Computer Interaction* 4(1989), 1–9.

In this paper, the author focuses on the use of nonspeech audio to communicate information from the computer to the user. He discusses figure and ground in audio, sound and the visually impaired, function and signal type, audio cues and learning, perception and psychoacoustics, and the logistics of sound.

[2] J. Hereford and W. Winn. "Non-Speech Sound in Human-Computer Interaction: A Review and Design Guidelines." *Journal of Educational Computing Research* 11:3(1994), 211–233.

This article describes research on uses of computer sound and suggests how sound might be used effectively by instructional and interface designers. Following a review of general principles of interface design and basic research in auditory perception, the article examines two uses of sounds (earcons and sonitization). The role of sound in virtual environments is discussed and design guidelines are provided.

[3] D. Masten. "Silence of the Brands." *Business 2.0* (November 1999), 36–39.

The author describes how sound can benefit the user experience as well as the branding of web sites. He discusses the design challenges for audio design on the web and forecasts the sound evolution on the web as new technologies continue to evolve.

[4] W. Gaver. "Auditory Interfaces." In *Handbook of Human-Computer Interaction*, edited by M. G. Helander, T. K. Landauer, and P. V. Prabhu, pp. 1003—1041, NY: North-Holland, 1997.

This book chapter provides an extensive overview of a variety of auditory issues related to computer systems. Types of sound feedback used in interactive systems are addressed. Parameters of sound and hearing are discussed in detail. Systems using sound are presented and reviewed.

[5] S. Brewster, P. Wright, and A. Edwards. "An Evaluation of Earcons for Use in Auditory Human-Computer Interfaces." In *INTERCHI'93 Human Factors in Computing Systems* pp. 222–227, 1993.

The authors evaluated earcons to see whether they are an effective means of communicating information. An initial experiment showed that earcons were superior to unstructured bursts of sound and that musical timbres were more effective than simple tones. A follow-up experiment improved on some of the weaknesses of the earlier study and resulted in an improvement in recognition. Some guidelines for creating earcons are provided.

[6] M. Blattner, D. Sumikawa, and R. Greenberg. "Earcons and Icons: Their structure and Common Design Principles." *Human-Computer Interaction* 4(1989), 11–44.

In this article, the authors identify design principles that are common to both visual and auditory symbols and discuss the use of representational and abstract icons and earcons. They provide examples of auditory patterns that may be used to design modules for earcons, which may be assembled into larger groupings called families. In addition, issues concerned with learning and remembering earcons are discussed.

[7] W. Gaver. "Auditory Icons: Using sound in Computer Interfaces." *Human-Computer Interaction* 2(1986), 167–177.

This paper describes an approach to the use of sound in computer interfaces, one that emphasizes the role of sound in conveying information about the world to the listener. He emphasizes that the most important advantage of this strategy is that it is based on the way people listen to the world in their everyday lives. He describes how auditory icons can provide information about sources of data, in particular, by allowing the categorization of data into distinct families.

[8] E. Mynatt. "Designing with Auditory Icons: How Well Do We Identify Auditory Cues?" In *CHI'94 Human Factors in Computing Systems*, pp. 269–270, 1994.

This paper examines users' ability to identify auditory cues. An experiment is conducted in which subjects are asked to verbally describe a collection of short sounds that are typical in our everyday environment. The authors suggest that the content and accuracy of their identification can be used to shape a methodology for deciding how to use auditory cues.

[9] S. Jones and S. Turner. "The Construction of Audio Icons and Information Cues for Human-Computer Dialogues." In *Contemporary Ergonomics, Proceedings of the Ergonomics Society's 1989 Annual Conference*, pp. 284–289, 1989.

This paper describes a study that evaluated the use of different types of sound for feedback. They observed that subjects were better able to associate auditory icons to functions, but preferred earcons.

[10] C. A. Sikora, L A. Roberts, and L. Murray. "Musical versus Real World Feedback Signals." In *CHI'95*, pp. 220–221, 1995.

Sound families of earcons, communications sounds, and real-world sounds were designed to provide auditory feedback in a graphical user interface. Users mapped the sounds to functions and the sounds which mapped well to functions were then tested within the context of a business application. Although real-world sounds mapped most reliably to the functions, users consistently preferred earcons to the real-world sounds.

[11] C. A. Sikora and L. A. Roberts. "Defining a Family of Feedback Signals for Multimedia Communication Devices." *INTERACT '97*, pp. 76–81, 1997.

The authors describe the process through which a family of auditory feedback signals was created for multimedia devices. In three experiments, users 1) mapped sounds to functions and rated the sounds for pleasantness/appropriateness, 2) determined the best sounds for each function within the context of a business simulation and 3), made similarity judgments for the resultant family of sounds. Results demonstrated that, while auditory icons mapped most reliably to the functions, users consistently preferred musical sounds to the real-world sounds.

[12] C. A. Sikora and L A. Roberts. "Sounds Good to Me: Global Investigation of Auditory Feedback." *HFES/IEA '2000*, pp. 37–39, 2000.

Research investigated the use of auditory feedback signals in four countries. Subjective ratings were used to compute a scale value of desirability for the set of sounds. Findings indicated that the reliability of mapping sounds to intended functions does not vary across countries. However, the subjective ratings for the sounds indicated that, although all subjects rated the sounds above average, US subjects rated the sounds significantly higher than two of the three others countries. These differences were due to two function feedback sounds.

[13] L. A. Roberts and C. A. Sikora. "Optimizing Feedback Signals for Multimedia Devices: Earcons versus Auditory Icons versus Speech." *IEA '97 International Ergonomics Association, 13th Triennial Congress* 5(1997): 224–226.

The authors evaluated speech, earcons, and real-world sounds in two experiments. They observed that the speech stimuli mapped most predictably to 12 telecommunications functions. They also observed that, for both pleasantness and appropriateness ratings, speech and musical signals were judged more positively than real-world signals.

[14] G. Leplatre and S. A. Brewster. "An Investigation of Using Music to Provide Navigation Cues." In *ICAD '98*, pp. 1–10, 1998.

This paper investigates the viability of representing hierarchical menus with nonspeech audio. The authors describe an experiment in which a series of musical motives represented a hierarchy of 25 nodes, with a sound for each node. Participants were very efficient at identifying the position of the sounds in the hierarchy.

[15] C. A. Sikora and L.A. Roberts. *Mapping Auditory Cues to an Organized Structure.* Proc. SCI 2003 (Orlando, Florida, July 27–July 30, 2003).

The authors examined the appropriateness of mapping auditory cues to an organized structure with the intention of using those cues as feedback when navigating a web-based search structure. They found that the sounds were mapped with reasonable accuracy and that the hierarchical structure resulted in better performance that the linear structure. The authors suggest that this research indicates that mapping sound feedback to a web-based search structure could provide a meaningful navigation cue.

[16] D. Masten. "Sounds like Money—The Importance of Audio Branding on the Web." Cheskin Research. Available from World Wide Web (http://www.cheskin.com), 2000.

This article describes the potential power of sound on the Internet. In particular, he focuses on branding and audio signatures. He briefly describes some research indicating that sounds can carry the same level of brand recognition as does visual branding.

Nature

Brainwave Entrainment through Binaural Sound

Jeffrey Thompson

Human beings have used sound to access deeper states of consciousness, expanded awareness, and physical healing for thousands of years. Drumming, chanting, toning, playing Tibetan singing bowls, and invoking mantras are all examples of the use of sound for these purposes.

Major research institutions are increasingly exploring the neurophysiology of meditation, deep relaxation states and mind/body interactions. In one study, a simple meditation technique used for 20 minutes a day was shown to cause profound changes in blood pressure, stress handling ability, immune response, and feelings of well-being. Mainstream doctors are recognizing the benefits of pursuits like yoga and meditation and have begun prescribing these to their patients with positive results, especially where other therapies are either not available or have negative side effects.

The application of technology as an aid for the many people not trained in meditative traditions is an exciting area of inquiry. Preliminary results[1] indicate that by using these technological aids, patients may achieve deep levels of relaxation and experience benefits similar to those trained in traditional meditative techniques. Daily use of this technology for mind/body integration and stress reduction may be very beneficial.

---

[1] The following professionals have conducted research on binaural beats and their positive effect on brainwave entrainment: Holmes Atwater: Monroe Institute, Faber, Virginia; Dr. Suzanne Evans Morris, Ph.D. (Speech pathology); Dr Lester Fehmi (Director Princeton Behavioral medicine & Biofeedback Clinic); Dr Arthur Hastings, Ph.D.; Langley Porter, Neuropsychiatric Institute (University of CA at San Francisico) & Dr Joe Kiniya (Director Psychophysiology of Consciousness Laboratory); John Kiebeskind (UCLA Neurophysiologist); Candace Pert (Natl Institute of Mental Health); Suzanne Evans Morris PhD (Speech & Language Pathology); Tom Brudzinski (EEG brainwave expert); Dr. Gene W Breckopp (Medical researcher).

One promising phenomenon being explored is called brainwave entrainment. Brainwaves can sympathetically "lock on" to an external sound-pulse at a brainwave speed. This gives us the tools to gently guide brainwave function and states of consciousness into deeply relaxed and balanced states. This article explores the physiology of brainwave entrainment and its application in my audio recordings. Audio files and program examples are available on the CD-ROM accompanying this book.

1 Entrainment

Entrainment refers to the seemingly universal principal where one system will bring itself into dynamic equilibrium with another. One common example of this phenomenon is resonant entrainment when, for instance, a tuning fork resonating at 440 Hz is brought into the proximity of a 440-Hz tuning fork, initially at rest. The second tuning fork will begin to resonate sympathetically with the first in increasing amplitude until equilibrium is achieved. This sympathetic vibration or entrainment is one source of the richness of sonic multistringed musical instruments. Musicians damp the strings of their instruments when this phenomenon is undesired.

Entrainment is not limited to sympathetic vibration; many systems exhibit similar synchronizing behaviors, including biochemical systems. Electrically, it is the principle that allows the "tuned circuits" within radio receivers to operate. This article is concerned with entrainment within the neural activity of the human brain.

2 Binaural Beats

The definitive work on the discovery of the phenomenon of acoustic brainwave entrainment—the ability to change brainwaves and states of consciousness with sound—was done by Oster, a medical researcher at Mount Sinai Hospital. The October 1973 issue of *Scientific American*, entitled "Auditory Beats in the Brain," provides an easily readable account.

In this article, Oster outlined the research he had conducted which showed a brainwave entrainment response to something he called "binaural beats." These beats occurred when two separate tones were tuned slightly differently from one another in frequency—to be precise, within 18% of one another—a range called the "critical bandwidth." The speed of the beats was governed by the difference in the frequency of the two notes: A left channel tone of 100 cycles per second (Hz) and a right

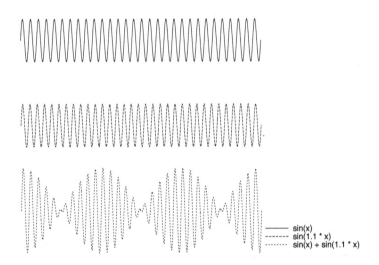

Figure 1. The sum of two pure tones of similar frequency results in a pulsed wave.

channel tone of 105 Hz would cause a 5-Hz pulse to arise as an interference pattern.

This is similar to the well-understood phenomenon called *heterodyning*, also responsible for the beats sometimes used to tune guitars. An already tuned reference string is *fretted* so that it will theoretically produce the same note as the *open* to be tuned. The two strings are struck and if the second string is tuned close to the correct frequency, a distinct beat is heard. This beat is actually a node heard as the two closely related tones slip in phase against each other sometimes periodically reinforcing and attenuating each other. (See Figure 1.) Adjusting the string being tuned will cause the period of the beat to slow down and eventually go away when proper tuning has been achieved.

In the guitar example, the beats are a physical phenomena, the interaction of two sound waves in air. However, in the previous example, if the 100-Hz signal is presented to only the left ear, and the 105-Hz signal is present to only the right, by means of a pair of headphones, the two sound waves never physically interact. The perceived beat pattern occurs completely in the brain and is the result of the neural representation of the two signals interacting with each other!

3   Brainwave Entrainment

When presented with an induced brainwave signal, the brain wave activity has a tendency to entrain, thereby inducing an altered state of consciousness. Oster also found that listening to these two frequencies through headphones caused not only the brainwave entrainment phenomenon, but a synchronicity of the electrical activity of the right/left hemispheres as well.

This phenomenon of hemisphere synchronicity is due to a quirk in how the brain processes information and the physics phenomenon of the critical bandwidth. When two tones are tuned within the critical bandwidth, the brain cannot distinguish two separate tones; it hears one single tone with a pulse within it. The speed of the pulse it hears is the difference between the two tones.

Through headphones, however, the opposite hemispheres, which process sound information from each opposite ear, have to compare information in order to hear the pulse. Actually, the brain is *manufacturing* the pulse out of thin air, moment by moment. When the brain hemispheres compare information, they synchronize their activity, which results in hemisphere synchronicity.

Brainwave synchronicity is associated with the "aha" moment, the moment when the answer to a problem pops into the mind, in times of great inspiration, and certain high states of reverie and meditation. With this new technological method of entraining brainwaves with binaural beats using headphones, it is possible to float the brain in this hemisphere synchronized state for prolonged periods of time. Each time we do this, it is like exercising a new brain function—which makes the brain more able to engage this function as its normal repertoire of behavior. It's kind of like going to a gym on the *inside* and working the muscle of your brain.

4   Musical Applications

Using sound in these ways, it is possible to make profound changes in brainwave patterns and states of consciousness, observable on brainwave mapping equipment (EEG), as well as in positive changes in the body, measurable with blood tests, bio-feedback equipment, and other biomedical procedures. It is also possible to influence the core balance and functioning of the brain and central nervous system as a whole.

In a series of recordings based on these principles, I have used sound frequency patterns—built into the music—that have been shown clinically to cause positive changes in consciousness, brainwave, and body function.

This process involves the use of digital technology, electronic keyboards, and computer programs which make it possible to take any recorded sound—instrument sounds, nature sounds, human voice sounds, etc.—and precisely alter the tuning of the right/left channels of these sounds (a precision of 100 steps of tuning between two notes on a piano) which causes an interference pattern of pulses to arise by the difference of tuning. If the speed of these pulses is calibrated to a brainwave speed (Delta .5–3.5 Hz, Theta 3.5–7 Hz, Alpha 7–13 Hz, Beta 13–30 Hz), then the brainwaves will follow the speed of these pulses and brainwave entrainment will occur. The slower Delta and Theta brainwave states are associated with relaxation, the higher brainwave states with increased alertness and ability to concentrate.

There are other methods for building pulse rates into soundtracks which cause brainwave entrainment not based on the idea of binaural beats. We can modulate the amplitude, filters, and pitch of the sound. This means we can build a pulsing loudness level, a pulsing bass/treble level, and a pulsing sharp/flat level in the sounds. All of these systems work to cause the entrainment response, but only the binaural beat through headphones technique causes the hemisphere synchronicity response in the brain.

5 Primordial Sounds

Many of the sounds you hear on these recordings are sounds you don't even notice. Certain sounds have the power to awaken deep levels of recognition in the subconscious mind; I call these sounds *primordial sound* because they are primordially recognizable to the subconscious mind regardless of race, sex, or language.

Our first sensory experience in life as a fetus in the womb is of sound and vibration. We float in body-temperature amniotic fluid—weightless. We have fluid in our nose and mouth which eliminates the senses of smell and taste. We have our eyes closed and are in the dark—no sense of sight. We have fluid in our ears pressed right up against the eardrum— but sound travels through water fives times more effectively than through air, therefore our sense of hearing is actually amplified. The symphony of sound patterns we experience at this time will be deeply imbedded in our subconscious mind for the rest of our lives—water swishing sounds, arterial pulse sounds, and voice sounds. These are our first experiences of primodial sounds.

Recordings of these types of sounds form some of the primordial sounds you hear on this recording (on the accompanying CD-ROM). Each of these sounds is intentionally altered and disguised by slowing them down and speeding them up. By changing the speed of these sounds, we can side-step the rational, thinking mind, which will no longer recognize the sounds, and tap into the subconscious directly, with sounds it deeply recognizes and to which it responds. In one sense, the organic/biological intelligence, the same intelligence which grew our entire body out of two cells, will certainly be awakened with recognition of sounds recorded from this body.

6   Acoustic Pacing

This has formed the basis for another method I developed for entraining the entire biological network in the body which I call *acoustic pacing*. In acoustic pacing, I am taking nature sound recordings—recorded with special binaural, three-dimensional, microphones (please refer to Hempton's article "Listening to Nature: Hearing is More than Meets the Eye" (see *Audio Anecdotes I*) for more information on binaural three-dimensional recording and the nature of listening)—and slowing these recordings down over time in the soundtrack. Since all the audio memories stored in the brain from past experiences are three-dimensional sound memories, a three-dimensional soundtrack fools the brain into assuming these nature sounds are real. Since, as part of the larger world phenomenon of "biological sympathetic oscillation," our bodies time themselves to larger nature cycles, when three-dimensional recordings of nature sounds are slowed down over time, the body automatically adjusts its internal timings accordingly and a global body-based entrainment of slowing down occurs. Brainwaves slow in response to the whole system slowing in this method.

7   Conclusion

It is best to listen to these recordings using headphones in a dimly lit room with your eyes closed to get the full effects of the three-dimensional sound and brainwave pulse-wave information. You will hear the sounds moving around you in three-dimensional space and hopefully experience an altered and relaxing state of consciousness.

Annotated Bibliography

[1] H. B. Adams. "A Case Utilizing Sensory Deprivation Procedures. In *Case Studies in Behavior Modification*, edited by L. P. Ullman and L. Krasner. New York: Holt, Rinehart & Winston, 1965.

[2] E. D. Adrian and K. Yamagiwa. "The Origin of the Berger Rhythm." *Brain* 58 (1935), 323–351.

[3] F. H. Atwater. *The Monroe Institute's Hemisync process: A Theoretical Perspective*. Faber, VA: Monroe Institute, 1988

[4] R. Bandler. *Using Your Brain-For a Change*. Moab, UT: Real People Press, 1985.

[5] T. X. Barber. "Experiments in Hypnosis." *Scientific American* 196 (1957), 54–61.

[6] F. Bremer. "Physiology of the Corpus Callosum." In *Proceedings of the Association of Research on Nervous Disorders* 36 (1958), 424–448.

[7] F. Bremer. "Cerebral and Cerebellar Potentials." *Physiological Review* 38 (1958), 357–388.

[8] G. W. Brockopp. "Review of Research on Multi-Modal Sensory Stimulation with Clinical Implications and Research Proposals. Unpublished manuscript. See Hutchison 1986.

[9] T. Budzynski. "Some Applications of Biofeedback-Produced Twilight States." In *Biofeedback and Self-Control*, edited by D. Shapiro, et al. Chicago: Aldine-Atherton, 1972.

[10] T. H. Budzynski. "Biofeedback and the Twilight States of Consciousness." In *Consciousness and Self-Regulation, Volume 1*, edited by G. E. Schwartz and D. Shapiro. New York: Plenum Press, 1976.

[11] T. H. Budzynski. "Tuning in on the Twilight Zone." *Psychology Today* August (1977), 38–44.

[12] T. H. Budzynski. "Brain Lateralization and Biofeedback." In *Brain/Mind and Parapsychology*, edited by B. Shapin and T. Coly. New York: Parapsychology Foundation, 1979.

[13] T. H. Budzynski. "Brain Lateralization and Rescripting." *Somatics* 3 (1981), 1–10.

[14] T. H. Budzynski. "Clinical Applications of Non-Drug-Induced States." In *Handbook of States of Consciousness*, edited by B. Wolman and M. Ullman. New York: Van Nostrand-Reinhold, 1986.

[15] T. H. Budzynski. "Hemispheric Asymmetry and REST." In *Restricted Environmental Stimulation*, edited by P. Suedfeld, J. W. Turner, Jr., and T. H. Fine. New York: Springer-Verlag, 1990.

[16] C. M. Cade and N. Coxhead. *The Awakened Mind: Biofeedback and the Development of Higher States of Consciousness*. New York: Delacorte Press, 1979.

[17] D. Cheek. "Short-Term Hypnotherapy for Fragility Using Exploration of Early Life Attitudes." *The American Journal of Clinical Hypnosis* 18 (1976), 75–82.

[18] R. J. Davidson, P. Ekman, C. D. Saron, J. A. Senulis and W. V. Friesen. "Approach-Withdrawal and Cerebral Asymmetry: Emotional Expression and Brain Physiology." *Journal of Personality and Social Psychology* 58 (1990), 330–341.

[19] A. Deikman. "De-Automatization and the Mystic Experience." In *Altered States of Consciousness*, edited by C.T. Tart. New York: John Wiley & Sons, 1969.

[20] A. Deikman. "Bimodal Consciousness." *Archives of General Psychiatry* 25 (1971), 481–489.

[21] D. N. J. Donker, L. Njio, W. Storm Van Leeuwen and G. Wienke. "Interhemispheric Relationships of Responses to Sine Wave Modulated Light in Normal Subjects and Patients." *Electroencephalography and Clinical Neurophysiology* 44 (1978), 479–489.

[22] F. J. Evans, L. A. Gustafson, D. N. O'Connell, M. T. Orne, and R. E. Shor. "Response during Sleep with Intervening Waking Amnesia." *Science* 152 (1966), 666–667.

[23] F. J. Evans, L. A. Gustafson, D. N. O'Connell, M. T. Orne, and R. E. Shor. "Verbally-Induced Behavioral Response during Sleep." *Journal of Nervous and Mental Disease* 1 (1970), 1–26.

[24] C. Evans and P. H. Richardson. "Improved Recovery and Reduced Postoperative Stay after Therapeutic Suggestions during General Anaesthetic." *Lancet* 2(1988), 491.

[25] A. Felipe. "Attitude Change during Interrupted Sleep." Unpublished doctoral diss., Yale University, 1965.

[26] D. S. Foster. "EEG and Subjective Correlates of Alpha Frequency Binaural Beats Stimulation Combined with Alpha Biofeedback." Ann Arbor, MI: UMI, Order No. 9025506, 1990.

[27] D. Foulkes and G. Vogel. "Mental Activity at Sleep-Onset." *Journal of Abnormal Psychology* 70 (1964), 231–243.

[28] J. Glicksohn. "Photic Driving and Altered States of Consciousness: An Exploratory Study." *Imagination, Cognition and Personality* 6 (1986), 167–182.

[29] E. E. Green and A. M. Green. "On the Meaning of the Transpersonal: Some Metaphysical Perspectives." *Journal of Transpersonal Psychology* 3 (1971), 27–46.

[30] E. E. Green and A. M. Green. "Biofeedback and States of Consciousness." In *Handbook of States of Consciousness*, edited by B. B. Wolman and M. Ullman. New York: Van Nosfrand Reinhold, 1986.

[31] G. F. Harding and M. Dimitrakoudi. "The Visual Evoked Potential in Photosensitive Epilepsy." In *Visual Evoked Potentials in Man: New Developments*, edited by J. E. Desmedt. Oxford: Clarendon, 1977.

[32] J. B. Henriques and R. J. Davidson. "Regional Brain Electrical Asymmetries Discriminate between Previously Depressed and Healthy Control Subjects." *Journal of Abnormal Psychology* 99 (1990), 22–31.

[33] Z. B. Hoovey, U. Heinemann, and O. D. Creutzfeldt. "Inter-Hemispheric 'Synchrony' of Alpha Waves." *Electroencephalography and Clinical Neurophysiology* 32 (1972), 337–347.

[34] M. Hutchison. *Megabrain.* New York: Beech Tree Books, 1986.

[35] M. Hutchison. "Special issue on Sound/Light." *Megabrain Report* 1:2 (1990).

[36] Iamblichus. "The Epistle of Porphyry to the Egyptian Anebo." In *Iamblichus on the Mysteries of the Egyptians, Chaldeans, and Assyrians*, translated by T. Taylor. London: B. Dobell, and Reeves & Turner, 1895.

[37] P. Janet. *L'Automatisme Psychologique*. Paris: Alcan, 1889.

[38] A. Koestler. *The Act of Creation*. London: Pan Books, 1981.

[39] K. A. Kooi. *Fundamentals of Electroencephalography*. New York: Harper & Row, 1971.

[40] L. Kubie. "The Use of Induced Hypnagogic Reveries in the Recovery of Depressed Amnesic Data." *Bull. Menninger Clinic* 7 (1943), 172–182.

[41] S. R. Lankton and C. H. Lankton. *The Answer Within: A Clinical Framework Ericksonian Hypnotherapy*. New York: Bruner/Mazel, 1983.

[42] K. Leman and R. Carlson. *Unlocking the Secrets of Your Childhood Memories*. Nashville, TN: Thomas Nelson, 1989.

[43] J. C. Lilly. *Programming and Metaprogramming in the Human Bio-computer*. New York: Julian, 1972.

[44] J. F. Lubar. "Electroencephalographic Biofeedback and Neurological Applications." In *Biofeedback: Principles and Practice*, edited by J. V. Basmajian. New York: Williams & Wilkins, 1989.

[45] A. Mavromatis. *Hypnagogia: The Unique State of Consciousness between Wakefulness and Sleep*. New York: Routledge & Kegan Paul, 1987.

[46] E. E. Miller. *Software for the Mind: How to Program Your Mind for Optimum Health and Performance*. Berkeley, CA: Celestial Arts, 1987.

[47] K. I. Moscu and M. Vranceanu. "Onelques resultats concernant l'action differentielle des mots affectogenes et nonaffectogenes pendant le somneil naturel." In *Psicofisiologia del Son no e del Sogno*, edited by M. Bertini. Milan: Editrice Vita e Pensiero, 1970.

[48] R. A. Moses. *Adler's Physiology of the Eye: Clinical Applications*. St. Louis, MO: Mosby, 1970.

[49] J. C. Nemiah. "The Unconscious and Psycho Pathology." In S. and D. Meichenbaum, pp. 4987. New York: John Wiley & Sons, 1984.

[50] G. Oster. "Auditory Beats in the Brain." *Scientific American* 229 (1973), 94–102.

[51] E. G. Peniston and R. J. Kulkowski. "Alpha-Theta Brainwave Training and B-Endorphin Levels in Alcoholics." *Alcoholism* 13 (1989), 271–279.

[52] A. Richardson and F. McAndrew. "The Effects of Photic Stimulation and Private Self-Consciousness on the Complexity of Visual Imagination Imagery." *British Journal of Psychology* 81 (1990), 381–394.

[53] E. L. Rossi. *The Psychobiology of Mind-Body Healing.* New York: W. W. Norton, 1986

[54] F. Rubin, editor. *Current Research in Hypnopaedia.* London: MacDonald, 1968.

[55] F. Rubin. "Learning and Sleep." *Nature* 226 (1970), 447.

[56] D. L. Schacter. "EEG Theta Waves and Psychological Phenomena: A Review and Analysis." *Biological Psychology* 5 (1977), 47–82.

[57] J. Schultz and W. Luthe. *Autogenic Training: A Psychophysiological Approach in Psychotherapy.* New York: Grune & Stratton, 1959.

[58] P. Sittenfeld, T. Budzynski and J. Stoyva. "Differential Shaping of EEG Theta Rhythms." *Biofeedback and Self-Regulation* 1 (1976), 31–45.

[59] J. M. Stoyva. "Biofeedback Techniques and the Conditions for Hallucinatory Activity". In *The Psycho physiology of Thinking*, edited by F. J. McGuigan and R. Schoonover. New York: Academic Press, 1973.

[60] S. H. Strogatz and I. Stewart. "Coupled Oscillators and Biological Synchronization." *Scientific American* Vol. 269:6 (1993), 102–109.

[61] A. Svyandoshch. "The Assimilation and Memorization of Speech during Natural Sleep." In Current Research in Hypnopaedia, edited by F. Rubin. London: MacDonald, 1968.

[62] E. Swedenborg. *Rational Psychology.* Philadelphia, PA: Swedenborg Scientific Association, 1950.

[63] A. J. Tomarken, R. J. Davidson and J. B. Henriques. "Resting Frontal Brain Asymmetry Predicts Affective Responses to Films." *Journal of Personality and Social Psychology* 59 (1990), 791–801.

[64] R. E. Townsend. "A Device for Generation and Presentation of Modulated Light Stimuli." *Electroencephalography and Clinical Neurophysiology* 34 (1973), 97–99.

[65] D. M. Tucker. "Lateral Brain Function, Emotion, and Conceptualization." *Psychological Bulletin* 89 (1981), 19–46.

[66] L. H. Van der Tweel and H. F. E. Verduyn Lunel. "Human Visual Responses to Sinusoidally Modulated Light." *Electroencephalography and Clinical Neurology* 18 (1965), 587–598.

[67] W. Van Dusen. *The Presence of Other Worlds.* London: Wildwood House, 1975.

[68] V. J. Walter and W. G. Walter. "The Central Effects of Rhythmic Sensory Stimulation." *Electroencephalography and Clinical Neurophysiology* 1 (1949), 57–86.

[69] I. E. Wickramasekera. *Clinical Behavioral Medicine: Some Concepts and Procedures.* New York: Plenum Press, 1988.

Introduction to Bioacoustics: Learning from Nature How to Create and Process Sound

Jeffrey Greenebaum

"A bird is an instrument working according to a mathematical law, which instrument it is within the capability of man to reproduce, with all its movements."

-Leonardo da Vinci
(1452–1519)

Looking skyward, Leonardo da Vinci carefully watched, then diagrammed, birds soaring overhead before drafting plans for his own flying machines. He believed animals were the ideal source of inspiration for new technology and that they, in effect, represented an existence-proof of what could be accomplished. Birds, like the flying machines taking shape within his notebooks, balanced weight with lift, kept drag to a minimum, and remained stable in air. The renowned inventor realized that if a bird routinely overcomes gravity's hurdles, man's own ascent need not be far behind.

Today, it is accepted that an engineer seeking to improve a robotic arm might study the elegant workings of the human elbow, forearm, and wrist for inspiration. Biomimetic Roboticists have created machines that walk upside down from ceilings by emulating flies. Similarly, biologists have discovered new antibiotics by studying bacteria-resistant plants.

Bioacoustics, the study of the interactions between sound and living organisms, is an interdisciplinary field that includes elements of biology, acoustics, and behavioral science. Researchers use anechoic chambers, parabolas, microphones, and sophisticated computers to isolate, focus, record and analyze sound waves. The resulting science demonstrates how organisms produce, discern, and use sound. In this article, we will briefly examine creatures great and small that use a variety of mechanisms to sonically communicate, map their environment, and even stun their prey.

Animal capabilities have improved over time due to the competitive forces of natural selection and rigorous necessities imposed by the laws of physics. Carefully observing animals, then, may prove to be a resource for acoustic engineers to gain insights by studying the elegant, precise, and highly efficient systems organisms have developed and optimized over the millennia.

We hope to encourage the reader to explore the rich field of bioacoustics when looking for acoustical inspiration! Please take a moment to look through the reference list at the end of the article, where you will find a wealth of sources on the subject.

> *"I do not invent my best thoughts, I find them."*
> -Aldous Huxley

1   Acoustic Capabilities of Animals

1.1   "Silent Thunder," or a Rumble in the Jungle

Generally, the most convenient way to compare sound intensities is the SPL decibel scale (described in Fouad's article "Understanding the Decibel" (see *Audio Anecdotes I*) and enumerated in Greenebaum's article "Sound Pressure Levels: Mine Goes to 11!" (see *Audio Anecdotes I*) A purring house cat contentedly registers 30 dB SPL, while a roaring lion generates a respectable 90 dB SPL [3]. A peal of thunder rumbles in at 110 dB SPL—much the same sound intensity with which an elephant (*Proboscidea*) is able to vocalize.

While an elephant's call can be as intense as thunder, it is not necessarily audible to humans. Indeed, most of the energy from the truly intense call is infrasonic, or below a human's range of hearing, which drops off precipitously at around 25 Hz. Energy below this frequency is experienced as vibration by the body, but not as sound by the ears. Katy Payne, who first discovered infrasonic sound in elephants, referred to this irony when she named her 1998 book *Silent Thunder: In the Presence of Elephants* [5].

In her book, Payne recalls a childhood memory of "felt" infrasound generated musically by a church organ at Cornell University's Sage Chapel.

Her long-remembered experience of sound waves sensed only as vibration leads Payne to suspect that the elephants at the Washington Park Zoo in Portland, Oregon were making vocalizations inaudible to the human ear: The elephants would lean against the concrete walls that separated them and, at these times, the air seemed to vibrate. "Is that what I was feeling as I sat beside the elephant cage? Sound too low for me to hear, yet so powerful it caused the air to throb? Were the elephants calling each other in infrasound?" she mused.

Payne returned to the Washington Park elephants equipped with new microphones and recorders that would test her theory. It was at Cornell, a few weeks later, that Payne and a colleague had proof: The spectrogram readings depicted infrasonic sound generated by elephants. It was unequivocal, since the recordings were taken at a time when there was no audible vocalization from the elephants—when Payne had merely felt a shuddering of the air.

Elephants have other surprising abilities. For instance, their hearing appears to be amazingly acute and their perception of pitch seems to be close to that of humans. A passage from *Van Nostrand's Scientific Encyclopedia, Eighth Edition* gives an interesting account [2]:

> *The extremely keen hearing of elephants has long impressed hunters and mahouts [the elephant keepers and drivers of India], but it was not scientifically studied until 1951. An elephant could distinguish one specific tone from six pairs of pure tones. In one case the various tones were just one note apart from each other. Elephants also learned simple melodies and rhythms that could be recognized independently of the instrument creating the music (i.e. whether the music was performed on violin, piano, organ, or xylophone).*

1.2 Long-Range Communication in Elephants

While a wide range of frequencies are found in elephant vocalizations, most of the energy tends to be concentrated in specific frequencies. Both the Asian elephant's (*Elephas maximus*) and African elephant's (*Loxodonta Africana*) calls contain significant energy that is usually tuned to a low frequency between 14 and 35 Hz. These bands, when coupled with high intensity signals, are extremely efficient for purposes of long-range communication.

Not so for high-frequency transmission such as those employed by the little brown bat (*Myotis luci fugus*), whose echolocation ability is based on an intense, 100-dB chirp signal, yet has a very short range when compared to the elephant. (Echolocation is the process of emitting high-pitched "chirps" and then interpreting the echoes reflected off of objects to determine the objects' position, direction, and relative velocity.) The difference in transmission distance is due to the frequency of the sound that is generated, not just its intensity. The frequency of a sound dictates how easily it propagates—how much is scattered and attenuated within a given environment. While the high frequency chirps of the bat travel for many meters, the long wavelength elephant calls are transmitted and received up to distances of 4 km.

Spreading loss, expressed by the inverse-square law of sound attenuation, dissipates the energy of all frequencies equally. High frequencies, however, tend to be strongly absorbed by air and can be adversely effected by such factors as air temperature, pressure, and humidity. Lower frequencies propagate with relatively little loss. Moreover, higher frequency sounds are much more easily deflected and absorbed by obstructions such as grass, leaves, boulders, and trees.

Animals living in scatter-rich environments benefit from using lower frequency bands, especially if they require long-distance communication. Physically large transducers are needed to efficiently generate or receive low frequencies; hence, large animals have the best chance of utilizing those bands. The largest terrestrial species, the elephant, grows to approximately 3 meters in height and weighs around 5.4 metric tons—a sizable advantage over the miniscule mosquito, for instance. This is bad news for your average mosquito (*Culicidae*), but good news for the African elephant, provided both animals might benefit from long-range communication.

1.3   Breeding and Other Uses for Communication

There are a variety of uses for high energy, low-frequency calls in the elephant world. Long-distance communication enables elephants to forage widely while keeping family-groups intact. It helps groups successfully avoid lone, aggressive males and even signals group-members when the herd is ready to move on toward better lands. Effective communication is also essential for breeding.

"Timing is everything," quips a *Boston Globe* article on animal mating seasons. *"An elephant's pregnancy lasts about two years and she is not receptive for about three years after the birth of her calf. That means that a female elephant is in the mood about twice a decade. It's a moment a*

male would not want to miss. 'Not this year darling, I have a headache.'''
Indeed, elephants have a unique and fascinating social system revolving around the perpetuation of the species.

A female elephant's receptive period, *estrous*, is fairly unpredictable and lasts for only two days. Meanwhile, females in estrous are generally found in geographically isolated groups, far from suitable male partners. Long-range vocalization, then, is the only means available for females to attract males during the two-day window. Vocalizations of female elephants in estrous have been measured at 117 dB at a distance of one meter from the throat. Dominant frequencies center at 30 Hz. Males in a similar state of sexual readiness known as *musth*, range solo for long periods, but emit rumbles that are as low as 14Hz.

Elephant calls are not uniform. Their overall band depends on a number of variables, including but not limited to, the type of call being issued and the individual signaler's physical characteristics. During the course of her research, Katy Payne identified vocalizations used by elephants that ranged from "trumpets" to "peeps." The Savanna Elephant Vocalization Project, based in Kenya's Amboseli National Park, places the number of distinguishable elephant calls at 70. Joyce Poole, a biologist with the project and a colleague of Payne's, maintains that the calls are used not for the practical matters of orchestrating herd movements and for mate attraction alone, but also to ensure social order and to express feelings of playfulness, anger, joy, or sympathy.

A basic distinction occurs with individual versus communal vocalization. Males tend to communicate individually. Female elephants are naturally social animals, which their "talk" reflects. Again, quoting Payne's book, "Females . . . make communal calls if they encounter a male in musth, or even a pool of his urine. They call collectively when a male sniffs a family member—loud vocalizations follow each test, and some of them run away screaming. They call collectively when they greet relatives, and when they reassure offspring, and when any one of them is mounted, and after mating. Families band together when one of their family members is in estrus, and the larger the group, the noisier" [5].

Long-distance communication is important for the wide-ranging social animals. Elephants recognize individual family member's voices. An individual's vocalization often elicits a response from another's a few kilometers away. In fact, social groups of elephants have been observed "silently" tracking each other for weeks or months, even when separated by kilometers of forest.

Elephants have another acoustic strategy that benefits them by further enlarging their communication range. They use the naturally occurring inversion layer, an atmospheric condition where cooler air sits atop warm air, to bounce their calls off the sky, down to otherwise inaccessibly distant places. Without the inversion layer, the call's energy would be radiated upward towards space. When the inversion layer is present, however, elephant calls may be heard at twice the usual range. David Larom and Michael Garstang, pioneers in the study of this phenomenon, describe it as bouncing vocalizations through an atmospheric "duct."

The boundary of dissimilar density materials creates an impedance mismatch that will influence the transmission of energy. When sound or any other energy propagating through a medium encounters a sudden transition to a denser medium, a portion of the signal is reflected with the angle of the reflection equaling the angle of incidence. This effect is particularly pronounced when the signal approaches the boundary at a shallow ("grazing") angle (see Figure 1).

Since this phenomenon is not limited to atmospherics, a variety of aquatic animals may take advantage of it. For example, a similar bound-

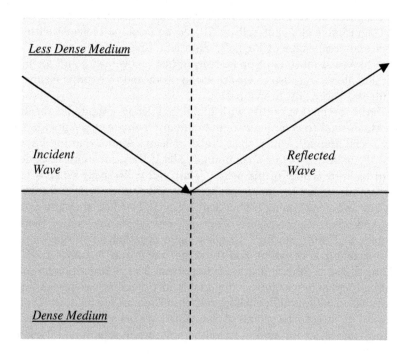

Figure 1. Grazing Angle: A sound wave is reflected at the angle of incidence when it reaches the border of a denser medium.

ary zone exists in lakes and oceans where cold water may sit on top of warmer water. Two distinct water temperatures means two distinct water densities and the opportunity to reflect sound. Later, we will see how another large mammal makes use of this aquatic boundary layer.

Elephants utilizing temperature inversions have been observed communicating up to 9.8 kilometers away from one another. Moreover, observations show that elephants increase their calling in the late evening and at night, precisely when the inversion layers are strongest. Females generally call in the late afternoon or early dusk, before the inversion layer is optimal, but also while predatory lions are still asleep: a compromise between distance and safety. Two other benefits for communicating from dusk till dawn are that winds generally die down and temperature variations are reduced between ground-level bodies of air, reducing background noise and distortion.

2   Flukes in Nature

Transmitting underwater is a much different proposition than transmitting in air. Sound waves travel at about 344 ms in the atmosphere, while underwater sound travels 4.4 times faster. Low frequencies (generally those under 100 Hz) still travel with less attenuation than high frequencies, therefore whales are able to use low frequencies to communicate over long distances underwater much the same as elephants are able to on land.

Land animals have difficulty producing sound efficiently because the impedance mismatch between the speed of sound in their sound-producing organs and the speed of sound in air is very different. A benefit to animals vocalizing in an underwater environment, compared with those on land, is that impedance matching becomes less of a problem. The organs generating sound are comprised of water—or at least substances much closer in density to water than air. As such, underwater animals transmit sound quite effectively, requiring far less energy when conducting sounds from their organs into the propagating medium, namely water.

Some land-based animals, such as frogs of the family *Ranidae,* utilize inflated throat sacks, in part to address this concern. Impedance between the end of the throat and the propagating medium of the atmosphere is great. The inflated structure couples the vibrations from the animal's laryngeal gateway to the atmosphere that surrounds it, easing the energy requirements for transmission.

Another contrast between air- and water-based signaling is imposed by medium absorption, the loss of energy to heat as sound propagates. In air, a 1 kHz signal suffers medium loss to the tune of 1.2 dB/100 meters. Raising the air temperature increases this effect. By contrast, medium absorption for the same sound wave in ocean water is only about 0.008 dB/100 meter, several hundreds of times less severe. Moreover, fresh water offers about 1,000 times less medium absorption than salt water. Factors of pressure and temperature of the water also have an effect, but no matter what the medium, high frequencies are always attenuated more than low frequencies.

2.1   Cetacian Variation in Frequency Usage

Whales (*Cetacea*) are mammals supremely adapted to the ways of the ocean. Many whales possess the ability to move very quickly underwater; all maintain their body temperature under very cold conditions, an important trait because 90% of today's whales feed and breed in the waters off Antarctica. Putting aside other impressive adaptations, whale species also command a number of sophisticated methods for transmitting sound waves.

Like elephants, some cetaceans utilize low frequencies to communicate at a distance. Many whale species also use very high frequency sound (ultrasound), especially while tracking prey with echolocation. The result is that the frequency ranges used by species of cetacean stretch over an astonishing range, from 15 Hz to 150 kHz.

Toothed whales (*odontocetes*) including the sperm whale (*Physeter catodon*) and Narwhal (*Monodon monoceros*) generally produce sounds near 1000 Hz for purposes of echolocation. These frequencies are very effective in hunting prey such as squid or fish. Cetaceans detect targets down to a tenth of a meter in size.

Pulses of ultrasound (sound with a frequency of 720 kHz or higher, and so above the threshold of human hearing) are utilized for echolocation. They are typically very short emissions lasting from 0.05 to 0.1 ms. They may be used for ranging a target or determining its shape, often at distances greater than aquatic vision would allow. Cetaceans have the ability to use echo spectra to determine the relative speed of their targets and information about the composition of their targets as well.

2.2   Communicating at a Distance

When it comes to long distance communication and intense signaling, the plankton-feeding baleen whales (*mysticetes*) are king. Not dependent on high-frequency echolocation signals to chase down prey, members of this suborder specialize in lower frequencies. Gray whales (*Eschrichtius robustus*) for instance, have been observed using 12.5 Hz signals. Their powerful moans are estimated to be 188 dB at one meter and can be detected for many kilometers.

One of the only whales that can out-produce the gray in decibel output is the blue whale, another species belonging to mysticetes. These blue-gray mammals can weigh more than120 tons and, likewise, can stretch more than 100 feet in length, making them the largest animals ever to inhabit land or sea. Blue whales produce correspondingly low and loud signals that, not coincidentally, also travel farther than those of any other known animal. These signals center around 20 Hz and are transmitted for periods of up to 30 seconds.

The blue whale's most notable competition for loudest animal in existence is the fin whale. The fin whale (*Balaenoptera physalus),* produces a shorter, but very pure, tone of 20 Hz that lasts about a second. The signal is repeated at very regular intervals, sometimes with a softer call following on the heels of the louder one. These "doublets" are categorized by the time intervals separating the components. Both the loud and softer signals exhibit a purity of tone comparable to that of a flute. Intensity levels reach a shocking 155 decibels, far louder than the take-off of a jet airplane.

Bandwidths for fin whale signals are small and precise. About 95 percent of the signal's energy resides within 4 Hz of the 20 Hz core. Roger Payne, a noted cetacean researcher and president of the Whale Conservation Institute in Lincoln, Massachusetts, suggests that 20 Hz is the perfect frequency for communicating while swimming under icebergs and icecaps, where fin whales spend much of their time. One principal reason is that this frequency is not absorbed by ice, as can occur with higher frequencies.

Whale vocalizations offer a number of behavior-related modalities with individual whales using different parts of the sound spectrum at different times. Gray whales, for example, have been observed utilizing distinct categories of sound only during migration. The sound categories contain frequencies ranging from 15 to 305 Hz, and each exhibits a distinct frequency-spectrum.

Like elephants, whales may reflect sound to extend their range. Humpback whales (*Megaptera novaena australis*), according to researchers, "select particular depths and bottom substrates, and channel sounds so that they are detectable hundreds of kilometers away."

Roger Payne has calculated that cetacean vocalizations likely traveled much further in preindustrial age oceans than they do today. He speculates that using deep currents as sound channels, a whale might have communicated all the way from Antarctica to the Aleutian Islands. That, however, was before the advent of modern ocean-going vessels that contribute a great deal of sound pollution to an already noisy ocean. The maritime engines of oil tankers and other large vessels significantly reduce the effective distance of communication achievable by many cetaceans in this day and age, their propellers emitting high-decibel sound at 20 Hz.

2.3   Whale Songs and Bubble Nets

Whale sounds range from powerful moans, to clicks, to very complex songs. Generally, even the simplest whale vocalizations are referred to as songs. Stanzas of complex songs average 15 minutes in length. Less sophisticated versions may be a single tone that is methodically repeated at a constant duty cycle.

Songs are repeated for many hours or days. Often a variation on a theme is introduced by one whale and then repeated by others as it is sent back and forth across the waters. Over the course of a few months, the song evolves, with passages altered, added, or deleted. At the end of one singing season, a song will sound very different from how it began. After many months of inactivity, the song is reincarnated with the new singing season, picked up from where it was left off. It has been observed that every whale of a group repeats the same song, but individuals tend to sing it for different lengths of time. Similarly, individuals may only sing particular parts of the entire song.

Speculation on the purpose of the songs varies. It has been theorized that they are simple homing beacons used to attract other whales at distance. Some perceive them to be content-laden communications of complex design. One possible use for the intense sounds generated by whales is to scare up edible fish from hiding places on the seabed.

Sound plays a part in orchestrating the movements of whales while they engage in sophisticated feeding behaviors. Sound seems integral to baleens, for example, when they organize for the formation of "bubble nets"—columns of bubbles are released by the whales while below a school of plankton and are used to coral the food supply into smaller areas for easier feeding.

In cases where groups of individual humpback whales conduct bubble netting jointly, there is a "continuous whining buzz" which lasts more than 30 seconds. At the occurrence of an upward inflection of the signal, the whales breach in unison. Also, the whales reach the surface in a precise array. These whales repeatedly utilize bubble net feeding behavior, often breaching many times during the course of a day. They always surface together and always with each whale in the same position relative to the others in the group. According to Roger Payne, this maneuver occurs in highly murky waters, ruling out visual coordination and making sound the most likely means of organizing the movements.

2.4 Anatomy Plays a Part

Whale sound is thought to be generated by the movement of air through the nasal passage and specialized membranes housed between the nasal sacks. Some of the sacks branch out into the head, and it is thought that they, along with the whale's skull, help reflect sound forward and into a specialized funneling organ known as the melon.

Embedded within the whale's head, the fatty structures of the melon act as an acoustic lens. Sound waves are focused as they transit through the melon, encountering successively slower-propagating areas as the material changes composition. The sound narrows, creating a directional beam that is then emitted from the whale and into the surrounding ocean (see Figure 2).

The melon offers a closer approximation to water density than the air passages which generated the initial vibrations. As such, it reduces the impedance mismatch, cutting down on the amount of uncontrolled and wasteful reflection and scattering of sound. The resultant sound waves, once emitted, can be highly directional.

Whales have the capacity to adjust the structure of the flexible melon, presumably altering the direction or even focal point of the transmitted beam. It is an interesting aside that the sperm whale, a predator, possesses the largest melon of all the whales. One hypothesis is that it uses a focused sonic beam as a weapon, so as to stun or confuse fish or squid at close range.

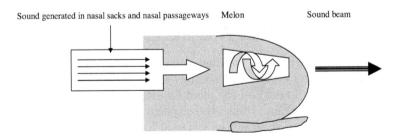

Figure 2. Lateral diagram of a whale head: The conical melon offers a means of focusing sound into a tight beam.

Another possibility is that the melon adds a strong directional component to conspecific communication. The more focused the sound, the simpler to home in on it once it has been located. As such, it would be a particularly useful tool in keeping together members of the same pod.

2.5   Assorted Findings

Although there is presently little knowledge on the specific mechanisms of whale hearing, a recent study has demonstrated that white whales, one of the *odontocetes*, have sensitive hearing capacity even at great depths and pressures.

Researchers selected two white whales and trained them to whistle when they heard a 500 ms signal transmitted from a hydrophone. Results demonstrated that the whales could hear the tones to the lowest depth and highest water pressure of the test— 300 meters, or about 30 atmospheres.

The hearing capacities of whales, when scientifically verified, closely correspond with the frequencies of their vocalizations. It is theorized that beaked whales might be able to amplify sounds once they reach the ear. Some scientists suspect many species of whales use their lower jaw to collect sound vibrations which are then conducted to the ears.

The flexibility of whale echolocation behavior has also been a subject of inquiry. The echolocation signals of beluga whales (*Delphinapterus leucas*), for instance, demonstrate adaptability to environment. The belugas in the study used lower frequencies when ambient noise levels were low and shifted to higher frequencies and intensities when ambient noise levels were high.

Similar versatility has been observed in false killer whales that have been trained to home in on man-provided targets. The animals slowly changed the frequency and duration of their clicks when adjusting to a new set of targets, in the process becoming more accurate in their targeting.

3   The Smaller They Are, the Harder to Call

An insect momentarily stops crawling along the stem of a plant and begins a rhythmic tap of its leg against a nearby leaf. Stoop down, cup your hand over your ear, and listen. Feel the plant for vibrations. Try as you might, you won't detect a thing. Unlike the elephant, whose call we can't hear because its frequency is below the range of human hearing, the insect's communiqué is too faint for human ears.

Sound pressure correlates to the volume of a medium—such as air or water—that a vibrator moves. Creatures that are capable of energetically affecting a great deal of a medium may produce low frequencies at high pressure levels. Small organisms have difficulty moving large amounts of anything; hence, they tend to generate lower sound intensities than their larger counterparts.

In the case of small land-based animals, the vibrating sound medium is most often air; however, water, soil, rock, or even organic structures such as plant stems can also be used. No matter what the medium, it takes a series of highly refined abilities for small organisms—and this includes insects—to make noises intense enough to propagate over significant distances. A number of creatures do manage the trick, however, by employing specially evolved organs for that purpose.

It is a key consideration that animals have trouble generating, or even receiving directionally, wavelengths that are any longer than their own bodies. If a small animal, say a cricket, is attempting to locate the direction of a potential mate's call, it can only rely on high frequencies. This is because long wavelengths interact weakly with much smaller objects (like a cricket's ears). Short wavelengths easily reflect off even very small objects and so are received by the small sound receptors of a cricket, located on the insect's front legs.

3.1 Vibration Multipliers

Although the twitch-rate of muscles (the fastest rate muscles can contract and relax under optimum conditions) is slow, higher frequencies are achieved through "vibration-multipliers." The larynx is considered such an organ because it vibrates much faster than the muscles (largely the diaphragm) responsible for exhaling the air that activates them. Even the fastest muscle is limited to a maximum of around 1000 contraction/relaxation cycles per second effectively limiting high frequency output to 1000 Hz far lower that the frequencies produced by the vocal cords' vibration. (Please refer to Bunnel's article "Introduction to Speech Acoustics" (see *Audio Anecdotes III*) describing the human vocal tract for more details.)

Vibration-multipliers have evolved independently within different species and are suited to that type of animal's capabilities and needs. The first two such systems will be mentioned without elaboration while the third, stridulation, will be looked at in some depth, largely because it is the principal means of communication for the smallest animals dealt with in this section. Stridulation also points toward some difficulties inherent for small animals in the business of making noise.

The larynx is the principal organ of sound for most mammals. It consists of two vocal cords, each covering roughly half of the whole trachea. These cords are held in place by cartilage and muscle. When the cords are closed by the interarytenoid muscle, and the proper tension is applied to them from the thyro-arytenoid and cricothyroid muscles, they shut off the flow of air. As air pressure builds, they open and close rapidly, causing vibration.

Variations on the mammalian vocal cords exist in other species. For instance, frogs and toads utilize a vocal cord to produce what amounts to a carrier wave (within the 100 to 200 Hz range), and subsequently modulate the sound through a second and independent vibrating structure. That structure sits on the sides of the trachea above the glottis and works to add vibration in the 1 kHz range. Because the two sets of vibrating membranes are not connected and are controlled by separate muscle groups, a great deal of control is achieved.

3.2 Arthropods

Suppose for a moment that a cricket has wandered into your home late one night, chirruping with fervency. Try as you might, you can't muffle the high-pitched noise that will not let you sleep. The noise seems too intense for a single insect to generate, yet he is your malefactor. For an animal the size of a cricket to be able make a large racket, a few interesting principles of acoustics must come into play.

The sound consists, like all sound, of the compression and rarefaction of its medium; in this case, air. The effect is the formation of longitudinal waves (the case for all sound waves propagating through air and water, but not necessarily for those propagating in solids, which are sometimes transverse) that range from 2 to 29 kHz. The most common cricket in the United States, southern Canada, and South America is the field cricket, (*Gyrrlus assimilis Fabricius*), utilizing a 4-kHz signal produced by stridulatory organs located on the wings.

Stridulatory organs are external appendages attached to opposing surfaces, used to effect sound through grating actions. In a crab, the rubbing of specially adapted portions of the front claw generates the sound. Another crustacean, the lobster, rubs the antennae against its head to achieve the same effect. Certain beetles have their stridulatory organs on the thorax and the leg. No matter where they are located, the stridulatory organs produce sound in a mechanical manner. In some ways it is similar to a metal comb being plucked by running a thumb along the teeth—no matter how hard the thumb's pressure on the comb, the responding vi-

Figure 3. A comb: Plucking the tooth of a comb produces a distinct frequency; no matter what force is imparted.

bration is the same frequency, dictated by the physical properties of the comb itself (see Figure 3).

Arthropods specialize in stridulation and their devices for this type of sound production vary, however, all of the forms of vibration have certain traits in common. The first of these has to do with the type of sound characteristically generated by the stridulatory organs themselves. To understand this, we must first make a brief accounting of the organs that generate the sound. Located on the upper side of the lower wing of a cricket is a hard, sharp ridge of material known as a plectrum. It forms the equivalent of a violinist's bow. The instrument itself, the file, contains many small teeth and is situated on the underside of the top wing.

As the cricket rubs, sound is produced. The plectrum sets in motion the teeth of the file, causing them to vibrate. Each tooth moves forward, then back, imparting motion to the air molecules that surround it. The resulting sounds combine to form the familiar "chirrup" we associate with crickets.

The sound generating mechanisms are dipoles, meaning their teeth vibrate in two directions along a single axis. As such, they impart sound energy more strongly along that axis. A peculiar aspect of sound fields created by dipoles is that the resulting sound field is directional. Thus, it is easier to home in upon.

Directional sound can be a great advantage for the cricket, which utilizes this sort of transmission to attract a mate. The disadvantage lies in that predators, too, can home in on the transmitter. This suggests a hungry small mammal might make lunch of the cricket or a larger, sleepless, and angry homeowner might successfully locate and destroy the marauding pest.

3.3   The Tool-Using Cricket

Another difficulty associated with small vibrating files is that of acoustical short-circuiting. The effect occurs when air molecules "leak" from one side of the file's teeth to the other, rapidly equalizing air pressures on both sides. The result is a reduction of sound pressure. Without short-circuiting, rarefaction occurs on the receding side of the tooth of a file while compression occurs at the other. With short-circuiting, the two pressures equalize before another duty cycle begins. This is especially true with the generation of lower frequencies, where the duration between duty cycles is great.

Small animals, such as insects, that use stridulation are naturally prone to difficulties arising from short-circuiting because the teeth of their sound organs are tiny, reducing the distance that molecules have to travel in order to leak. Insects that use dipoles therefore need a means to contend with acoustical short-circuiting, without which the sound would be compromised at its source.

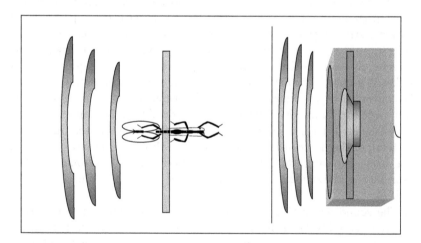

Figure 4.   Left: The leaf as a baffle. A lateral view of a leaf being used as a baffle by a tree cricket. Neozabea has extended its body through a hole in the center of the leaf. The cricket must first draw its wings parallel to the leaf (away from the perpendicular position that is depicted in this diagram) and then rub them together, producing sound. The leaf's structure provides for a reduction in acoustic short-circuiting of the sound waves. Right: A man-made baffle. A simplified transducer/speaker arrangement utilizes a sound board as a baffle to reduce acoustic short-circuiting.

To reduce the problem, small animals speed the rate and number of duty cycles, creating higher frequencies, which in turn reduce the amount of time air has to leak before another duty cycle starts. Another means is utilized by tree crickets, which construct a partial baffle out of tree leaves. This leaf-baffle acts the same way that another, and much more familiar, dipole baffle does—the sound board which backs a speaker's transducers (see Figure 4).

After going to the trouble of manufacturing the hole and wrestling itself into a seemingly uncomfortable position, the tree cricket is rewarded. Once situated properly in the leaf, short-circuiting is reduced. Overall sound pressure of the noise is strengthened because rarefactions on one side of the leaf are now undiluted by compressions on the other.

Another variation on the baffle theme is utilized by the *Oecanthus*, a close relative to the *Neozabea*, where the shape of the baffle is different, but the general principle is the same. Interestingly, people debate whether man is alone in the role of tool-maker. Here we see that the humble insect instinctively creates and utilizes a rather sophisticated tool.

4 Legislating the Kingdom: Rules for Effective Communication in Animals

If bioacoustics shows us anything, it is that evolution provides ingenious methods for overcoming environmental hurdles. Indeed, whenever an acoustic engineering difficulty is identified, a prudent investigator might do well to see if an animal is exploiting a partial, if not total, solution. Nature, given evolutionary significant time periods, is adept at overcoming environmental hurdles.

Yet, if we are to see competition among animals as part of the overall environment, an added level of complexity becomes apparent. Animals evolutionarily selected for optimum acoustic design are not only constrained by physics, but also by the challenge of competing organisms. Organisms may take different paths when responding to evolutionary pressures. One may control its vocalizations to limit its vulnerability to being located by predators. Another may increase the acuity of its hearing in order to improve its chances of obtaining prey or escaping from predators.

Issues like these are linked to the consideration of cost/benefit in animal communication—a subspecialty which is studied by a number of bioacoustic scientists and which utilizes the branch of mathematics known as game theory.

Signal content, form, and function are intertwined in complex ways. A simple and important example is evident with mate-attraction signals. By their very design, these transmissions take a great deal of energy and effort to accomplish. Over time, the evolutionary process has undoubtedly balanced the inherent costs of the energy expenditures with the potential rewards. In the case of mating calls, physically superior males can broadcast to a larger number of possible mates.

The use of energy by a male to attract a female also makes sense for the female. The longer and more strenuously an individual male animal calls, the more likely it is that he is in good physical condition. The more information a female knows from the call of a male, the less energy she will have to utilize investigating the wrong type of mate.

Signal design "rules" state that the mate-attracting signal type be long-range. The longer the range, the more potential mates can be alerted to the presence of an opposite-sex animal. Furthermore, the signal must be locatable by the potential mate and contain information specific enough to at least distinguish the transmitting animal from related species. These signals are of the lowest possible frequency or utilize a band where there is little competing noise. They are repeated often for long durations to make it as easy as possible for the originator to be located by potential mates.

Design rules exist for other types of signals as well. When marking or defending territories through vocalization, animals must use transmissions with ranges roughly corresponding to the size of the territory. As such, their signal intensity must vary according to the circumstances. Territorial calls—those which ward off dangerous competitors—will likely be of long duration, but only repeated infrequently during the course of the day. This, of course, limits the amount of energy expended for unseen and possibly nonexistent threats.

Extraordinary balances are struck by animals living in nature. Design features and design rules, however, demonstrate that they gravitate toward systems which are effective for multiple applications and suitable over the long term.

5 Conclusion

"What is man without the beasts? If all the beasts were gone, man would die from a great Loneliness of the Spirit."

-Chief Seattle

The Earth's surface vibrates with the sounds of life. Elephants trumpet while muted insects chatter. High-decibel whale songs permeate our planet's oceans. Resonating amidst those same waters is the ceaseless, lulling drone of the microscopic organisms that live, on a tiny scale, within the biotasphere. (See Hempton's article "Listening to Nature: Hearing is More than Meets the Eye" (see *Audio Anecdotes I*) for his description of the sound of dawn.)

The ever-present diversity and abundance of life on this planet has inspired mankind in more ways than one. Native Americans saw themselves as connected with the spirit of the animals that surrounded them. Observing animals in nature, likewise, brought scientists like Leonardo da Vinci closer to unlocking the secrets of the universe. In turn, as one of Mother Nature's greatest and most attentive students, Leonardo would later become an inspiration himself to thousands of scientists and artists that followed in his footsteps.

Today, the methods and goals of researchers in the field of bioacoustics range greatly. Specialists among these scientists attempt to understand portions of every biome and to put the pieces of a puzzle together that touches every continent and sea of the planet. Simultaneously, the field of bioacoustics helps scientists conserve some of the world's most fascinating animals. It would be an enormous and disturbing irony to lose the elephant and whale to extinction, even as we near a much fuller understanding of these majestic animals.

The biotasphere provides an abundance of inspirational models for today's inventor—just as the study of birds in flight inspired wonder and inquiry in the renowned Italian master, Leonardo. But, innovation, now as in the past, begins with the inquiring mind. This article has touched on but a few examples within the rich field of bioacoustics. The topic should be further explored, in all of its intricacy. In an effort to make pursuit of this knowledge an easier task, the end of this essay includes a list of excellent references.

Annotated Bibliography

[1] Jack W. Bradbury and Sandra Vehrencamp. *Principles of Animal Communication.* Sunderland, MA: Sinauer Associates, Inc, 1998.

This is a landmark survey of animal communication, useful for undergraduates and graduates alike. The text is notable for its excellent diagrams and for its clear articulation of the principles of bioacoustics. An added bonus is the extensive bibliography.

[2] Douglas M. Considine and Glenn D. Considine, editors. *Van Nostrands Scientific Encyclopedia, Eighth Edition.* New York: Van Nostrand Reinhold Co., 1999.

A compilation of articles touching upon all manner of scientific inquiry. Entries relating to acoustics are both thorough and thoughtful.

[3] Neville H. Fletcher. *Acoustic Systems in Biology.* Oxford, UK: Oxford University Press, 1992.

This text is a quantitative approach to bioacoustics, well detailed and suitable for advanced graduate-level courses.

[4] S. L. Hopp, M. J. Owren, and C. S. Evans, editors. *Acoustic Communication in Animals.* New York: Springer-Verlag, 1998.

This text is an excellent resource with many essays on bioacoustics by experts in the field.

[5] Katy Payne. *Silent Thunder: In the Presence of the Elephants.* New York: Penguin Group, 1999.

Scientific observations are coupled with personal anecdotes from the pioneer who discovered the use of infrasound among elephants. The book proves that good science can result from imaginative sources of inspiration.

[6] Roger Payne. *Among Whales.* New York, NY: Bantam Doubleday Dell Publishing Group, Inc., 1995.

The world's leading cetacean scientist introduces his field of study to laymen while eloquently communicating the great need for whale conservation. Characteristics of whale vocalization and hearing are treated in depth.

Glossary of Audio Terms

Accidental: A sharp (#), flat (b), natural, double sharp (x), or double flat (bb), placed in front of a note to either raise or lower the pitch of that note by a specific amount. For example, a sharp placed directly in front of middle C raises the frequency (pitch) of that note by one semitone. Middle C is typically tuned to 261.6 Hz. Raising its pitch by one equally tempered semitone will result in a frequency of 277.2 Hz (C-sharp). A natural cancels the effect of a previously placed accidental in any given measure of music. A double sharp raises the pitch of a note by two semitones (one wholetone), and a double flat lowers the pitch of a note by two semitones (one wholetone).

Acoustic: Pertaining to sound as a physical event, in contrast to "auditory" (pertaining to sound as a psychological event).

Additive white Gaussian noise: A model of noise as a zero-mean Gaussian random process. Used to represent noise in a system from thermal motion of electrons through all electronic circuit elements.

Advanced Audio Coding (AAC): The new digital compressed audio format proposed as part of the MPEG-2; it's an improvement over the MP3 format.

Aeolian mode: The sixth mode derived from the major scale; the same as the natural minor scale. The aeolian mode uses the exact same notes from a major scale, but begins and ends on the sixth note of the major scale (i.e., A up to A with the key signature of C major).

Alias-free: Describes a digital signal which is constructed by summing a set of sine waves, each of which has a frequency which is less than or equal to 1/2 of the sampling rate. See bandlimited.

Aliasing: According to the Nyquist theory, a sine wave can only be represented by a digital sample stream with a sampling rate twice the frequency of the sine wave. In the case where the sampling rate is less than twice the frequency of the wave, the energy from frequencies that are above the Nyquist rate, SR/2, must go somewhere so they appear as phantom tones below the Nyquist Rate. This phenomenon is referred to as "aliasing." For frequencies between SR/2 and SR, the frequency of the aliased signal is (SampleRate - OriginalFrequency). Thus, a signal with a frequency of 40,000 Hz recorded with a sample rate of 44,100 Hz would sound as an audible tone at 4,100 Hz. This is an important consideration when recording or synthesizing audio because complex signals in the audible range can easily have harmonics that extend far above the Nyquist Rate.

Allophone: A variant of a phoneme that is acoustically distinct, but does not constitute a phonemic difference in a language.

Allpass filter: An IIR filter whose gain is unity over its entire frequency range, but whose phase response is variable.

Ambience synthesis: The process of creating a distinct sonic atmosphere through the use of "background" sounds.

Ambient microphone: A microphone placed in a room or hall in such a way as to pick up acoustical properties of the space, especially its reverberant properties. (These properties are sometimes called the "ambience" of an acoustic space.)

Amplitude: The extreme range of pressure levels exhibited by a sound wave, voltage in an electrical signal, or digital value in a digital signal.

Amplitude modulation: See modulation.

Amplitude spectrum: See spectrum.

Analog: 1. In recording, refers to the process of putting sound on tape resulting from data that are collected by measuring continuous variations in sound pressure level or voltage. (see digital). 2. In general, refers to any process by which data are represented as measurements along a continuous variable. Analog radios, for example, allow you to tune stations by turning a knob (continuously) that changes the frequency selectivity of the receiver continuously.

Analog synthesizer: A sound-generating device containing circuits that operate over a continuous range of voltages. The components typically include oscillators, filters, amplifiers, envelope generators, etc. The modules produce varying voltages and are also controlled by voltages and can thus be interconnected in complex patterns to create novel sounds. Some well-known brands include Moog, Bucchla, Arp, Serge, and Oberheim.

Analog-to-Digital (A/D) converter: A device that converts samples of a signal to a numeric representation. In some cases, the sampling process is included in the A/D converter.

Assimilation: The systematic shifting of the articulation of one speech segment when in the context of another specific segment.

Asynchronous granular synthesis: A type of granular synthesis where grains are distributed in time according to one or more stochastic parameters.

Adaptive Transform Acoustic Coding (ATRAC): The digital compressed audio format used in mini discs; operates typically at rates between 64 kbps (ATRAC-3) and 384 kbps (ATRAC-1 and 2).

Attack time: The time it takes for an audio compressor to reduce its gain when the output signal exceeds the threshold.

Audification: The use of realistic, short-duration sounds to communicate the occurrence of an event. See Auditory icons and sonification.

Auditory branding: Sounds or brief songs (jingles) are often used to enhance the emotional or cultural image associated with a company or product. Successful auditory branding includes the NBC chimes, the AT&T "sparkle tone" and the "you deserve a break today" McDonalds jingle.

Auditory icons: Auditory icons use environmental sounds that have a strong link with the objects or actions represented by the sounds. Examples include the sound of trash being emptied into a trash can, traffic noises, or the sound of a door shutting.

Auditory masking: Effect in which the presence of one sound precludes perception of another.

Auditory Scene Analysis (ASA): Forming separate representations of the individual sounds that are present in a mixture of sounds, given only the sound created by their mixture.

Auditory stream: A set of sounds that are perceived as coming from the activity of a single acoustic source over time.

Augmented fifth: A fifth that encompasses eight semitones (i.e., C up to G-sharp).

Augmented fourth: A fourth that encompasses six semitones (i.e., C up to F-sharp). This interval is diatonic to the major scale between notes 4 and 7 (i.e., in the key of G major, the notes C and F-sharp). This interval is also called the tritone because it encompasses three wholetones (six semitones).

Augmented second: The interval of a second that is one semitone larger than a major second. It encompasses three semitones. An augmented second (C up to D-sharp, for example) occurs between the sixth and seventh notes in the harmonic minor scale. It is one of the intervals that gives the harmonic minor scale such a distinct sound.

Augmented sixth: A sixth that encompasses ten semitones (i.e., C up to A-sharp). This interval is not diatonic to any major scale, but it is an integral part of the augmented sixth chord. This is a complex family of chords used primarily in 19th-century Romantic music in the western European tradition.

Augmented triad: One of the basic triad types (along with major, minor, and diminished). An augmented triad consists of a root, a major third, and an augmented fifth.

Balanced modulator: An analog device which combines two signal frequencies and produces only their sum and difference frequencies.

Band-limited: Describes a signal consisting of sine wave partials whose frequencies are all below the Nyquist Limit (SR/2) for a given sampling rate. Band-limiting is desirable because frequencies above the Nyquist Limit can alias back into the audible range and cause undesirable artifacts. See alias-free.

Band-passed: Filtered so that only a certain range of frequencies (the "pass band") is present with substantial amplitude in the output of the filter. Other frequencies are attenuated.

Bandpass waveform: Waveform suitable for Radio Frequency (RF) transmission. A bandpass waveform is frequency translated by a carrier frequency to a frequency much higher than that of the baseband waveform.

Bark scale: Nonlinear scale of frequency scale based on human frequency resolution in which auditory excitation is usually measured. Sounds which are separated by more than about one Bark unit are generally resolvable as separate sounds and do not interact with each other at a sensory level.

Baseband waveform: Waveform suitable for a transmission channel. It is created from the incoming binary (in this case) data commonly by pulse code modulation.

Bass clef: Also called the "F clef." This is the clef that identifies the lower pitches in the grand staff, and is written on the bottom staff of the two staves in the grand staff. The bass clef identifies the pitch F3 (F below middle C).

Beam: A part of music notation. The beam functions as a type of grouping device that shows the beat units in a measure of music. This is especially useful when there are lots of eighth-notes and sixteenth-notes in a measure of music.

Bilinear interpolation: An interpolation that occurs in two dimensions. An example is combining multiple look-up tables to compute a function of two variables. You use the first variable to interpolate between adjacent entries within a table, and then use the second variable to interpolate between the results from two adjacent tables.

Bilinear transform: A nonlinear transformation of a continuous time system to a discrete time system. The output of the frequency response mapping between the two time systems has an arctangent relationship and is very close to linear for frequencies less than half the Nyquist frequency. An example of its use is when a passive or active R-C-L filter is bilinear transformed in order to implement a similar filter on a DSP using discrete time stepped operations.

Bit: An abbreviation of "binary digit." Signals such as sound waves can be represented by strings of numbers. In the decimal system, such numbers (0 to 9) are called "digits." In the binary system, the numbers 0 and 1 are called "bits." In information theory, a "bit" is the amount of information that one must send to a listener (or decoder) so that the latter can tell which of two equally likely alternatives it should choose.

Bit rate: The rate at which bits are transmitted in a communication system.

Bit reversed: A binary number written so that the least significant bit is at the left and most significant at the right. Used in the FFT process.

Bode plot: A method of quickly plotting frequency response by using poles and zeros.

Boundary tone: A marker of certain syntactic boundaries. Examples include the rising intonation at the end of a question or the falling intonation at the end of a sentence.

Bow: A wooden stick strung with horsehair used to play instruments of the viol and violin families. The tension of the hair is varied by means of an adjustable nut attached to one end of the stick.

Brick wall: A term used to describe a filter whose frequency response cuts off very abruptly. A graph of the response resembles a brick wall.

Bridge: In string instruments, a slender wedge-shaped wooden device that holds the strings in place and transmits string vibration to the table for amplification by the body of the instrument.

Brightness: A quality of the timbre of sound in which the sound seems high or sharp. It is correlated with the greater intensities of high frequency components in a sound relative to its low-frequency components. The opposite is often referred to as dullness.

Buzz core opcode: A core opcode in the MPEG-4 Structured Audio standard for creating pulse waveforms with dynamic spectral movement. Also see MPEG-4, structured audio, and pulse waveform.

Chirp: A short windowed sinusoid or bank of sinusoids, where the frequency of the sinusoid(s) changes from one value to another over the course of the window's duration.

Chord: A group of notes played at the same time that have a musical relation to one another and are intended to be experienced as a group. Notes may be played together (a block chord) or melodically unfolded (arpeggiated).

Chorus effect: Produced when a delayed signal is mixed with its original nondelayed version. The delay is modulated randomly or periodically, usually in the 10-40 millisecond range (see modulation). A number of independently delayed and modulated copies of the same signal can be mixed together to "thicken" the chorus effect.

Chromatic: Literally means "colorful." Chromatic typically refers to a note (or notes) that uses an accidental to raise or lower its pitch level in relation to a given key signature. For example, in the key of C major (neither sharps nor flats in the key signature), the note F# (F-sharp) is chromatic: It is not a naturally occurring note in the key of C major. It is not diatonic to the key of C major. The term "chromatic" is often used synonymously with the term "accidental." An accidental refers to a specific sharp, flat, natural, double sharp, or double flat that is used in a musical passage. The term "chromatic" typically refers to a larger section of music or to an entire musical composition.

Clef: A notational convention that allows the musician to interpret the grid of a musical staff in terms of the pitch content. For example, in the treble clef, the bottom line is where the pitch E4 (E above Middle C) is placed. In the bass clef, the bottom line is where the pitch G2 is placed (G an octave and a fourth below Middle C). There are many different clefs, but the treble and bass clef are the two most common. The other clefs are moveable C clefs (they determine where on the staff Middle C will be written), and are (from high to low musical range) soprano clef, mezzo-soprano clef, alto clef, tenor clef, and baritone clef.

Clipping: A form of distortion where the normally sinusoidal waveshape is clipped at a maximum amplitude level. Clipping is caused when the dynamic range of the signal exceeds the range of the equipment. Clipping causes both harmonic and intermodulation distortion.

Co-articulation (anticipatory/carryover): Temporal overlap of articulatory movements for multiple phones. Anticipatory is influence of a subsequent phone; carryover is influence of a prior phone.

Cochlea: Spiral, snail-shaped organ of the inner ear, in which acoustic waves are converted to electrical impulses.

Codec: A coder and a decoder of sound. The coder converts the sound to a numerical code and the decoder converts the code back into sound. Also, it converts digital audio signals from one form to another and back.

Communications sounds: These are relatively simple sounds derived from traditional electronic tones, used primarily in telecommunications products. Examples include telephone rings, the signal that a telephone line is on hold, and the call waiting tone.

Comparator: A function that takes two inputs, A and B, and outputs a logical TRUE if A>B or FALSE if A<B.

Complex: A procedure which uses complex numbers (real and imaginary parts) and the associated mathematical rules for operating on them.

Compound time: A type of meter. In compound time, the beat naturally subdivides into three faster rhythmic values. In compound time, the printed note-value equal to one beat will always be a "dotted rhythmic-value." For example, in six-eight time, there are two beats, dotted quarter-notes, and each beat naturally subdivides into three eighth-notes.

Compression: Audio dynamic range compression is the use of an automatic variable gain control system to reduce or compress the dynamic range of an audio signal, i.e., to reduce the difference between the loudest and quietest portions of an audio program. Not to be confused with methods used to compress or reduce the data needed to transmit or store an audio signal (data rate compression).

Compressor: An amplifier whose gain decreases automatically as its input signal level increases. A compressor combines both a fixed gain amplifier for input signals staying below a preset level (threshold) and variable gain amplifier that compresses the input signal automatically when it exceeds the threshold level.

Computational Auditory Scene Analysis (CASA): Carrying out Auditory Scene Analysis by means of a computer program.

Concatenation/stitching: Concatenation is stitching together words and phrases to make sentences and/or a continuous stream of words, phrases and sentences to provide an ongoing commentary for (color), and/or a description of (play by play), and/or reaction to (input response) events as they occur. More simply put, it is producing interactive speech by concatenating specially designed and prepared speech segments.

Consonance: The perceived stability of two or more musical tones sounding together. Consonance has an acoustical definition, and a musical definition. In music, the context of the event in question determines whether that sound is considered a consonance or a dissonance. The syntax of the music, especially in terms of the historical era in which the music was produced, is a large part of how any given sound is perceived.

Continuous spectrum: A spectrum exhibiting nonzero amplitude for one or more broad regions of the continuous frequency spectrum. This is the kind of spectrum that is found for aperiodic sounds, that is, sounds that do not repeat any pattern at all. The "ideal" aperiodic sound is an impulse, that is, a sound consisting of a single instantaneous pressure spike. The impulse is a sound which has equal amplitude at all frequencies. See also line spectrum and harmonic spectrum.

Contrapuntal: A term used to describe the musical texture in a musical composition or musical passage. Contrapuntal music is constructed in such a way as to consist of several melodic lines that occur simultaneously. Any of the fugues by J. S. Bach are examples of artfully crafted contrapuntal compositions.

Convolution: A linear method for multiplying the frequency response of two systems in the time domain. The output of this mathematical operation is waveform in the time domain that acts as though the frequency response of one of the input waveforms has been filtered by the frequency response of the second waveform. The convolution operation is independent of which waveform is chosen to be convolved about the other.

Coproduction: Like co-articulation, but the term is intended to emphasize the overlapping, but independent, articulation of speech segments.

Core opcode: A library function for audio synthesis in the structured audio standard.

Cue: 1. A feature of a sensory input that gives evidence pertaining to the interpretation of that input. For example, in vision, the desaturation of the colors of an object is a cue for the distance of the object. 2. To seek to a location in a linear access medium like a tape.

Cycle of fifths (circle of fifths): A pattern that organizes the major or minor scales into a circle. Each individual scale is a perfect fifth higher or lower than the scales directly adjacent around the circle.

dB Lp: A measure of the loudness of a sound relative to a reference intensity of 10^{-12} watts/m^2. For a measured sound intensity I, DB Lp is calculated as dB Lp$= 10 \log_{10}(I/10^{-12})$.

dB SPL: A measure of the loudness of a sound relative to a reference sound pressure level of 20 μPa. For a measured sound pressure level p, dB SPL is calculated as dB SPL$= 20 \log_{10}(p/20)$. Zero dB SPL is near the threshold for hearing and each dB SPL increment in amplitude is roughly one just noticeable difference in loudness.

dBm: A measure of the level of a signal's power relative to a reference level of 1 milliwatt. Power cannot be measured directly, but must be inferred by measuring a voltage across a resistive load. A standard resistive load of 600 ohms is assumed when inferring power levels for dBm. The voltage level corresponding to a power level of 1 milliwatt across 600 ohms is 0.7746 volts. Given a measured voltage v across 600 ohms, dBm is calculated as dBm $= 20 \log_{10}(v/0.7746)$.

dBv: A measure of the level of a signal's amplitude relative to a reference level of 1 volt. For a measured voltage level v, dBv is calculated as dBv$= 20 \log_{10}(v/1)$.

Decay time: The time it takes for an audio compressor to increase its gain, when the output signal is below the threshold.

Decibel (dB): A unit of measure that expresses the relative levels of two like quantities. Decibels are used to measure sound levels based on acoustic measurements of sound pressure level or sound intensity. The decibel is a logarithmic measure expressed as dB $= 10 \log_{10}(I_2/I_1)$, where I_1 and I_2 are the values being compared. Often I_1 is a reference value like the smallest sound perceivable or a certain voltage. A change of 3 dB corresponds to a ratio of 2x power and 10 dB corresponds to 10x power. A decibel is actually 1/10 Bel which was named after Alexander Graham Bell. Decibels are used because their logarithmic nature allows them to describe vast ranges of value easily and human perception has a natural logarithmic sensitivity (see also dB Lp, dB SPL, dBM, and dBv).

Decimate: **1.** Systematic removal of samples by picking, for example, one out of N consecutive samples. Down-sampling can be used as a synonym. **2.** To divide a single group of samples into a number of smaller groups.

Declination (speech): The tendency for F0 to gradually decline over the course of an utterance.

Delay line: An entity that stores the past values of a signal so they can be later retrieved to reconstruct a delayed version of the signal. Digital implementations of delay lines usually employ a circular buffer into which samples are written.

Delay Tap: A signal derived from a delay line with a fixed or variable delay relative to the input of the delay line. When the delay time is not necessarily an integer multiple of the sampling period, some form of band-limiting interpolation is necessary to achieve an alias-free signal.

Diatonic: Any pitch that naturally occurs within a given key. For example, in the key of C major (neither sharps nor flats in the key signature), the pitch G-natural is diatonic. That is, it is a member of the collection of pitches that occur in the key of C major. The pitch G#, is not diatonic to C major. G# is not a member of the collection of pitches that occur in the key of C major.

Diatonic harmony: The manner in which the individual chords that occur in any given major or minor key interact in the context of a piece of music. Diatonic harmony means "conforming to the practice of using notes and chords that conform to the key signature." In other words, diatonic harmony does not use chromatic chords. The study of diatonic harmony is fundamental to the understanding of the way western European music evolved, and is a prerequisite to the study of chromatic harmony.

Digital: Of or pertaining to a process of representing a signal as a series of discrete numerical values, typically created by sampling an analog signal (see synthesis for all digital techniques). To obtain a digital representation of a signal such as a musical waveform, two processes are involved. The first step is to sample the signal by systematic measurement of the signal strength at even intervals (the sampling interval). If this process is carried out on a band-limited signal which contains components up to B Hz, an exact representation is possible if measured at least 2B times per second. The second step is the digitization, which is an approximation of the signal samples to a discrete set of possible amplitudes. The amplitudes are represented by integers, which in turn can be expressed by binary numbers. The digitization process is often called quantization and causes quantization noise. The level of the quantization noise depends on the quantization step size, which is a consequence of the allowed dynamic range of the signal and the number of bits used to represent each sample. The Nyquist theorem and Fourier transform prove, theoretically, that digital representations will be indistinguishable from analog representations providing that the sampling rate is high enough. In practice, cost cutting designs with low-bit sampling, poor antialiasing, and little dithering cause sometimes noticeable and undesirable distortions.

Digital filter: A filter which performs arithmetic operations on digital signals.

Digital-to-Analog (D/A) converter: A device that from a digital signal representation outputs signal samples.

Diminished fifth: A fifth that encompasses six semitones (i.e., C up to G-flat). This interval is diatonic to the major scale between notes 7 and 4 (i.e., in the key of D-flat major, the notes C and G-flat). The diminished fifth is the inversion of the augmented fourth (and vice versa). This interval is also called a tritone because it encompasses three wholetones (six semitones).

Diminished fourth: A fourth that encompasses four semitones (i.e., C up to F-flat). This is not diatonic to any standard major or minor scale.

Diminished seventh: A seventh that encompasses nine semitones (i.e., C up to B-double flat). This interval is used in the diminished seventh chord between the root and seventh, but is not diatonic to any standard major or minor scale.

Diminished seventh chord (diminished-diminished seventh): Also called diminished-diminished seventh chord because it consists of a diminished triad with a diminished seventh added to it. All diminished seventh chords consist of a root, a minor third, a diminished fifth (diminished triad), and a diminished seventh.

Diminished triad: One of the basic triad types (along with major, minor, and augmented). A diminished triad consists of a root, a minor third, and a diminished fifth.

Direct Current (DC): A signal component that remains at a steady voltage, either positive or negative.

Dispersion: Any phenomenon in which the velocity of propagation of a wave is wavelength-dependent.

Dissonance: The perceived instability of two or more musical tones sounding together. Dissonance has an acoustical definition, and a musical definition. In music, the context of the event in question determines whether that sound is considered a consonance or a dissonance. The syntax of the music, especially in terms of the historical era in which the music was produced, plays a large part in how any given sound is perceived.

Dominant seventh chord (major-minor seventh): Also called major-minor seventh chord because this chord consists of a major triad with a minor seventh added to it. All dominant seventh chords consist of a root, a major third, a perfect fifth (major triad), and a minor seventh.

Doppler modulation: Changing the apparent pitch of a sound by moving it away from and/or towards a recording instrument, creating a "Doppler shift" in the wavelength of all the component frequencies. (See modulation.)

Dorian mode: The second mode derived from the major scale. The Dorian mode uses exactly the same notes from a major scale, but begins and ends on the second note of the major scale (i.e., D up to the next octave D with the key signature of C major).

Dot: A part of music notation. A dot on a note simply makes the note length longer by one more of the next shorter rhythmic value. For example, a quarter-note is equal in length to two eighth-notes, but a dotted quarter-note is equal in length to three eighth-notes. Conversely, an eighth-note is equal in length to two sixteenth-notes, but a dotted eighth-note is equal in length to three sixteenth-notes.

Double flat: The accidental that lowers the pitch of a note by a wholetone.

Double sharp: The accidental that raises the pitch of a note by a wholetone.

Downbeat: In the most general sense, downbeat means the beginning, or onset, of any beat in a piece of music. For example, in four-four time, each measure has four beats, therefore, each measure has four downbeats. In a more specific sense, downbeat means the first beat in any measure. It is also used to designate the first beat of a music composition (the downbeat of "Row, Row, Row Your Boat").

Duple: Describes the number of beats in a meter. Music in simple-duple time has two beats in each measure, and the beats are simple, in that they naturally subdivide into groups of two faster note values. Music in compound-duple time has two beats in each measure, and the beats are compound in nature, in that they naturally subdivide into groups of three faster note values.

Dynamic range: The range of loudness of sounds, from the softest to the loudest, usually measured in decibels (dB).

Earcons: Earcons refer to abstract sounds that are musical in origin. The signals may be described as very short snippets of "program music" that are intended to steer the emotional reaction of the listener in support of the desired image.

Eighth-note: A type of rhythmic note-value in music notation. The eighth-note is the next shorter rhythmic value in relation to the quarter-note. There are two eighth-notes in a single quarter-note.

Electroglotograph (EGG): A device that measures impedance across the vocal folds during speech using a surface electrode on either side of the larynx. When the vocal folds are in contact with one another, the impedance is relatively low and when the folds are abducted, impedance is high. For this reason, the EGG signal is essentially measuring vocal fold contact area. The EGG signal is also inversely related to air flow: When contact area is low, air flows; when contact area is high, air cannot flow.

Enharmonic: A convention in music notation where two notes with the same frequency (pitch) are spelled differently (i.e., C-sharp and D-flat). The conventions used in music notation to determine which enharmonic spelling is the correct spelling at any given moment are quite complex, and are dependent upon the style of music.

Ensemble timbre: An emergent timbre, arising from the combined sound of an ensemble (group of voices or instruments played together), which is distinct from the timbre of any one instrument or voice.

Entropy: Amount of information carried by a signal; it is a function of the probability distribution for that signal. The information is theoretically infinite for noiseless signals, but is finite if the signal is quantized or has some other noise component.

Entropy coding: Encoding of a signal based on knowledge of the probability distribution for that signal.

Envelope: An imaginary curve (E) that can be fitted to another time-varying curve (T) such that it touches T at its highest (or lowest) points. A temporal envelope of an acoustic wave has two parts: the curve that touches the highest points over time and another that touches the lowest points. It represents the time changes in the amplitude. A spectral envelope is a curve that touches all the points in a spectrum (i.e., points that represent the intensities or amplitudes of all the frequency components). A *smoothed* envelope comes as close as possible to the points it should touch, given the constraint that it should be smooth.

Envelope generator: An algorithm or device for producing a waveform to represent a slowly varying contour of a sound quality such as amplitude or brightness.

Equalization (EQ): The application of gain or attenuation to particular frequency bands of an audio signal. Simple equalization controls are available on most car and home stereos as the bass and treble control, which allows for adding or subtracting energy at fixed points along the frequency spectrum (typically around 200 Hz and 3500 Hz, respectively). Parametric equalizers allow the user to specify the center frequency that is being affected, as well as the width or "Q" around that center frequency. Among audio engineers, some believe in an ethic that "no EQ is better" because equalization can lead to audible distortions of the signal in terms of phase shifts.

Equalizer: A device that incorporates a set of filters, each of which can be controlled separately. Its function is to shape the spectrum of the sound.

Expander: A device that increases the dynamic range of an audio signal. Usually used in conjunction with a compressor to restore the dynamic range removed by the compressor.

FFT Order: Log base 2 of N where N is the number of samples transformed. Also the number of passes through the data arrays required to perform the transform.

Filter: 1. A mathematical operation or physical device that intentionaly changes the frequency content of a signal, usually for the purpose of attenuating or accentuating a range of frequencies. For example, a low pass filter will pass frequencies below a certain cutoff frequency and attenuate those above the cutoff frequency. 2. A device that alters the amplitude spectrum or phase spectrum of a sound.

Filter bank: A set of filters that are applied simultaneously to the same signal.

Finite Impulse Response (FIR): When referring to a system, this generally indicates a filter that only responds to present (current) and past input signals, and does not employ feedback. In DSP systems, FIR filters are less efficient compared to IIR filters but are easy to design, are unconditionally stable, and can easily be made to have a flat phase response.

First In First Out queue (FIFO): Also known as a Silo. Commonly used to buffer the flow of data between a producer and consumer.

Flap: A speech segment produced by rapidly tapping the tip of the tongue against the alveolar ridge.

Flat: The accidental that lowers the pitch of a given note by one semitone.

Focus (Speech): The placement of special prominence (including pitch accents, changes in duration, and changes in amplitude) on certain words in a sentence for pragmatic reasons such as to emphasize a particular contrast with a prior utterance.

Formal Language for Audio-Visual Object Representation (FLAVOR): A formal language developed by Columbia University for describing compressed bitstream syntax, especially the bitstreams representing multimedia objects.

Formant Wave-Function synthesis (FOF synthesis): A technique developed by Xavier Rodet and collaborators for the synthesis of sounds that are characterized by the existence of pronounced formants in their spectrum, such as vocal sounds. The technique employs trains of damped or enveloped sinusoids whose envelope characteristics can be modulated to affect the formants of the resulting signal.

Foot: A rhythmic unit in speech consisting of a stressed syllable and any immediately following unstressed syllables (definition for English).

Formant: 1. A peak (region of enhanced amplitude) in the spectrum of a sound. The intensities and arrangement of formants, and their change over time, alters the timbre of the sound and helps the listener to distinguish between different musical instruments or different speech sounds. 2. A spectral prominence resulting from a resonance in the vocal tract. The average spacing of formants is largely due to the length of the vocal tract and the exact frequencies at which formants appear are determined by the shape of the vocal tract. Formants are normally referred to as F1, F2, F3, etc., meaning the first, second, third, and so forth formants from lowest to highest frequency.

Formant transition: Change in frequency of a formant typically associated with the change in articulation from one phonetic segment to the next.

Four-four time (Simple-quadruple meter): There are four beats in each measure, and the quarter-note is equal to one beat.

Fourier Transform: Forward: Conversion of a sample set from the time domain into a spectrum (the frequency domain). Inverse: Conversion of a spectrum (frequency domain) into a sample set in the time domain.

Frame: The number of digital audio samples presented at one time. One for a mono signal, two for a stereo signal, four for quad, etc.

Frequency component: That part of a complex wave having a particular frequency, amplitude, and phase. If the wave is periodic, each frequency component will be a harmonic.

Frequency modulation: See modulation.

Frequency Modulation (FM) synthesis: A technique for generating sound that involves adding the output of one sine wave generator known as the "modulator" to the frequency control input of another sine wave generator known as the

"carrier." Traditionally, this was accomplished using a voltage-controlled oscillator, but may now be accomplished purely digitally. Harmonically rich sounds
can be generated inexpensively by controlling the depth of modulation and the
frequency ratios of the carrier and modulator. Multiple oscillators, typically 2
to 6, can be combined in patterns referred to as "algorithms." This technique
was patented by John Chowning of Stanford University and licensed to Yamaha
for use in their popular DX-7 line of synthesizers. See modulation.

Frequency response: **1.** A complex valued function of frequency which indicates the modification performed by a filter on a sinusoid of a given frequency.
The frequency response can be split in a magnitude response (the magnitude of
the frequency response), which is responsible for amplification or attenuation
of the different frequencies, and a phase response, which is responsible for relative delays of different frequency components. **2.** The frequency response of
the highest quality audio systems vary less than 1 dB over the range of audio
frequencies from 20 Hz to 20kHz.

Frication: The broadband turbulent noise source we use in spoken sounds like
/s/ and /f/.

Friction: Force that appears, for example, whenever one surface rubs against
another.

Fugue: A specific type of contrapuntal composition.

Fundamental frequency (F0): The fundamental frequency is $1.0/T0$, that is, the
inverse of the period. Normally, we express F0 in units of cycles per second or
Hz. This can be slightly confusing since we often express T0 in units of ms.
You must remember to multiply T0 by 1000.0 if it is expressed in ms to arrive
at F0 expressed in Hz. For complex sounds, F0 will normally be the frequency
of the first, or lowest, frequency harmonic. See harmonics.

Fusion (Perceptual): Hearing a set of concurrent sounds—which might otherwise
be heard as separate sounds—as a single sound.

Gate: **1.** An electronic circuit that either does or does not allow an input signal
to appear at the output, depending on the state of another signal that controls
the gate. **2.** An amplifier whose gain decreases automatically to zero (at a
preset rate of decay) as soon as its input signal level drops below a certain
threshold value that has been set in advance.

Gated reverberation: Reverberation passed through a gate that attenuates it as
soon as the reverberation level drops to a threshold that is set so that it will
occur shortly after the onset of the reverberation. This produces a dramatic
ambient effect, used most often on drums and percussion to increase their ex-
plosive quality and loudness.

Gibbs phenomenon: The ringing and overshoot that can occur when constructing a waveform by adding together harmonics and abruptly stopping the harmonic series after a finite number of terms. The ringing can be reduced by gradually tapering off the harmonics being used. It also refers to the ringing that can occur when using a brick-wall lowpass filter that effectively chops off high frequency partials in the same manner.

Grand staff: The combined staves of the treble and bass clef. The grand staff is the most commonly used full-range musical grid, and is the clef used for piano music (as well as concert harp, marimba, and others).

Group modulation: A variation of gain, time delay, frequency, or phase that is applied equally to a number of independent sound streams.

Half-diminished seventh chord (diminished-minor seventh and/or minor seven flat-five): Also called a diminished-minor seventh and/or a minor seven flat-five chord. This chord consists of a diminished triad with a minor seventh added to it (thus, the diminished-minor designation). It is also possible to conceive of this chord as a minor seven chord with a lowered fifth (flat five). All half-diminished seventh chords consist of a root, a minor third, a diminished fifth (diminished triad), and a minor seventh.

Half-note: A type of rhythmic note value in music notation. The half-note is the next longer rhythmic value in relation to the quarter-note. There are two quarter-notes in a single half-note.

Harmonic: 1. A frequency component of a periodic waveform having a frequency of I/P where P is the period and I is any positive integer. 2. A line (or near-line) in the spectrum of a periodic (or near-periodic) signal that can occur at any integer multiple of the fundamental frequency. In a harmonic spectrum, the harmonics are spaced F0-Hz apart.

Harmonic consonance: A sound comprised of at least two musical tones that produces a consonant (pleasant) effect in the context of a piece of music.

Harmonic dissonance: A sound comprised of at least two musical tones that produces a dissonant (tense or unpleasant) effect in the context of a piece of music. The V7 chord, in traditional Western classical music, is perceived as a dissonance that produces harmonic tension. This tension is resolved when the chord changes to the I chord (in a major key). This movement from dissonance to consonance is called a cadence.

Harmonic distortion: Distortion of an audio signal caused by a nonlinear process that produces unwanted harmonics of the original waveform. Usually expressed as a percentage of power, high-quality audio equipment will have a small fraction of a percent harmonic distortion.

Harmonic minor scale: A form of the minor scale. The harmonic minor scale has one chromatically altered note from the natural minor scale: The seventh note is raised in pitch by one semitone. This alteration creates an augmented second between the sixth and seventh notes of the scale. This augmented second gives the harmonic minor scale its characteristic sound. The scale is historically derived from the combination of the tonic subdominant, and dominant chords (i, iv, and V) used in musical compositions written in minor keys during the Common Practice era (1600-1900) in western European music history.

Harmonic relation: The relation between frequencies when they belong to the same harmonic series. Good harmonic relations are produced when the frequencies (or fundamental frequencies) of two simultaneous sounds form a simple ratio to one another (e.g., 1:1, 2:1, 3:2, 4:3 ...). These ratios are those that relate the component frequencies of a harmonic series.

Harmonic series: A summation of sine waves, f, $2f$, $3f$, $4f$, $\ldots$, whose frequencies are integer multiples of a base frequency, f, called the fundamental of the set of harmonics. The waveform produced by a harmonic series yields a strong pitch sensation.

Harmonic spectrum: Similar to a line spectrum except that sounds giving rise to harmonic spectra are not purely periodic, but only approximately so. Such sounds produce a harmonic spectrum in which the lines have some discernible width. As sounds deviate increasingly from true periodicity, their spectra deviate increasingly from line spectra to approach a continuous spectrum. For example, any sound that has finite duration is not strictly periodic. Many natural sounds, like the human voice, are quasi-periodic in that the sound deviates in a variety of ways from one period to the next. See also line spectrum and continous spectrum.

Harmonics: Most sound can be analyzed into a number of frequency components. These components are called harmonics when their frequencies are all multiples of the same frequency (which is called the fundamental frequency of the set of harmonics.

Harmonizer: A digital signal processing device that generates copies of the original signal transposed in pitch by a specified musical interval(s). It does it by writing and reading audio data at different clock rates and compensating for any resulting changes in signal duration.

Helmholtz motion: Characteristic motion of a bowed string whose name derives from the physicist who discovered it. In it, the bow sticks to the string for the longest part of the period, slipping only once every cycle. It is the motion that every player tries to achieve.

Hertz (Hz): Frequency expressed in cycles per second.

Imperfect consonance: Two tones that encompass one of the "imperfect" consonant intervals: major or minor thirds, and major or minor sixths.

Impressionistic transcription: Identifies all perceptible speech features.

Impulse Response: The output of a system, usually a filter, in response to an impulse at the input. An impulse is an infinitesimally brief input pulse. The impulse response is a mathematical representation of the system in the time domain and is directly related to the frequency and phase response. The Fourier transform converts between the time domain and the frequency domain, i.e., between the impulse response and the amplitude/phase response of a system.

Infinite Impulse Response (IIR): 1. When referring to a system, this generally indicates a filter that responds to both present (current) and past input signals, as well as past output signals. An IIR system employs feedback and has an impulse response that is, in theory, infinite in duration. In DSP systems, IIR filters are more efficient compared to FIR filters, but are more difficult to design and can be unstable. 2. A signal process that changes the frequency response by implementing poles and zero using a feedback loop.

Intensity: The power per unit area at a distance from a sound source.

Intermodulation Distortion (IMD): Distortion of an audio signal that contains two or more tones caused by a nonlinear process that produces the unwanted sum and difference frequencies of the original tones. Because the new tones are not harmonically related to the original tones, intermodulation distortion is very noticeable and objectionable. Usually expressed as a percentage of power, high-quality audio equipment will have a small fraction of 1% intermodulation distortion.

Interonset time: The time between the onsets of adjacent events in an ordered event series.

Interval: The distance in pitch between two notes. Intervals are categorized by size and quality. The size is a number which represents the number of generic note letter-names between the two notes (C up to G is a fifth: count C, D, E, F, G=5). This is often called the diatonic size of an interval. The quality represents the relative amount of consonance and dissonance in an interval, which we determine as the number of semitones encompassed by the given interval (C up to G encompasses 7 semitones which equals a perfect fifth).

Inversion: Literally "flipping something upside down." To invert an interval, take the bottom note, transpose it up one octave, which makes it the top note of a new interval. One can also invert an interval by transposing the top note down one octave, which will make it the bottom note of a new interval.

Ionian mode: The first mode, same as the major scale.

Isochrony: 1. Taking the same time. 2. The notion that the intervals between stressed syllables in a stress-timed language should be equal.

Just Noticeable Difference (JND): The smallest change that a subject can differentiate. Any change smaller than the JND is indistinguishable from the original. Knowledge about the JND of various domains allows algorithms like lossy compression to distort a signal in ways that are undetectable.

Key signature: The pattern of sharps or flats written at the beginning of a musical composition, and at the beginning of every line of music. The key signature is a notational shorthand that communicates to the individual musicians the key of the music.

Lagrange interpolation: Fitting of polynomials to make the resulting polynomial function exact at the data points. If N data points are given, an N-1 degree polynomial can be applied

Laplace domain (S domain): Continuous time domain.

Laplace transform: Method of transforming a continuous time function to the Laplace domain.

Larynx: The cartilagenous structure above the trachea containing the vocal cords. It is within the larynx that much of the sound for speech is generated.

Leading tone: The note that is a major seventh above the tonic note in any given key. This note derives its name from the practice of melodically moving the leading tone to the tonic at an authentic cadence (V-I in a major key or V-I in a minor key).

Leakage: An artifact of Fourier transform-based spectral analysis caused by transforming nonperiodic waveforms or waveforms having a nonintegral number of cycles in the analysis record. When present, strong frequency components in the analysis spread out and obscure weaker components even if far away in frequency. See window.

Leger line: A short horizontal line that extends the musical staff above or below the standard five lines. Leger lines are used to accurately distinguish the pitches that are either too high or too low to fit within the musical staff regardless of the clef being used.

Leslie loudspeaker: A loudspeaker system employing a rotating horn-type transducer at the top and a rotating low-frequency transducer at the bottom of a wooden enclosure. Its characteristic time-varying polar pattern due to the rotation produces spatial and spectral modulation able, for example, to enrich the sound of a Hammond organ.

Lexical stress: The pattern of syllabic prominence that is specifically identified with a word. It is primarily a lexical stress difference that distinguishes the verb conVICT from the noun CONvict (upper case representing the stressed syllable).

Line spectrum: The kind of spectrum that is found for sounds that are purely periodic, that is, for sounds that repeat the same pattern infinitely. Each line in a line spectrum is an harmonic of the fundamental period of the waveform and represents a sinusoid at a particular frequency and amplitude. Line spectra are the ideal case of harmonic spectra. See also harmonic spectrum.

Locrian mode: The seventh mode derived from the major scale. The locrian mode uses the exact same notes from a major scale, but begins and ends on the seventh note of the major scale (i.e., D up to D with the key signature of C major).

Lossless compression: A compression technique in which the original data can be recovered exactly.

Lossy compression: A compression technique in which the original data can only be approximately recovered.

Loudness: The perceptual correlate of amplitude. Equal steps in loudness are roughly equal to logarithmic steps in amplitude.

Loudspeaker panning: A spatialization technique whereby the level of sound emanating from a set of loudspeakers is manipulated to give the listener the impression the sound is emanating from a particular point or region in space.

Low-pass filter: A filter that passes low frequencies and attenuates high frequencies.

Lydian mode: The fourth mode derived from the major scale. The lydian mode uses the exact same notes from a major scale, but begins and ends on the fourth note of the major scale (i.e., F up to F with the key signature of C major).

Major scale: The scale that is comprised of this specific interval pattern above a tonic note: wholetone, wholetone, semitone, wholetone, wholetone, wholetone, semitone. Constructing an ascending collection of pitches based on this interval pattern will result in the creation of the major scale. The major scales can be easily organized into a memorable pattern called the "circle of fifths" (or "cycle of fifths"). Each major scale has a unique key signature, which is the pattern of sharps or flats contained in that specific scale.

Major second: The interval that is equal in sound to a wholetone. A major second is the interval of a second (adjacent letter named notes) that encompass two semitones (i.e., C and D). It is also the diatonic interval between the tonic and second notes of any major scale.

Major seventh: A seventh that encompasses eleven semitones (i.e., C up to B-natural). This interval is diatonic between the tonic and seventh notes of a major scale.

Major seventh chord (major-major seventh): Also called major-major seventh chord because this chord consists of a major triad with a major seventh added to it. All major seventh chords consist of a root, a major third, a perfect fifth (major triad), and a major seventh.

Major sixth: A sixth that encompasses nine semitones (i.e., C up to A-natural). This interval is diatonic between the tonic and sixth notes in a major scale.

Major third: A third that encompasses four semitones (i.e., C up to E-natural). It is also the diatonic interval between the tonic and third notes of a major scale.

Major triad: One of the basic triad types (along with minor, diminished, and augmented). A major triad consists of a root, a major third, and a perfect fifth.

Manner of articulation: The classification of speech segments on the basis of the type of articulation needed to produce the segment such as stop, fricative, glide, etc.

Masking: The ability of an interfering sound (the masker) to make a listener unable to detect the presence of a target sound (the masked sound).

Measure: A notational convention consisting of one instance of the metric pattern in a given music composition. The printed measure is identified by the placement of a vertical bar-line printed through the five lines of the musical staff at the end of the metric pattern. For example, in two-four time, there are two beats in every measure, and the quarter-note is the rhythmic value equal to one beat. Each measure will have two quarter-notes (or their rhythmic equivalent, such as four eighth-notes) before the bar-line is printed.

Mel scale: A logarithmic scale of frequency based on human pitch perception. Equal intervals in Mel units correspond to equal pitch intervals.

Melodic minor scale: A form of the minor scale. The melodic minor scale uses two chromatically altered notes, only in the ascending version, from the natural minor scale. In the melodic minor scale, the sixth and seventh notes are raised by one semitone in the ascending version of the scale, and are returned to their original pitch level in the descending version of the scale.

Meter: An organized hierarchical system of beats into regularly occurring patterns. These patterns are called measures. The first beat contains the most gravitational weight, and is therefore the most important beat in the measure. It is the psychoacoustic perception of the first beat that makes the pattern recognizable to the listener.

Meter signature: A notational convention consisting of two numbers, one printed directly on top of the other, that communicates to the musician the type of meter for a given music composition. Synonymous with time signature.

Metronome: An electronic or mechanical device that outputs a regular "click" sound at selectable speeds. A metronome is commonly used as a learning tool during practice sessions when a musician is learning to play a piece of music at a specific tempo. Metronome markings are also commonly used in music notation to indicate the tempo at which a specific composition should be performed.

Middle C: The C that is approximately in the middle of the piano keyboard. Middle C is written one leger line below the staff in the treble clef, and one leger line above the staff in the bass clef.

Minor scale: Also called the natural minor scale. The scale that is comprised of this specific interval pattern above a tonic note: wholetone, semitone, wholetone, wholetone, semitone, wholetone, wholetone. The minor scales can be easily organized into a memorable pattern called the circle of fifths (or cycle of fifths). Each minor scale has a unique key signature, which is the pattern of sharps or flats contained in that specific scale.

Minor second: The interval equal in sound to a semitone. Minor seconds are distinct in their spelling because they always encompass adjacent note names (i.e., C and D-flat, as opposed to C and C-sharp). Therefore, all minor seconds are intervals of a second (adjacent letter named notes), that encompass only one semitone.

Minor seventh: A seventh that encompasses ten semitones (i.e., C up to B-flat). This interval is diatonic between the tonic and seventh notes of the natural minor scale.

Minor seventh chord (minor-minor seventh): Also called minor-minor seventh because this chord consists of a minor triad with a minor seventh added to it. All minor seventh chords consist of a root, a minor third, a perfect fifth (minor triad), and a minor seventh.

Minor sixth: A sixth that encompasses eight semitones (i.e., C up to A-flat). This interval is diatonic between the tonic and sixth notes in the natural minor scale.

Minor third: A third that encompasses three semitones (i.e., C up to E-flat). It is also the diatonic interval between the tonic and third notes of a minor scale.

Minor triad: One of the basic triad types (along with major, diminished, and augmented). A minor triad consists of a root, a minor third, and a perfect fifth.

Mistuning: Altering the pitch of a sound (e.g., that of a musical instrument) so that it is not related to other sounds by a good harmonic relation.

Mixolydian mode: The fifth mode derived from the major scale. The mixolydian mode uses the exact same notes from a major scale, but begins and ends on the fifth note of the major scale (i.e., G up to G with the key signature of C major).

Modality: In perception, the particular sense used in perceiving something. (e.g., the visual modality, the auditory modality).

Mode: One of the forms of scale typically derived from the major scale. By building a scale using the exact same pitches from a major scale (called the parent scale in this context), but starting and ending on a different note, one is constructing a modal scale. Since there are seven different pitches in every major scale, there are seven distinct modes that can be derived from the major scale.

Modes: The family of scales derived from the major scale which is thought of as the "parent" scale. These modes are Ionian (same as the major scale), Dorian (second mode), Phrygian (third mode), Lydian (fourth mode), Mixolydian (fifth mode), Aeolian (sixth mode and the same as the natural minor scale), and Locrian (seventh mode).

Modulated Lapped Transform (MLT): Similar to Fourier and cosine transforms, with the exception that the MLT functions extend beyond block boundaries, overlapping orthogonally with the functions from adjacent blocks. Also known as the MDCT (modified discrete cosine transform), the MLT is used in most digital compression formats, including MP3, AAC, ATRAC, etc.

Modulation: The change, over time, of some property P of a sound, often in a periodic (repetitive) way. If the modulation is periodic, it can be viewed as a wave that is "modulating" (changing) property P. If P is amplitude, the process is called amplitude modulation (AM) and when P is frequency, it is called frequency modulation (FM). See also side-bands.

Motion Picture Experts Group (MPEG): The ISO/IEC working group that determines standards for coding digital audio and video.

MP3: File format for the MPEG-1 Layer III audio compression system. It provides good-quality stereo audio encoding at bit rates of 128 kbps and above.

MPEG-4: The latest set of standards for audio and video compression issued by the MPEG committee.

Multirate systems: Systems where more than one sampling frequency is involved. A digital interpolator where the input and output sampling frequencies are different is a typical example.

Murmur: The low frequency and low amplitude energy found during the closure interval of a consonant.

Natural: The accidental that cancels the effect of a previously placed sharp, flat, double sharp, or double flat, in a measure of music.

Natural Minor Scale: see minor scale.

Nine-eight time (Compound-triple meter): There are three beats in each measure, and the dotted quarter-note is equal to one beat.

Node (FFT): A graphical representation of the fundamental unit of computation in the fast Fourier transform.

Noise-to-Masking Ratio (NMR): A measure of the noise level of an audio signal with respect to the masking threshold; an NMR of 0 dB means that the noise is barely audible. High-fidelity digital audio systems should have NMRs of several dBs negative.

Nyquist frequency: One-half the sampling rate.

Nyquist rate: This is equvalent to the necessary sampling frequency for obtaining an aliasing-free representation of a band-limited signal. If the signal is band-limited to B Hz, the Nyquist rate (or frequency) is equal to 2B. For digitally sampled representations, the Nyquist rate is one-half the sampling rate. Any energy of frequency higher than the Nyquist frequency will alias down into the audio range and cause undesirable artifacts.

Octave: **1.** The interval between two notes of the same name whose frequencies exhibit a 2:1 ratio (i.e., A4 @440 Hz and A5 @ 880 Hz). The interval between these two specific notes is an octave. **2.** A popular signal processing library.

Oscillator: An algorithm or device that generates a periodic waveform signal, usually a sine wave. See voltage-controlled oscillator.

Partial: Fourier theory tells us that any sound can be constructed by adding together a sufficient number of sine waves of the appropriate frequency and amplitude. Each sine wave is a "partial." If the ratio of the frequencies of two partials is a whole number (2, 3, 4,...), then the higher one is said to be a "harmonic" of the lower one. Some sounds, like pipe organs, have partials that are mostly harmonically related. Percussive sounds, like bells, are often rich in enharmonic (not harmonically related) partials.

Pascal: A unit of air pressure measurement named after the physicist and mathematician, Blaise Pascal, that is used to establish an absolute reference for comparing loudness or intensity of sound waves. The standard reference of 0 dB SPL corresponds to 20 uPA or 20 micro Pascals. One thousand Pascals or 1 kPa = 0.145 PSI = 7.52 mm Hg.

Perceptual Quality Audio Measure (PQAM): An audio quality metric that includes measurements such as NMR and others. It is an important metric for digital audio systems, for which traditional measurements such as SNR are not meaningful.

Perfect consonance: A consonance that is comprised of one of the "perfect" intervals: unison, octave, perfect fifth, or perfect fourth. This is a mathematical definition. In practice through most of the Common Practice era (1600–1900), perfect fourths were treated as a dissonance when the lowest sounding tone of the interval was found in the bass part of the musical ensemble. The implications of this are beyond the scope of this book, but are worth mentioning nonetheless.

Perfect fifth: A fifth that encompasses seven semitones (i.e., C up to G). This interval is diatonic between the tonic and fifth notes of a major scale.

Perfect fourth: A fourth that encompasses five semitones (i.e., C up to F). This is the diatonic interval between the tonic and fourth notes in a major scale.

Period: For a repetitive waveform, the time between repetitions.

Period (T0): The duration of a single complete cycle of a periodic waveform. We sometimes refer to the period of a signal as T0.

Periodic: A waveform that continually repeats its shape in time.

Phase: The time relation between two sinusoidal waveforms having the same frequency or the relation between one sinusoidial waveform and a fixed reference.

Phaser: A function that corresponds to the phase angle of a rotating vector mapped into the range -1.0 to +1.0. It can be used as the phase input to a band-limited oscillator and looks like a "sawtooth wave."

Phonation (Voicing): The periodic impulsive sound source that is characteristic of all vowels and many consonants.

Phonemic transcription: Identifies just sounds that are phonemic in a language.

Phonetic feature: Minimal characteristics of segments which distinguish one speech segment from another (e.g., voicing, stricture).

Phonetic transcription: Identifies allophones as well as phonemes.

Phrase final lengthening: The tendency for the final syllable of phrases to be substantially longer in duration that the same syllable would be in a phrase medial position. We use the drawing out of syllables at the end of phrases (and to some extent, smaller units as well) to signal the presence of a boundary.

Phrygian mode: The third mode derived from the major scale. The Phrygian mode uses exactly the same notes as a major scale, but begins and ends on the third note of the major scale (i.e., E up to E with the key signature of C major

Pitch: 1. A perceptual quality—running from "low" to "high"—that is a function of the repetition rate (or frequency) of a sound wave (inversely proportional to the sound's wavelength). Higher repetition rates are heard as higher in pitch. For example, as one moves to the right on a piano keyboard, the notes produced by the keys are considered to be higher and higher in pitch. Humans can hear a wider range of frequencies than that to which they can attach a strong sense of pitch, however, with the range of strong pitch roughly spanning the range of the keyboard, from approximately 40 Hz–3500 Hz. 2. In humans, the ability to vocally reproduce a stable tone at the same frequency that a recently heard tone occurred is considered one of the criteria in determining one's sense of pitch. 3. Pitch also means the specific pitch of a given note. For example, the note middle C, is also the pitch middle C. The pitch that is 440 Hz is the "A" above middle C on the piano. **4.** (Speech) The perceptual correlate of frequency. Normally, the pitch of a complex sound is a function of its F0. Equal steps in pitch are roughly equal to logarithmic steps in frequency.

Pitch accent: A prominence-lending peak or trough in the intonation contour of an utterance. Pitch accents mark words for special emphasis and guide listeners in interpreting the meaning of utterances.

Pitch class: One of the 12 distinct names of pitches regardless of octave and of enharmonic. For example, the letter name C is a pitch class regardless of which octave any given C occurs. Consequently, there are seven letter-named pitch classes that correspond to the musical alphabet (letters A through G). Also, the notes C-sharp and D-flat belong to the same pitch class because they are enharmonic.

Pitch period: The waveform associated with a single closing and opening cycle of the vocal folds. Each pitch period contains information about both the sound source generated in the larynx and about the structure of the vocal tract about the larynx.

Pitch shifting: The process of changing the apparent pitch of a signal without noticeably altering its temporal evolution. The musical analogue of pitch shifting is transposition. Algorithms for pitch shifting are related to those used for time stretching.

Pitch smearing: An audio effect that results in the smearing of frequency components across the spectrum of a signal.

Pitch synchronous granular synthesis: A technique for synthesizing periodic tones with one or more formant regions developed by Aldo Piccialli and Giovanni De Poli. Grains are generated at a rate related to the fundamental frequency of the tone and are overlapped and added to create smooth spectral transitions. The content of the grains is generated by filtering a pulse train according to parameters acquired from analysis of an existing musical signal.

Pitch Synchronous Overlap Add (PSOLA): A method for operating on speech in the time domain that allows timescale modification and pitch modification.

Place of articulation: The location of primary constriction needed in the production of a speech segment.

Pole: **1.** Signal processing terminology used to describe the characteristic of attenuating frequencies. **2.** An element of a linear system that causes the frequency response to increase in magnitude. For instance, if we were to describe the frequency response of a system with $h(\omega) = 1/(1-\omega)$, the point at $\omega=1$ would represent a pole because the graph would clearly show the frequency response approaching infinity as ω approached 1.

Polyphonic: Referring to music in which two or more concurrent parts are meant to be heard individually (at least sometimes), and no part is simply an accompaniment of another.

Power: The amount of energy per unit time being emitted by a sound source. Power is usually measured in Watts. A power level of one Watt is equal to one Joule of energy per second.

Psychophysicist: A scientist who attempts to establish the relationships between physical variables, such as the amplitude of an acoustic pressure wave, and psychological variables, such as the loudness of the perceived sound.

Pulse wave: An idealized oscillator waveshape that can be drawn with a series of straight lines whose intersections make right angles (add sketch of a pulse, if possible). See oscillator.

Quantization: Approximation of an arbitrary real value by the nearest entry in a finite table of values. It is a key step in audio data compression.

Quantization error: Errors that emanate from the limited precision of digitally represented numbers during mathematical operations.

Quarter-note: A type of rhythmic note-value in music notation. In the majority of popular music, the quarter-note is the written value that is equal to one beat.

Record: A group of consecutive samples representing a short segment of sound.

Release burst: The "explosion" of air at the release of a stop consonant. The burst is a brief period of frication which may be followed by a period of aspiration.

Resonance: Oscillations that are self-reinforced by the dynamics of a system, causing an increase in response.

Reverberant: Having high amplitude and a slow decay of reverberation.

Reverberation: **1.** The persistence of a sound after its source has stopped, caused by multiple reflections of the sound reflecting off surfaces within an enclosed space. This term usually refers to the later reflections, in which individual copies of the sound (echoes) cannot be heard because the sound is a mixture of so many repeated reflections from a variety of surfaces. **2.** The total description of all reflections, echoes, and spectral qualities of sound in an enclosed space. **3.** The application of delays and echoes by use of a signal-processing device to achieve the simulation of particular acoustic spaces.

Ring buffer: An efficient implementation of the FIFO queue. Also known as a cyclic buffer.

Root Mean Square (RMS): Square root of the mean of the squares. Found by squaring a function, calculating the mean, then taking the square root. Also known as the effective value, the RMS value is important because it represents the *average* power of a waveform and also closely represents the perceived loudness of a waveform. Note the RMS value of a current, voltage or pressure is proportional to the *average* power. The term RMS power, while widely used, is strictly speaking, *not* correct.

Roundoff error: Computational error resulting from the limited number of bits (digits) used in the computation.

Rubato: A style of playing employed by soloists in which they deviate slightly from the note durations that are shown in the musical score, sometimes leading and sometimes lagging behind the other musicians.

S domain: Laplace domain for continuous time systems.

Sample: The amplitude value of a signal measured at an instant of time (see frame).

Sample accurate: Presenting a digital signal at the closest audio frame position to the intended time. This is the finest granularity of timing available when presenting a digital signal. For professional 48 KHz audio, this is approximately +/- 21 μSeconds. Also implies that the system will not drop audio samples causing quality and timing issues.

Sampling: The process of systematic measuring analog (time continuous) signals at regular intervals. If a signal is sampled at the Nyquist rate, the representation is theoretically exact.

Sampling frequency: The number of samples per time unit employed is sampling. If the time unit is seconds, the sampling frequency is measured in Hz.

Sawtooth wave: A repeating waveform commonly used in audio synthesis that resembles the edge of a saw. It has a straight section that rises or falls punctuated by a sharp edge. It can be constructed by adding even and odd harmonics of a fundamental frequency.

Scale factor: An assumed multiplier applied to one or more numerical values.

Score: A generic term for any musical composition that is written in standard musical notation. Lots of popular music is not written in music notation, and therefore has no score, in the traditional sense of the word.

Search for Extra-Terrestrial Intelligence (SETI): Relies on gigantic Fourier transforms of radio signals received from space to detect periodicities that may indicate an intelligent origin.

Segmental: Having to do with individual speech sounds or phonemes. Syllables can be broken down into a sequence of segments. For instance the syllable (and word) *sat* consists of three segments, "s," "a," and "t."

Semitone: The smallest interval in the western equally tempered scale. A semitone is the difference in pitch between any two adjacent keys on a piano keyboard, regardless of color (black or white). A semitone is often called a "half-step" in music slang. Physically, moving the pitch of a note upward by a semitone is equivalent to multiplying its frequency by about 1.06 (i.e., the twelfth root of two).

Series summation: A method of describing a function as the sum of many component functions.

Seventh chord: A four-note chord consisting of a triad with an added seventh. All seventh chords consist of a root, third, fifth, and seventh. There are five basic types of seventh chords: major seven chord, minor seven chord, dominant seven chord, half-diminished seven chord, and diminished seven chord.

Sharp: The accidental that raises the pitch of a given note by one semitone.

Side-bands: When a periodic modulation is applied to either the frequency or amplitude of a wave, it creates side-bands (other frequencies that were not present in the unmodulated sound). The frequencies of these added frequencies are related to the frequency of the wave that is modulated (the "carrier") and to the frequency of the wave that is modulating the carrier (the "modulator").

Signal-to-Noise Ratio (SNR): Usually measured in decibels (dB). High-quality sound reproduction will feature an SNR better than 60 dB which is a power ratio of $1x10^{-6}$.

Simple time: A type of meter. In simple time, the beat naturally subdivides into two faster rhythmic values.

Sinusoidal: A waveform having the shape of a sine wave. A sine wave is heard as a pure tone.

Six-eight time (Compound-duple meter): There are two beats in each measure, and the dotted quarter-note is equal to one beat.

Sixteenth-note: A type of rhythmic note-value in music notation. There are two sixteenth-notes in a single eighth-note, and there are four sixteenth-notes in a single quarter-note.

Sonification: The mapping of data to sound in order to acoustically display information, such as trends (the acoustic analog to visualization). For example, pulse rate is conveyed aurally with a hospital-monitoring device.

Spatialization: Creating illusionary or virtual sound sources that are perceived to have a direction and distance relative to a listener.

Spectrogram: A two-dimensional visual representation of the intensity of a sound or series of sounds. It has time as its x-axis and frequency as its y-axis. It depicts the intensity of the acoustic energy at each point of frequency and time by the darkness (and sometimes the color) of the spot that represents it.

Spectrum: A description of a sound, giving some measure (m) of each of its frequency components. Usually presented as a graph with frequency as the x-axis and the measure m as the y-axis. The measure can be amplitude ("amplitude spectrum"), power ("power spectrum"), phase ("phase spectrum"), etc.

Square wave: A pulse waveform whose high and low sections are constant values of equal length (add sketch of a square, if possible). An ideal square wave contains the fundamental component and only odd harmonics. See pulse wave.

Staff: The grid upon which musical notation resides. The staff contains five horizontal lines with four spaces between them. Musical pitches of specific rhythmic duration are placed on the staff to represent the sound of the music. Staff lines are always counted up from the bottom. The first line is always the bottom line.

Steady-state sounds: Sounds that stay constant, over time, in all their properties.

Stochastic: A description of signals or sets of values that possess random characteristics defined by (usually) nonuniform probability distributions. In generative contexts, a *stochastic parameter* is defined in terms of the statistical distribution of its possible values rather than its actual value.

Structured audio: A part of the MPEG-4 standard, for coding sound as an algorithm. The compressed version of the audio consists of a computer program that, when executed, generates audio output. See MPEG.

Subdivision: The act of dividing the beat, or pulse, into faster regular rhythmic divisions. This is a human response to rhythmic stimuli and a skill all trained musicians master.

Subtractive synthesis: A sound synthesis method, which works by dynamically filtering a static, harmonically rich waveform.

Suprasegmental: Characteristics of speech such as intonation and timing that are defined over syllable and larger sized units.

Syllable coda: The final consonants of a syllable.

Syllable nucleus: The vocalic portion of a syllable.

Syllable onset: The initial consonants of a syllable.

Syllable rhyme: The nucleus plus coda of a syllable.

Systematic transcription: Identifies all acoustic differences known to be systematic in a language.

Tempo: The rate at which the beats progress in a piece of music. Humans respond to tempo in relation to one's heart rate. The perception of "fast" and "slow" passages in music depends upon the tempo of the music in relation to the heart rate of the listener.

Three-four time (Simple-triple meter): There are three beats in each measure, and the quarter-note is equal to one beat.

Tie: A part of music notation. A tie is a curved line that connects different rhythmic values of the same pitch together into a longer sustained note or sound.

Timbral: Of or related to timbre. For example, "timbral variation" refers to variations in timbre.

Timbre: That quality of sound that distinguishes two instruments (or voices) sounding at the same pitch and loudness. Also known as "tonal color." Timbre encompasses differences in attack, steady state, and decay of a musical tone. It is what makes a trumpet sound identifiably different from a clarinet, for example, when both are playing the same tone. Sounds are said to be different in timbre when their perceived qualities are different, even though their pitches, locations, and loudnesses are the same.

Time freezing: An audio effect that creates the illusion that the passage of time in an audio signal has halted. Since audio signals only exist in time, time freezing essentially involves the generation of a signal with a constant or quasi-constant spectrum that reflects the spectrum of the input signal at the time it was frozen. This effect can be implemented in a number of ways including looping, granulation, and additive synthesis.

Time signal: The description of a sound in the time domain as fluctuations in some physical property like pressure over time. Often, because the pressure fluctuations have been transduced by a microphone or other measurement instrument, we have converted pressure fluctuations to voltage fluctuations over time.

Time signature: A notational convention consisting of two numbers, one printed directly on top of the other, that communicates to the musician the type of meter for a given music composition. Synonymous with meter signature.

Time smearing: An audio effect that smears the content of an audio signal forwards and/or backwards in time. Reverberation can be thought of as a type of time smearing, although the latter term is more general. Depending on the application, this effect can be the result of artifacts in certain types of processing (such as some types of overlap add resynthesis,) or as an intended outcome as is the case with reverberation or granular time smearing.

Time stretching: The process of altering the perceived passage of time in an audio signal without the intention of modifying its spectral characteristics, such as changing its pitch for example. Implementing generalized time stretching is difficult to achieve without introducing audible artifacts. However, in some musical contexts, artifacts may be acceptable, or even useful, as they add additional spectral interest when stretching ratios are large.

Time varying filter: A filter where the components/coefficients are time-dependent. This means that the output signal from a given stimulus will generate different outputs depending on the onset in time of the filtering.

Tonic: The most important note in any given major or minor key. The pitch that gives the key its name (i.e., the note C in the key of C major). The first note of a major or minor scale (i.e., the note E in the E minor scale).

Top-down: Perception, memory, attention, and other mental activities can be influenced by the prior knowledge of the class of signals that the person may encounter and also by the cues provided by the signal itself. The former are called "top-down" influences because they are assumed to come from higher parts of the brain, whereas the latter are called "bottom-up" influences because they are assumed to originate at lower levels of the nervous system (the sense organs and the early processes that operate on sense data).

Torsional waves: Waves in which the displacement of the medium is a twist in a plane perpendicular to the direction of propagation of the wave. For example, when a bow is drawn across a violin string, the string twists and a torsional wave travels down the string.

Track: In audio recording, a specific instrument or group of instruments is often recorded together on a "track" and this track is later mixed with others.

Transducer: A device that changes a signal from one physical form to another. For example, a microphone changes the signal from a pressure wave in the air to an electrical voltage whose values change over time in exactly the same pattern as the pressure wave in the air does. Because of the one-to-one correspondence, the original signal can be recovered from the transduced signal.

Transduction: The activity of a transducer.

Transfer function: An equation describing the system given by output/input.

Transients: Rapid changes in a signal (e.g., at the onset of sounds).

Transpose: To move a note (or notes) to a different pitch level. If a melody starts on the note C, and one wanted to transpose the melody up a perfect fifth, the new starting note would be the G above the original C. By continuing this process (moving each note up a perfect fifth), one can transpose a given melody up a perfect fifth. It is possible to transpose pitch information by any interval up or down.

Transverse waves: Waves in which the displacement of the medium is perpendicular to the direction of propagation of the wave. For example, when a bow is drawn across a violin string, the string moves in a direction perpendicular to the excitation and a transversal wave travels down the string.

Treble clef: Also called the "G clef." This is the clef that identifies the higher pitches in the grand staff, and is written on the top staff of the two staves in the grand staff. The treble clef identifies the placement on the staff of the pitch G4 (G above middle C).

Triad: A specific type of three-note chord. All triads consist of a root, a third, and a fifth. The root of the chord is the note that gives the chord its name (i.e., the note C in a C major triad). Triads come in four basic types: major, minor, diminished, and augmented.

Triangle wave: A repeating waveform commonly used in audio synthesis that has a rising straight section followed by a falling straight section. It can be constructed by adding odd harmonics of a fundamental frequency in the proper proportion.

Triple: Describes the number of beats in a meter. Music in simple-triple time has three beats in each measure, and the beats are simple, in that they naturally subdivide into groups of two faster note-values. Music in compound-triple time has three beats in each measure, and the beats are compound in nature, in that they naturally subdivide into groups of three faster note-values.

Two-four time (Simple-duple meter): There are two beats in each measure, and the quarter-note is equal to one beat.

Uniform sampling: The process of sampling at regular intervals, usually called the sampling interval. CD recordings use uniform sampling with 44100 samples per second, which indicates that the sampling interval is equal to $1/44100$ s = 22.67 microseconds.

Unison: Two notes with the same frequency are in unison. This can be an aural event, as when a musician tunes his/her instrument to a given pitch, and can be a visual event, when two notes of the same pitch-class are written on the staff (two middle C quarter-notes, for example).

Upbeat: In the most general sense, upbeat means the portion of a beat that occurs after the downbeat. Typically, upbeat refers to the second half of an individual beat. For example, in four-four time, there are four quarter-notes. Each quarter-note can be subdivided into two eighth-notes.

Virtual acoustic environment: A sound field created by spatializing a set of sounds (see spatialization).

Voice Onset Time (VOT): The time from the release burst of a stop consonant to the onset of voicing for a subsequent voiced segment.

Voltage-Controlled Oscillator (VCO): An electronic component that generates a sine wave whose frequency can be varied via the input control voltage.

W function: A complex function of a real angle, $i/N : W(i) = \cos(2 * \pi * i/N)$, $\sin(2*\pi*i/N)$. It is the fundamental multiplier used in the fast Fourier transform and represents a pair of "probe waves" 90 degrees apart.

Waveform: Sounds are pressure waves in the air. The sequence of instantaneous pressures that passes a fixed point in the air or other medium, over time, can be plotted as a wave. The shape of this wave is called the waveform. Sounds may also be encoded as time-varying voltages, currents, or approximated by a series of numerical sampled values.

Wavetable: This term most accurately describes an area of memory containing a single cycle of a sampled or synthesized periodic signal that is usually used in oscillator synthesis. In a common corruption, wavetable is used synonymously with "stored sample" to describe any sequence of audio samples stored in computer memory for use in sample-based synthesis techniques.

Wavetable synthesis: A technique for generating repetitive waveforms of an arbitrary shape. A simple phase accumulator is used to index into an array (table) that contains the shape of the desired waveform. The output is usually generated by interpolating between adjacent values in the table. The term "wave table synthesis" is also sometimes used incorrectly to refer to sample playback systems which play a digital recording of a sound.

Whole-note: A type of rhythmic note-value in music notation. There are two half-notes in a single whole-note. There are subsequently four quarter-notes in a single whole-note.

Wholetone: The interval that encompasses two semitones (keyboard steps). It is often called a "whole step" in music slang. Physically, moving the pitch of a note upward by a wholetone is equivalent to multiplying its frequency by approximately 1.12.

Window: A special kind of amplitude envelope or weighting curve given a signal before Fourier transformation in an effort to reduce spectral leakage. See leakage.

Windows Media Audio Compression (WMA): The digital audio component of Microsoft's Windows Media product; it can represent high-fidelity stereo signals at about the same bit rates as AAC.

Z domain: Discrete time domain.

Zero: An element of a linear system that causes the frequency response to decrease in magnitude. For instance, if we were to describe the frequency response of a system with $h(\omega) = (1-\omega)$, the point at $\omega=1$ would represent a zero because the graph would clearly show the frequency response approaching zero as ω approached 1.

Contributor Biographies

Stuart Allman is an electrical engineer with Cypress Semiconductor and a frequent contributor to industry publications. Stuart has a passion for music and the beauty of mathematics. He foremost enjoys grasping knowledge that drives new innovation and provokes thought.

Maribeth Back is an award-winning researcher and designer who builds and writes about real-world, socially informed exploratory applications for new technologies. Her background includes theory and audio system design for virtual and computational environments as well as sound design and engineering for music, live theatre, radio, museums, and CD-ROM. She has created prototypes of experimental musical instruments, informatics for advanced medical research systems, and public interactive installations, both solo and collaborative. She has also built a number of innovative electronic reading devices, exploring the intersections between digital systems and the reading and writing of text. Back completed her doctorate at Harvard's Graduate School of Design in May 1996. As a senior research scientist at Xerox PARC (1996 - 2002), she worked with the RED group exploring emerging technologies.

Chris Bagwell is a software developer for telecommunication equipment. In his spare time, he contributes software to various open source projects. Two of the more popular projects he maintains are SoX, an audio file format conversion program, and the Audio File Format FAQ.

Ronen Barzel received his undergraduate and Masters from Brown University then completed his Ph.D. at Caltech in computer graphics, researching physically based modeling techniques. He has worked at Pixar on production of the first *Toy Story* movie (among other things, he built the Slinky Dog model) and in R & D of modeling and lighting software. He is the editor-in-chief of the *Journal of Graphics Tools*.

Chris Bore is a respected signal processing expert and speaker. He has authored many books and seminars on signal processing. Bore and his company, BORES Signal Processing, are located in the South of England.

Phil Burk is a designer and developer of music systems. His projects include an early experimental music language called HMSL, the first DSP-based sound synthesis system for the 3DO video game console, a music synthesis API for Java called JSyn that allows composers to embed interactive computer music pieces in a web page, a client/server system called TransJam that supports multiplayer interaction and performance on the web, a multiplatform audio I/O API for Java called JavaSonics, a MIDI ringtone engine for embedded systems, and, with Ross Bencina and others, a cross platform audio API for C called PortAudio.

Mike Caviezel is a sound designer, composer, producer, and engineer who has been making sounds for multimedia since 1994. His sound design credits include works for Disney Interactive, Sierra Entertainment, Sound Ideas, the Hollywood Edge, and Best Service, among others. His original music productions have appeared in such television shows as MTV's *The Real World*, *Tough Enough*, and *Live Through This*, as well as NBC's *Providence* and the WB's *Jack and Jill*. Caviezel holds a Bachelor of Science degree in music and audio technology from Indiana University and is currently employed by Sierra Entertainment as a staff composer/sound designer.

Hal Chamberlin studied at North Carolina State University where he received a B.S. degree in electrical engineering and a Master of Science degree. His Master's thesis, "Design and Simulation of a Digital Sound Synthesizer," predates a number of prominent articles and patents in the field by several years. He went on to found Technology Unlimited in 1971 and later Micro Technology Unlimited, which is still in business today. In 1986 he joined Kurzweil Music Systems as a hardware/software systems engineer where he is currently on assignment in South Korea. Chamberlin has written numerous articles and started one of the first amateur computer publications, *The Computer Hobbyist*, in 1974. He is the author of the classic book, *Musical Applications of Microprocessors*, which is still in demand today. Presently, he is pursuing alternative keyboards and instrument controllers as well as additive synthesis.

Perry R. Cook received a B.A. in music from the University of Missouri at Kansas City Conservatory of Music, a BSEE from UMKC Engineering, and a master's and Ph.D. in electrical engineering from Stanford. He is an associate professor of computer science (jointly in music) at Princeton University, researching physics-based sound synthesis and control, auditory display, and immersive sound environments. He was senior research scientist of media vision and technical director for the Stanford Center for Computer Research in Music and Acoustics. Cook has worked in DSP, image compression, sound synthesis, and speech processing for NeXT Inc., Media Vision, Interval Research, and others. He has published extensively, including two books: *Real Sound Synthesis for Interactive Applications* (2002) and *Music, Cognition and Computerized Sound* (1999).

Hesham Fouad has been involved in various aspects of audio for the past 15 years. After receiving a doctorate in computer science in 1997, he founded VRSonic, Inc., a company focused on developing new techniques for creating compelling virtual auditory environments.

Jeffrey Greenebaum is an award-winning journalist and has spent the past six years as a reporter and weekly newspaper editor-in-chief. Presently, he resides in suburban Baltimore County, teaches, and occasionally writes freelance.

Ken Greenebaum is a software engineer who has developed digital media applications over the past 15 years for companies that include Silicon Graphics and Microsoft. His research interests include the creation of reliable, sample-accurate, low-latency media engines; language systems to describe time-varying behavior of sound, video, and graphics; and temporal optimization based on human perception. He is an adjunct member of the DigiPen Institute of Technology faculty where he develops and teaches the interactive audio for gaming curriculum.

Gordon Hempton currently provides location recording services, sound design, and audio fulfillment to a broad range of businesses. He also maintains one of the largest libraries of quiet natural ambiences in the world. Hempton originally financed his passion for recording by working as a bike messenger—and purchased his recording equipment after 13,500 deliveries. In 1989, he received a grant from the Charles Lindbergh Fund to reconstruct the wilderness soundscape of Washington State as it existed in 1889. He has also been the recipient of a Rolex Award for Enterprise, a National Endowment for the Arts grant, and an Emmy award. He has taught at the Olympic Park Institute and produced two series of nature CDs, *Earth Sounds* and *Quiet Places*.

John Lazzaro is an associate research specialist at the University of California, Berkeley, where he currently does research in multimedia, networking, and VLSI models of biological computation. He received a Ph.D. and M.S. degree in computer science from Caltech in California and B.S. degrees in electrical engineering and computer science from the University of Pennsylvania.

Ville Pulkki received the M.S. degree in engineering from the Helsinki University of Technology (HUT), Espoo, Finland. Between 1994 and 1997 he majored in studies at the Musical Education Department at the Sibelius Academy, Helsinki, Finland. He completed his Ph.D. at HUT Laboratory of acoustics and audio signal processing in 2001. He has been a visiting scholar at Center for New Music and Audio Technologies at University of California, Berkeley.

Linda Roberts is currently a distinguished member of technical staff at Bell South's Science and Technology Center in Atlanta, Georgia. Prior to her move to Bell South, Roberts was a researcher, technical manager, and director at Bell Labs for 18 years, first with AT&T and subsequently with Lucent technologies. She has done research in a variety of areas, including music perception, auditory displays, speech recognition, response time, documentation, telephone design, and web design. She has a Bachelor's degree in music and an M.S. and Ph.D. in experimental psychology. She has been doing research in music and auditory perception since 1982.

Gary Scavone is technical director and research associate at the Center for Computer Research in Music and Acoustics at Stanford University, where he received a Ph.D. in computer-based music theory and acoustics and a Master of Science degree in electrical engineering. His music technology research includes physical modeling of musical instruments, sound synthesis software development, human-computer interaction, and psychoacoustics. Dr. Scavone is also a saxophonist specializing in the performance of contemporary concert music.

Cynthia Sikora is a technical manager of the Usable Solutions Engineering group at Bell Labs, Lucent Technologies in Holmdel, New Jersey. She has been a Certified Human Factors Professional (CHFP) since 1993 and has been doing human factors work since 1984. Previously, she conducted human factors research and development for Honeywell, McDonnell Douglas, and Unisys. Her Master's degree is in psychology and her dissertation work is in information and cognitive sciences and pertains to the use of multi-modal cues for enhancing web search memory. Sikora has been doing research in the area of auditory feedback at Bell Labs since 1994.

Rob Tannen has researched the use of auditory displays to convey information and improve usability in contexts ranging from web surfing to Air Force fighter cockpits. Dr. Tannen is currently a lead human factors analyst with Electronic Ink, a digital design firm in Philadelphia.

Jeffrey Thompson is recognized worldwide as an expert in the field of brain-wave entrainment frequencies and their incorporation into musical soundtracks. He is also a consummate musician and composer. He is currently a member of the faculty of the California Center for Human Studies in Encinitas, California.

Benjamin Tomassetti received the Bachelor of Music degree in music composition from Shenandoah Conservatory of Music and both the Master of Music and Doctor of Musical Arts degrees in music composition from the University of Oregon. He is currently the coordinator of the Music Engineering Technology Program at Hampton University in Hampton, Virginia.

John Wawrzynek is a professor of electrical engineering and computer sciences at the University of California, Berkeley, where he teaches courses in VLSI design and computer architecture. His current research interests include reconfigurable computing, multimedia and networking, and VLSI circuits and systems. He received his Ph.D. from the California Institute of Technology in 1987, where he worked under Carver Mead, and holds a Masters of Science in electrical engineering from the University of Illinois, Urbana-Champaign.

Index